BLACKPOOL FOOTBALL

BLACKPOOL FOOTBALL

The Official Club History

Robin Daniels

With a Foreword by
SIR NEVILLE CARDUS

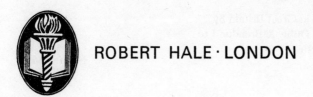
ROBERT HALE · LONDON

ISBN 0 7091 3501 7

Robert Hale & Company
63 Old Brompton Road
London, S.W.7

Set in 10 on 11 pt Intertype Times

Printed in Great Britain by
Clarke, Doble & Brendon Ltd.,
Plymouth

I dedicate this book to
ALAN ROWLANDS
to whose teaching and gentle goodness
I owe so much

*What is the rôle of the teacher? It is to help
the student find out what he loves to do.*

J. KRISHNAMURTI

ACKNOWLEDGEMENTS

Blackpool Football is a joint effort. I am most deeply thankful to:

My mother, the grammarian of the family, who for many years kept me fed and watered; and my father, the historian, who introduced me to the game of football and taught me the principles of good sportsmanship. As a spectator, he has the supreme advantage over me: he saw the peerless Arsenal team of the thirties. . . . A nice, impartial way to begin a book about Blackpool!

My teachers, at various times of my life: Mrs Jacqueline Suitor, H. W. F. Franklin, the late J. P. ("Mick") Walker, Miss Kathleen Hoare, Roy Stanton, D. A. Sandeman, F. C. Chown, David Potter, Mrs Homer Croy, Alan Rowlands, Rev. and Mrs A. H. Bray.

Everyone connected with Blackpool Football Club—officials, spectators, players (past and present)—for unstinting help at all times. I am especially grateful to the Chairman, Frank Dickinson, and his Board of directors: C. A. Sagar (Vice-Chairman), I. Gibrail, T. H. Lane, D. J. Lewin, W. S. Lines, G. S. Parr, R. Seed, Ald. A. E. Stuart J.P.; Des McBain, the club secretary, who has been the book's godfather; the Blackpool F.C. Development Association, for its generous support; Fred Jones, a former secretary; George Sheard, the Press Officer.

All those who so willingly agreed to be interviewed: Alan Ball, Tony Green, Jimmy Armfield, Peter Doherty, Bob Stokoe, Sir Stanley Matthews, Stan Mortensen, the late Joe Smith, Frank Dickinson, Syd Bevers, Harry Johnston, Des McBain, Bill Stewart, Eddie Shimwell.

Ellis Tomlinson, a follower of Blackpool football for more than 40 years, who helped—at schoolboy level—several of the players mentioned in this book. During the preparation of the manuscript, he was a liberal supplier of facts, statistics, anecdotes, newspaper cuttings, and memories of past players and matches. No one could have a more loyal friend; and no writer a more valuable guide.

Dr Ernst Menhofer, Press Attaché of the Austrian Embassy,

London; Bob Battersby, Blackpool's Director of Attractions and Publicity; Alan Hardaker and A. H. Johnson of the Football League; J. Carr of the Football Association; Brian Collins, Phil McEntee, Don Creedy, and the late Clifford Greenwood, of the *West Lancashire Evening Gazette*; Stan Whittaker of the *Lancashire Evening Post*; Bob Oxby of the *Daily Telegraph*; Phil Rising of *World Soccer*; Mrs M. Mann, who produced the typescript —cheerfully, accurately, and speedily; Mrs I. Vincent and Mrs P. Fountain of Rita Moore's Agency, and Miss G. E. L. Consentius, who shared the tape-transcription work; Maurice Golesworthy; William Blundell; Giles Woodforde; Mr and Mrs A. H. Fisher; the ever-patient staff of the British Museum Reading Room and Newspaper Library; and the staff of the Central Library, Blackpool.

My publishers, Robert Hale. I am particularly grateful to Gordon Chesterfield, Bill Bloodworth and John Gittens. Mr Chesterfield has been the ideal referee, allowing the game to proceed at an even pace with the minimum of stoppages, and, as the second half drew to a close, giving his players ample warning of the blowing of the final whistle.

ROBIN DANIELS

CONTENTS

ILLUSTRATIONS

FOREWORD
By Sir Neville Cardus

I must confess to some surprise, as I find myself writing the Foreword to this book. Until I saw the manuscript of it I had not heard of Robin Daniels, except as a voice on the telephone. Moreover, though soccer was the first of my loves of games, as a boy, I have not seen a first-class match these last four or five decades. I "gave up" soccer as soon as it began to encroach noisily and multitudinously on the cricket season; and as soon as players began to kiss and embrace at the scoring of every goal. I can't imagine "Billy" Meredith, of Manchester City, at the turn of the century, kissing a colleague on (or off) the field of play. Anyhow, his toothpick would have got in the way. Also, I lost interest in soccer, in general, because individual genius became more or less frustrated by a collective and defensive strategy. I still dote on the Bobby Charltons, the George Bests; but they are, I gather, rarities.

On the whole, soccer hasn't produced a permanent library of literature. It is a game too quick and brief of action; there is no time for a player to present, or expose, himself to the writer's scrutiny. There have been, still are, splendid descriptive pens at work telling us of a match's excitement and result: Geoffrey Green, Brian Glanville, and an *Observer* Hazlitt, whose name at the moment escapes me. But no book of perennial interest has yet been inspired by soccer; it has given us no Nyren, no Robertson-Glasgow, no Bernard Darwin, no Henry Longhurst. Maybe Robin Daniels will contribute to the vacant bookshelf. I at once smack my reader's palate with anticipation of pleasure when I read, "Blackpool, in yearly number of visitors, is now the world's most popular seaside resort, a town of show business, slot machines, holiday camps, and donkey rides: a free-swinging town, windblown—even in the height of summer. It is not surprising to find that Blackpool's football is entertaining, open, breezy, fluctuating."

You see, Robin Daniels relates a great game to its environment, its climate. He does not see it in a *vacuum*; the game for him is a matter of local character, of *habitat*. The style, for him, is the man; the crowd is a protagonist. Soccer in this book is part of Blackpool's air, temperature, Blackpool's *life*. And the book is entirely about Blackpool soccer. Mr Daniels himself describes the intent of his book, unique of its kind: *"Blackpool Football* portrays the men and the players who made Blackpool the most attractive football team in Britain, and also features those who are now trying to recapture old glories." So he rises to the heights of his heroic (and affectionate) theme with portraits of Stanley Matthews, Mortensen, Joe Smith, Armfield, Alan Ball, Johnston, Ernie Taylor ("Tom Thumb of football of his day"), Jackie Mudie, and others. One sentence, in particular, of Mr Daniels will whet your appetite: "Matthews seldom headed the ball. Football, for him, was *foot*-ball." Again, "Stanley Matthews used to score goals about as frequently as the arrival of leap-year, but he was too original a player to be judged by ordinary standards. He had not the goal-scoring urge of Meredith or Finney. But no one has excelled Matthews in his ability to feed the goal-scoring urge of others." I am content to leave my recommendation of this book at that—a Daniels come to judgement, with love of the game and pride in the artists who, for Blackpool soccer, have made it worth fine and historical writing.

INTRODUCTION

The First Division without Blackpool is like strawberries without cream.

BILL BECKETT

They [Blackpool] would look as strange in the Second Division, as would Callas playing Blackpool Pier.

BRIAN GLANVILLE

I was born in a large house on Hornby Road, in the middle of an air-raid. The conditions of hygiene at my birth were primitive: doctors of today would have gone on strike. I left Blackpool at the age of three weeks—too young to qualify as a "sand-grown 'un" [someone who was born and bred in Blackpool].

I spent my childhood in San Francisco, most characterful of all cities in the United States. Like Blackpool, San Francisco is by the sea, free to go its own way and find its own pleasures, not caring about what New York or Chicago or Texas thinks.

California, in the late forties and early fifties, was a Promised Land, rich in natural beauty. The industrial potential was enormous, and hundreds—perhaps thousands—of families came every week to live in the state. Since then, many of the lemon and orange groves have gone. You no longer find silver dollars in your change. The old wooden bridges, dating from pioneer days, have been burned and replaced by concrete monstrosities, slick and characterless. The swing-doors at the entrance to bars—known to everyone who has seen a cowboy film—have gone. This was before John and Robert Kennedy and Martin Luther King were shot. Before Black Power. Before the Kent State massacre. Before the bloodstains of Vietnam.

During the summer vacation, we would stand on Irving Street, next to an up-turned crate, and sell orange squash for 10 cents a glass. Free enterprise was in our veins. We were—our one claim to fame—predecessors of the hippies. We scandalized the middle-aged by wearing fluorescent socks, green on one foot and red on the other. It was *chic* to turn-up one trouser leg slightly higher than the other.

We were young patriots, proud of our young country. Every morning, at school, we hoisted the American flag, and then saluted it, right arms raised, chanting: "I pledge allegiance to the Flag of the United States of America and to the Republic for which it stands, one nation indivisible, with liberty and justice for all." "Chant" is not quite accurate: we *meant* what we were saying. We had a simple childlike trust in America's future. A lot—such a whole lot—has changed.

My first love among sports was baseball. I could recite all the batting records of "Babe" Ruth and Lou Gehrig, just as my English counterparts knew in detail the exploits of Compton and Washbrook. Minor-league baseball was played every week-end in Golden Gate Park, 50 yards from our house. One Saturday, I was shuffling around the stadium twenty minutes before the start of a game, dressed in a blue shirt and blue jeans, the colour of the local team. The manager came up to me. "D'ya wanna job, Sonny? We need a bat-boy." "Sure thing," I replied. When a batter made a hit, he threw his bat to one side, and scampered towards first base. My job was to run onto the pitch (or, more correctly, the diamond), pick up the bat, and put it on a stand, in the correct batting order. At the end of the afternoon, the manager gave me 50 cents and two used baseballs. I ran all the way home to show off my prizes.

I place importance on those early years of my life, because my love of football—and of Blackpool football in particular—owes a lot to baseball and to my father. We went to baseball games together, and he taught me to be an alert spectator. We went to Golden Gate Park, and he taught me how to throw and catch and hit. "Watch the ball, move your feet, and *swing*", he used to tell me. He was infinitely gentle and always encouraging. I owe much to my father for my enjoyment of sport.

The Daniels family returned to England in the summer of 1952. I celebrated my 11th birthday on the boat. At that time, I had never *heard* of the game of association football. The name *Matthews* was unknown to me. And—I blush a deep purple as I write this—I didn't know where Blackpool was.

My arrival in England coincided with the beginning of the 1952–53 season, the season in which Blackpool won the F.A. Cup. Within weeks of setting foot in England, I was one of the staunchest Blackpudlians in the country. I collected newspaper cuttings and compiled statistics. I wrote reports of matches I'd seen—imitating

"A mellifluous voice. . . . A contagious breath"

Bloomfield Road

Henry Rose or Frank Coles or one of the other football corres-
pondents of the day—and I wrote pen-portraits of players I
admired. *Blackpool Football* was in embryo.

With every passing week, I became increasingly sure that I
should concentrate on *people*, and not fall prey to the formal
historical approach—one chapter for each decade. I remembered
a sentence in Neville Cardus's *English Cricket*. His wise words are
true of any sport: "In the long run the game is the sum total of
the character of the men who take part in it."

A few years ago, Blackpool, clearly the more skilful, if less
direct, side, were booted out of the Cup after playing on a sluggish,
muddy pitch. The Blackpool captain, when questioned about his
team's defeat, said, "We just can't change our style. We always try
to play good football, whatever the conditions."

There are, surely, links between a football team and its home
town. When the football club was founded, in July 1887, Blackpool,
with a population of 14,300, was described as a "fashionable watering place". Blackpool, in yearly number of visitors, is now the
world's most popular seaside resort,[1] a town of show business, slot
machines, holiday camps, and donkey rides: a free-swinging town,
wind-blown—even in the height of summer. It is not surprising to
find that Blackpool's football is entertaining, open, breezy,
fluctuating.

Blackpool is the club that gave birth to the Atomic Boys; the
club that christened one of its stands "The Scratching Shed"; the
club with the wing-half who sauntered out for a cup-tie and reached
the middle of the field before he realized he was still smoking a
cigarette; the club whose winger was sent off for a witty reply to a
referee. When asked his name—the referee had intended to book
him; not send him off—the player replied, "You've got a programme, haven't you?" Blackpool is a club that survived poverty
and a tough childhood: more than once, when travelling to away
matches, club officials had to persuade a booking clerk to give them
tickets on credit.

For years, the name of the club was not to be seen on the stand
that faces the main road; and strangers to Blackpool, strolling along
Bloomfield Road, used to ask, "Is this the rugby-league club's
ground?" There is not an ounce of ostentation in Blackpool Football Club. You'll find only modesty, tinged with an unspoken pride.
The cordial atmosphere stretches out invitingly; the great blue
doors are usually open. You wander in, and onto the deserted kop.

---

[1] As recently as 1960, the number of British people going to Blackpool
for their holidays was twice as large as the number who went to the
Continent.

Behind you, the Tower stands against the horizon, overlooking Blackpool with a steady, paternal gaze. Sea-gulls glide overhead, screeching and hungry. Then you think back. You begin to day-dream: of Cup Finals and of memorable goals; of internationally-known players and loyal club-men; of waddling mascot-ducks, tangerine-dyed.

If to sum up an era is a sure mark of greatness, then Blackpool in 1953 paraded a great team. The members of that Cup Final XI are, to a man, clear-sighted, articulate, and grateful to Blackpool Football Club. They consummated the Age of the Individual and made way for the Age of Systems. Gross financial incentives, play-the-man, win-at-all-costs, lack of control of self: these were the warts of later years, not often seen in the 1953 approach and attitude. Of course they wanted to win. But not at the expense of adventure or grace, or entertainment, or flair. Football in the early fifties was aglow with panache, and, virtue of sporting virtues, geniality.

The fulfilment of Blackpool's ambition—F.A. Cup victory, in 1953—is best seen against the background of the early history. After unsuccessful attempts in 1894 and 1895, the club was finally elected to the League, Division II, in 1896, and, though not re-elected three years later, regained admission in 1900, after amalga-mating with South Shore. Blackpool, in the early days, lived more on hope than money. More than once, their ground rights for a cup-tie were sold. "Blackpool will never be promoted", the cynics used to sing. Then, when Blackpool became Champions of the Second Division in 1930, the cynics had to change their tune. No other seaside resort in England had ever offered First Division football; and, to this day, no other seaside resort has done so. Over 30,000 voices cheered the Champions on their way to the Town Hall. The crowds were ecstatic, and the players had to be half-helped, half-dragged, from the coaches and up the steps. The police only just managed to prevent a friendly invasion. Three hard seasons later, Blackpool dropped back into the Second Division. The club was not ready for first-class football. Yet.

At last, in August 1935, there arrived a manager to rescue Blackpool from obscurity: Joe Smith the eager. The very next season, Blackpool, runners-up this time, rose again to the premier Division, and stayed there for 30 years. During the war, when many prominent players guested for the club, Blackpool's Augustan age began. In several post-war seasons, Blackpool could boast the most popular team in Britain, and one year the club regularly fielded nine internationals. In the 1960s Blackpool and England found a leader and a model sportsman. That "unspoken pride" can hardly contain itself when you mention the name of Jimmy Armfield. At his peak, he could have gone to any of the wealthier clubs in the country, but he stayed with Blackpool, and led them back into the First Division. His loyalty and his patience were rewarded. His quiet dignity typifies all that is best in Blackpool football. Countless are the clubs with more honours, more money, a larger ground, more cups on the boardroom mantelpiece. But no club surpasses Blackpool in *spirit*.

Bloomfield Road, like all football grounds, is used as a scribbling-pad by young fans. A few summers ago, these slogans were easily visible to the passer-by:

> *Long Live Chopper.*[2]
>
> *Banks out; Taylor in.*[3]
>
> *Tony Green for Mayor.*

And less printable ones, such as:

> *F — — — off, Villa.*

And chants like:

> *Ha-La-La Leslie Lea.*

And reminders of star-players of the recent past, such as Alan Ball and "Big Em" Hughes. And, beneath the top layer of green paint on the doors, and in fainter lettering on the stone-work, a careful observer would find names of an earlier generation of Blackpool players, enshrined, by young supporters, on the walls of their stadium. Bloomfield Road and young people are synonymous. Few League clubs give, or have given, so much encouragement to local football: to amateurs, as well as to youth and school teams.

Blackpool Football portrays the men and the players who made Blackpool the most attractive football team in Britain, and also features those who are now trying to recapture old glories. "There is properly no history," wrote Emerson, "only biography." Courage, loyalty, strength of character: they appear again and again in these portraits. There is the manager who acted as ball-boy during a Cup Final; the full-back who seldom trained in Blackpool, but always reported 100 per cent fit; the goalkeeper who ignored the many loud-mouths who told him he didn't know how to catch the ball; and the forward who received a tempting offer to return to his homeland—but refused.

[2] John McPhee, a Scotsman, a hard-tackling wing-half of great courage and versatility, who was Blackpool's Player of the Year in 1965 and 1968.

[3] This was written by an optimist, who was suggesting that Taylor, Blackpool's goalkeeper, should replace Banks in the England team.

All the interviews were willingly and generously given. Those meetings are here recorded, as spoken. If only it were possible, by some special means of notation, to convey—to the reader—phrasing of sentences, accentuations, inflections of the voice, warmth of tone. Why should composers of music have sole rights to expression-marks?

It is fascinating to compare the words and ideas of players of different generations. Read what Alan Ball and Peter Doherty say about the need for 100 per cent effort. Compare the wise words—by Johnston, Armfield, and Ball—on captaincy. Different personalities, different age-groups: linked by a love of football and the desire to excel. You will be reminded, again and again, that football, *au fond*, is *still* a simple game.

The man most fitted to write a history of Blackpool Football Club was the late Clifford Greenwood. He could see much further than a football team's week-by-week performance, and his writing at all times combined deep knowledge with a sensitive response to events and to people. Clifford Greenwood has left, with all who knew him, the memory of a large and gracious nature, and of a man, of Christian tolerance and a gentle sense of humour, who always wanted to find the Good in others. Once, after being thanked for a kindness, he looked away, blushing slightly, and muttered, "Oh, it's all part of the service." Service was a quality he exhibited in war, in his work, in his friendships, and in maintaining a grace and dignity of human relations. Thank you, Cliff, for advice and encouragement: eagerly sought; selflessly given.

R.N.D.

London
June 1972

1

THE SEASIDERS
A History to be Proud Of

Why *The Seasiders*? Blackpool Football Club has three nicknames. Three, that is, in general use and fit to put in print: "The Pool"; "The Tangerines"; "The Seasiders". Not one of them is Blackpool's sole property. There are other Pools, both greater (Liverpool) and smaller (Hartlepool). Other clubs play in tangerine. And other seaside resorts provide League football: Brighton, Torquay, Southend, Southport, and Bournemouth. But none of these seaside-resort clubs—however spirited their efforts—have approached Blackpool in sustained achievement. Blackpool, alone among seaside-resort clubs, has played in the First Division. Blackpool, alone, has won the F.A. Cup, been runners-up in the League Championship, and won the Second Division title.

Of all seaside resorts currently offering first-class football, Blackpool was the first—by a couple of decades—to be elected as a member of the Football League. I have no wish to stimulate inter-town rivalry. Blackpool Publicity Department is well able to trumpet its own propaganda. A few years ago, Blackpool claimed to have the finest summer shows in England, and a rival resort threatened the town with the Trade Descriptions Act.

I am not content with the World Cup, the Welsh Cup, the Watney Cup, the European Champions Cup. When will a Pontin or a Butlin sponsor a Seaside Resorts Cup? It would be played on a home-and-away basis in the summer months. Miami v. Majorca? Blackpool v. Bondi Beach?

So far as we now know, the first football club in Blackpool was the Victoria Football Club, founded in 1877 with the Rev. James Wayman as president. The first meetings were held in the classroom of the Victoria Street Chapel, and, for the club's first game, walking-sticks served as goal-posts on a piece of waste land at South Shore. Three members took part in this historic game: one player in each team and a "jack of both sides". After further practice games, the Victoria Club travelled to Fleetwood, for its first proper match, in a hired waggonette with an awning and side curtains. Eventually, the Victoria Club was disbanded, and football in Blackpool was continued by the St John's team, consisting mostly of old boys of the school.

Blackpool Football Club was founded on July 26, 1887, at the Stanley Arms Hotel. The club was not formed by a breakaway group. Members of St John's F.C., and others, wanted to form a club bearing the name *Blackpool*.

Blackpool F.C.'s first-ever match was won, 2-1 at Chorley, on September 17, 1887. In that first season, Blackpool won the Fylde Cup and the Lancashire Junior Cup. The first balance-sheet has a quaint look. The two major items were:

Share of stand and gate receipts   £108   12s.   2d.
Payment to players, travelling, etc. £103   14s.   9d.

These two figures, when added together, come to less than Blackpool's current income from programme sales on a single Saturday afternoon.

We tend to think that worker representation is a product of our own day. It is interesting to note that, in the 1880s, the first-team captain and vice-captain were given a place on the club Committee, forerunner of the Board.

Nicknames for players were more freely used than now. The players of Blackpool's early years offer some delightful examples: "Lal" and "Tricky" Wright, "Tishy" Hull (was this the nineteenth-century version of "dishy"?), "Tich" Winstanley, "Skill" and "Pank" Parkinson, "Jubba" Hardman.

Blackpool were among the founder members of the Lancashire League, and the club had eight successful seasons in it, only once finishing below fifth place. Blackpool were runners-up in four of the eight seasons, and won the Championship in 1893–94. In 1892–93, Blackpool and Liverpool ended with identical playing records, but Liverpool, in spite of defeats at home and away by Blackpool, won the Championship on goal-average.

In May 1896, Blackpool F.C. became a limited company, and a few months later played in the Football League for the first time. Blackpool's first-ever League match, a Division II game at Lincoln City on September 5, ended in a 3-1 defeat. The Blackpool team on that baptismal day was: Douglas; Bowman, Parr (Captain); Stuart, Stirzaker, Norris; Clarkin, Donnelly, J. Parkinson, R. Parkinson, Mount. There is disagreement among the local newspapers of 1896 on whether Harry Parr played right- or left-back, but they do agree that the crowd numbered about 2,000. In the second half, a free-kick for hands led to Blackpool's first-ever League goal. Stuart put the ball smartly across, and Charles Mount volleyed it. The ball hit the underside of the bar and cannoned into the net. The *Athletic News* commented that "Blackpool's weakness was in front of goal". And 75 years later, when Blackpool were relegated to Division II, these same words were chorused by every national newspaper. "The more things change, the more they are the same."

In the early 1890s, Blackpool played in the Competition Proper of the F.A. Cup for the first time. The well-heeled players of today would be on strike if they received the same treatment as their forefathers before a cup-tie: "because of the trainer's forbidding eye, tobacco and intoxicants were partaken of, after being adroitly smuggled into bed." For their first-ever cup-tie victory—against Burton Swifts in 1896—the Blackpool players received a win bonus of 10s. each. The aristocrats from Burton had been offered a bonus of no less than 50s.

A Blackpool match in 1910 might provide an idea for the churches, now desperately seeking ways of becoming involved in community life. The match was refereed by the Rev. W. Marsh, and one of the linesmen was a fellow-clergyman. No bookings nor dismissals-from-the-field are recorded. And no conversions to the faith, either.

Blackpool played an unobtrusive part in the competitions held during World War I, but one match set a club record: the 11-1 defeat by Burslem Port Vale in November 1916. Blackpool had the services of so many Blackburn players that the war-time team became known as "Blackpool Rovers". One of the guest stars was Bob Crompton, the famous England right-back and captain. So great was the number of imported players that, at one time, only one of the Blackpool XI—the left-back—was a registered Blackpool player.

The years just before and just after the turn of the century harassed Blackpool's patience and her financial resources. Because of small gates—small compared to most other clubs in the Second Division—Blackpool were unable to pay the maximum wage, and few players received summer pay. During the season, most of the Blackpool first team were part-time footballers.

Lack of capital spun the club round and round in a cruel, never-ending circle. Small gates brought little money. Lack of money forced the club to sell its star players. Losing star players weakened and unsettled the team. No success on the field-of-play kept the gates low. And so on and so on.

Many people advised the directors to take Blackpool out of the

Second Division for a few years: "Join one of the minor leagues. Reduce your overheads for a while, and consolidate." But Blackpool chose the harder route: more painful, but more rewarding. No praise can do justice to the foresight of the directors and officials of those early years. Happily, some of them lived to see Blackpool play in the First Division.

Blackpool had reached the Promised Land, but their passports did not guarantee an indefinite stay. In the inter-war period, a couple of directors used to pay some of the wages out of their own pockets. And today, because of the abolition of the maximum wage, Blackpool are again in a financial strait-jacket. The city clubs have become bigger and richer; the town clubs—all of them—are struggling. Who are the men who have dedicated their lives—and often their fortunes—to Blackpool Football Club? They—no less than all the well-known, well-loved players—deserve their place in the history of Blackpool football.

Directors who have given long and devoted service to Blackpool F.C. include: Sam Butterworth, Harry Evans, Albert Hindley, and Albert Hargreaves. But two families have predominated: the Seeds and the Parkinsons. Leonard Seed was a member of the club's first-ever Board of directors in 1896. His brother, Fred, served Blackpool for thirty years, as director, Chairman, and President. Fred Seed's son, Richard, has been a director since the mid-thirties, and for several years was club Chairman. During his directorship, Richard Seed has held the post of hon. secretary: the only *hon.* secretary in the top two Divisions of the Football League. Blackpool F.C. has never had a more faithful and hard-working servant.

The Parkinson family also has associations with Blackpool football dating back to the last century. Sir Lindsay Parkinson was playing for South Shore well before the amalgamation with Blackpool in 1899. He later became President and Chairman of Blackpool during the eventful years in the club's history. He was succeeded, as Chairman, by his brother, Colonel William Parkinson. The family's representative today is the Blackpool F.C. Hon. President, Teddy Parkinson, son of Colonel William.

Three men now at Bloomfield Road joined Blackpool F.C. in the thirties: two directors, Richard Seed and W. S. Lines; and Harry Glossop, originally a trainer of the junior teams and now the dressing room attendant. The longest-serving member of the present staff at Bloomfield Road is Harry Smith, whose association with Blackpool Football Club dates back to 1919. He looks after the boardroom and the directors' room, and makes a strong contribution to the club's nation-wide fame for hospitality.

In seventy-five seasons in the Football League, Blackpool have had only seven club secretaries. T. A. Barcroft took the job on a temporary basis, and served for thirty years. For a long time—like Richard Seed, in later years—Barcroft was the only *hon.* secretary in the top two Divisions. He kept people amused with a flow of anecdotes, and a straw hat was his trade mark. One week-end, Blackpool failed to pick up the first-team goalkeeper at Preston station, and arrived at Leicester a vital player short: the club wasn't rich enough to take a twelfth man. Tom Barcroft kept goal that day, and he gave all the spectators within earshot a running commentary on the game.

Dozens of former Blackpool players have been lured back to the friendly atmosphere of Bloomfield Road: Ron Suart and Stan Mortensen, as managers; Harry Johnston and Eric Hayward, as assistant managers; Sam Jones, as assistant secretary; Paddy Sowden, as youth manager; as coaches or as trainers—Bert Tulloch, J. Charles, W. Tremelling, Harry Wilson, W. Benton, "Shorty" Mee, L. Cardwell, R. Finan, A. Roxburgh, Jackie Wright, Hugh Kelly, and Dave Frith; as scouts—W. Thorpe, A. Watson, D. Blair, A. Munro, W. Rickett, M. Butler, E. Sibley. And many more.

Eric Hayward can claim one of the finest single examples of loyalty to Blackpool. A few days before Blackpool went to Wolver-hampton for the fifth round of the F.A. Cup in 1950, Hayward was selected to play for the Football League. He was overjoyed. For several years, he had been denied the international recognition he deserved. Here, at last, was his chance. But the cup-tie ended in a draw. Blackpool needed him for the replay. Without hesitation, Hayward asked to be withdrawn from the Football League team.

The longest-serving Blackpool supporter is William Blundell, a "sand-grown 'un", who was born on November 5, 1880. He first watched Blackpool play when he was about eight years old. The club was founded in 1887, and so Mr Blundell has witnessed virtually the whole history of Blackpool football.

As a child, he used to live near Raikes Hall Gardens, which was then Blackpool's home ground. On a match-day, he and his pals used to wait for the players to arrive. "Carry your bag, sir?", the boys used to ask. The lucky boy went in with the player, carrying his kit for him, and had a free view of the match. The boys, who didn't get in by this method, clustered around the entrance until half-time. When the gates—or what served for gates—were opened, all the boys rushed in. He recalls going to Bury's ground when he was a youngster. The pitch was roped off. Inside the rope, there was a fearsome man with a whip. He used to thrash any boy who tried to get in without paying.

Mr Blundell can remember "Lal" Wright, Blackpool's first-ever goalkeeper: "He was quite a short fellow. He always wore a cap to cover his bald patch. If ever the cap was knocked off during a match, the spectators would laugh and clap." Mr Blundell considers Harry Bedford—Blackpool's leading goal-scorer in the early twenties—to be one of the best marksmen he has ever seen: "He never did a great deal of running, but he was always in the right place when the ball came over from the wing." The best Blackpool team he has seen *so far* was the one that did so well during World War II.

Mr Blundell speaks with equal affection of Blackpool players of the 1970s. He and his wife are people of Victorian charm of manner. I went away greatly encouraged by his memory, his clarity, and his dignity. As I left, he helped me into my coat. William Blundell—a young man of 90.

In the first ten years (1887–1897), Blackpool played at Raikes Hall Gardens. The club was forced to move to the Athletic Grounds (August 1897–January 1899) and then resumed at Raikes Hall. After amalgamating with South Shore in December 1899, Blackpool moved to Bloomfield Road, which had been South Shore's home ground. In the early twenties, the ground was known as "Gamble's Field", after Billy Gamble who once owned it. He used to let a pigeon out of a basket—with instructions to fly home with the news—every time Blackpool scored. At Blackpool's scoring-rate during the sixties, a pigeon would have had a lazy time on most Saturday afternoons.

Blackpool's goal-scoring *has* occasionally hit the headlines. Stan Mortensen, Blackpool's centre-forward, once gave away an own-goal, when he had gone back to help his defence. An own-goal by an Aston Villa player—in a match against Queen's Park Rangers, at the end of the 1967–68 season—prevented Blackpool from winning promotion to the First Division. In a match in August 1950, Blackpool's wing-halves, Harry Johnston and Hugh Kelly, scored three of the team's four goals. A couple of years later—in a 5-2 win at Wolverhampton—every member of Blackpool's forward-line scored. Shortly before Christmas 1955, Blackpool were 4-0 down in a League match at Highbury. Just before the end, a spectator blew a whistle. The Arsenal full-back, Dennis Evans, pleased at having had a good game against Stanley Matthews, joyfully kicked the ball into the Arsenal net. But the game wasn't over, and so he had scored a goal for Blackpool.

History sometimes repeats itself. Two of the most bizarre goals in Blackpool history have remarkable similarities: both were scored by full-backs, at Bloomfield Road, in fourth-round cup-ties; both owe something to the elements; and, in both years, Blackpool reached the Cup Final. In 1948, against Chester, Eddie Shimwell made a 60-yard clearance. The ball hit a rut in the frozen turf, and bounced, over the 'keeper's head, into the Chester goal. In 1953, against Huddersfield, the ball rolled to Tom Garrett, who was standing just a few yards inside the opponents' half. He decided to loft the ball high into the goal-mouth. The wind carried the ball on and on, and into the Huddersfield net. It was the only goal of the match, and helped Blackpool on their way to Wembley.

Blackpool F.C. has had its fair share of weather-hit matches: the Cup replay against West Ham in 1925, a match against Sunderland six years later, and, more recently, the 1963 cup-tie against Norwich that was postponed eleven times, while the Blackpool team played football—on ice-skates—on Bloomfield Road's frozen pitch. Not to forget the match at White Hart Lane in January 1963. Snow began falling half an hour after the start, and howled over the pitch with ever-increasing fury, temporarily blinding the players, who looked like blurred figures in a snow-scene paper-weight. The spirit of the game was lost, on one occasion, when a linesman insisted that Waiters re-take a goal-kick from the proper spot, and with the ball motionless. Once, twice, half-a-dozen times, Blackpool's goalkeeper ran forward to kick, and each time the ball, like a young child enjoying attention, would roll away. At last, with the help of a divot and the co-operation of the wind, the kick was taken. The game continued, and Waiters peered into the blizzard like an Arctic explorer who has lost his way.

The Blackpool–Chelsea match at Bloomfield Road on October 29, 1932, was in every way a stormer. The game looked more like water polo than football. The Chelsea walk-out, in the last fifteen minutes, has no parallel in football history. Four of their exhausted players left the field, unassisted, in the closing minutes, leaving the team—whose left-half had retired with cramp at half-time—with only six men at the end of the game. Blackpool won 4-0. Three of Blackpool's goals were scored while the teams were still evenly matched. These three goals came in the first forty-five minutes, when Blackpool, not Chelsea, faced the sterner wrath of wind and rain. Only 6,000 brave spectators watched history being made. None of Blackpool's XI reported for treatment the next day: a triumph for the club's trainer.

One year after the Blackpool–Chelsea "water polo" match, a gangling young Irishman joined Blackpool. Within a few seasons he was one of the most beloved, talked-about, sought-after players in English football. Peter Doherty was the Alan Ball of his day, always in the game, master of the long pass, and capable of firing accurate shots at goal from all angles. His long-striding pace was deceptive: much faster, in fact, than it looked. He could read the game well. He was often half-way to the ball—on the quiet—before anyone had seen him start running. He had an alertness—a sportsman's sixth sense—that is given to few men. A swimmer's last spurt for victory; the tackle that prevents a winning try; a boxer's sudden man-felling right hook; a horse's wild gallop over the final furlong—sport is the art of The Moment.

Doherty will for ever be remembered as one of the bravest forwards of all time. He played in an era prolific with hefty defenders. He would run, at, through, or over them; never shirking a tackle. Even the crudest of tackles delayed his flow of genius only momentarily. If he was felled thirty yards from goal, he would spring to his feet, shake the mane of tawny hair out of his eyes, dodge a few more scything tackles, and still manage to put in a shot at goal. But, mostly, mind and body reacted quickly enough for him to avoid, or swerve away from, a direct challenge.

Doherty was the most lethal penalty-taker of his generation, preferring the well-placed kick to the net-buster. He took a run-up of only a few paces, and usually persuaded the bewitched goalkeeper to dive the wrong way. Blackpool brought him to England and then, needing money, sold him to Manchester City for £10,000. As goal-maker and goal-scorer, he guided City to the League Championship in 1936–37, and, immediately after the war, gained an F.A. Cup-winners' medal with Derby County. Peter Doherty was an artist-footballer, never afraid to commit his gifts to the hurly-burly of professional football. He gave himself freely—his skill, his energy, and his imagination—to every team he played for. He played, and schemed, and scored goals, without apparent effort. There was a natural, sinuous, totally Irish charm about him. Genius does not labour—or at least does not show signs of labour.

Doherty's most famous team-mate at Bloomfield Road was Jimmy Hampson. When Blackpool officials went to Nelson to sign Hampson, they were informed that he was in a cinema. They persuaded him to come out, and within an hour he had become a Blackpool player. A year or so later, Arsenal offered £10,000— only a few hundred pounds short of the record transfer fee between English clubs. But Blackpool kept him, and no wonder. In his ten years by the sea, he set a club record: 247 goals in 360 League games. He used to head the ball about as often as Stanley Matthews did—in other words, about once a year—but, on the ground, he was devastating. In seven representative matches—for England and the Football League—he scored fourteen goals. Hampson had the misfortune to be a contemporary of Dixie Dean. In almost any other era, he would have been an automatic choice for the England team.

At 5ft 6in, Jimmy Hampson was small for a centre-forward, but he made up for lack of height with a compact, sturdy build and a superb sense of balance: he could wrong-foot a centre-half with a subtle sway of the hips. His assets were acceleration, uncanny anticipation of a centre or a through-pass, and his ability to make space for himself in a tight situation. He had a bullet-like shot in both feet—though he preferred to kick with his right—and caused terror among goalkeepers if they saw him, with the ball at his mercy, anywhere in or near the penalty-area. Jimmy Hampson could not be intimidated: if a couple of defenders were closing-in on him, intending to tackle or "sandwich" him, he would keep the ball under tight control and shoot low, on the run.

In Blackpool's first promotion season (1929–30), Jimmy profited from the passes of Tremelling, an attacking centre-half. Tremelling would follow behind, give a quiet whistle, and then slide the ball, either past Hampson—on his right side—or just behind him. Hampson had a sixth sense for the second type of pass—the one to his heels. He would swing his right leg backwards, and scoop the ball forward. Tremelling's passes were always timed so that Hampson was a yard or two on-side. He broke Blackpool's all-time goal-scoring record, in that promotion season, with 45 goals in 41 League games.

On the field, Jimmy was one of the most feared marksmen in England. Off the field, he was quiet and unassuming, never keen to talk about himself, and without bitterness at the rough treatment he received from opposing defenders: "I've to expect this," he said. He was idolized in Blackpool. When he was drowned in a boating accident, in January 1938, grown men wept. His body was never recovered.

From the day of his signing for Blackpool, he was a perfect servant of his club. His skill as a footballer won him admiration at grounds all over England, but he never gloried in fame or in himself. One night, in May 1930, the team was returning from a drawn match at Nottingham Forest. Blackpool, for the first time, had won the Second Division Championship. The train stopped at Kirkham, and a porter entered the carriage. "There are thousands of people in Blackpool waiting to welcome you," he told the team. There was one player, in particular, whom the crowds in Blackpool wanted to see, and that was Jimmy Hampson, the top goal-scorer in the whole of the Football League. "I'll get out here," said Jimmy. "I'll wait for the next train to Central." And he meant what he said. Had it not been for the forceful protests of his team-mates, Jimmy Hampson would have walked onto the empty platform and gone home alone, leaving his friends to receive all the applause.

Peter Doherty and Jimmy Hampson cost Blackpool a total of £2,500. Blackpool's first big transfer deal was the selling of Jack Cox to Liverpool for £150. In 1898, that was a headline-making fee. Blackpool astonished the football world in March 1920 by selling three players—Joe Lane, George Wilson, and Peter Quinn—for a total of £10,200. In the mid-twenties, Herbert Jones went to Blackburn Rovers for £4,000, a colossal fee at that time for a full-back. Then there was 1938–39, the last pre-war season, when Blackpool signed five players for a total cost of £30,000, and transferred five for £19,750. These transactions produced one of Blackpool's best-ever teams: the team that won the first three matches of the 1939–40 season, and whose hopes of winning the Championship were put to an abrupt end by the advent of war.

Many of Blackpool's transfer deals—both to and from the club—have set records, but the inflation that hits the housewife's weekly budget applies to football as well, and few record fees remain records for very long. In 1950, Blackpool paid East Fife £26,500 for the services of Allan Brown, an established Scottish international. This was the highest fee that had been paid to a Scottish club. Twenty years later, Everton paid six times that amount for Henry Newton, a half-back in his mid-twenties who had never played for his country. And, even with a price tag of £150,000, Newton did not become an automatic choice for Everton.

It was Everton again who were so keen to sign Gordon West that they paid Blackpool £27,500, a British record fee for a goalkeeper. Four years later, Everton paid Blackpool £112,000 for Alan Ball, a record transfer between two British clubs. Emlyn Hughes became British football's most expensive full-back and most valuable teenager when he moved from Blackpool to Liverpool for £65,000. The £30,000 fee that brought Pat Quinn to Hibernian was the highest ever paid by a Scottish club to an English club. Tony Green—sold to Newcastle for £150,000—became the most valuable Scottish player in football history. And Blackpool created a British record fee for a winger when they paid Stoke City £11,500 for Stanley Matthews. Few clubs of Blackpool's size have played such a large part in football's transfer market.

Six-figure transfer fees are a product of recent years, but competition for players was also very keen before the Second World

War, and many amusing stories can be told of how one club tried to outwit another. In the late thirties, Wally Lines, a Blackpool director, and Johnny Lynas, who was then the club's assistant trainer, went to watch a representative match in Liverpool. The trainer went onto the stands and the director went into the paddock: they agreed to look up at each other every twenty minutes, so that they could indicate their impressions of any particularly promising players. A mere nod of the head, by the two Blackpool officials, was all that was needed to convey their joint admiration for Tommy Buchan, a wing-half with a Scottish junior club, who was having an outstanding match. The Blackpool director was on his way to the tea-room at half-time when the Burnley Chairman nudged him, and said, "I like yon right-half." "So do I," replied the Blackpool director, "but I wish he was ten years younger. He's getting old." "I thowt so," murmured the Burnley Chairman. The Blackpool director hurried to his meeting-place with the club trainer. *They* knew that Tommy Buchan was still in his early twenties. He looked older than he was. Within forty-eight hours, he had become a Blackpool player—for £200. Thereafter, the Blackpool officials had no need to tell jokes to one another. They simply nodded at each other: that was enough to send them into fits of laughter.

One signing, made by Blackpool, rivals James Bond for panache and daring. Blackpool and Belfast Celtic both wanted to sign Malcolm Butler, an Irishman. A small posse of Blackpool officials arrived at the rendezvous—a small pub—and found, to their consternation, that the Belfast Celtic manager was in the bar, also waiting to see Butler. Unknown to the men at the bar, the landlord had locked the much-hunted player in an upstairs bedroom. The Blackpool officials crept up the stairs, completed the necessary forms, and escaped by way of the bedroom window, taking Butler with them. Not until a couple of hours later did the Belfast Celtic manager—his face red with impatience—learn what had happened. The happy sequel to this story is that Butler later became an Irish international.

A total of twenty-eight Blackpool players have won full-international honours: thirteen Englishmen, nine Scotsmen, three Welshmen, and three Irishmen. It is illuminating to discover that, in all the seasons up to World War II, only ten Blackpool players were capped; compared with eighteen in the post-war period. 1939-45: these were the years of Blackpool's Renaissance.

The first Blackpool player to be capped, F. Griffiths, played for Wales when Blackpool was a non-League club. That was at the turn of the century, and not for another twenty years was a Blackpool player invited to wear his country's jersey in an international match. Since the Second World War, a number of Blackpool players have helped to win thousands of friends for British football: Jimmy Armfield, captain of England on fifteen occasions; Alan Ball, outside-right in England's 1966 World Cup victory; Stanley Matthews, who continued to grace the England team until he reached his early forties; Tony Green, of Scotland, who made a splendid Wembley début in May 1971; and Stan Mortensen, who can claim one of the best goal-scoring records ever achieved by an England player: 23 goals in 25 matches.

Several players made their international débuts after leaving Blackpool, but the club deserves some credit for the honours they received. They include: Jack Cox, H. P. Hardman, F. Pentland, G. Wilson (who captained England), J. F. Mitchell, Herbert Jones, Jack Hacking (who left Blackpool on a free transfer), L. Stoker, W. Slater, Gordon West, and Emlyn Hughes.

Most locally-born players have joined Blackpool F.C., but a few well-known footballers never played for their home-town team: Maurice Webster, who won England caps around 1930 while he was with Middlesbrough; Frank Swift, Manchester City and England goalkeeper, once a coke-keeper at the Blackpool Gasworks, who might have joined Blackpool if his elder brother, Fred, also a goalkeeper, had not previously signed for the club; Malcolm Barrass, England international, centre-half for Bolton in the 1953 Cup Final against Blackpool, son of Matt Barrass, a Blackpool inside-left; George Eastham Jr, many times capped by England, another son of a Blackpool player; and John Hurst, strong midfield player of Everton, who has captained the England Under-23 XI.

Several foreign-born players have been on Blackpool's books. The most recent recruit from abroad was Fred Kemp, a wing-half, who was born in Salerno, Italy. In September 1960, the club's "A"-team forward-line consisted of an Englishman, a Scotsman, a Chinaman, a South African, and an Irishman. The Chinaman was Cheung Chi-doy, who sacrificed his chance of playing in the 1960 Rome Olympics, in the hope of making a career at Blackpool. He made only a couple of appearances for the club, but etched his name in history by becoming one of the few Chinamen ever to play in the Football League. One day some of his Blackpool teammates were teasing him. "Who are you?", they asked. "Where are you from?" The retort came without hesitation: "Scotland. Can't you tell by my accent?"

Over the years, Blackpool F.C. has attracted a small colony of South Africans. Blackpool began the 1961–62 season with four

"I surrender", mutters the player on the left, as Jimmy Hampson, highest
goal-scorer in Blackpool history, shows his speed

Blackpool F.C. 1929–30, Champions of Division II. *Left to right*. Back row: H. Wilson, W. M. Grant, H. Pearson, S. Ramsay, G. Wolf, A. Watson, W. Benton; middle row: A. Ure (Trainer), C. Quinn, J. Lauderdale, W. Tremelling, W. J. Upton, P. Downes, J. Charles (Assistant Trainer); front row: C. R. Rattray, S. Tuffnell, C. Broadhurst, J. Hampson, J. Oxberry, R. M. Neal, A. W. Ritchie

South Africans in the team: Peter Hauser (right-half), Des Horne (outside-right), Brian Peterson (inside-right), and Bill Perry (outside-left). Four other South Africans have played for Blackpool: Gordon Falconer, Bernard Levy, Peter Smethurst, and Keith Peterson, brother of Brian. The most successful of them all was Bill Perry. He was the first foreign-born player, in post-war football, to win full England honours, and is one of the few players born outside Britain to score a century of goals in English League football. His spectacular, long-range goals are still talked about, with awe, by Blackpool supporters.

Blackpool have a reputation as innovators. The Blackpool-Bolton match, at Bloomfield Road on September 10, 1960, was the first Football League match to be televised live. ITV billed the programme as *The Big Game*. Cinema-managers and owners of public houses, in many parts of the country, complained about a slump in business that evening. The "gate", according to viewer-audit figures, was the biggest in League history: 2,350,000. To this day, no other League match has been televised live.

A year later, Blackpool again made football and television history when Stanley Matthews signed for Stoke during the BBC's *Sportsview* programme. This was the first live televising of a footballer's transfer.

Blackpool was the first club to fly to a Football League match (to Arsenal, for the game on Good Friday, 1957) and the first club to fly to a League fixture on the day of the match (to Cardiff, March 1961).

But there are two "firsts" of which Blackpool may be particularly proud. After the Munich disaster, in February 1958, Blackpool was the first club to offer to lend players to Manchester United. And, in 1961, Blackpool became the first Football League club to be complimented by the Football Association for not having a caution administered to any of its players during a season. The Disciplinary Committee, at a meeting in Hastings, resolved: "that the Secretary convey to the Blackpool officials and their players the Committee's appreciation of the exemplary conduct of the club's players—no adverse report having been received regarding any member of the club during the Season." Not even the threat of relegation—and Blackpool came perilously close in season 1960–61—tempted the players to try rough or unfair tactics.

For many years, Blackpool was unique—among English League clubs—in wearing tangerine. Albert Hargreaves, a Football League referee and a Blackpool director, noticed the colour when refereeing an international match in Amsterdam. Blackpool adopted tangerine in the early twenties, and it has been the club's

c

main colour ever since; except for a spell in the thirties when Blackpool players wore Oxford- and Cambridge-blue stripes. Blackpool have been known as "The Tangerines" for such a long time that it comes as a surprise to discover two nicknames of long ago: "The Stripes" and "The Reds" (*pace* Liverpool).

Good club-spirit and an attractive style of play have made Blackpool a popular touring side. Few League clubs have travelled more widely than Blackpool. Blackpool have played in Europe, Asia, Africa, North America, and Australasia—every continent except for South America. In the mid-thirties, a North African tour failed to materialize, and in 1937 an F.A. ban on tours of Russia kept Blackpool at home during the summer. After the war, Blackpool began globe-trotting in earnest: Scandinavia in 1947, and again in 1948; Switzerland in 1951; Alsace in 1954.

In 1958, Blackpool embarked on a world tour, one of the longest and most successful ever undertaken by a British club. After a visit to Hollywood and a 13-2 trouncing of the Los Angeles All-Stars, Blackpool became the first English League club to visit Australia. Blackpool played eleven matches—including five test matches against Australia—and won them all. The all-conquering tourists then flew to Hong Kong and beat the national side 3-1. A local official alleged, in public, that Blackpool had been lucky to win. He was silenced a day or two later when Blackpool played a Combined Chinese XI, also in Hong Kong. Blackpool pride was at stake. On paper, this was a more difficult match than the first one. Blackpool won 10-1.

The tours continued: Africa in 1960, winning seven out of eight matches; the Orange Bowl Trophy in Valencia, 1962; the Costa del Sol tournament in Malaga, 1963; exhibition matches in 1965 against Sheffield United—the first time that two First Division clubs had played a series of matches in New Zealand.

Many stories—some amusing, some poignant, some flattering—could be told of Blackpool's tours: of the young footballers in Africa who were seen practising in their bare feet; the Swiss team that unexpectedly brought on three substitutes; the match in Barcelona that finished at 12.25 a.m., and the *Spanish* newspaper, the next day, that accused the referee of being unfair to Blackpool; the dozens of goals scored on tour by Ray Charnley; the local newspaper in Alsace that referred to Blackpool's star players—Matthews, Mortensen, Johnston, and others—as *Les Incomparables*; the promoter, worried after a previous and unsuccessful visit by an English team, who requested that Blackpool should begin their tour with a victory "in doubled (*sic*) figures, if possible".

Blackpool won the F.A. Cup in 1953, but did not gain entry

into a European competition: the Cup-Winners' Cup did not begin until 1960–61. A few weeks after being relegated to the Second Division, Blackpool F.C. won at its first attempt in European football: the 1971 Anglo-Italian Inter-League Clubs Competition. Here was tangible proof of Blackpool's fine club-spirit. Blackpool charmed the partisan crowds with fluent, attacking football: a rare sight in Italy, where defence is god. Blackpool, top scorers in the Competition, won 2-1 in the final against Bologna, a team reputed to have cost £1½ million. One of Blackpool's star players was goalkeeper John Burridge. Only a few weeks earlier, he was on the books of Workington, a Fourth Division club.

Blackpool excelled not only in results but also in goodwill. The players obeyed manager Stokoe's instructions not to provoke the crowds or the opponents. This meant no tackling from behind, no charging of the goalkeeper, no challenging of a referee's decision. The first series of matches was played in England, and, off the field, Blackpool F.C. upheld the town's reputation for warmth and hospitality. For this, much credit was due to the efficiency and foresight of Des McBain, the club secretary. After the final, Alan Hardaker, secretary of the Football League, heaped praise on Blackpool: "They have made a lot of friends in Italy, by their behaviour both on and off the field. Everybody has been delighted with Blackpool. They have been England's finest ambassadors in football, and tremendous ambassadors of the Football League."

Bob Stokoe is the latest addition to the line or cavalcade of Blackpool managers. I can see them now, one by one, as though in a gallery of portraits: some strict, some lax; some humorous and some dead-pan; some inspirational and some technocratic. The grandfather of them all—Blackpool's first full-time manager —was Bill Norman. He came to Blackpool just after the First World War, having trained Barnsley—F.A. Cup victors in 1912. His wax moustache, and the Spartan training routines he organised, earned him the nickname "Sergeant-major". He was not a tactician; training was his forte. His teams were notable for speed and fitness: they ranked among the fittest in the whole of the Football League. When Norman was manager of Blackpool, the club's trainer was Allan Ure, his son-in-law. At the end of season 1922–23, they both decamped to Leeds United; Bill Norman as manager. Allan Ure returned to Blackpool several years later, and was trainer of the 1929–30 promotion team.

In direct contrast to Norman was the next manager of Blackpool, Major Frank Buckley. As a football tactician, Buckley was years ahead of his time. Not everyone believed in him or in his methods. His was an original mind, and he believed in himself. That, for him, was probably all that mattered. I have heard an eye-witness account of his handing-out of pep pills, in the Blackpool dressing-room, before a cup-tie in the mid-twenties. For years, he was the most controversial manager in League football—and, by way of compensation, the highest-paid.

Buckley was a commanding figure, both to look at and to listen to. He was well educated and well spoken, nearly a six-footer, and had a distinctly military bearing. He invariably wore plus-fours, and could easily be mistaken for a farmer. Buckley had strong self-discipline—he was a non-drinker and a non-smoker—and he expected the same sense of dedication from his players. His critics said that he lacked humour, but he was not as daunting or forbidding a man as you might imagine.

He was a track-suit manager. He trained with his players, and arranged informal discussions on tactics. He had a far-sighted youth policy: it was no big event if he signed half-a-dozen juniors in a single day. He encouraged his team to play golf, as a means of relaxation from football. They disliked golf at first, but eventually came to share his enthusiasm.

He left Blackpool in 1927, to become manager of Wolverhampton Wanderers. This was an era of contrasts. At a time when Buckley was devising a new style of management, many footballers —Blackpool players among them—lacked security. No five-year contracts for *them*. At the end of each season, all the players at Bloomfield Road had to wait in a queue to hear if they were to be signed on again. Each one would leave the ground, either rubbing his hands gleefully or hanging his head in disappointment.

Sydney Beaumont, a former Preston player, left Blackpool in the spring of 1928. His managership lasted less than a year, the shortest in Blackpool history. Blackpool were, as usual, short of money, and decided to do without a paid manager for a while. A club director, Harry Evans, acted as honorary team-manager during several momentous seasons, including promotion to the First Division in 1929–30. His service to Blackpool football spanned most of the club's triumphs: he was Chairman at the time of the 1953 Cup Final victory. Harry Evans was a prosperous self-made businessman, frank and outspoken at all times. He had a prodigious memory for the facts and figures of the club: from players, and their transfer fees, to match results.

Alex ("Sandy") Macfarlane, who had been a Scottish international before World War I, signed a two-year contract just before the start of the 1933–34 season. He was one of the foremost authorities on the game during the inter-war period, and a quick and accurate judge of a player. He made some astute signings during his short spell as manager of Blackpool, but it is as a tactician that he is best remembered.

The first-team goalkeeper was slow in getting down to low balls, so Macfarlane asked one of the directors, who was a cricketer, to stand in the penalty-area and throw tennis balls at the 'keeper, from all angles. That is one example of Macfarlane's originality and his *determination* that every player should strive for higher and higher standards. He was a perfectionist, a relentless perfectionist. That was his strength as well as his weakness.

Smiles took over from sternness when Blackpool appointed Joe Smith as manager in August 1935. Joe led the club to greatness. Age alone stopped him, almost 23 years later, and brought to an end the longest and most successful reign of any manager in Blackpool history. Joe helped players to believe in themselves. And *he* believed in Blackpool: he often used to say, "The two best teams in the country are Blackpool and Blackpool's reserves."

Joe Smith was one of the *characters* of Blackpool and Lancashire football, with an entirely original sense of humour, a wonderful way with people, and warmth and humanity beneath the blunt surface. Joe was larger than life. His days as Blackpool's manager still live in the minds of all who knew him or played for him. Once, before the team left for an away match, Joe made a half-hearted attempt at a roll-call. He stood up at the front of the coach and asked, "Is Morty here?" "Yes, Joe." "And is the Maestro here?" A hesitant "Yes" came from the back of the coach: Matthews was too modest to enjoy being called "Maestro". "Let's go," said Joe Smith. "We've got at least half the team."

When the players had their rub-down at half-time, Stanley Matthews always insisted on being rubbed-down by Joe Smith. Joe would talk non-stop: "You can beat this full-back. Try and take him inside, now and then. You can beat the daylights out of him." Depending on how the team had played in the first half, Joe would be either encouraging or caustic. One afternoon, his key inside-forward was making no impact on the game. "What time did you go to bed last night?" Joe asked. "I was in bed by ten, Joe. Honest." "Yes, but *whose* bloody bed?"

One Saturday Blackpool went south for a particularly vital match. Blackpool left the field at half-time 2-0 down, and the players knew that there would be some verbal fireworks in the dressing-room. Joe called Harry Johnston, the captain, to one side, and whispered a few words in his ear. Harry then said, "Lads, the manager wants to talk to you." The players stood up and shuffled to attention. They knew what to expect—or thought they did. Joe said, "We have to catch the first train back to Blackpool, so get changed as quickly as you can after the game." He walked towards the door. Some of the players sighed with relief. Some looked at each other, as if to say, "Has the manager gone soft?" As Joe Smith got to the door, he turned round. He looked at his players and said, with chilling irony, "And if you intend to play as badly in the second half, as you did in the first, you might as well get changed now." The Blackpool team went back onto the field and won the match.

Joe Smith was succeeded by one of the full-backs of his post-war team, Ron Suart. Suart was the first former Blackpool player to return as manager. A sincere, quietly-spoken man, with a keen eye for young talent, he had the misfortune to be manager during the first years of the no-maximum wage. Blackpool and the other town clubs suffered, while their big brothers in the cities flourished. The fatality rate of Blackpool managers increased.

In February 1967, when Blackpool were anchored to the bottom of the First Division, Stanley Mortensen took over. The football world rejoiced: because Morty was one of the most popular players ever to represent Blackpool and England. He had the potential to become a highly successful manager. In April 1969, his contract was terminated. Was there a vendetta?

Morty very nearly took Blackpool back into the First Division in his first full season as manager: the record book is his best defence counsel. His departure brought to a close one of the saddest chapters in Blackpool F.C. history.

Les Shannon, a former Burnley player, was manager from May 1969 until October 1970. In his first season at Bloomfield Road, he helped Blackpool win promotion. A few months later, the club was heading for the Second Division again. On October 24, 1970, Bloomfield Road staged an extraordinary match. At half-time, Blackpool were winning 3-0 against Chelsea, holders of the F.A. Cup. When the final whistle was blown, Blackpool had lost 4-3. Three days later Les Shannon resigned.

In December 1970, Blackpool persuaded Carlisle to release their manager, Bob Stokoe, who had been a member of Newcastle's 1955 Cup-winning team. But it was too late, even for miracles. Blackpool had already lost too many points, and, lacking penetration near goal, slipped quietly back into the Second Division. A few weeks later, thousands of tangerine-scarfed fans welcomed the team's return after victory in the Anglo-Italian Inter-League Clubs Competition. Bob Stokoe's achievement, within six months of becoming manager, was true to Blackpool traditions. The promotion campaigns of many clubs have been the result of years of careful planning and team-building by the manager. Not so at

Blackpool. The club has been promoted three times—from Division II to Division I—and each occasion was an instant success for the manager. In 1929–30, Harry Evans led Blackpool to promotion in his second season as honorary team-manager. In 1936–37, Blackpool won promotion in Joe Smith's second season as manager. In 1969–70, Les Shannon went one better by guiding Blackpool back into the First Division in his first season as manager. Two seasons earlier, Stan Mortensen, in his first full season as manager, took the club to within a hand's grasp of the First Division. Only goal-average foiled him.

A number of seasons—all through Blackpool F.C. history—have reached a flash-point of interest and tension. Blackpool lived dangerously between the wars. Three times in seven seasons, the club narrowly escaped relegation to Division III (North). The third —and the most tense—occasion was in 1927–28 when Blackpool finished 19th in Division II, saved from the Third Division by only two points. Blackpool gave the Bloomfield Road fans sleepless nights by leaving the jump to safety until the last match of the season, at home to Fulham. Relegation threatened the losers. Jimmy Hampson produced his best form that day—when it was most needed—and scored three goals in a 4-0 win.

Two years later, Blackpool were playing with more consistency than ever before. After the matches of April 12, 1930, the top of the Second Division read :

	Played	Points
Oldham	37	51
Blackpool	37	51
Chelsea	37	49

Only Chelsea, in third place, had a realistic chance of catching the leaders. Blackpool and Oldham were competing not only for promotion but also for the Championship. A mischievous demon in the fixture list forced Blackpool and Oldham to meet twice at Easter. At Bloomfield Road on Good Friday, Blackpool won the first encounter 3-0. The next day, two goals by Hampson steered Blackpool to victory over Bradford City.

The fans were given a day of rest on Sunday, before the return game at Oldham on Easter Monday. The Blackpool team that travelled to Oldham, for this third match in four days, was : Pearson; Grant (captain), Watson; Wilson, Tremelling, Tuffnell; Rattray, Broadhurst, Hampson, Oxberry, Neal. There was no score at half-time. Ten minutes after the interval, Jimmy Hampson missed a penalty. Determined to make amends, he gave Blackpool the lead a few minutes later, and then set up a goal for Oxberry.

Blackpool's 2-1 win ensured a place for the club in Division I for the first time. But who would win the Championship? On April 26, Blackpool went down 3-0 at Swansea. The positions at the top were now:

	Played	Points
Blackpool	41	57
Chelsea	41	55
Oldham	41	53

Blackpool were due to play at Nottingham Forest; and Chelsea at Bury. Blackpool needed one point to be certain of winning the Championship. If Blackpool lost and Chelsea won, Chelsea would win the Championship on goal-average. Blackpool gave the supporters a nail-biting afternoon. Harry Wilson was injured early in the match, and Hampson had a goal disallowed. At the end of ninety minutes, the score was 0-0. Blackpool, with a team that had cost not a penny more than £8,000, returned home as Division II Champions.

In Blackpool's first season in Division I, the club secretary, T. A. Barcroft, accompanied the team to a match in London. For him, this was no ordinary match. To go with the team to London, to play against this famous club, was the consummation of a lifetime's dream and ambition. On arriving at the ground, Barcroft asked to see one of his friends, a director of the home club. "Oh no," came the reply, "he's not here today. He only comes to the *important* matches."

Blackpool's defence caved in almost every week-end in that first season in Division I: 3-7 at home to Leeds; 1-7 at Arsenal; 1-7 at Sheffield Wednesday; 1-10 at Huddersfield. And so on. The Saturday editions of Blackpool's local newspapers were all but edged in black, as a sign of perpetual mourning. The sceptics went about muttering, "I told you so," and, when Blackpool lost 6-2 in the second-last match of the season, their faces beamed at the prospect of relegation—their forecast come true.

The scene was set for a dramatic finale. The last match was played at Bloomfield Road on May 2, 1931. Blackpool needed one point to avoid relegation. Ten minutes from the end, Manchester City were leading 2-1. Blackpool, in desperation, put Albert Watson, a wing-half, into the forward-line. A couple of minutes later, Jimmy Hampson found a gap in the City defence. He squared the ball to the right, and Albert Watson shot a 20-yarder into the top of the net. Blackpool's defence held firm, and the old rivals drew 2-2. Watson's goal—his only one that season—became known as the "£10,000 goal", because Blackpool were assured of at least one more season of lucrative First Division gate money. On the field that day was Blackpool's S. Tuffnell (5ft 2½in), one of the smallest half-backs ever to play in League football. City's right-half was Matt Busby.

A year later, Blackpool needed to win at Sheffield United in order to escape relegation. United took the lead in the first minute, but Blackpool won convincingly, 3-1. In the second successive season, Blackpool finished in 20th place and escaped Division II by a single point. At the end of the 1932–33 season, Blackpool won at Newcastle, but other relegation candidates also won. And so Blackpool, after three torturous seasons in the First Division, dropped back into the Second. But not for long.

We move now to 1937, Blackpool F.C.'s golden jubilee year. Blackpool played at Coventry, on April 17, and this was the team : big Jock Wallace in goal; Butcher and Witham at full-back; Farrow, Cardwell, and S. Jones—the best half-back line in the Second Division; little Munro on the right wing, with the immortal Jimmy Hampson at inside-right; Bobby Finan, the free-scoring Scotsman, at centre-forward; Tom Lyon at inside-left; and Frank Hill, a strong and influential captain, on the left wing. This was not a team of star players, or glamour boys, or internationals, but it was a *team*.

Munro scored for Blackpool in the 12th minute and Finan made it 2-0 in the 48th. Coventry scored four minutes later, and forced Blackpool onto the defensive for most of the last half-hour. In those last tense minutes, Joe Smith, Blackpool's manager, is reputed to have chewed—to pulp—two expensive Havana cigars. Jimmy Hampson, genius of the 1929–30 promotion side, gave a masterly display. Blackpool won the match 2-1 and regained First Division status. There was no champagne in the dressing-room. Even if Blackpool had been given a dozen bottles, no one would have had time to enjoy them, because the players and officials had to be on the homeward-bound train half an hour after the end of the match. Now for the Championship. Then the champagne would flow.

The top of Division II now read :

	Played	Points	Goals For	Against
Blackpool	41	54	87	52
Leicester	40	52	83	55

Neither Bury, who were in third place, nor Plymouth, who were fourth, could catch Blackpool. Blackpool's last match was against Doncaster Rovers, at Bloomfield Road on April 24. Victory for Blackpool would almost certainly win them the Championship.

Even if Leicester gained four points from the last two matches, Blackpool would come first because of a better goal-average. Surely all this was unnecessary speculation? What did Blackpool have to fear? They had been at the top of the Second Division for months. Doncaster were at the bottom, already doomed to relegation.

The Blackpool selectors caused a surprise by changing a winning team. Danny Blair, who missed the Coventry match because of injury, replaced Butcher at right-back. Henry Bowl, who had been scoring goals in the Central League, was preferred to Lyon at inside-left. Dick Watmough, who was left out of the Coventry match, was given back the outside-right position, to the exclusion of the lively Munro. Watmough was brought back for sentimental reasons. The selectors thought it would be ungracious to leave out a forward who had been a first-teamer for most of the season. Anyway, what did it matter? Blackpool would get a cricket score against the unfortunate Rovers.

The Blackpool fans, in their thousands, invaded Bloomfield Road. Like a holiday crowd going to a bull-fight, they were lusting for Doncaster blood. The band played *Yes, we have no bananas*, which for years was Blackpool's signature tune; but the words should have been rewritten for this particular day—*Yes, we shall have no champagne*. Doncaster opened the scoring in the 32nd minute. All Blackpool was dumbfounded. Five minutes later, they cheered Henry Bowl's equaliser. Now for the winner. . . . But the winner never came, and the match ended in a 1-1 draw. It remains —to this day—one of the most bizarre results in Blackpool F.C. history. A few days later, Leicester beat Tottenham and won the Championship by a single point. Blackpool finished the season with a better goal-average than Leicester. That 32nd-minute goal by the bottom club had cost Blackpool the Championship.

Blackpool enjoyed an uninterrupted stay in the First Division from 1937–38 until the end of season 1966–67. At the time of relegation. Blackpool were the second-oldest inhabitants of the Division: second only to Arsenal. It was a proud record for a club that has never been a member of the wealthy élite. Blackpool hoped for a quick return, and that hope very nearly came true after only one season. The 1967–68 promotion race was one of the closest in Division II history. Six consecutive wins had kept Blackpool in the top three, and the day of reckoning came on May 11, 1968. On that Saturday, Blackpool played at Huddersfield, and Queen's Park Rangers at Aston Villa. If both Blackpool and Queen's Park won, then Queen's Park would win promotion on goal-average, and Blackpool would remain in Division II.

The Huddersfield–Blackpool match toyed with the emotions,

but, throughout the afternoon, there were also fervent Blackpool chants of support for Aston Villa. The Blackpool fans were in Huddersfield, but their thoughts and hopes often strayed to the equally important match at Aston Villa. A few minutes after the start of the second half, the electronic score-board at Huddersfield began to flash the half-time scores in other matches. The one that mattered was match "B" in the third group of scores to be shown. The second group disappeared, and then the score-board began chuckling to itself: Villa 1–Q.P.R. 2 . . . 3 . . . 4 . . . 5. Villa 4–Q.P.R. 3. At last the fickle score-board settled for Villa 1–Q.P.R. 0. The Blackpool supporters laughed and cheered.

Blackpool, meanwhile, were playing with Mortensen-like spirit, and had a 3-1 lead. Minutes from the end, a rumour spread through the crowd that Villa were 2-0 up. The referee blew his whistle and hundreds of Blackpool fans ran onto the pitch, like the splash of a great tangerine-coloured wave. Thinking that Blackpool had won promotion, they stood beneath the directors' box and chanted "MOR-TY", "MOR-TY".

Then the final, sad twist. Villa 1–Q.P.R. 2. Official. Villa had conceded a controversial goal and then gave away an own-goal. The manner of Queen's Park's victory was heavy with irony. A fortnight earlier, they had gained a point at Ipswich with a penalty and a last-second free-kick. When the Villa–Q.P.R. result was announced, the Blackpool cheering stopped. The waving and the clapping stopped. The rattles and banners were put down. And the Blackpool fans slouched slowly, sadly, away. Several girls were in tears. A memorable season for Blackpool had come to an end.

Jimmy Armfield, Blackpool's valiant captain, was the first to board the coach. Stan Mortensen, the Blackpool manager, was the last to leave the ground. By great force of personality, Morty had imbued his team with new purpose, determination, and will-to-win. In each of their last two matches, the Blackpool players fought back—undismayed at being a goal down—to win 3-1; and both games were away from home. Although Blackpool were not the Champions, at least they had the consolation of having looked and played like Champions.

A year later, Blackpool were thinking more about escaping relegation to Division III, than about winning promotion to Division I. On September 20, 1969, Blackpool languished in sixth-from-bottom place in Division II. There were a number of early-season injuries, and Blackpool's best forward, Tony Green, missed the whole of the campaign because of an operation to an Achilles tendon.

After losing to Bristol City at the end of November, Blackpool were unbeaten in League matches until the middle of March.

Blackpool gained five points—out of a possible six—at Easter, played an uninspiring draw at home to Queen's Park, and then, on the evening of April 7, met Swindon Town (away). Swindon were also challenging for promotion, but they needed a win; a draw would virtually ensure Blackpool's return to the First Division. Blackpool, with goalkeeper Harry Thomson at his best, absorbed constant pressure in the last twenty minutes and managed to draw 1-1.

Promotion became a certainty when Blackpool went to Preston on April 13 and won 3-0, thanks to a hat-trick by Fred Pickering. To the Blackpool team, it didn't feel like an away match, because more than half of the 34,000 spectators had travelled to the game from Blackpool. The player with special reason for celebrating was the captain, Jimmy Armfield, who, after many years' service, had at last won a major honour with his club. The Blackpool team that day was: Harry Thomson, an acrobatic Scot, in goal; Jimmy Armfield, a former England captain, and Bill Bentley; John "Chopper" McPhee, Glyn James, a Welsh international, and Dave Hatton; little Mickey Burns, who had scored the vital goal at Swindon, at outside-right; the hard-working John Craven, loyal Blackpool club-man; Fred Pickering, former England centre-forward; Alan Suddick, a graceful inside-forward, feared by goal-keepers throughout the country for his "banana" shot; and, on the left wing, Tommy Hutchison, one of the most gifted ball-players in Britain.

And so we come to the end of our Cook's tour of Blackpool F.C. history. Cynics claim that only summer football or a millionaire patron will restore Blackpool to her post-war greatness. But, greatness or no greatness, Blackpool F.C. will continue to make its own special contribution to English League football. Blackpool's future will be as absorbing as the colourful past: absorbing to spectators as well as to historians. We can be assured of surprise transfers and financial struggles, days of depression and days of triumph.

I have so many memories of Blackpool and of Blackpool football. I suppose—and hope—that I shall go on accumulating them for the rest of my life. I remember a little group of cockneys who sang *Oranges and Lemons* as the Blackpool players came onto the field in their bright tangerine shirts. I recall the modesty of Stanley Matthews. Everton once asked him if he would like to accompany them on their tour of North America. "I'll come," replied Stan, "if the rest of the lads at Blackpool can come too." No Blackpool fan will forget Cheung Chi-doy, who played for Nationalist China before coming to England: "I come half-way round world to play football, not to find girl friend. English girls very nice, but not for keeps." The spontaneous wit that crackles (or cackles) from the Blackpool kop, Saturday after Saturday, would fill a whole shelf of books. In a home match, during their relegation season of 1970–71, Blackpool were having a particularly unhappy time. "Look at all those sea-gulls on top of the stand," said one supporter to his neighbour. "They aren't sea-gulls, lad. They're vultures."

In all my travels I have never met waitresses more sympathetic (in a strictly confined-to-the-restaurant sense) than those in Blackpool. And Blackpool's taxi drivers are among the most articulate in the world—fit to be compared with their talkative cousins in Paris and New York. I have met taxi drivers in Blackpool, ranging from "sand-grown 'uns" to the old fellow who reminisces about India of colonial days: elephants, rajahs, and all the opulent rest.

Any Blackpool taxi driver, who is part of the unofficial Speakers' Union, will, in no more than five minutes, tell you his life story, give advice on the best shows in town, ask solicitously about your train journey, speculate on the next political conference, and philosophize about the pressures of making a living in Blackpool. They offer you gems like this: "Blackpool is a grafting town. You've got to work for everything, and you're always working while others are playing. You can't have a quiet 35-hour week up here." And poetic similes are part of the repertoire: "We are like squirrels. We have to collect our nuts when the weather is fine, and then go into hibernation."

"Saw them last season. Not worth a light," a Blackpool taxi driver baited me, in the summer of 1955, after Blackpool had narrowly missed relegation. "They'll be back at the top, before long," I replied. A year later, I arrived at the station and waited my turn in the taxi queue. Who should drive up but my downhearted friend of the previous summer? He recognized me immediately. But he said not one word. He took my case and gestured to me to get in, and, as he did so, he winked and made an apologetic nod of the head. This time, Blackpool had finished as No. 2 team in the First Division. Blackpool soccer is like a fickle woman: welcoming and unpredictable. Therein lies nine-tenths of her charm.

2

PETER DOHERTY — in an Interview
Already a Legend

Peter Doherty is one of the greatest players in football history. He is a man of modesty and charm, deeply interested in other people and in the game of football. Blackpool brought him to England, and gave him a foundation on which he built his career. That career has become a legend. Here is Peter Doherty's own story:

I began to get keen on football when I was ten or eleven. Football was always my main sport: perhaps one of the reasons is that I was one of ten children. I had six brothers and three sisters. We used to have a clocking-in room! In our neighbourhood, there were other large families. Football is a cheap game to play, because 22 players can mill around one ball. If I had twopence to go to a matinée at the cinema, I felt rich. So football was really our only recreation. Other sports weren't available. Cricket, for example, is not popular in Ireland. If we had had an opportunity of playing other sports, I would almost certainly have joined in.

We had no such thing as a school football team. In fact, if we played football in the school yard, we would have got the cane, because we might have smashed a window. After school, we used to play football: one street against another, with coats or bricks for goal-posts.

When I was a boy, a football was my best pal. I was never away from a ball. I developed my ball control around the age of ten to fourteen. I used to dribble around bricks or pieces of stick. I would run with the ball, and imagine I was Alex James. I used to imagine that the right-half was coming at me, and I would swerve out of his path. I used to do all these sort of things on my own. A row of houses overlooked the big field I used to play in: I saw old women watching me. I bet they used to say, "Isn't he mad?" I never dreamt that, by doing all this, I would one day become a professional footballer.

Even when I had become an international, I still used to practise my ball control. I used to go out with a ball and run left, right . . . pretend to pass . . . then, all of a sudden, turn. . . . Imagination is a great thing in training. It's important in shadow-boxing. It's important for those fellows on the stage who juggle. If you practise with a ball regularly, constantly, you'll get better and better. My school-days—*that* was my foundation. That's when footballers are made; plus, later on, when they meet people who really know the game.

When I was a boy, I was always shy about talking football with my Mum and Dad. Dad loved the game. He was keen for me to be a footballer, but he never talked to me about it because he knew I was shy. I knew that, when I was promoted or did well, he was pleased and would talk about it to other people. But we never discussed football. I kept my thoughts to myself. I think it's because there has always been a tinge of humility in me.

When I was about thirteen, I joined Station United, which was a very good junior side. I played against men. People said that I would get killed because these men were twenty or thirty years old. And I was not yet fourteen. Station United was a prominent junior side in Coleraine. The gentleman in charge of us was a fellow called "Heedy" Brown, a Scot. He had quite a knowledge of the game, although he had never been a professional. He was very keen on soccer. He was wrapped up in it, like most officials at junior levels. They give their heart and soul to the game they love.

My father and mother insisted that I have a trade. I became an apprentice to a local builder. In those days—back in the twenties and thirties—all Mums and Dads used to say, "A trade will take you anywhere. It's the passport to success." The wage I got was 7s. or 8s. a week. All the apprentices wanted to work with the best tradesman. There was one particular gentleman who was an outstanding tiler. We used to toss up to see who should work with him, because we all wanted to learn. The job didn't work out too well for me. I felt the strain of having to do a labourer's job: having to carry half-hundredweight blocks of cement, and so on.

I had an uncle who was pretty well off. He lived in Portstewart, which is a seaside resort $3\frac{1}{2}$ miles from my town, Coleraine. He operated a bus service, and he wanted me to come and work for him—which I did, as a conductor. I worked on the buses for two or three months, but my uncle had to stop me. I couldn't get a licence. You had to be seventeen, and I wasn't nearly seventeen.

Coleraine F.C., a professional club, asked me to come to them for a trial. I was only a mite at the time. I was joined, at this trial, by a big fellow, an ex-Guardsman. He was a six-footer, and I had

to look up at him. We went along, not sure if we would be asked
to play. Luckily for me, the outside-right, Norman Lynn, hadn't
turned up. He missed the train at Belfast. My name was called out,
over the loudspeaker, so I went to the dressing-room, and they
said, "Come on, you're playing." When I went onto the field, the
game had started. I played outside-right, which was not my position: I was an inside-left. I didn't play for more than twenty or
thirty minutes, and I only kicked the ball twice. At half-time, I
was told to take my jersey off; Norman Lynn had arrived. When
they passed round the lemon slices, I was ignored. In other words,
I was nothing. I was useless. I remember vowing to myself—in
my childish mind—that I would never play for Coleraine again,
even though an uncle of mine was a director.

My next step was Glentoran. Billy McSevenny, whose brother
was a well-known full-back, got me a trial. At first I refused to go,
because it meant being away from home for a night. That shows
you how "countrified" I was. They arranged for me to go there
on a Saturday. Billy took me, and brought me back after the game.
I must have done well, because in a very short time I was in the
first team. I was about seventeen.

They sent me a telegram to tell me that I was to play in the
League side: it was a match against Cliftonville, which was an
amateur club in a professional League. When I got the telegram,
I didn't know what to do. I didn't know what day it was. I was
very shy with Mum and Dad. I kept very quiet and humble. I
didn't want them to think I was big-headed. When I signed professional for Glentoran, I got a signing-on fee of £24. £24! I thought
I had the world. I'd never dreamed of playing professional football. I'd only been playing because of my love for the game.

When I was with Glentoran, I heard a lot of rumours about
English clubs who were looking for players in Ireland. You heard
that so-and-so was after you; but we heard so many rumours that
we took very little notice of them.

One day, when I'd been with Glentoran for a couple of seasons,
I decided to go and watch my town team, Coleraine, play at
Windsor Park, Belfast: just as you might go to watch Blackpool
play at Bolton or Preston. I didn't know which tram to take, so I
asked a fellow who was coming from the direction of the shipyard.
"Excuse me," I said. "Could you please tell me the best way to
Windsor Park?" He said, "Come with me. I'm walking it, and I
know a short cut which will take us there in no time."

As we walked to the ground, the first thing he said to me was,
"Do you know that fellow Doherty who plays for Glentoran?" I
said, "No." "Did you know," he said, "he went to Celtic Park

Frank O'Donnell. Scottish international centre-forward, who joined Blackpool from Preston in November 1937

The legendary Peter Doherty in 1935, the year of his international début

Blackpool F.C. 1936–37, Division II runners-up. *Left to right.* Standing: J. Smith (Manager), J. Hampson, T. K. Lyon, G. Farrow, J. Wallace, R. Witham, S. Jones, T. W. Jones, L. Cardwell, H. Wilson (Trainer); sitting: R. Watmough, D. Blair, R. J. Finan, F. Hill, A. Munro, W. Cook

with a pair of boots under his arm? He asked them for a trial, and they wouldn't accept him. He went from there to Windsor Park, and they turned him down too. Then he went to the Oval, and Glentoran took pity on him and signed him. Now, all the English clubs are after him." I still didn't let on who I was. We reached the officials' entrance and I went in. I left him there.

To this day, I don't know if he realizes that he had been speaking to Peter Doherty. I don't know who he was, but I would love to know. In fact, his story wasn't very accurate. It just shows you how these tales can get around. I can still picture that fellow. He had overalls on. I didn't know him from Adam, but I remember he came from the shipyard. This was the first real intimation I had that English League clubs were interested in me.

Soon afterwards, I was asked to go to the Abercorn Hotel in Belfast. I met Sandy Macfarlane, Blackpool's manager, and Sam Butterworth, a director. I didn't know that Blackpool had been watching me. Within minutes, I was a Blackpool player.

Many years later, I became assistant-manager at Preston. It was only then that I learned that Preston might have got my signature before Blackpool came along. Preston had a representative in Ireland. He sent them a number of names that proved to be of no use. Eventually, he told them about me. But Preston were so fed up with being given useless names that they didn't go to see me.

I came to Blackpool in November 1933. I arrived on Armistice Day: I remember it so well. I was met by Jack Charles, the assistant-trainer, and Louis Cardwell, a big centre-half with whom I played for many years.

I was only a young man, and I'd never been away from home before. So you can imagine what an ordeal it was for me to leave Ireland. I arrived at Heysham, and it was about 6.15 in the morning when I caught the train to Blackpool. I looked out of the window and I saw, far away in a field, the advert that shows two men, one at each end of a distemper board. I thought they were two men walking to work. I said to myself, "By God, they get up early in the morning, around here." As you can see, I was very "countrified".

The Blackpool dressing-room made a terrific impression on me. It had "discipline" written all over it. The strip was neatly arranged on numbered pegs. The dressing-room was spotless, very different from Ireland, where, if you went into a dressing-room, you'd find clothes and boots all over the place.

I am very pleased that I went to Blackpool. This was the best thing I could have done. They built a foundation for me of discipline and character, moulding me into good footballing habits. Blackpool was—and still is—a very good club.

D

Sandy Macfarlane did a lot for me. He was not a popular manager, but he was a very *good* manager. He was getting on in years. He wasn't a track-suit manager any more. Had he been younger, I am quite certain he would have taken Blackpool a long way. Sandy Macfarlane was a tactician of the highest quality. He was years ahead of his time.

I thought such a great deal of him, because of his *knowledge* of the game; knowledge commands respect. He was always immaculately dressed. He always looked as though he had come straight out of Burton's. When he appeared on the scene, amongst the players, you could have heard a pin drop.

Before we went for a team talk, we used to congregate in the passage at Bloomfield Road. We would all be talking, and then someone would whisper, "Sandy is coming!" We used to call him "Mr Macfarlane", but, when he wasn't about, we used to refer to him as "Sandy".

We had several Scots at Blackpool. They use to wear "bumfreezers"—underwear that was buttoned up the back, but revealed the backside. Jock Wallace, a big goalkeeper, came to Bloomfield Road from Scotland. He was quite a character. One day, Jimmy Hampson—bless him—was chatting to Jock, telling him, "We call the manager 'Sandy'." A minute later, Mr Macfarlane came out of the boardroom and walked up the passage. Big Jock called out, "Good morning, Sandy." And Mr Macfarlane turned round and said, "You silly big clot."

When we reported at the ground in the morning, smoking was definitely out. Mr Macfarlane had a professional sprinter for us, taking us individually. We used to have tactical talks. Mr Macfarlane would stand at the head of the table, with the trainer. We used to try and hide down so that he wouldn't pick on us. He would say, "Doherty. We're attacking on the right wing. Set out the team on the board." It was an ordeal for me, or for any young player, to think deeply about tactics. We were shy about having to explain our ideas to the others. We were afraid of making a mistake, and afraid of being laughed at. But, in these sessions, we learned a lot about the game.

There were only two teams in those days. When the team-sheet for the first team was put up, everyone used to rush in to have a look, even though a lot knew that their names would not be listed. Then, as soon as the second-team sheet was put up in the other dressing-room, we all rushed in there. If your name wasn't on either list, you were in the "stand" team.

I was drafted into Blackpool's League side quite quickly. I made my début at Bradford Park Avenue on December 23, 1933. I was playing at inside-left. We won 2-1. In those days, we used to play three games at Christmas. I didn't do so well, and I was soon back in the reserves. I didn't get a very good report from the second-team trainer. At our tactical talk, the first thing Mr Macfarlane said to me was, "You didn't try a leg, did you?" I took a terrible battering from him. Eventually, I fought back and said, "Well, if you think that, you're wrong; because I did try. I probably just had a bad game." Then I said, "And I'll tell you another thing. I don't want to play in your first team, because it's no pleasure to play in it."

Mr Macfarlane bullied me. If I hadn't been able to fight back, or take all he gave me, I think I would have failed. But even though he hounded me, at least it showed he was interested in me. He bullied me more than he did the other players. He knew I had potential.

My best friend was Sam Jones, a left-half. He arrived at Blackpool about three weeks before I did. One Saturday, a goal by Sam Jones put us on the road to victory. A short while after the game I saw Sammy, and he was as white as a sheet. "What's the matter?" I asked. And Sammy said, "The manager had me in. He told me I shouldn't have been in the penalty-area."

If I had been talking to my future wife, and Mr Macfarlane had walked past, he would have had me in. He would have said, "What do you mean by this? Do you want to be a football player? You can leave women out of your life for a while."

One day, after a reserve match, we were having a tactical talk, and Sandy Macfarlane turned to me and said, "I hear you were holding on to the ball. We'll have to give you one of your own." My team-mates teased me unmercifully about this.

Sir Lindsay Parkinson was Chairman in those days. We were aiming for promotion. Blackpool would have given a great deal to get out of the Second Division. So every game was a needle game. Every point we lost was a tragedy. Mr Macfarlane gave vent to his feelings, and it was usually the players who suffered. He was sparing with praise. After a particularly hard match against Bury, which we had done well to win, all he could say was, "You should have won it an hour earlier."

The press were very good to me. I especially remember Clifford Greenwood, who came to most of our games. He was a fine man. The press can make or break a player. The press will always favour an *honest* player, the fellow who—even if he lacks ability—*gives* all he has to the game. The fellow who idles, the fellow who couldn't care less, the fellow who degrades the game: this is the sort of player who deserves all the bad publicity he gets.

I have always had a great affection for Blackpool as a town. It's an exciting town. But I kept away from the places—such as the Palace and the Winter Gardens—that I thought might tempt me or harm my career. Not that there was anything wrong with these places: they just weren't places for me. I dedicated myself to my profession.

My home life, as a child, was very helpful to me. I had a very strict upbringing—a Christian way of life—and I tried to carry it out, to the letter. In fact, I met my wife in church. My upbringing helped me tremendously in my career as a professional footballer. I never wanted to see or taste alcohol. I never stayed out late. And I didn't smoke until I was twenty-five or twenty-six.

We were all pals at Blackpool. The lads at Bloomfield Road were a grand crowd. My best pal, Sam Jones, was similar to myself—dedicated to the game. We were fitness-fanatics. We went everywhere together. We walked mostly; seldom took a bus. We used to do deep-breathing exercises: in-two-six, out-two-three; in-two-three, out-two-six. It was called the Swedish Breathing Drill. That deep-breathing, plus avoiding the things that would harm my body, gave a tremendous boost to my stamina. I could run and run. When a game was over, I still felt like playing on.

When Sam and I arrived at Bloomfield Road in the morning, for training, the rest of the lads used to chant: "They don't drink. They don't smoke. They don't go out with women. What do they live for?" There was a one-word answer to that—football.

There was another Jones at Blackpool: an inside-forward by the name of T. W. Jones. He had come from Burnley. Tommy, Sam, and I, were in the same digs. We were known as "The Three Musketeers". Tommy was a good player, but I had come as a youngster with a promising future, and I took his place in the team. Tommy took the news like a gentleman.

There were two great inside-forwards at Blackpool while I was with the club: Bobby Finan, who was a Scot, and Jimmy Hampson. Jimmy was an idol in Blackpool, and he was even featured in Louis Tussaud's Waxworks. He wasn't as good in the air as he was on the ground. His shooting power was his great asset. His right foot, particularly, was lethal. *Hampson* was a household name in Blackpool because of the number of goals he scored, and the way he scored them. Compared to Jimmy, we were only *learners*. He was a good team-man, the type of chap who would pass the ball for others to fire in. Jimmy was a very dry-humoured person. He was very modest, quiet, and humble.

In the third round of the Cup, in 1934, we played against Cheltenham Town. I was playing at centre-forward that day. Cheltenham was better known for its rugby union team. We were the first League club ever to play in the town. There was a big crowd waiting for us. They put detonators on the track, and, as our train came into the station, the noise was terrific.

Cheltenham were only a team of part-timers, but they scored in the fifth minute. I can hear the cheers even now: they must have lasted for several minutes. That ovation is still ringing in my ears. It was still 1-0 to them at half-time. In the end, we won 3-1. I scored Blackpool's third goal.

It was only a matter of time before we got those three goals against Cheltenham. There was plenty of effort in the Blackpool side. There were no shirkers. The Blackpool team, at around that time, was Jock Wallace in goal; Wassell and Grant at full-back; Bobby Dougall, a Scottish wing-half, a very good player; Phil Watson, another Scot, at centre-half; with Sam Jones, my best pal, at left-half. Among the forwards were Jimmy Hampson, Bobby Finan, Tommy Jones, and Alan Hall, a centre-forward from Tottenham.

In the next round, we played at Stoke. We lost that one. Stanley Matthews scored Stoke's first goal. He was a truly great player. Even in those early days, he was one to watch. Two years later, we played Margate in the Cup. Like Cheltenham, Margate was a non-League club. There was a lot of tension before these two matches, because Blackpool had everything to lose. We beat Margate 3-1.

We got paid on a Friday, and I used to send my mother £2 every week. I knew that she needed it. I could picture her waiting for the postman to come. When I joined Blackpool, I signed for £7 in the first team, £7 in the reserves, and £6 in the summer. The maximum wage was £8. I was a young boy who never dreamed that he would make Blackpool's first team. It was a *great* wage in those days: a tradesman was getting only about £3 5s. or £3 10s. I felt like a millionaire. But money is not the thing you think about most, if you are going to be a successful player. Those who love the game will generally get more success out of it than those who are always looking for money.

Sir Lindsay Parkinson, Blackpool's Chairman, had practically taken over the club. He was a wonderful person. Once, when he was ill, he sent for me. He said, "Peter, remember these words. While I'm alive, you will not leave this club." And I said, "I never want to leave Blackpool, sir." He once said to me, "I will look after you when your playing days are over. You can work in my firm." I was very happy at Blackpool.

I was having lunch one day at my digs, and someone came to

the door and told me to report to Bloomfield Road. My first thought was, "What have I done wrong?" I went to the ground and saw Ted Crabtree, the club secretary. "What is it, Mr Crabtree?" "Sir Lindsay has died," he said. "We want some money, and you are the only one we can realize it from."

I said, "I won't go. I don't want to leave Blackpool." I was about to get married to a girl who had been brought up in Blackpool. We had bought a house, on mortgage, at South Shore.

"Will you," he asked, "at least *see* the people who have come to buy you?" I hadn't even asked which club it was. It turned out to be Manchester City. I was introduced to Mr Bob Smith, the City Chairman; Mr A. Alexander, a director; and Mr Wilf Wild, the manager. All three of them are dead now, bless them.

When I told them that I didn't want to leave Blackpool, Mr Alexander said, "You ought to be *proud* to come and play for Manchester City." "I mean no disrespect to your club," I replied. "I'm getting married, and I'm very happy at Blackpool." So Mr Bob Smith said, "We will not interfere with your private life. You can live in Blackpool, if you wish." That put a different complexion on it, and I eventually signed for City at a wage of £8 a week. City paid £10,000 for me. In those days, a player didn't get a percentage of the fee. All I got out of the deal was £231, my accrued share of benefit.

I went straight into the Manchester City first team. I took over from Jimmy Heale, who was injured. I had an awful day on my début. 1 wasn't in the game. I remember a wag shouting out: "£10,000? You mean 10,000 cigarette cards!" I can hear that as if it was yesterday. But I didn't let it affect me. In the long-term, the City crowd was great. There's no support like football-fans' support. One minute, they're calling for your guts. By the next minute, they've forgotten all about it.

The best side I ever played for was Manchester City in 1936–37, the team that won the League Championship. Frank Swift stands out in my mind, not only as a great goalkeeper, but as a great personality. He was a man six feet tall, with hands as big as shovels, but he was only a boy at heart. He was one of the *characters* of football, great in the dressing-room. The fun we used to have! There was Eric Brook, England outside-left, a great character, a Yorkshireman; Freddie Tilson at centre-forward; Toseland at outside-right; Bobby Marshall and Jackie Bray at half-back; Bill Dale and Sam Barkas at full-back. A great side.

The most praise I got from a football crowd was at Derby in the mid-forties. I was as humble as anybody, but I used to love applause. Every player responds to it. At Derby, there was one big cheer when we had the ball: until it went out of play or until we put it in the net. This cheer urged us on. Without atmosphere, a team can't do its best.

My finest-ever partnership was with Raich Carter at Derby. We had an unbelievable understanding. Not from the very beginning, but as we went on, as we got to know each other. We could have found each other without looking. I used to try to get the ball to his dynamic left foot. I used to run with the ball to his side of the field—or he would come over to my side—and I would back-heel the ball, *knowing* he would be there waiting for it.

Raich was a *great* inside-forward. He was a prolific goal-scorer. He used to score wonderful goals, marvellous goals. In or near the box, he was like dynamite. As soon as he hit the ball, that was it. It was in the net. I'd always say to myself, before a game, "Well, we'll get a few today. Raich is playing."

I believe that if a footballer looks after himself, and avoids the things that will harm his body, he should be able to play until he is forty. His experience will compensate for his loss of speed. When I was at Doncaster—as player/manager—I moved from inside-left to the wing. I was in my late thirties, and I needed to conserve my energy: I knew I could still do a useful job, because playing on the wing isn't as demanding as inside-forward. If I hadn't had an accident during the war, when I was in the R.A.F., I could have played on, even longer.

I was at a rehabilitation centre. I was out training my squad one morning. They didn't need a lot of discipline. We were trying to get them well: they would have run over the roof for us. The squad lined-up at a farm-house. The farmer used to give us bottles of milk. While I was talking to him, I said, "Well then, lads. A-ten-shun! Right turn. Quick march." So off they went. When they were about 100 yards away, I said "Cheerio" to the farmer, and ran like hell to overtake them. I went to the right of the last man in the squad. A van came round the corner, and I ran straight through the window. They took me to Loughborough Hospital. I was due to play in an international on the Saturday, and I did. But I shouldn't have played so soon. That accident shortened my career.

While I was at Blackpool, I made my début for Ireland. Your first cap is something very special. It was against England at Goodison Park, and we lost 2-1. In those days, the team was selected from Northern Ireland and Southern Ireland. The outstanding memory I have of that day is the telegram I was given after the game. It said that I was to come home immediately: my brother Joe had had a leg amputated.

He was playing in a junior game. There was a lot of "needle" in this particular match. He went into a tackle, and his leg was smashed. Gangrene had set in, and I asked Mother to wire me if he had to lose his leg. The press said I had heard about the amputation before the match; but I didn't. They didn't give the telegram to me until after the game—which was wise. Thanks to the kindness of Sir Lindsay Parkinson, I was able to make the trip home. I went to Ireland that same night, and I saw Joe the next morning. While I was in Ireland, Sir Lindsay cabled to wish Joe a good recovery.

The name I made in England—as a football player—I lost playing for Ireland. Ireland had some good players, but the organization was poor. We would arrive, in ones and twos, the night before an international. On occasions, I've seen players arrive on the *morning* of an international. We were strangers. We didn't always have a tactical talk. I've openly criticized the Irish F.A. for its lack of foresight. I don't think they love me too much! I always enjoyed being selected for Ireland; but, although I always tried my best, I never played my true form in internationals.

I was Ireland's manager for seven or eight years, and I took them to the World Cup Finals in 1958. Later on, I had to resign from the job. My wife was going to have an operation, and the team was going abroad for about a fortnight. I didn't want to leave my wife, so I resigned; and Billy Bingham took over. Ireland has produced some talented players, such as Georgie Best, and will continue to produce talent in the future. But we don't have many international-class players at any one time, and that makes it hard for us to compete against other countries.

On a Saturday, I used to have breakfast at 11 o'clock. I would very rarely eat again before the game. I had one or two little superstitions. I never liked to put my left boot on. I always put my right boot on first. I used to be keyed-up before a game: alert; raring to go; can't get out quick enough; where are they? I think this helps you to play better. Almost all players are keyed-up before a game. If they're not, they're unnatural.

I had terrific self-confidence. I didn't care who I was playing against. This is something I try to impress on young players: "Ability on its own is not sufficient. What's also important is the *application* of ability plus *confidence* in your ability. You can't have one without the other."

I was a completely two-footed player. I could play inside-right or inside-left, but I preferred inside-left. The all-purpose player is nothing new. Even in my early days, a club manager always wanted a player who would be in his own penalty-area one minute, and in the opponents' area the next minute; but it wasn't easy to find someone like this. It still isn't easy. You see a lot of mid-field players—even today—who are all right going forward, but cannot destroy in defence. They cannot *win* the ball. They are luxury players. It is useless having two luxury players at inside-forward. Managers in my day—no different from today—were looking for a fellow who could win the ball, a fellow whose work-rate was good. A player whose work-rate is not good is shifted about from club to club. He is not wanted.

Football hasn't changed a lot. The only big difference, compared with pre-war days, is that players are better trained today: they have greater variety in their training. We used to do continuous lapping; we hardly saw the ball. If we had had today's training methods, we would have been better players. There are some very good coaches today; but, at times, coaching is overdone. A lot of players cannot absorb certain things that are taught them, and coaching only destroys their natural abilities.

These days, coaches and managers shout at their players from the touch-line. I don't believe in this. If someone had shouted at me, during a game, I would have said, "Come on, mate. *You* play." I don't think it's good for the game. A lot of players resent it. It belittles a player, humiliates him. A lot of coaches do it to show people how knowledgeable they are. If I was a manager, and I wasn't able to tell my players what I wanted—throughout the week, before the game, and at half-time—then I would resign.

Football has become very defensive. First we had 4-2-4. Then they brought in 4-3-3, which makes the game even more defensive. I maintain that the best way to goal is by the wing. Today, we're bunching everybody in the middle of the field. Only a team of great players, like Real Madrid, can get to goal through the middle. But almost every team is trying to do the same thing. The Crewes and the Workingtons are trying to do it, and so is Leeds. This is farcical.

You've got to have method in your play, but football is still a simple game. When I was a manager, I used to give each of my players simple directives. I'd tell my full-backs: "Get into the tackle—hard. You can commit murder, so long as you play the ball. If the winger is good at coming inside, then keep him on the line. If he's good at going down the line, then make him come inside. Use your head." To my right-half, I'd say: "Your man is their No. 10. When we have the ball, forget him; let *him* worry about *you*. But when we lose the ball, sort him out." Little things like that: two or three to each player. Football is *still* a simple game.

Good play is habit-forming. It's like bringing up a son: you bring him up to be a good citizen. If a young player loses the ball, you get him into the habit of trying to retrieve it. If the ball has gone out of play and the enemy has the throw-in, then you have to get quickly into your marking formation. You get onto your bloke quickly: that is good habit-forming. If you want goals, you mustn't stand waiting for them. You have to go and seek them, where angels fear to tread: that's a good habit.

If I am helping a youngster, I give him three or four qualities which will make him a better player. And I see that he carries out my advice. But there are so many distractions today for young boys. We are not getting through to them. We are failing to produce as many good players as we should. I've been writing a thesis on why we have so many failures. I've got some of the answers; but not all. It's a long story.

To be a good manager, or a good coach, you've got to have so many qualities. Sandy Macfarlane didn't know much about psychology. He classed everybody alike, and that's dangerous. When I'm coaching a boy, I like to find out what makes him tick. I like to find out what I *can* say to him, and what I *shouldn't* say to him.

This is what I tell young players: "Make yourself super-fit. Then, when you go onto the field, you will *feel* superior to anyone. Football is not a difficult game to play. It only becomes difficult when you are playing with difficult players. Difficult players are those who don't think; those who stand still after they've passed the ball; those who allow themselves to be marked tightly; those who don't want the ball—who hide when you are in possession."

Some of the great players of my era couldn't write their own names. You don't need to go to high school to play football. But you need courage. That's vital. Then you've got a *player*. Then you've got a Bremner or a John White: good players; workers; grafters. Even if they're having a bad game, the crowd will be with them.

The will-to-win covers a multitude of things, from looking for goals to trying to retrieve the ball when you've lost it. The will-to-win has to be in every fibre of your body. You run and you run till you fall down dead. I used to say, "The football field is a great place to die."

In my playing days, if a fellow was going to hit somebody, he'd do it so that few people would see. He would do it at the right time. Today, a player fouls at any time. Everyone can see what he's doing. I can cite so many cases of this. A little while ago, I saw a player—from one of the big Scottish teams—run 20 yards to have a kick at somebody. Television, of course, has brought this sort of thing into everybody's front room.

Fouling, today, is done so openly. We had the "professional foul" in my day, but the referee very rarely saw it. I remember playing against Aston Villa one afternoon, on a heavy pitch. I fell, and an opponent ground his heel (with three studs) into my hand, and broke two bones. Nobody saw it. I had to wear a plaster cast for weeks. Before we went onto the field, there were always one or two players who would say, "Who do you want me to sort out, today?" There was far more dirty play in my day than there is now.

I took quite a lot of punishment from defenders. Managers paid particular attention to inside-forwards—who are key men. If I was at inside-left, the right-half—I'm sure—had instructions to bite hard in the tackle. This can be a good thing for a player because it makes him more alert. It makes him seek more space. Football is brain against brain. Whoever has the best brain will win in the long run.

Because I was closely marked, I was always alert, always trying to be a yard quicker than the defender. I made myself into a perpetual-motion player: this is what I ask young kids to do now. I remember Ken Willingham of Huddersfield, an England winghalf. Ken used to say, "Why don't you ever stand still? I don't know why you ever got an international cap." And I would reply, "It's thanks to playing against mugs like you, Ken!" There are so many stories like that, which supporters never hear about.

I think the British referee is the best in the world. I have never known a British referee to be unfair, knowingly. But I think the standard of refereeing may be falling a bit. They should be fitter than they are, so that they can keep up with the play. This is vital. And they're using too much whistle. Stopping the game, so often, annoys the crowd and annoys the players. Players get very annoyed at a referee who doesn't use the "advantage rule". If I foul you, and you beat me and are still in possession of the ball, then you will want to play on. If the referee blows his whistle, you're being penalized a second time. So you feel angry, the spectators feel angry, and the "advantage rule" has not been used to advantage. The *good* referee is the one who uses his whistle the least, and keeps the game alive.

I used to call linesmen "the greatest inside-forwards in the game" because they anticipate too often. I'll give you an example. A halfback has the ball, and is about to send it through the middle. The linesman sees somebody, at that instant, in an off-side position.

But, by the time the half-back actually kicks the ball, the fellow who was off-side has moved back, and someone else moves through, from an on-side position. You'll see that flag half-up.

I was only once chastised by a referee. It was at Swansea. This referee was well-known in the game. When he came onto the field, he used to get a bigger cheer than the teams got. I had a free-kick given against me. I kicked the ball away—which was wrong. He made me pick the ball up and bring it back, and he gave me a long lecture. Sometimes, I've lost my temper over a decision, and said, "Oh, *referee*." But I still say that the British referee is the best and fairest in the world.

The player of today is very fit, but he *has* to be fit. His life is hectic—with booze and women in many cases—so he *has* to train hard to keep himself up to scratch. The game is getting more physical. First, because of this extra fitness. Secondly, because of the systems: 4-2-4, 4-3-3, and so on. Through playing without wingers, there are more players congregating in the middle of the field. Obviously, in this confined space, you get more bodily contact. Thirdly, because of bigger bonuses and keener competition between clubs.

Football will have its day of reckoning. It's OK for the select few, but who has catered for the Crewes and the Doncasters? For the good of our game, they should have put a ceiling on wages. When a manager tries to sign a player, he finds that John Jones wants as much money as the top players.

Real Madrid was the first glamour club of the new era. They collected really good players from all over the world. To play a friendly match against Real, you had to give them a guarantee of £10,000 or more. And then the Italian clubs started to pay big money. But you can't base the Football League on Real Madrid. Ninety per cent of British clubs are in poverty. If it hadn't been for the pools and development associations, half of the clubs would be out of the League by now. I'll bet that 50 per cent of the clubs—or more—are mortgaged up to the hilt. Directors have been putting in thousands of pounds—of their own money. Would they run their own businesses like that? Can it last?

I married very early in my career. Because I had a family to support, I became a better, more determined player. My wife has been a marvellous companion. My first concern, after an away match, was to get home. After a home match, my wife would be waiting for me. We'd go out for a meal—to a nice little place where no one would recognize us.

Especially when I was with Manchester City, I often used to go away with my club for Cup training. And later on, like every manager, I had bad times and good times. My wife knows it all. She has shared the ups and downs of my career.

I'm a home bird. I value my home very highly. Home is something that I have always cherished. There's only my wife and I now. Our son is grown up, and is on his own. We have a little doggie. I love dogs. I love all animals. We like walking, my wife and I. We walk for miles, with our doggie.

I get a lot of invitations to give talks. I'll tell you what I have always wanted to do. I want to go to Ireland—because it is *my* country—and I want to lecture on football to the young players. The Irish boy doesn't get the same chances as a boy in England. He doesn't have many amenities. He has to fend for himself. One day I'll go back to Ireland and help those kids: help them to know more about the game. This is something I would love to do.

3

WORLD WAR II
Blackpool's Rise to Power

> *A centre-forward should be thinking about goal as
> soon as he leaves the centre-circle, and his shot
> should be hitting goal as soon as he arrives at the
> penalty-area.*
>
> JOCK DODDS

Blackpool were invincible in the 1939–40 season. The club had a
100 per cent record—having beaten Huddersfield, Brentford, and
Wolves—and led the First Division. On the Monday morning
following the Wolves match, the advent of war left the staff of
Bloomfield Road, like the whole of England, fearful of what was
to become of them and their families. Training was abandoned.
The players stood around, looking at each other, not knowing
what to say. Within weeks, many of them had been posted abroad,
and some never came back.

The gates were closed. They were soon opened again. The game
had to go on. The first war-time season stretched from October
1939 until June of 1940. By winning only one point from the last
three games, Blackpool threw away their chances of winning the
Championship of the North-West, and had to be content with third
place. Many more opportunities of footballing fame were to be
offered to Blackpool during the later years of the war, and the
club was not so wasteful again.

Blackpool had a rigidly controlled black-out, to prevent lights
being seen from the air, and some fire bombs were dropped on
the town. But Liverpool and Manchester presented much more
inviting targets to the Germans, and the people of Blackpool could
hear the drone of enemy planes flying their lethal cargo towards the
big industrial centres of Lancashire.

In this war, as in the 1914–18 war, the R.A.F. made use of
Blackpool. The town had accommodation unlimited and also a
splendid Promenade, which, especially near South Shore, was used

for square-bashing [drill]. The R.A.F. virtually took over Blackpool and requisitioned whatever buildings were needed. Included among them was Bloomfield Road. The R.A.F. converted parts of the stadium into offices; Blackpool F.C. were allowed use of the boardroom. The club had a £30,000 overdraft when the war began. This overdraft—the then-highest-ever in Blackpool's history —was all but repaid during the war years, because the R.A.F. rented Bloomfield Road and loaned the ground to the club on Saturdays.

The club's mid-week headquarters were at an accountants' office in Birley Street. Harry Evans, a director, and Joe Smith, the manager, selected the team. Colonel Parkinson, the Chairman, acted as liaison-man between the club and the R.A.F., and he received unfailing co-operation from Air-Commodore E. L. Howard Williams, Air Officer Commanding the R.A.F. in Blackpool.

The townspeople treated the R.A.F. with traditional Blackpool friendliness. Food was not scarce, at least in the first few years, and the proprietors were glad that their hotels and guest-houses were being used. Blackpool continued to have a holiday season, and some of the stalls on the Golden Mile were open, but business was quieter than usual because the R.A.F. had absorbed so much of the town's accommodation.

Many features of the war-time game were similar to peace-time football. The League arranged the fixtures and appointed referees. The price of admission was about the same, and the R.A.F. left the turnstiles intact. The size of the crowd at Bloomfield Road varied little from week to week. The ground always seemed quite well filled: 15,000 was an average gate. Although the matches were keenly contested, the atmosphere at Bloomfield Road was less partisan than in peace-time. Local supporters were joined by men in R.A.F. blue who had come from all over Britain and owed no allegiance to Blackpool. This made no difference to the results: Blackpool were unbeaten—in League matches at Bloomfield Road —from October 1939 until December 1941.

There was no official registration of guest players. In theory, it was necessary to get permission from a player's own club, but, in practice, if a player was on leave, he simply turned up on a Saturday at the local club and said, "What about a game?"

Ron Suart and Eric Hayward often travelled to Blackpool on a Saturday, but most of the team was recruited from within the town: the R.A.F. gave the fullest possible co-operation to Blackpool F.C. The servicemen played mid-week football with their own units, but only met as Blackpool F.C. on a Saturday. Blackpool had no shortage of players. At times, there were many more potential first-teamers than places in the team. The final line-up was often not decided until the morning of the game. If someone, who had been pencilled-in to play, did not arrive on time, there were always other players of First Division calibre eager for a game.

Because of the shortage of paper and the last-minute team selection, match programmes were seldom published. The teams, if known, were announced in the local press. Football fans, brought up on banner headlines and many columns of match reports and comments, had to be content with a few paragraphs. For Blackpool followers, especially, this was a pity, for the club was always newsworthy during the war years. Almost every Saturday was a "V-B" day.

In three consecutive seasons, Blackpool won the League Championship of the North: 1941–42, 1942–43, 1943–44. In those three campaigns, Blackpool scored with a relentless fury that the club has never matched, before or since: in 54 matches, Blackpool conceded 67 goals, and scored 224. Blackpool's scoring rate of over four goals a match will make today's supporter gasp with envy.

Double-figure victories were not unusual for Blackpool. The club achieved six during the war:

May 13, 1940	Oldham Athletic	H	11-2
September 13, 1941	Southport	H	10-1
February 28, 1942	Tranmere Rovers	H	15-3
March 7, 1942	Burnley	H	13-0
September 19, 1942	Bury	A	11-1
October 28, 1944	Southport	H	10-2

In addition to winning the League Championships, Blackpool did well in the War Cup (North). The Cup matches, during most of the war years, were on a home-and-away basis. Blackpool won the 1942–43 Final against Sheffield Wednesday, and lost to Aston Villa, by the odd goal in nine, in the 1943–44 Final.

On May 15, 1943, at Stamford Bridge, Blackpool (Cup winners of the North) met Arsenal (Cup winners of the South) in a match billed as the "Championship of England". Arsenal were so confident of winning, so the story goes, that they had a photo taken of themselves with the Cup—before the match began. Arsenal took the expected lead and were soon two goals in front. But goals from Dix, Burbanks, Dodds, and Finan, won the day for Blackpool.

Soon after the war began, a match at Bloomfield Road was broadcast on the radio for the first time: the troops in France heard a commentary on the second half of a high-scoring game. It was during the war that Mortensen made his international début

Eddie Shimwell (*far left*) makes history. With this penalty, scored in the 14th minute of the 1948 classic against Manchester United, Shimwell became the first full-back to score in a Wembley Cup Final

King George VI meets the Blackpool team before the 1951 Cup Final. The players are (*left to right*): Harry Johnston (Captain), Tommy Garrett, Bill Slater, Bill Perry, Stan Mortensen

—for Wales; that Blackpool were accused of "regularly borrowing men for box-office purposes", and were criticized for using a
coach to take the team to Manchester. It was also during the war
that Blackpool, because of a ban on Services' travel, once had to
withdraw from the Cup.

Blackpool's goalscorer-in-chief during the Second World War
was Jock Dodds, a 13-stoner, a great solid oak of a man, fear-
somely strong of thigh and neck. He scored well over 200 goals in
war-time matches for Blackpool, and in one memorable cup-tie
he scored eight. His three goals at Hampden Park, on April 18,
1942, inspired Scotland to a 5-4 defeat of England.

Dodds was injured before one particularly important cup-tie,
but Blackpool needed him, if only to frighten the opposition. A
Blackpool team without Dodds was unthinkable. And so Dodds
hobbled onto the pitch to take up his usual position at centre-
forward. Although his injury reduced him to walking pace, he
won the match for Blackpool, who were 1-0 down with ten minutes
left. He scored twice from standing free-kicks: both taken from
almost the same spot, 40 yards from goal. Dodds put one in each
corner of the net.

In another match, Dodds found the ball accidently gripped
between his thighs, about fifteen yards from goal. He shuffled
forward, charging off anyone who impeded him. The defenders
couldn't play the ball, so they had to try to shoulder him off, and
few men could do that. When he was two yards from the goal-
line, he let the ball drop to the ground and then scored. After
that, he used to try it occasionally as a deliberate ploy. I recall a
match at Bolton in the late fifties in which Ray Parry, who joined
Blackpool a year or so later, rushed in, unmarked, to a centre
from the right wing. The ball got lodged between his thighs. Parry
was two yards from goal, and, in the excitement of the moment, he
simply couldn't find the ball. It dropped behind him and was
cleared.

During one of those war-time matches in which Blackpool
scored almost at will, Jock Dodds, having netted four times, said
to Mortensen, "You have a go at centre-forward." And Morty
proceeded to help himself to four goals.

E

4

THE ATOMIC BOYS
Wonderful Entertainers

*. . . when the game was a reflection of the life and
character of Lancashire, humorous as could be,
humorous without knowing it was ripe with comedy
of the soil.*

SIR NEVILLE CARDUS

The Angel of Good Humour hovered over the cradle of Syd
Bevers. He was born to give pleasure to others, not as a clown, a
comedian, or an actor, but as a football supporter. He is a naturally
kind and gracious person, sensitive, impeccable in his good manners, a man with a truly creative imagination, and the gift of making,
and keeping, friends. He speaks of himself with a delightful
absence of self. He is forever smiling. He has a Churchillian
craving for cigars. And he has been a Blackpool supporter, for
many faithful years, who has been admired and loved by managers,
players, and spectators, all over England.

I said he was neither a clown, nor a comedian, nor an actor;
but he has in him many of the qualities of all three. He is a born
mimic. I once saw a lanky, bearded youth amble into his fancy-
goods shop, behind the Golden Mile. "Robinson Crusoe!", Syd
exclaimed, and he proceeded to act the part of Man Friday, with
appropriate bowings and scrapings. Children adore him, especially
when he addresses the young boys as "Sir", and the young girls as
"Madam".

Syd will always be remembered, in Blackpool and football
history, as the founder and creator of the Atomic Boys, whose
antics brought laughter to a war-worn nation. Syd used to lift the
front of his kilt to reveal a sign that read "The New Look": this
was the catch-phrase of the times. The Second World War was
just over. Those who had served in the forces, and those who had
patiently borne the austerities at home, and the young boys who
were first entering school when war broke out: they all marched

eagerly through the turnstiles. Football crowds soared in number and in enthusiasm. People wanted competition and struggle, but they wanted peaceful competition and bloodless struggle. The Atomic Boys expressed a national mood that sought an outlet in colour, imagination, good humour, and freedom: freedom of dress, word, and action. English football had never seen anything or anyone like them. And never will.

The growth of the Atomic Boys owed its roots not only to a national need, but to the town of Blackpool, whose citizens, during the forties and fifties, exulted in one of the most pleasure-giving football teams in England, if not in Europe. The sense of fun, the bright colour and bright sound, of the Atomic Boys took much inspiration from the football team—The House That Joe Built; the team that triumphed and found its final reward in the Wembley Cup Final of 1953.

The sight of the Atomic Boys enlivened many a Saturday afternoon of winter and English spring. Often, you might have thought you had come to a circus instead of to a football game. Into the arena they prance, like clowns, bulbous of nose, shoes of size 24, foot-wide bow-ties, wigs and braids. Here comes a headless man, carrying in his hand the head and helmet of a policeman. And look, the one with the fez and long side-boards is praying to the east. Kilts they wear, and tangerine jackets, great baggy trousers, vividly-striped suits. And enough variety of head-dress to fill a hat-shop: boater, top hat, fez, turban, metal helmet, tammy, sailor's cap; caps cloth, caps peaked, caps plumed.

Listen to the sound they make. The Hallé Orchestra has nothing on the Atomic Boys, with their bugles and bells, cornets and drum, rattles and recorders, and the famous pair of bellows, with horn attached, that sound like a ship's fog-horn. And there is Syd Bevers, in the front, in all his tangerine finery, robes embroidered and sequined. And sprinkled among the whole throng are the words "UP THE POOL"—on poster and banner—and scarves, tangerine and white, proudly worn.

Syd Bevers formed this squad, and used for its name the word "atomic" which was on everyone's lips after the bombing of Japan. The Boys numbered twelve or fifteen—they were augmented for cup-ties—and included a hotelier, a clown, and a Blackpool-rock maker. The clown was George Sayers from the Tower Circus, and towering above him, 6ft 7in from the ground, was the fellow who used to dress up as a woman, all skirts and gold braids.

"The idea to form the Boys came to me in February 1946," says Syd. "I was watching a Cup replay between Blackpool and Middlesbrough at Leeds. I thought there was something missing.

'I'll see if I can put something together,' I said to myself. I wanted to get more support for Blackpool, especially at away matches, and boost the morale of the team when they came onto the field. I really went to town on the idea. I never missed a cup-tie in sixteen consecutive years.

"We did our act at grounds all over the country, and put on a really big show for Cup matches. I would write to the secretary of the away club for permission to perform, and we were very rarely refused. We used to raise funds by holding dances, and by a small subscription paid by the Boys. One or two wives helped with costumes. Occasionally, we had to buy. The police lent us helmets and coats, and we obtained dummy faces and heads from the waxworks.

"Sometimes we travelled by coach, sometimes in cars. At every ground we visited, we did a little something. We used to have meetings to discuss our parts. There were a lot of slogans to be made up, and signs to be written. Sometimes we picked out a prominent theme or player from the opposing team. Another time, we would highlight a Blackpool player: for example, we called Eddie Shimwell 'The Minister of Defence'. We did an act about the suggested knighthood for Stanley Matthews, some years before he was knighted. We did a take-off of Tommy Trinder; and one of Henry Rose, the debonair sports-writer, with his moustache and bowler hat. We performed before the kick-off and during the interval, and we used to do a parade of the ground."

Syd Bevers used to distribute leaflets at football matches for the Blackpool Publicity Department. His work was entirely voluntary. Before a match, he would also give away sticks of rock—to children, and to invalids in wheel-chairs—"just to create goodwill". The Atomic Boys helped to collect thousands of pounds for charities by performing at balls and other events. They were known all over the country, and several television appearances spread news of their good works and good humour.

For the '53 Final, the Atomic Boys travelled south on the Friday night. The next morning, in full regalia, they paraded along the streets of London. They went to Trafalgar Square, joined by a number of other Blackpool supporters, and photographers. Nelson's Column had never seen anything quite like the Atomic Boys. Dozens of coloured balloons, printed with Blackpool slogans, were given to the wind to bear across London.

Just before noon, Syd Bevers called at No. 10 Downing Street, clutching a 12lb stick of rock lettered *Sir Winston*. Unfortunately, the Prime Minister was not at home. Afterwards he wrote a letter to Syd Bevers to say how sorry he was not to have seen him, adding that if Blackpool was as good as the rock it must be a fine place.

Syd Bevers brought out his mascot duck, for the last time, at Stanley Matthews' farewell match. Syd presented a huge stick of rock, lettered *Stanley Matthews*, to Di Stefano, the great inside-forward. The Atomic Boys were disbanded. "It's gone now, mainly because of hooliganism," he says. "I wouldn't dare walk about now, in my old outfit, in another town. They'd be after me, wouldn't they? Around 1963, I could feel that some spectators were getting out of hand. There's trouble not only in football, but in the streets as well. There's trouble not only in this country, but in other countries. I can't explain why. I did try to help another group of lads to get started, but nothing much came of it. The public probably didn't realize the toil and effort we used to put into the preparations for our show. The Atomic Boys always tried to comply with the rules and regulations; we never abused our privileges. I always told the Boys never to ridicule a policeman.

"We had four ducks in all: Donald, Douglas, Stanley (named after Stanley Matthews), and Puskas. One of them was given to us by a film company, as a publicity stunt. Our first duck came from Reggie Young, a gipsy boy who was employed on the Pleasure Beach. It was his own idea for a mascot. We tried to dye the duck tangerine, but the feathers wouldn't take an ordinary dye. Eventually, we got a good tangerine dye: it was the one used for colouring smoked haddocks!

"On one or two occasions, we were twenty or thirty miles from Blackpool, going to an away match, before we realized we'd forgotten the duck. We couldn't be without our mascot: we just had to go back for it. At one time, because of fowl-pest restrictions, I was not allowed to take the duck out of the Fylde, without a permit from the Chief Constable.

"Ducks aren't very tidy animals to keep. They're quite a job to look after. I never read any books about handling ducks. I just learned from the lads who keep farms. They used to tell me: 'Plenty of water, plenty of bread, and Quaker Oats!' Puskas could drink beer. When we pulled up at a pub, on the way to a match, we put the duck on the bar counter. It would drink out of a pint glass, wobble about, and then, embarrassingly for us, do a little business.

"As the players came out, I used to put the duck on the centre-spot, and the duck was there while the captains shook hands and tossed the coin. If the duck got a fright, it became airborne for about twenty yards. Sometimes, on a muddy ground, I had to dive to catch it.

"During matches at Bloomfield Road, I used to put the duck on a perch near the broadcasting hut. One Saturday the duck disappeared. It was eventually found, after a nation-wide hunt, in an actor's dressing-room in a London theatre. It had been a publicity gimmick."

For one of the Blackpool Cup Finals, Syd Bevers had to smuggle the duck into Wembley. He had written to the authorities and was told that no mascots were allowed inside the ground, and that no one would be allowed to go onto the field. "There were so many requests from the Blackpool public that I just had to put the duck in the middle. I got away with it, after a little effort. I don't think Jesse Owens could have caught me! While I was queuing up—I'd put the duck in a shopping bag that had a zip fastener—I had to open the top to let his beak out for a bit of fresh air. I thought to myself, 'If he quacks, I'll have him.'

"I met some great players at Blackpool Football Club: Morty, always very humorous; Matthews, an elusive one, but always nice to meet. As soon as the whistle went, Matthews was first off the field. I've seen him sign autographs: I've seen it become too over-powering for him at times. I've met Tom Finney; Peter Doherty; Sir Matt Busby, one of the greatest men in the game—he always has a word for everybody; Joe Smith, a man who called a spade 'a spade'—a rough diamond, but he knew his football. I got on really well with all the boys at Bloomfield Road."

On the Saturday nearest to Clifford Greenwood's silver-wedding anniversary, Syd Bevers went up to the press box at Bloomfield Road and presented him with a bunch of flowers. "He was a little surprised. He showed his feelings and thanks all over his face. Cliff was a wonderful gentleman. We could do with a few more like him, today: not only in football, but in all walks of life. He would never belittle anyone."

5

A TEAM OF FRIENDS
Blackpool's Glory-day

I am told by many that I was the match-winner.
But I say that we had eleven match-winners.
SIR STANLEY MATTHEWS

Heroes are made, not born. Why do some historians seek to glorify one man and (p)raise him far above his fellows? No artistic or social movement, no revolution, no triumph, no discovery, has been the work of one man. Every man of achievement owes a few laurels of his fame to all the people who, throughout his life, have been a source of education, advice, support, and influence. Every architect has his draughtsmen. It is the duty of history to reveal these draughtsmen and win them recognition.

On the golden day of Blackpool football—May 2, 1953—the club sent six England internationals into battle: Matthews, Mortensen, Joe Smith, Shimwell, Garrett, and Johnston. Joe Smith I include because he played, on that Queen-graced day, as hard as any man on the field, and in the excitement of the second-half actually performed as ball-boy, so anxious was he that not a moment should be lost, as Blackpool's football rose to a crescendo of skill and power.

Joe was never a believer in time-wasting. Once, as captain of Bolton, he saw one of his players, Billy Jennings, hesitating over a throw-in. Jennings was a Welsh-international wing-half, but that made no difference to Joe. He charged up and roared: "For God's sake, Billy, stop watching the smoke puffing out of the factory chimneys and get on with the bloody game."

In addition to the six men of England, Blackpool fielded a Scottish international, George Farm. The club's two other Scottish internationals, Brown and Kelly, were kept on the side-lines by injuries to leg and ankle. Ernie Taylor had to wait until a fateful day in November[1] for his first cap, and by 1956 Mudie had

---
[1] The Hungarians achieved a 6-3 victory at Wembley.

represented Scotland; and Perry, England. The two reserves, Wright and Crosland, had both played for England "B", and Ewan Fenton, right-half and Scotsman, was honoured by the British Army during his period of National Service. Cyril Robinson, in the other wing-half position, was making his second and gallant appearance in a cup-tie. Robinson had a brief career with Blackpool, spanning a handful of years and a couple of dozen first-team matches. I hope he will allow me to devote the word-portrait, of Blackpool's left-half, to the long-serving Hugh Kelly,[2] whose number of appearances help to swell the careers' total of League and F.A. Cup matches for Blackpool, of the fifteen post-war players featured in this book, to 5,316. Has any other club inspired such loyalty?

The whole of the Cup Final XI cost £50,000. All but Farm, Shimwell, Matthews, and Taylor, had been recruited from junior football. How much would they be worth today? A million pounds? More? It seems scarcely more than two or three years since the two Lancashire teams, in their long-sleeved shirts and quaint baggy shorts (Taylor's seemed to droop almost to his ankles), produced one of sport's historic matches. In 1953 men counted more than systems. Blackpool fielded a team of thirty-three men: eleven players, eleven friends, eleven personalities. Several of them, such as Mortensen and Shimwell, you would probably describe as "characters". No drab defensive tactics from these men. They attacked. They risked all. They let in three goals but scored four. They showed not only the good humour and the confidence, to be found only in the truly great sides, but also the courage. Injuries could not dismay them; and they enjoyed fighting back, after allowing the other side a goal-or-two's start. Blackpool earned a reputation for the grandstand finish after their late winners, in previous rounds, against Arsenal and Spurs; not forgetting Mortensen's hat-trick in the 1948 semi-final, also against Spurs. His first goal was scored in the last minutes of proper time, and he headed two more during extra-time. And now, here were Blackpool at Wembley, 3-1 down, with barely half an hour left.

Garrett suffered a broken nose on the Saturday before the Final. Mortensen had been out of the team for weeks, following a cartilage operation, and Matthews did not play for several months, early in that season, because of knee trouble. Just before the Final, Matthews was given a pain-killing injection for a thigh injury. And then there were the two internationals sitting on a bench, watching helplessly: Hugh Kelly, who later became club captain,

[2] The eleven 1953-vintage players, featured in *Blackpool Football*, formed the team that competed for the F.A. Charity Shield, against Arsenal, in October 1953.

and Allan Brown, who bravely and unforgettably scored the winner against Arsenal in the sixth round. Adversity strengthens. Twice, in 1948 and 1951, Blackpool had slumped off Wembley's pitch, defeated. Now, in 1953, with faces dazed and uncomprehending, they received winners' medals. Matthews was near to tears. Each man had played for the other ten, and for Joe Smith, and Johnny Lynas, the trainer, and for the two injured Scotsmen, and for the Blackpool faithful, on the terraces, or at home in front of television, or next to a radio at full excited volume. One of the spectators was a young man called Jimmy Armfield.

The '53-Final XI was *the* Blackpool XI, as a team and as individuals. In what positions were the players not the most outstanding in the club's history? Blackpool have never had a sounder goalkeeper and right-back than Farm and Shimwell; no more brilliant an outside-right than Matthews; no more poised a captain and centre-half than Johnston; no more valiant a leader of the attack than Mortensen; and no more penetrating a left-winger than Bill Perry. For inside-forward, wing-half, or full-back, you may be able to make claims for other players. *May* be able to. Find a place, if you wish, for Armfield, Benton, Farrow, Doherty, Dodds, Ball, or Hampson. For me, the 1953 XI is inviolable.

We saw Farm recover from his tense beginning, and with increasing admiration we watched the full-backs, Shimwell and Garrett, so resourceful in defence, with Shimwell making an occasional foray in order to prompt the attackers and cross a centre for them. Johnston proclaimed his sportsmanship when, twenty minutes after the interval, he kicked into touch so that the injured Lofthouse could receive attention. Johnston, with the effortless mastery of Frank Woolley at the crease, always seemed to have so much time, and his calmness gave strength to the less-experienced men who flanked him.

Matthews, at 38, showed a speed of acceleration that a player of any age would have been proud of. His sudden burst down the wing, before crossing the ball for Mortensen to score Blackpool's second goal, is one of the enduring memories of the game. Taylor and Matthews: they were inseparable. Taylor played the game of his life—his art full of subtleties, beyond anticipation—goading Bolton with light-footed brilliance, and finding Matthews with passes of uncanny precision. To this spectacle, Mortensen added his fabulous loose-limbed pace and jinking body-swerve, and he scored three fine goals. The first, which Hassall deflected into his own net, was aimed just inside the far post. The second goal Morty forced home from among a ruck of players, and the third he cracked-in from a free-kick, taken just outside the penalty-area.

The ball seemed to hit the back of the net before Mortensen had moved.

The Blackpool sections of the crowd roared their delight, producing great waves of cheers, like film extras at the *Ben-Hur* chariot race. And they made themselves known to all England when Bill Perry scored the winner in the last minute. His partner, Mudie, was everywhere, working all through the game, and he came up smiling after several hefty tackles. Bolton's best goal was their third, a centre perfectly placed for Bell to nod in. The response to Blackpool's victory was free and uninhibited. The Mayor of Blackpool, sitting only a row or two behind the Queen, threw his hat up in the air and shouted, "We've won!"

The game knew no pattern. At every turn, there was the unforeseen and the memorable, such as Blackpool's classic triangular move on the right wing shortly before their fourth goal. The keeper of the giant scoreboard became so flustered, towards the end, that he once made the score 4-4. The referee used the "advantage rule" intelligently, but there were only two bad fouls in the whole ninety minutes, a tribute to two teams who had so much wanted to win and had chased every loose ball. The Bolton defence deserves all credit for its stout-heartedness, and for refusing to be shaken by the injury to Bell. Neither side dominated until the last fifteen minutes. Then Blackpool overwhelmed Bolton. Was this the greatest of all Cup Finals? I do not know. I make no claims, except to declare that those last thirty-five minutes are without equal for thrills and for genius in the art of football.

In the greenhouse of every mansion of human endeavour—in politics, in sport, in the arts, in commerce, and in scholarship— teams are formed; or, rather, they form. A *good* team forms only when a number of trends converge, like rays of light, onto a single point of time and place; when there is an atmosphere that is both friendly and stimulating; when talented individuals want to work for a common purpose; when there is balance of temperament; when there is a strong leader. A *great* team has all of these, and something more. That "something more", although beyond verbal description, is instantly seen and felt. A great team forms only once or twice in a generation; sometimes, even less often. It happened in the fifties, in Blackpool.

6

JOE SMITH — in an Interview
Fun but Firm

I went to Bolton as a boy of eighteen, in 1908. I became captain
after I'd been there a couple of years. When I first went there, I
got 50s a week in the second team, and £4 in the first team. That
was the top limit. We were well paid: that was a lot of money in
those days. We used to get lodgings for 15s a week. Now, players
want 15s a minute.

Inside-forward, I fancied. Later in life, I played centre-forward
sometimes. In my prime, I was about 11 stone and 5ft 7½in or
5ft 7in. I used to volley balls into the net from a few feet off the
floor. I was deadly with them. And do you know how I developed
that? When I was a junior, my mother used to make rag balls for
my brother and I. We couldn't afford a real ball.

We used to play against a wall, and kick from the street, about
twenty yards out. Quite a few people used to watch us every time
we went there. My mother could make a decent "ball" with stock-
ings, and fill it up with rags. We'd chuck it out of the hand, and
you'd have to volley it before it dropped to the floor. We didn't
dribble with it. It was just for chucking out, just for shooting.
That's how I developed my goal-scoring.

I put a ball right through the net one day. I think it was against
Manchester City. We'd got a penalty. The week before, I'd missed
one. I didn't miss many. I put it down. Then I went to this ball, I
went straight to it, and it went through the net. Mind you, the
net must have been in a bad way, because I'm not saying I was
good enough to break any net. The crowd roared, "He's missed it
again!" It hit the railings at the back of the net, and the referee
had to go and have a look. If anyone asked me how to take a
penalty, I would say: "Pick your spot in the bottom of the net,
and hit it hard." I didn't tell Eddie Shimwell how to take penalties.
Eddie was a beautiful kicker of a ball. They don't need advice,
fellows like him.

When we were at Bolton, that team was picked up for practically next to nothing. It was run that way. They started as juniors and grew up with the team. Bolton had a good side. We won two Cup Finals. It was the same at Blackpool: a good many of those players were juniors when I signed them. Ted Vizard and I played together seventeen years in the first team. I could have found Ted Vizard with my eyes shut when I'd got the ball.

I never copied any manager. In the same way, I made my own style as a player. We finished runners-up twice, and third and fourth: that was my four years as manager at Reading. Only one team went up from the Third Division in those days. Ted Crabtree, who was the Blackpool secretary then, told me that the job was vacant, and they offered it to me. I said, "Well, I'll think it over." I went back to Reading, and they didn't want to let me go. I had a bit of a job to get away.

It's a very healthy place, Blackpool. I'd lived near here, at Bolton. I'd been to Blackpool several times. I fancied coming here. I never fancied one or two of the southern crowds, somehow. They'd saunter about, even if it was two or three minutes before the start of a match. They'd walk along as if next week would do. Whereas in the north, they'd run to the ground, frightened of missing the match.

As I remember Blackpool, when I was a Bolton player, they were just a bottom-of-the-Second-Division team. They went from an ordinary side to a good side in a few seasons. We really stood out in war-time football. I was here all through the last war. Before the cup-winners' challenge match in 1943, Arsenal had a photo taken *with* the cup. Afterwards, I went in and said, "Where's the cup? We won the bloody thing." I don't know where that cup is now. I think it's probably in the Arsenal boardroom. . . .

Quite often people used to ask me: "What do you say to them at half-time, Joe?" I'd reply, "That's *my* business." I could tell you millions of stories about little Ernie Taylor. As I walked into the dressing-room, he'd look up and say, "Me again?" "You again," I'd reply, "you little so-and-so." Before he went out, I'd say, "Now Ernie, you're the brains of this side. Get 'em moving."

Matthews was an object-lesson. He didn't say a lot, but he always looked after himself. Jimmy McIntosh: now he was a good centre-forward. Something went wrong—war-time or something. He never made half the player he ought to have done. When he was about seventeen, he looked like being a brilliant player. He had the build. He had everything. And Jackie Mudie. He could hit 'em, I tell you, for a little fellow. Then there was George Farrow, a good thrower of a ball. It was better than a corner-kick, when he took a throw-in. We got many a goal from this.

I used to go in the dressing-room at half-time, and either play hell with them or congratulate them. I used to play steam with them sometimes, if they weren't pulling their weight. We could get down to serious talking, but we never fell out. You could ruin a side if you got on to them too much. I always got them moving again for the second half.

There was one particular cup-tie in the south. I went in the dressing-room at half-time, and I said, "You're playing like a lot of b—— old women." I thought I'd start with —— first. "You," I said. "You're frightened to death. You're frightened to go near this full-back." And —— said, "He's fast." I said, "You can give him ten yards in a hundred." And they went out for the second half, and they won.

I used to drill into them: "The ball runs badly sometimes; sometimes it runs as sweet as can be. It'll come so that you can trap it and take it away. Other times, it's coming a bit too near for you, or a bit too far away." The run of the ball . . . it's the same in billiards or snooker. I always drilled into my players that if they worked hard, they made up for that off-day. Eleven grafters, all working, want a lot of beating. Let them play their natural game, but they've got to play as a team. Plans, plans . . . a load of old tripe. How do you know what the other team is going to do?

We never trained on the sands. It's too soft. I think it tends to make you slow. The Blackpool directors never interfered with the team. I had the running of the team. After the meeting—we'd meet about different things: advice and what-not—I'd say, "That's the team, Gentlemen."

You hear about players grumbling when they've gone out of the manager's office. But I never had any rows. With all my players, I was the boss, and that was it. If they had to have a rest, that was it. Even if they were internationals, on top of the world, it didn't matter to me.

Loyalty has to be inspired from the top. If the manager's all right, and the club's all right to them, the players grow up with a happy spirit. If you haven't got that, you haven't got a chance. They were all friends at Bloomfield Road. We were a very happy crowd.

7

STAN MORTENSEN
The Lionheart

The name *Mortensen* has become a synonym for courage. When Stanley was a small boy, his father died. Stanley left school and went to work in a timber yard. Then he and Blackpool discovered each other, and they have never parted. In his early days with Blackpool F.C., he was one of the slowest players in the club. Yet he became the fastest centre-forward in the game. Twice, during the war, he narrowly escaped death: once, while making a practice parachute jump; once, when his Wellington crashed. A head injury forced him to endure insomnia for several years. Suffering will ennoble a man *if* he has sufficient courage, and Mortensen has that courage. He never spared himself on the field. He laughed at danger, and he mocked injury. He walked onto Wembley's lush pitch, for the 1953 Final, not long after two cartilage operations, and he had played in only one cup-tie all season. He was a few weeks short of his 32nd birthday, an age when centre-forwards are supposed to be past their best. Within two hours Stanley Mortensen had become the first player of the century to score a hat-trick in a Cup Final.

His third goal, an equaliser, from a free-kick late in the game, was a triumph for optimism. Ernie Taylor shouted, "You'll never do it!" But Mortensen saw a small gap. He shot and scored, and Blackpool went on to win the Cup. In February 1967, as Blackpool were nearing the end of the most calamitous season in their history, Mortensen, always ready for a challenge, accepted the managership, his first ever. For several years he had been absent from football, but his heart had never stopped pumping out a love for the game. The very next season, Blackpool came to within an own-goal of promotion. Mortensen gave the club new hope, by re-enacting the spirit of his centre-forward rôle—in the manager's office.

Mortensen's paternal grandfather was a Norwegian sailor, and he inherited a Viking's tenacity and driving sense of purpose. "I could never imagine any team I played for being beaten." Politicians practise the art of the possible; Mortensens practise the art of the impossible. His personality ranges from the shrewd to the adventurous, from optimist to realist. He is a practical optimist. He is consistent: whenever you hear someone speak of him, about something he has said or done, you find yourself nodding in agreement, and thinking: "Yes, that's Morty all over." His loyalty to Blackpool is absolute: a shining thing. "I'm not only football daft, I'm Blackpool daft." There is latent power in his voice. He expresses himself fluently, and gives the listener a sense of urgency. Above all else, Mortensen has the gift of the Positive. To all that he does, he brings enthusiasm and this enthusiasm spreads to all around him. I once heard a player say, at the beginning of a new season, "I hope we do well—for Morty's sake."

In the early fifties, he offered one of his Cup medals to an injured first-team player of a Wembley-bound club. His generosity is everywhere acknowledged. He has been untiring in his work for charity. He was popular with his team-mates, of Blackpool and England, and a favourite of spectators throughout the country. Few footballers have been awarded so many nicknames (all of them complimentary!) from press and public. He was known as "Spring-heeled Jack", "The Mighty Atom", "The Blackpool Bombshell", "The Electric Eel". To most people, he was, and still is, known as "Morty". You have only to walk down the street with him to realize that he knows half the population of Blackpool, by name; and, of course, the whole of Blackpool knows his smile. He has a quick sense of humour. One winter's morning, a day or so before Blackpool were due to play in a particularly important match, I asked him if he had selected his team. "Yes," he said. "And do you want to know who's playing?" Whereupon, with a perfectly straight face, he began, "Tom, Dick and Harry. . . ."

Mortensen on the field was a quite unforgettable sight. The game of football, and the way he played it, expressed the man: dynamic, non-stop, loose of limb, strong-shouldered, resilient of spirit, inexhaustible of energy and of hope. He had the opportunist's eye for the half-chance, and could score from the most acute angles. A Mortensen goal from twenty or thirty yards was commonplace. Few players have so consummately combined strength with speed; and he was admired for the agility of his leap and the perfection of the timing of his headers, a product of his schoolboy days as centre-half. He was noted also for his ability to launch himself parallel to the ground for a torpedo-like header. He had a sinuous body-swerve. His acceleration was remarkable. So quick was his sprint from the kick-off that he would arrive in the opponents' penalty-area almost before the ball had rolled the regulation distance of its own circumference. Mortensen needed no special atmosphere: his passion for the game caught fire at the mere sight of the ball. He did not *play* football. He revelled in it.

Matthews for centres; Mortensen for goals. There are dozens that he will be remembered by, but none surpassed his two great hat-tricks: the Hall of Fame hat-trick in the 1953 Final, and the one he scored in the 1948 semi-final against Spurs. How's that for sense of occasion? These were the only two hat-tricks he ever scored in cup-ties.

Blackpool spotted him on Easter Monday 1938, when he was playing for a team of former schoolboys from South Shields. The month of May will always have a special significance for Mortensen. He was born in May; became a professional in May; made his England début in May; and scored a hat-trick in a Cup Final in May. He joined Blackpool at the same time as his right-wing partner, Withington. Some years after the war, Joe Smith told me: "Dick Withington was a good player, but he hadn't the guts of Morty."

War deprived League football of Mortensen when he was in his early twenties, but he was seen as a guest player, at grounds all over the country. During the war he had his first taste of representative football: with the Royal Air Force. Also, he made his international début—for Wales! Mortensen, Engand's reserve, was called-on to replace the injured Ivor Powell; Wales lacking a substitute. Such was the friendly atmosphere of most war-time international matches. In 1945, Mortensen and Matthews formed the right wing for "Arsenal", in the side that played, one foggy London day, against Moscow Dynamo. This was the partnership that was to become known as "The Terrible Twins".

In his first full international for England, against Portugal in 1947,[1] Mortensen joined a forward-line that boasted Matthews and Finney on the wings, with Tommy Lawton at centre-forward and Wilf Mannion at inside-left. A year later, in May 1948, against the Italians, Mortensen sparked off a historic England victory: he opened the score inside five minutes, shooting almost from the goal-line. He averaged very nearly a goal a game in his full internationals. Off the field, too, he was a lively member of an England party, and his clowning with Frank Swift helped to keep spirits buoyant.

And so Mortensen took his place in, and enriched, the noble line of Blackpool centre-forwards: Joe Lane, the first player to receive a four-figure share of his transfer fee; Harry Bedford, League's

---

[1] Mortensen scored four goals against Portugal, which is almost certainly the most by an England player in his international début: it is definitely the highest-scoring début since records have been kept.

The Atomic Boys on their way to No. 10 Downing Street, before the 1953 Cup Final. Syd Bevers (*third from right*) clutches a massive stick of rock, a gift for the Prime Minister

Captain Joe Smith (holding ball) leads the Bolton team onto the field for the 1926 Cup Final

Manager Joe Smith (*front row*, *far left*) leads the Blackpool team onto the field for the 1953 Cup Final *against* Bolton

top scorer in two successive seasons; Bill Tremelling, who went on
to captain Preston, from centre-half, in a Cup Final; the immortal
and modest Jimmy Hampson; battler Bobby Finan; big Frank
O'Donnell; Jock Dodds, prolific goal-scorer during the Second
World War; Mortensen; Jackie Mudie, wee Scottish international;
and Ray Charnley, the bargain-buy from Morecambe.

When he joined Hull City, in November 1955, Mortensen chose
to stay in Blackpool, and he was given permission to continue to
train at Bloomfield Road. Later, he played for Southport, Bath
City, for whom he had guested during the war, and Lancaster;
but he and his wife, Jean—a Blackpool girl, and an ardent supporter of the club, one of whose grandfathers played for South
Shore—still kept their home in Blackpool. As businessman and as
town councillor, and by his unceasing work for charity, Mortensen
strengthened his links with Blackpool.

Then, all of a sudden, in February 1967, he found himself back
at Bloomfield Road, as manager, taking over from Ron Suart, a
former club-mate. Blackpool were bottom of the First Division.
Many a man would have flinched at the hopelessness of their
position, and turned away, but Mortensen wanted to repay the
club and the town that had given him so much. There can be few
managers who, from the day of their appointment, so commanded
the faith of players and supporters alike. "I want 100 per cent
effort. I want players to have a pride in the team—and they've got
to go all out." Mortensen was back.

A successful manager has to be part-diplomat, part-psychologist,
part-strategist, part-public-relations-man, part-father. He needs to
have learnt the art of timing, and must know when to buy a new
player, and for which position; when to bring in a youngster from
the reserves; when to rest an established first-team player; when to
send-on a substitute in a tense match; when to be firm, and when
to be gentle. And in all his decisions, a manager must, at least to
every outward appearance, be decisive. Mortensen was humble
enough to set about learning his new trade. He encouraged the
younger players, and he gave the older ones new faith in themselves. In his own career, Mortensen had known the importance of
confidence. Now he showed the ability to give confidence to others.
These two gifts are not always allotted to one and the same person.

Mortensen enjoys coaching, and youngsters respond to him
readily. He can express himself clearly, in words and in action,
and his pungent sense of humour makes a lasting impression on
young people. One day, he went to coach at a local school which
at the time had two strong XIs. The boys had been winning everywhere, and they felt—how shall we say?—a little proud of them-

F

selves. They began to "sir" Morty, who would have none of it. "To you, I'm Stan," he said. "First of all, we'll have a look at penalty-kicking and the importance of accuracy." So he took the 20 boys—the two XIs, minus the goalkeepers—to one of the goals, and said, "You'll have three kicks each. I'll be in goal." Morty walked towards the posts, and when he reached the goal-line, instead of turning to face the penalty-spot, he bent over, presenting his backside as a target.

"When taking a penalty, you should always pick your spot. You'll score one point every time you hit me. I represent a space." Each boy took his turn, and, every so often, between kicks, Mortensen would move to a different spot on the goal-line, and bend over again. The boys, between them, scored eleven hits out of a possible sixty, and no boy scored more than one out of three. A lifetime of words and theories and manuals could not have taught them more.

Only an own-goal by an Aston Villa full-back[2] thwarted him from leading his club back into the First Division, in his first full season as a manager. But there was triumph in defeat. By astute signings, and by force of personality, he resurrected a team that a season earlier had been crucified. In 1967–68, Blackpool amassed 58 points: equal-highest total in her history. The year before, Blackpool had finished with only 21 points, the lowest the club had ever gained in a 42-match season. During a training session, early in the year of near-promotion, I saw Morty walk, chatting, across the Bloomfield Road pitch, with his arm, like that of a friendly uncle, on the shoulder of his club captain: an inspired Armfield played through all the season as though his one mission in life was to captain Blackpool again in the First Division.

At the end of the season, while Blackpool were playing with Mortensen-like spirit on the Leeds Road ground, Huddersfield, my thoughts wandered again and again to Morty, sitting (standing?) in the directors' box. I knew that he would be deeply moved by the drama of the occasion. Here, unfolding before him, was a rebuff to the fulfilment of his dream—"to put Blackpool at the top, where they belong". This would be only a temporary check. Morty was confident.

[2] In 1967–68 Blackpool missed promotion by goal-average of 0.21. An own-goal by Bradley, right-back of Aston Villa, gave Queen's Park Rangers victory, eight minutes from the end of the last match of the season, and Blackpool failed to go up: despite a final surge that brought seven consecutive wins; despite having an away record that was unsurpassed in all four Divisions of the League; and despite scoring 58 points, the number that gave Blackpool the Division II Championship in 1929–30. Never before, in the history of the Second Division, had a team that scored 57 points (let alone 58) failed to gain promotion.

8

STAN MORTENSEN
— in an Interview

Stan Mortensen was manager of Blackpool from February 1967 until April 1969. He inherited a relegation side, but he soon gave the players new life and new hope. Only tragic bad-luck prevented him from bringing them back to Division I at the first attempt. Everyone who played for Morty speaks well of him. This interview —which he gave while he was manager—has been left intact, as a tribute:

I was quite happy to play anywhere, as long as I was playing in the team and playing football; and if Joe Smith had come to me and said: "You'll play full-back," I would have played full-back.

My preference was centre-forward, although as an inside-forward I was still an attacking player. I was naturally right-footed, but I was never frightened to have a shot with my left foot. Lots of players get the ball on their bad foot, as it were, and they are not prepared to have a crack at goal. In fact, shooting at goal has become a bit of a dying art. Most players want to take the ball in too far, before they're prepared to have a crack at goal with it.

A player has got to have the confidence to hit balls from outside the penalty-area, and I was encouraged in this art by my manager. It was instilled into me that if I'd missed a couple of chances, well, I'd got to make up for it; and the only way to do this is to have the confidence to try more shots at goal. You find nowadays that if a player has a couple of shots and he misses, all he wants to do is to pass the ball to his own players, and let them have the responsibility of scoring.

I was very slow in my early days at Blackpool. Georgie Mee and Bobby Finan helped to speed up my game a bit. [*This is English understatement at its best.*—R.D.] I think the most important thing about it was that determination came into it, eventually. When opponents had given up a ball as going dead, I chased it and sometimes caught it, right on the dead-ball line; and at times managed to score. This was a tremendous boost to my confidence. I used to try and pull out everything I could in catching those impossible balls.

Take Rod Laver, the tennis player. He goes for impossible balls, where another fellah would say, "I have no chance for that." If you hesitate for a split second, while going for a difficult ball, the chance is gone. But if your reactions are to go for it, and you don't make it an impossible ball—if you think, "I *can* get this"—you've got chances of retrieving it. The most important thing in football is confidence: the confidence to try things off your own bat, and the confidence to take on opponents and beat them, and confidence whether you're taking free-kicks, penalties, or shooting at goal. It's an attitude of mind. Rod Laver doesn't say, "Now, can I get that?"

That free-kick in the 1953 Cup Final? This is what happened. Jackie Mudie was going through and he was brought down. I used to take most of the free-kicks around and about the penalty-area. Ernie Taylor picked the ball up, but I walked up and said, "Give it to me. I'm going to have a bang." And Ernie Taylor looked, and he said, "There's no gap." And I looked at the wall myself and I couldn't even see the goal-posts. And I said, "Well, gap or no gap, I'm going to have a bang at this." So I put the ball down, and, as I walked back towards my own goal, I saw Eddie Shimwell running up the field, and I thought, "He's going up to the far post. I'll pretend to hit this ball, and then I'll float it over to him." So I turned round. I'm running up to the ball now. From seeing absolutely nothing of the goal, I could now see a post standing outside of a Bolton player. And what had happened, and people who were behind the goal tell me this: when I turned my back onto the line-up and walked away, in order to have a run-up to the ball, a Bolton player went from one end of the line to the other. So therefore one post wasn't covered. There was a gap of one man. As I was running to the ball, I changed my mind. The chip has gone out of my head. I'm now going to hit it. This is what wins or loses matches: split-second decisions. I'm not going to be big-headed and say that this was a wonderful shot. Believe me, although the ball went into the net, I could have tried that kick a million times and the ball would have gone anywhere but in the net. The true interpretation to the story is that a gipsy on the Golden Mile that year had said that Blackpool were going to win the Cup, and as I ran to the ball I thought that she cast a spell over the arena and picked the ball up and threw it in the net, and then brought everyone back to life; and I got the credit for the goal.

I've had experience, all my life, of dealing with people. I think that the most important thing in a manager's life is to be on good relations with his players. And the players have got to have confidence in the manager: that the things he tries to do are going to be for their benefit. Those are the two most important rules. And, of course, to be fair with your players. I always try to be fair with them, and, whenever I do anything, I try to have my players in mind, first. Ever since I came here as a young boy, we've had a wonderful team-spirit, and the atmosphere at Blackpool has always been 100 per cent.

To me, the name *Blackpool Football Club* is the most important thing in the world. We're part of a wonderful organization. And I say to my players, time after time: "Whenever you're playing away from home, wherever you are, you're looked upon as ambassadors of Blackpool Football Club." These lads have got names in the game. If one of my players steps out of line or does something wrong—which an ordinary man-in-the-street could do without any publicity being showered upon him—the worst interpretations are put on his actions. Not only does it go against him; people will say, "Oh, Blackpool Football Club."

I came to Blackpool as a young boy of sixteen, from an area in the north-east which wasn't particularly blooming at that time. Any opportunities I have had in life were created in the first place by coming to Blackpool Football Club as a young lad. I married a Blackpool girl, and fell very much in love with the town. Before I came back to the club as manager, I had opportunities to leave Blackpool many times, to go to other clubs, but I wasn't interested in leaving. I don't quite see my coming back to the club as a repayment, because, by saying "repayment", I would seem a bit big-headed: in thinking that I could repay Blackpool for everything they've given me. But I know that whatever Blackpool Football Club asked me to do, in the good interests of Blackpool, I would most certainly do. At all times, I place the Football Club right at the top.

A manager stands or falls on the players' abilities. Lots of managers who get badly criticized are at clubs which can't afford to spend money. The same manager, put in a club which had untold wealth, could possibly become a great manager, because he could buy players, and probably have a lot more assistance. A lot of managers make decisions which go wrong. A lot of managers make decisions which on the face of things appear to be right and are still wrong. There's a tremendous amount of luck in this game of football: you pull a player out, and put someone on to take his place and he clicks for you.

Lots of times, the praise a manager gets is undeserved and the blame he gets is undeserved. There's been an outcry about the number of managers who have been sacked over the years, but to be a manager of a football club is essentially no different than being the manager of a big store or shop: you've got to be able to have good relations with people. I think that a lot of managers who have been sacked would have found it a struggle to be a success as a manager, whatever job they'd been in.

I think we have become too methods-conscious. Lots of times we don't take the full responsibility which we should have to the people who pay to watch us every week. At times, we've cut out entertainment by putting in systems which contribute to negative football. Although I appreciate that clubs have sometimes got to play defensive football, I have never been a negative football player. I've been an attacking player all my life. People pay to see entertainment. They want good entertainment.

At Wembley in 1953, the Hungarians were better prepared for us, tactically, than we were for them. This was the time when systems were coming. This was the time of the ball being pushed inside the full-back. They realized that we had a flaw in the team —we were playing the full-backs fairly square onto the wing men —and they kept pushing the ball inside of the full-back, and their wing man was beating him. The full-back was out of the game then. Harry Johnston, who was playing centre-half, kept having to move out to the wing, and, by Harry having to move out of the middle, we were getting exposed. Tactically, they were the better team.

We tend to think, when we look back: "My goodness, players aren't as good now as they were in my day." I'm not a great believer in this. I think that the players today are better-equipped tactically, than we were in my era, so they have the chance to become better players. Footballers are fitter now, than when we played: there have been tremendous changes in the training facilities and techniques.

There are probably not as many individual players now, as in my day, but this comes obviously from playing in systems. They don't bring out great personalities, like the Matthews' and the Finneys, the Mannions and the Carters, and the Hagans, and the Peter Dohertys . . . and you could go on listing the names of the great individualists. I always want to give my players individuality.

All the best players are in the centre stand. I remember once playing for Blackpool against Arsenal. I got the ball in the middle of the field, and a voice out of the centre stand shouted, "Give it to Taylor." So I gave it to Taylor. And then, about five minutes afterwards, I got the ball again in the middle of the field, and the same voice shouted, "Give it to Matthews." So I gave it to Matthews. A couple of minutes later, I got the ball again, but this time there were three Arsenal players around me, so I looked up at the stand, and the voice came back, "Use your own discretion."

9

ERNIE TAYLOR
Football's Court Jester

Ernie Taylor, who reigned over Bloomfield Road from October 1951 until February 1958, is a remarkable figure in Blackpool history. Not only was he the Tom Thumb of football of his day, he was also the Puck. At 5ft 4in, in his voluminous white shorts and boots of size four, he was usually the tiniest player on the field. Also the cheekiest. He had in him something of the court jester. To please the lords and ladies of his audience, he would sway as though about to dribble round an opponent; then, another trick from the hat, he would push the ball between the defender's legs. I once saw him dribble past several players, including the goalkeeper, before side-footing the ball into the unguarded net. Then, with mock courtesy, he presented the ball to the 'keeper, as if to say, "Well, *now* you can have it."

Taylor restored humour to the game. I am reminded of an afternoon, in November of 1932, when Blackpool beat Liverpool 4-1, and, a few minutes from the end, Jimmy Hampson scored one of the most impudent goals ever seen. He outran the whole Liverpool defence and had only the goalkeeper to beat. Elisha Scott, the Irish international, was forced to leave his goal in order to narrow the angle. Instead of diving at Hampson's feet, he chose to take an almighty kick at the ball, and, missing his aim completely, he landed flat on his back. Hampson found himself almost on the penalty-spot, with the ball at his feet, facing an empty goal. While Scott clambered from the ground, and the rest of Liverpool's defence stood rigid and helpless, Jimmy Hampson, at a leisurely pace, edged closer to goal, and then, after a taunting pause on the line, as if he longed to shout "Come and catch me if you can", he nudged the ball into the net.

By selling the dummy at speed, or by a close dribble, Taylor would outsmart several opposing players in a matter of seconds. He reminded older spectators of Alex James and Patsy Gallacher.

Taylor's football was original, quick-witted, delicate, regal, and impertinent. He was always prompting his forwards, for he had great reserves of energy. So often during a game, absorbed by goalmouth excitements, I would pinch myself and mumble, "Where is Taylor?" And there he would be, unmarked, with an impish grin on his face, ready to take the ball out of defence.

He was a connoisseur's footballer, an artist of the game, as nimble of mind as of foot. He was the supreme tactician, always thinking, and yet his schemings seemed always natural and instinctive: such is true art. I doubt if he ever hesitated to attempt a bold move, out of fear of failure. So often, like Matthews, he seemed reluctant to shoot at goal, but a surprising power of shot could explode from this tiny, weightless man, and he had the gift of scoring vital goals in vital matches.

Taylor scored the equaliser against Arsenal, in the sixth round of the Cup in 1953, and from one of his passes Brown scored the winning goal. It was Taylor's goal against Sheffield Wednesday which sent Blackpool victoriously through an earlier round. Three years later, at Maine Road, he scored thirteen seconds after the kick-off: one of the quickest goals ever recorded in a cup-tie in the competition proper. It would have counted as an official club record, had not a dense fog caused the match to be abandoned. Probably his best-remembered pass was the back-heeler to Milburn, who scored from long range to clinch victory for Newcastle against Blackpool in the 1951 Final. Taylor never saw Milburn score. When Taylor had turned round, the ball was bouncing joyfully in the back of the net. Six months later he became a Blackpool player.

Joe Smith never made a better capture, and he obeyed the manager's dictum: "If you can't beat him, buy him." Taylor came to Blackpool at the height of his creative and mischievous powers. He and Matthews formed one of football's truly well-blended partnerships. They soon developed an uncanny understanding. Taylor could judge his passes to the last centimetre. I used to imagine that a piece of metal inside the ball was lured to magnets in the toe-caps of Matthews' boots, so reliably did Taylor's passes reach him, beautifully-placed passes which skimmed over the turf for Matthews to meet smoothly, without falter of stride.

The wonder was that Taylor was given only one chance to play alongside his wing partner in an England international: the 6-3 defeat by Hungary, at Wembley in November of 1953, when Taylor became one of the smallest players, forward or defender, ever to represent England. You cannot pass judgement on a player after only one display, especially when his team has been brutally and totally overcome. In 1955–56, a good season for Blackpool,

Taylor's form failed to charm the selectors, and he had to be content with a "B" international in March of 1956, and an England v. Young England exhibition-match a year later. Still, Taylor had his Bloomfield Road audience to attend to, and delight.

A few days after the Munich air crash, he joined Manchester United, to act the uncle to a patched-up young team. Taylor went to Wembley with them that year: his third Cup Final, with his third League club. Not many months later, he moved to Sunderland, the club of the town of his birth.

Taylor was once told to keep the Queen and 100,000 spectators waiting. As the Bolton and Blackpool teams lined up for the start of the 1953 Final, Taylor suddenly knelt down, and fumbled with a boot-lace. He took his time. The referee, B. M. Griffiths, told Taylor to undo the lace again. A Wembley Final had to begin at exactly 3 o'clock. They were a minute early.

10

HARRY JOHNSTON
Great Strength of Character

Harry Johnston captained Blackpool's three Cup Final teams. That alone ensures him a place in our portrait gallery. He is a man large of nature. Have we a canvas broad enough? The quality of his leadership places Johnston not only among the outstanding captains of English post-war football—Mercer, Harvey, Wright, Carey, and Barnes—but among the finest captains that the game has known. There exists in Johnston something of the perfectionist. He played football with devotion. Tactful handling of his players, strong sense of fair play, a tactician's approach to the game, a belief that his club deserves a man's effort until he has spent his last drop of sweat, insistence on fluid team-movements and on skilful football attractive to watch, and a smile and quiet confidence when faced with long odds: these are the qualities of good captaincy in football, and Johnston has them all, in abundance.

The 1953 Final was the high point of all his years as a player. He steered Blackpool to Wembley. He rallied his side in the semi-final against Spurs, and Blackpool might not have reached even the fourth round had he not played so toweringly against Sheffield Wednesday. Supreme was his bravery in the Cup a year later, at Villa Park, in the second replay of a marathon against Luton. After an hour's play, he tore a ligament in his left ankle, and moved to centre-forward. Four minutes from the final whistle, he scored the equaliser which saved Blackpool, the Cup-holders, from the humiliation of defeat by a Second Division team. Johnston had shot and scored with his injured left leg.

Johnston is a gentleman who happened to be a footballer. He always gave the impression of being easefully in control: of himself, of his team, and of his opponents. Nothing could shake his composure. You had only to probe a short way below the surface to find the determination and strength of will that together directed his actions. The sight and sound of Johnston on the field, with his

rolled-up sleeves, his long throw-in, and his words of encouragement, leave enduring memories. He was, and is, a believer in
attacking football; having no time for negative, or merely defensive, tactics. Some observers thought that wing-half suited his style
more naturally than centre-half. He played in either position, to
suit his club or his country or a colleague (he once switched flanks
to help a Blackpool team-mate), and he appeared on the left wing
for Blackpool a couple of times before the war. His best season for
goals was in 1950–51 when he scored seven in League matches.
At the end of that same season, he was elected Footballer of the
Year, and received the statuette on Cup Final eve. Newcastle
triumphed. Johnston and Blackpool had to wait another two years
for their, and all football's, day of glory.

The boy who was destined to captain Blackpool, for a decade,
spent the early years of his childhood under the shadow of the
ground and home of Manchester City, but he more often went with
his Dad to Old Trafford, to watch the United. Eventually, as a
young man of fifteen, he joined Blackpool's ground-staff. The pay
was 50s. a week. He made his League début at Deepdale, on
November 20, 1937, soon after his eighteenth birthday. At the
time, he was one of the youngest players ever to appear in Blackpool's first team. As left-half, he marked one of his idols. George
Mutch, and when Sam Jones was injured, Johnston moved to
centre-half, facing Frank O'Donnell, who signed for Blackpool
ten days later. By the next season (1938–39), Johnston had become
a fully-fledged and regular member of Blackpool's team. The war
cut short the life of the 1939–40 season, only three matches old.

He played left-half—part of one of Blackpool's finest half-back
trios: Farrow, Hayward, Johnston—in the cup-winners' challenge
match against Arsenal in May 1943, and, after serving in the
Middle East came back to England. Now he was poised for greatness. Before the war, Johnston was marked out as a future international, but he had to wait until November of 1946 for the chance
to wear England's colours. His performance in his first international, a thumping 8-2 win over Holland, delighted all those who
had been calling for his selection, and he was chosen for England's
next match, against Scotland in April. He did not play again for his
country for another four years. But for the presence and the consistency of Billy Wright, Johnston would have won many more
caps. Who knows? But for Wright, he might have become captain
of England. Johnston's last appearance in an England side was in
May 1955, when, at the age of thirty-five, and joined by Mortensen
and Matthews, he played in an exhibition-match, against Young
England, on Cup Final eve. The veterans won 5-0.

Johnston is a man much honoured in football. No player has been more deserving of honours, and no one has received laurels with more profound modesty. No player has given longer service to Blackpool. With Joe Smith, he formed one of the longest player-manager partnerships in League history. In January of 1953, he became the first Blackpudlian to have made 300 appearances in the First Division. His final career tally, 424 first-team games, was a club record at the time of his retirement as a player.

He played in his last League game for Blackpool in April 1955, and in November of that year, after several clubs had invited him to become manager, he accepted an offer from Reading. By coincidence, Joe Smith took his first managerial post at the same club. In April 1967, Johnston returned to Blackpool F.C. as chief scout. As a player, Blackpool had been his only League club. The spell at Reading forms but a short chapter. Johnston is a Blackpool man through and through.

The old firm of Johnston and Morty was in action again. Morty became Blackpool's manager less than two months before Johnston's return. The careers of these two friends have run parallel. Both were born in the north, and both joined Blackpool, initially as amateurs, in the thirties. Both became England internationals in the 1946–47 season. They played together in three Wembley Cup Finals, and contributed to, and shared in, Blackpool's golden years. They both left the club one day in November 1955, within a few hours of each other, and only a few weeks separated their return, early in 1967.

Thirty-and-more years previously, James Haslam went to a game in order to assess the potential of Jim McIntosh, a centre-forward who was scoring a lot of goals for Droylsden Athletic. A half-back caught Haslam's eye.

"That left-half is promising," he said.

"I think so, too," said the man standing next to him.

"He'll be famous one day," said Haslam.

"I think so, too," said the other man.

Soon afterwards, Harry Johnston signed as an amateur for Blackpool. James Haslam, who later became a Blackpool F.C. director, befriended the man who agreed with him. That man was Harry Johnston's father.

11

HARRY JOHNSTON
— in an Interview

A calm attitude of mind is something you're born with, or at least it was with me. I've always been this way: taking things calmly— water off a duck's back—and not letting them affect me. I think it's essential. You can't be a manager or a leader or a captain if you are continually losing your temper. The players won't appreciate you, and I know the crowd won't. If you lose your temper, the crowd will never forgive you. You've got to be of a stable nature, haven't you? All through life, I've tried to be that way. No! on second thoughts, I've not tried to be; I have been. It's not something I've tried to cultivate. It's something I was born with. I was captain of the school team. I was always the same then.

I came to Blackpool in 1935, and I left in 1955: about six months short of twenty-one years. When I came here, there were players at Bloomfield Road that most of the present-day generation haven't a clue about. But to me, a youngster of fifteen, they were like giants: Jimmy Hampson; a lad called Phil Watson, a Scotsman; Jock Wallace, the goalkeeper; Bobby Finan. These were names I'd read about, and I thought I'd never meet them. When you first come to rub shoulders with such players, you look at them with a certain amount of awe. But you find out that they are just human beings. They were very good to me: Danny Blair, Bobby Finan, and those fellows.

At Bloomfield Road there was an atmosphere in which young players could develop—very much so. In those days, taking 15-year-olds on the ground-staff was unheard of. Nowadays it's commonplace. Blackpool took on two or three ground-staff boys, not long after I joined. Clubs were always alive to the need for youngsters, but it wasn't as cut-throat as it is today. In those days, members of an England-international schoolboy team could just drift away after they'd played, and never become footballers. But nowadays all the scouts are there, and they won't let these promising youngsters out of their sight. The scouts are soon at the parents' home. This never happened to me until Blackpool came for me.

The story about Jim Haslam meeting my father is quite true. Actually, it was Bill Willett, a Blackpool scout in the Manchester area, who recommended both Jimmy McIntosh and myself to the club. Bill was working for the Gas Board in those days. Blackpool's secretary and another chap, David Ashworth, the club's chief scout, an elderly man, a helluva nice fellow, came to my house to sign me on. And that's how it all came about.

I preferred wing-half to centre-half. I was freer at wing-half. I didn't like to be shackled down at centre-half, but I played the last few years of my football career in that position. Blackpool had no centre-half when both Crosland and Eric Hayward got injured, so I went there. I must admit I enjoyed it to some extent, and it helped to develop the defensive side of my game. But I preferred wing-half, always. I liked to be attacking: up and down. I'm like that song *Born Free*.

George Farrow had a very long throw, and I developed a fairly good one. He and I used to go out practising with a medicine ball. This was a heavy thing: I don't know how much it weighed. You can throw it only about 15 to 20 yards. The secret is in the timing, and in the way you stand, arch your back, and then fling. George and I played many years together: he was at right-half, and I was at left-half. This throw was more like a corner-kick, and we scored quite a number of goals from it. It was dangerous as long as there was the element of surprise. There'd be no sense in doing it at every throw-in. Tommy Gardner, a wing-half from Burnley, who was a guest player at Blackpool during the war, had a tremendous throw. He used to talk to me about the technique of throwing. A nice lad was Tommy.

Professional footballers don't usually get up early. When I first started my newsagent's shop, I wasn't a good getter-up. Six o'clock in the morning seemed the end of the world to me, but it's amazing how soon you get used to something. You've got to get up in some part of the morning, and whenever you wake up, you wake up tired, rubbing your eyes. After a short while, getting up at 6 or 6.15 a.m. didn't trouble me. It's something I knew I had to do, and I did it. In time, it's just like getting up at 8 o'clock. Nowadays, I don't so often have to get up early, because my in-laws live there. Stan Mortensen used to say, "Harry had a lie-in this morning. He didn't get up till half past 6!"

Training methods have changed tremendously since my playing days. This is one of the good things about present-day football.

Training is better now, if only for one thing—much more variety. When I first played at Blackpool, we used to lap the ground for fully an hour before we did any ball-work. We just kept running around, running around. This was the old-fashioned way to get fit. You've still got to run now, to get fit, but present-day coaching and training methods are definitely an improvement. We didn't have a lot of weight-training. This is one other good thing that has been developed recently. The cloth-cap-and-muffler era has gone.

Nowadays, the ball is out more or less straight away. There are so many different exercises and varieties of training that the morning goes as quick as lightning. Much more thought is put into training. I'm certain the players appreciate this; I know I would have done.

Players of both eras got to the same goal, come the start of the season. Don't ever imagine that the players of fifteen and twenty years ago were not fit. They had to be fit. Although the advent of television has brought more prominence to the game, football was a national sport then. In my day, the Cup Final was televised, and that was about all. Now, football has been brought to the homes. During the season, you can see it every week.

You had to report injuries on Sunday mornings. You'd have treatment if you were injured. Even if they were fit, some of the players would still come down to the ground, on a Sunday morning, just to have a natter. I'll describe a typical week at Bloomfield Road, when the season had started and when we were completely fit. I'm not going to talk about when we first started training, because then we were at it every day.

Monday used to be a day off—morning, anyway. On Tuesday we would have a practice match, starting about 10.15 and finishing about mid-day. Tuesday afternoon we would be free. Wednesday would be a hard morning's training. We'd do about 45 minutes of hard lapping, followed by ball-practice. Then we might finish up with a five-a-side. Thursday was another hard morning of the same type of training; perhaps not as long doing lapping, but still a concentrated session. As on the Wednesday, we would do sprints intermingled with the lapping. We'd have a ball out after that, and work on individual skills or collective skills (working out a move). Friday would be an easy morning, confined to a few laps, if you wanted to, or some sprints; and then in for a shower or a massage.

So, you see, we did all the things they do today, but it wasn't as interesting, or in the same variety, as now. There would be no loosening up on the Saturday. One or two players might feel a bit stiffish and want a massage, but it wasn't a recognized thing. You'd

The 1953 Cup Final. The Duke of Edinburgh meets the Blackpool team

The 1953 Cup Final. Blackpool's first goal: by Mortensen out of Hassall. Mortensen is in the centre, full length on the ground

just report three-quarters of an hour before the kick-off, and get yourself ready in your own time. I used to put my left boot on first; not that I was really superstitious. It became a habit, and I never changed it. Morty was always last into the dressing-room: we were all getting stripped when he arrived.

Films were not used for post-mortems in my day, but we certainly held post-mortems amongst ourselves. Often, on the Tuesday morning, during training, we'd walk around the pitch and talk about Saturday's match. It wouldn't be a terribly serious discussion, and we wouldn't go and sit in the boardroom. Only on very rare occasions would that happen.

We have a rule-book at Bloomfield Road now that is very much the same as we had when I was playing. I'll read you extracts. "Players must report on the ground every morning at 10 am, and are under the instructions of the manager for the remainder of the day. In case of sickness or injury, players, if unable to attend the ground, must report their indisposition to the club, immediately." I'm skipping through them.

This is rule 8: "Players are forbidden to smoke on the ground before or after training. Smoking is strictly forbidden on match days after breakfast. Any player found smoking in the saloon will be severely dealt with." And rules for match days are also covered. "Dancing after Wednesday evening, during the season, is forbidden. Players are expected to be in their homes no later than 11.30 pm any evening, and definitely not later than 10.30 pm on a night before a match. Permission cannot be given to players to ride motor-cycles. Gambling of any description is strictly forbidden. The captain shall report to the manager, after every match, any case of misconduct while on the field of play." Of course, the captain wouldn't do that unless something really nasty had been done on the field. These rules have been going ever since I came to Blackpool in 1935. Some of the rules have been altered slightly, for night-clubs and all this. We never had night-clubs here when I was playing.

We talked a lot, among ourselves, before the '53 Final. We'd played Bolton so many times: we knew them and they knew us. You get to know footballers as you go through season after season, just as tennis players and cricketers get to know the strengths and weaknesses of other players. We had to watch certain players, such as Willie Moir, their inside-right, and Hassall, their inside-left. I had the job of watching Lofthouse. We all had these special jobs to do. We were told to do them, but not to the detriment of our own game. It would be no good my marking Lofthouse, and saying, "Well, that's it. Finished. That's all I'm doing." We said, "We'll

G

mark these men, and then, when *we* get the ball, it's their job to find us."

This is what made Blackpool such an attractive side in the fifties. We were a good defensive side and could turn defence into attack, in a split second, with such players as Matthews, Mortensen, Taylor, Bill Perry, and Jackie Mudie. He could dispossess a Bolton player and—bang—we were on the attack straight away. Then they were worried about us.

I don't believe in saying, "You'll mark him, and you can forget all about your attacking qualities." That's no good, because you're playing right into the opponents' hands. If you play complete defensive football, you are saying to your opponents, "Right. You can have the ball. You try to score the goals, and we'll try to stop you." I think that's wrong. I'd rather say, "You're entitled to the ball sometimes, but we're going to mark you tightly and try to stop you getting that ball. Then, when we get the ball, you're going to start running after us." I still think this is the best rule in football.

Many teams, nowadays, when they go to an away match, say, "We're going to play a defensive game." At half-time, it's still 0-0. Then, ten minutes after the interval, the home side scores a goal. 1-0. Right from that moment, the team that went to play defensive football suddenly decides to attack. And then they start to look dangerous. And I say, "Why? Why give the home side the benefit of having the ball when, possibly, you are as good as they are, if not better?"

If you stay on the base-line all the time against good tennis players, you'll win nothing. You've got to attack, whatever sport you play. In golf, you've got to attack the pin. It's no good attacking the green, because you can finish 30 or 40 yards short. When I say "attacking football", it isn't all-out attack, with everybody going up. You've still got to have a basis of defence.

We were playing 4-2-4 in my day, but it wasn't called 4-2-4. There was no fuss and palaver about it. Hughie Kelly was the defensive wing-half, and I was the attacking wing-half. I backed up Stan Matthews and Stan Mortensen. Ernie Taylor and I were the mid-field links. Eric Hayward stayed back with Hughie Kelly and the two full-backs. It was as simple as that.

I don't think the duties of a captain have changed. I wanted to do the captain's job properly, both on and off the field. I was captain of a side containing fellows who were older than I was, but I soon got over the nervous opening of the first two or three months. I tried to become a captain in the true sense of the word. I felt this way: "If I can do it, so can they." It would have been no good shouting at them to "Do this and do that" if I just stood back and did nothing myself. I used to say, "Look, I'm doing this, running about, struggling like hell to help. You can do it, and you *will* do it." It is of great importance for a leader to prove that he can do it; and then the other ranks—or the other players, or what have you—will follow suit. They'll say, "He's showing us. He's doing it by example as well as by mouth."

You've got to prove by example that you're the captain. I always tried to do this. I never gave up until the referee blew the final whistle, and I hated anybody else to give up. I never wanted to be second best: I think this is the only way to get anywhere in life. It's the same now. I've taken up golf very seriously, and I hate to be second best. But don't get me wrong: I'm not a bad loser. If I've lost 2 and 1, I pay up my money gladly. I'm a good loser. But I'll only admit defeat when the game is finished, when the final whistle has gone.

Off the field, the duties of a captain are very much varied. For example, I often used to accompany players, who had complaints, on their visits to see the manager. I didn't go every time. If I felt a player was wrong, I'd say, "No. I'm not going. If you want that for yourself, you go and see him." If I thought it was just a bit of ego coming out, with the player wanting more limelight than the other players, I wasn't interested. But if I felt a player was right, and that he had a rightful grumble, I would support him all the way.

I saw Joe Smith nearly every day. I often used to drive him down to the ground. Joe used to walk part of the way to the ground, every morning. He used to walk down Palatine Road, and my shop is right at the bottom. I'd come out at about a quarter to ten, and he'd be waiting for a bus, so I'd give him a lift down, and we'd natter on the way: nothing very serious, just a little natter.

The Blackpool team were, on the whole, easy to handle. I now realize how much we meant to each other. From what I've heard, after my playing days were over, they appreciated me as captain. I didn't realize this when I was playing, but now I realize it from the things one or two of the players have said since we've finished. It's a nice feeling. As captain, I was a bit on my own at times. You have to be on your own, if you're a captain, a manager, or a leader of any kind. But it never worried me: it's something that's born in you.

You have to adapt your tactics to suit the player. One man you can really get into and rollock, and let him know how you feel, whereas with another player you've got to get at him in a different why altogether: you pat him on the back and say, "Well, come on.

You can do better than this." We had one player—he eventually left Blackpool and went on to play for England—who was very touchy when he first came here. You had to be a bit careful with him. But later on in his career, when he was playing for his new club against Blackpool, I realized how much he'd learnt. He'd got as tough as the rest.

Sometimes I had to lay down the law, on the field. One particular occasion that I remember was against Liverpool. We'd played them in a sixth-round cup-tie on the Saturday, and we'd lost 2-1 in the last ten minutes. On the following Wednesday we played them, again at Anfield: this time in a League match. I had occasion to bawl out one of our fellows: Willie McIntosh. He was so incensed at me, for having had a go at him, that a minute later he collected the ball, forced his way through, and helped to create a goal for Jackie Mudie. Willie came up to me and said something like, "Now I've shown you." He probably used much stronger language. And I replied, "I don't care *how* you've shown me. You've done it." It was a fairy-book ending because he had made the winning goal. That's just one illustration. Willie was a helluva nice lad. He's back in Scotland now. He was the type of man you could really get *into* on the field and know that he wouldn't sulk. Some players would sulk if you rollocked them, so you had to be careful.

Joe Smith wasn't a tactics man, at all. He wasn't one who believed in tactical talks and things like that. But he knew a player when he saw one. He got a good team together, and he more or less let it take care of itself. He wasn't the type of man to interfere when things were going well. He was a tremendously good loser—a terrific loser, this chap. It never seemed to bother him; obviously it did, but he never seemed to show anything.

I think his greatest asset was to leave well alone, and not interfere when things were going well. He wasn't the man to say to himself, "Well, I'm the manager, and I must say something, just for the sake of saying something."

He had a happy knack of picking out a good player. He had a fair amount of luck, which is something you've got to have in all sports. He wasn't one who would have the blackboard out three and four times a week. He would rather have the practical side than the theory. How he would get on today, I don't know. His results would have to prove him. A lot of present-day soccer is full of talking and theory. The Joe Smith types are dying out. I think it's a little unfortunate.

Joe got his team together—got a good team together—and left it that way. He only said things when he had to. In the dressing-room, he was a great asset with his jokes. He always had a joke.

He used to tell jokes till the cows came home. He cracked jokes many a time at Wembley, the three times we went there. Relieving tension is part of a manager's job.

There are a lot of little, human things that go to make a good manager. You don't have to be a great disciplinarian, cracking the whip all the time. You don't have to be always proving that you know football theoretically. I'm a great believer that a good manager doesn't necessarily have to be a young manager. Joe Mercer, for example, learnt a lot from his first attempts: at Aston Villa and Sheffield United. I had seven years as manager of Reading. I think I'd be more ready to be a manager now, because I've got that experience behind me. Tolerance grows in you.

You have to go with players' weaknesses. You'll never improve a great weakness in a player. You might tell him about it, and try to help him. But nowadays we believe you should concentrate on a player's strengths, rather than keep on to him about his weaknesses. Because, if you keep on to him about his weaknesses, you could create an inferiority complex.

Joe Smith, in his blunt way, had a positive approach with his players. He wasn't a man for long speeches or theory. He wasn't a man who said, "You *will* do this, and you *will* do that." But if I was marking somebody, and I wasn't marking him tight enough, Joe would tell me. It's a manager's job to spot things during the course of a game. During the week, he seldom interfered, because things were running so well. The players had a lot to do with it. We had a good, well-balanced side and a wonderful atmosphere, all the way through.

We had a perfect example of two full-backs in Eddie Shimwell and Tommy Garrett. One full-back—Garrett—was poised and polished and calculating; the other—Shimwell—was strong and determined, tough but not dirty. Who would say which was the better full-back? I would say they were both right. And here is where Joe scored. He got this balance, without making a lot of fuss and palaver about it.

We had some close matches on the way to the 1953 Final. In the third round we played Sheffield Wednesday, and we won 2-1. It was a hard match. Stanley Matthews had a particularly good game, even though he hadn't played for three months. We played Huddersfield next, and won with a fluky goal. There was a gale-force wind blowing throughout the match, and it was blowing right down the field. We were against the wind in the first half, and we hardly got out of our own half of the field. After the interval, we did almost all the attacking. Tommy Garrett kicked the ball from just inside the Huddersfield half, and it floated into the net: a fluky goal, if you like, but it put us through. This was an example of the luck you've got to have in order to achieve anything.

Southampton was another difficult one. We played them at Bloomfield Road, and drew. Southampton played very well, and we were lucky to draw. We went to Southampton, and they almost ran us off the field in the first half, down at the Dell. They should have been at least three up; instead of that, they were one up at half-time. As soon as we got into the dressing-room, I had a go at the team, and then Joe Smith came in and took over. We went out for the second half, and Stanley Matthews began to turn it on. In the end we won 2-1, and deservedly so. At the finish, we were playing like a First Division side, but it could have been all over at half-time. Early on, they had knocked us completely off our stride. Then we got to grips with it.

We beat Arsenal in the sixth round—a great match—and the semi-final was against Tottenham Hotspur at Villa Park. We beat them with the famous Alf Ramsey back-pass. All our Cup matches were very close that season, and we had some high-tension, nail-biting finishes. Often, we scored in the last fifteen minutes of a match. We always kept going, right to the final whistle. We were a very fit team, and we knew it.

Before the Cup Final, we went down to Lytham Green to train for two or three days. We wanted to get the feel of lush grass at that time of year, because our pitch—like most others—was bare. In those days, few clubs had a practice pitch to help keep their home ground in perfect condition. By the end of the season, most grounds were very bare down the middle and hard.

We had quite a strenuous week before the Final. We went through the usual motions. We still did our fair share of training. At that time of the year, you're fit. If you're not fit in April and May, you shouldn't be playing football. We didn't need to do terrifically hard training. It was just a matter of keeping loose and supple. There were a lot of photographers naturally, with it being Cup Final week, and a lot of pictures were taken.

Waiting from semi-final to Final was the worst period of the season, and the team's performance didn't quite live up to its high standards. The biggest fear was the fear of getting hurt, and miss-ing the Final. Unfortunate things happened: Allan Brown broke his leg in the sixth round, and Hughie Kelly also missed the match, because of an ankle injury. I think we tended to play things a bit carefully in the six weeks before the Final. The match immediately before the Final was agony because of the thought that there was only one more match to play, and a chance that one of us might get hurt. We felt we had to try and put up some sort of a show, because we had the paying customer and the press coming to watch us play.

We couldn't take our minds off the Final. We'd lost two. We didn't want to lose this third one. We were thinking all the time, "We *must* win this one." We were optimistic all the way through: more so, funnily enough, before this third one than before the previous two. The Blackpool v. Manchester United Final, I still believe, was one of the best, as a football spectacle, that was ever played. It was sheer good football, and United were worthy winners on the day. We were not 4-2 worse. 4-3, or something like that, would have been a fairer score, but they deserved to win the Cup.

Before the '53 Final, I had no idea what the score might be. I had no idea what a tremendous last twenty minutes it would be. All I can say is that I felt confident we would win. Don't ask me why. I don't know to this day. Naturally I was a little bit worried at 3-1 down, but, even then, I don't think *any* of us had given up hope. I still felt that we were in with a chance, and when Stan Mortensen scored Blackpool's second goal, I thought, "Well, that's it. We're going to *win* this." We'd started shouting words of encouragement to each other, and I can remember shouting to Ewan Fenton, "We can do it! We can do it!" The 100,000 spectators could never have imagined that they were going to see such a finish. Everybody still talks about the 1953 Cup Final: it was like a boy's book, a children's fairy-story, something you dream about.

Just before the match, Joe Smith's last words of advice were: "Don't be put off by the occasion, nor by the fact that we've lost two previous Finals. Go out and play your own natural game." He always said that. "Just try to be your own normal selves," he continued, "and let's win this one."

Joe was quite good to us at half-time. I think he felt like most of us: "We're in with a chance." We were losing, but we were playing quite well. We just weren't getting the breaks in front of goal. He never said anything about the silly mistakes that we had made. Having since been a manager myself, I know he must have thought a lot, and what he could have said at half-time is nobody's business. All he wanted to do was gee us on a little bit.

I felt convinced we'd win, especially with some of the Bolton players going down with cramp. It helped us tremendously to see that we were looking fitter than they, even though we were 3-1 down. They were carrying an injured man, which was unfortunate, but he scored their third goal. The Wembley turf is a heavy drag on muscles if you're continually chasing the ball; it's not so bad if you're in possession. Having sampled the turf before, in Finals and in international matches, most of us knew this. This experience made us each think, "We're looking fitter than Bolton, and I'm damn certain I feel fitter than most of them." This led us on.

Little Ernie Taylor came on to a great game. This also inspired us. He was one of the best inside-forwards in the game at that time. He was only about 5ft 3½in or 5ft 4in, but what a player! Once Ernie started to turn it on, we all felt that things were clicking. The only thing that bothered me was time running out. Then Morty and Perry got those great goals.

I've thought a lot about the finish. I've never really found a logical explanation. All I can think is that we had so many exceptionally good footballers in the side, and this gave us confidence. The fact that Stanley Matthews was playing for Blackpool could undermine the confidence of any opposing team, and, if Stanley was on his best behaviour, he would paralyse a defence, with no trouble. We had the two Stans, and Mudie, and Ernie Taylor, and Bill Perry, who was a flier; and the attack was backed up, all the time, by a strong defence.

We had a strong and skilful side. Looking back over the years, I sometimes wonder why we never won the League. We had a great chance, one season. We were lying about third at Easter, with games in hand. But we blew our chance away. I'm convinced that our side was good enough to have won the First Division Championship, and it's one of my chief regrets that we never did.

After the match, the Queen congratulated me. This was her first Cup Final as Queen. She said, "Well done. It was a tremendous game." She didn't say very much else. We were all too excited, anyway. It was a great moment to receive the Cup from the Queen in her Coronation year. Our victory couldn't have happened at a better time.

Out of all the teams that competed, Bolton and Blackpool were the last two. The Bolton players were very sporting losers. You've got something to be thankful for in that you got to Wembley. I think most professionals, when they get to a final—of football or rugby league or what have you—are sporting losers. A final is the showpiece of the season. Both teams want to make it a good game. Naturally, both teams want to win. When it's all over, the losers come and shake hands and offer their congratulations; and the winners say, "Bad luck. Let's hope that you can do it one day." Bolton were very good: wonderful, in fact, considering that they had been 3-1 up. They'd all but won the match. They were tremendously good sports, and so was their manager, Bill Ridding.

After the match, Joe Smith was walking about like a man in a dream. The champagne was flowing. Joe was running around like an excited schoolboy. Although the admin side of each club would have made separate arrangements, we both booked the Café Royal. One was up above and one was below. Then the Blackpool team went on "What's My Line?". Gilbert Harding guessed the identity of Stanley Matthews in no more than two questions. Stanley had insisted that we all appear on the programme, since it had been a team victory. We had a tremendous reception on the way home to Blackpool—all the way up the line.

Winning has always been important, but perhaps some of today's bonuses are causing a bit of concern. I think it was wrong to do away with the maximum wage. I said this at the time. The players were talking about going on strike. I was manager of Reading at the time, and I said to our Chairman, "Give the players an increase, by all means, but I don't think the maximum wage should be done away with." I'm not trying to be wise after the event. I stick to what I said at the time.

Nowadays, with the gates as they are, only a few clubs can pay their way from what comes in through the turnstiles. Today, most clubs have got to be subsidized by supporters clubs and development associations. Club loyalty has virtually gone. Without my mentioning names, you know the number of players who have refused to sign on, and want an increase in wages. What have they done to deserve an increase?

I think players were—and are—entitled to a good wage, because a footballer's life is short—very short—and he should make enough money so that he is able to buy a business, or something like that, and insure for a rainy day. When your football career is over, you are soon forgotten. But the transfer market has got all out of proportion.

I think my generation was happier, but I'm sorry we missed playing in European competitions. We had quite a few tours; and friendly matches, at home, against foreign teams; but the European Cup, for example, is a great Competition. I think we were happier because we were all on the same wage. We each knew what the other was getting. Nowadays, you and I could be playing for Blackpool, and if you don't care to tell me what you're getting, and I don't tell you, we would both be saying to ourselves, "I wonder what he's getting?" It's human nature to want to know what someone else, *in the same team*, is earning.

Although the wages were adequate when I was playing, they still weren't enough. But at least we *knew* that we were all getting the same money. I've never been jealous of another man in my whole life. Whatever a man's got—if he got it by the sweat of his brow and by sheer hard work and dedication—I say "Good luck" to him.

If there'd been no maximum wage in my playing days, and one man was getting £40 a week and one was getting £80, there'd have been a right shemozzle among some players, because they were both in the same team. There must be doubts in a lot of players' minds today, and then they start to get selfish or jealous. I'm not talking about a lad who's come out of the reserves for the first time. He's got to prove himself, and, when he has done so, I'm certain he'll get his rise in wages. I'm talking about the man who is a regular first-team player. I think they should all be on the same wage.

There are far too many tantrums now from some players. Fists are raised: I don't like to see it. I'm talking generally. There are always the exceptions, like Bobby Charlton, who never lose their self-control.

I used to play hard. I used to tackle hard. I used to try and play good, constructive football when I was in possession. But I never played dirty. When I was manager of Reading, I used to say to the team, "You don't play dirty. You play hard. There's a big difference. I don't mind how hard you go for the ball, as long as you go for the ball and not for the players' legs." I tried to put across my football experience, verbally, to my players at Reading. I wouldn't tolerate kicking.

The challenge match against Arsenal, in 1943, was a tremendous game. There were 55,000 spectators at Stamford Bridge, a big crowd for war-time. We had a really good side, an all-star forward-line. We'd won everything in the north. This was a challenge match to end the season. They tell me it is true that Arsenal had a picture taken with the cup, before the match, but I didn't see it. They were confident of winning. So were we, but we didn't pre-judge the issue. Let's put it that way.

Arsenal had a great side as well. They were 2-0 up in less than ten minutes. It *looked* all over bar the shouting, and Arsenal were going about as though it *was*. I couldn't blame them. In those first few minutes, they hit us with everything, and I thought, "Oh God, it'll be about 7-0 the way they're going." Then we suddenly clicked. We won well in the end. It was 4-2 at the finish: a tremendous achievement and a great match. It really was. Arsenal took defeat very well. They were very sporting. It was one of the best games I played in for many a long day, a match that will live in my memory for ever.

I played ten times for England. In my first full international we beat Holland 8-2 at Huddersfield. My first match against Scotland stands out in my mind: but not for personal reasons, because I had a poor game. It stands out because this was my first full international at Wembley, and playing against me was a pal of mine called Andy McLaren: we were stationed together in Egypt during the war. The game I played left a lot to be desired, and I didn't play again for England for four years.

In my second game against Scotland, we lost 3-2 at Wembley. We played most of the match without Wilf Mannion, who had suffered a terrific cheek-bone injury. He was carried off; blood all over the place. We didn't deserve to lose. We played a tremendously good game, with ten men. We attacked Scotland. We took the game to them. But we couldn't put the ball in the net. It was the good work of Cowan, their goalkeeper, that stopped us from winning.

I played for England on the 1953 summer tour. The match against Argentina was abandoned after 20 minutes. There were 100,000 spectators. The score was 0-0. There was a thunderstorm, and the rain was cascading off the stands, like waterfalls, all around the ground. At the finish, we were ankle-deep in water.

We beat Chile 2-1. I can remember, so vividly, flying over the Andes. I thoroughly enjoyed the game against Uruguay, out in Montevideo, which we lost 2-1. That was at a time when Uruguay were a great side. We put up a magnificent performance.

We played the U.S.A. at Yankee Stadium. It was a tremendous experience to play at a baseball ground. We felt that we'd have to win this game, because they'd beaten us in Belo Horizonte. For the first twenty minutes, we were a little bit worried, because the Americans went at us, and played well. We beat them 6-3 eventually. Tom Finney had an exceptionally good game that day.

I enjoyed the matches against Wales and Ireland later that year, but the outstanding match was the one we lost 6-3 to Hungary. I enjoyed that game tremendously, funny as it may seem. I felt I had a good game that day. We were up against what at that time was the greatest international side ever known. They'd licked everybody. I don't think there's been another international side that played so much like clock-work. Hungary haven't done it since. They've been nothing like that since. That was their Everest. [*As he said this, Johnston brought his hands together, to indicate a peak.*—R.D.] I was proud to play in that match.

There was too much emphasis placed on the fact that this was England's first home defeat by a Continental country. This emphasis on England didn't do just credit to Hungary, because this was *the* greatest side. If you play opponents at Wembley, you're bound to lose some time. They played to a different system. Later on, we in England started to use the system. We went overboard, though the deep-lying-centre-forward game was played by Don Revie at Manchester City, with some success. But the difference in tactics between the two teams wasn't the only reason for our defeat. We gave away some silly goals. To my mind, free-kicks from thirty-five yards out shouldn't be goals; but they scored one.

I thoroughly enjoyed playing against such great players as Hidegkuti and Puskas. They had eleven talented players, from goalkeeper to outside-left. I was marking their inside-right, who was coming through. Somebody else was marking Puskas. Hidegkuti was playing well back. I found myself having to go over to help my full-backs a lot. I think we did well to score three goals against them. We weren't disgraced.

I enjoyed all my international games. I enjoyed the tours I went on. I met some great fellows in the England team, and in the teams we played against. I thoroughly enjoyed my football career. . . . I wish it was starting again.

12

TOMMY GARRETT
Fearless Full-back

Full-backs come in all shapes and grades: burly or tiny, slow or fleet, fair or crude. Rare, and to be prized, is the stylish full-back. Tommy Garrett, the miner who became an England-international footballer, could number stylishness among his qualities. He was fearless, consistent, resourceful: an accomplished performer on either flank. Pressure-of-the-moment never dismayed him. He could produce a quick burst of speed, when necessary, and his canny northern nature taught him to keep wingers hemmed in near the touch-line, thus restricting their room for manœuvre. His height, and hours of heading practice as a youngster, gave him command in the air. I remember with affection the last time I saw Garrett play. He knocked himself out when brilliantly intercepting, and heading for a corner, a dangerous through-ball.

While he was playing for Horden Colliery, in a football-daft area of the north-east, Garrett was spotted by a Blackpool scout. He joined the seaside club in 1942, signed professional forms two years later, and worked his way up, through Blackpool's junior teams. Although he made his senior début in April 1947, it was not until a couple of years later, following the departure of Ron Suart to Blackburn, that he commanded a regular first-team place. Garrett once had ambitions to score, rather than to discourage, goals: as a junior with Horden, he played at inside-right; and he played centre-forward half-a-dozen times for Blackpool, including one cup-tie victory. His switch from forward to defender might almost be said to have given him an unfair advantage of knowledge, as with a robber who becomes a policeman, or a tax inspector turned accountant!

By winning a 1951 Cup Final place beside the mighty Shimwell, Tom Garrett, like many, was swept along in the harvest of Blackpool's success, contributing much and also reaping personal rewards. He soon gained international recognition. His début for his country was an impressive one—at left-back as partner to Ramsey, in April 1952—but only two more caps were added to the shelf; the last, for an appearance at right-back against Wales, in October 1953. That summer, he had toured South America with the England team.

Again he joined Shimwell in a Cup Final, despite suffering a broken nose the week before. This time it was Blackpool's all-conquering year. Not for this alone will Garrett's name be recalled; nor only for his famous goal against Huddersfield, earlier in that triumphant Cup run, when the Blackpool breezes converted a lob, from around the half-way line, into a winning goal. Tommy Garrett will especially be remembered for his determination. His devotion to training, and courage—such as he often displayed on the field—enabled him to win back a first-team place after several serious injuries. He had a few enforced spells in Central League football, and a number of graduates of the reserve team of those years have cause to be thankful for his guidance.

In his last playing years, he was forgotten neither by his club nor by the selectors of teams for representative matches. In October 1957, he was chosen for the Football League side, after several years' absence. Football made one more parting gesture. In October 1960, Blackpool recalled him to the colours, after he had been out of the first team for 13 months. The club were in a desperate plight. This, they reasoned, was a time to make use of experience.

Garrett's quick-wittedness and his intelligent positional play made up for flagging speed, and he was a vital force in Blackpool's battle against relegation. He played right-back in the thrilling 2-1 win over Newcastle which ensured First Division football at Bloomfield Road, at least for another few seasons. Several days later, April 19, 1961, was to be his farewell, against Manchester City, this time at left-back. He was versatile to the end. He had just turned thirty-five. Cool-headedness and a sure sense of timing allowed him to continue in first-class football for a year or two beyond normal expectations.

When the no-maximum wage came into being at the end of the season, Garrett refused the terms offered him. Probably he thought that his days in First Division football were numbered. Blackpool immediately, and considerately, placed him on the free-transfer list, and Millwall did not tarry in signing Garrett, who was promptly appointed captain of his new club. He had played more than 300 times for Blackpool, in Cup and League. "Some people have called me a good club-man. That is what I always tried to be. A good club deserves good service." An endearing player, was "Whaur Tam".

13

JACKIE MUDIE
A Terror for his Size

John Knight ("Jackie") Mudie, who like Ewan Fenton was born in Dundee, played at inside-forward for Lochee Harp, a local club. Not long after the war, a shy, ambitious youngster of sixteen travelled south for the first time, Blackpool-bound. With all his natural ability, he could not fail to do well in the trials. Because of his light build, he could move swiftly; and his eye for a half-chance was destined to confound Alf Ramsey and send Blackpool to their 1953 Wembley triumph. Most important of all, the young Mudie showed Blackpool his gift of ball control.

He joined as an amateur, and arrangements were made for him to serve as an apprentice with a firm of decorators. One day, he packed his bags and went back to Scotland. He was homesick. Blackpool, with fatherly understanding, gave him time to make up his mind about his future. Mudie had a return-ticket in his pocket, and a few weeks later returned to Bloomfield Road, inspired by a young man's dream of becoming a great footballer.

Mudie signed professional forms in June of 1947, and he represented the Royal Air Force during his National Service. He often led the reserve attack in season 1949–50, and he contributed more than one-quarter of the goals that brought Blackpool the Central League championship for the second time in the club's history. As centre-forward, he capped a most promising first-team début, at the age of nineteen, by scoring the winning goal at Liverpool, on March 8, 1950. Nothing could stop him now.

Little more than a year later, Mudie played at inside-right in the Cup Final against Newcastle, and Matthews was quick to praise his young partner. A few months afterwards, Blackpool paid a large fee for Ernie Taylor, one of the players who had contributed to Newcastle's victory. For a while, Taylor and Allan Brown prevented Mudie from gaining a regular place. Soon, Blackpool were again striving to reach Wembley.

In the sixth round of the 1952–53 Cup competition, Blackpool, in one of her finest hours, defeated the Arsenal at Highbury. Allan Brown broke his left leg in that game, when scoring the winner two minutes from time, and Mudie took over the inside-left position for the semi-final against Spurs at Villa Park. This was not one of Blackpool's better days, and only because of a tragic error by Spurs' full-back, Alf Ramsey, did Blackpool leave the field victorious. Ramsey's pass, back to his goalkeeper, was pounced on by the alert Mudie, who nipped in to score in the last minute, to the full-throated, rattle-whirling approval of the Blackpool fans. And so to Wembley, where Mudie played skilfully alongside Bill Perry.

Mudie moved to centre-forward when Stan Mortensen left for Hull City, just after the start of the 1955–56 season. Many asked: "How can this little fellow of 5ft 6in replace Morty the irreplaceable?" "This little fellow" answered the critics with goals. He played in every League match and scored 22 times. In addition, he had a four-goal feast in a friendly match at Hull. Blackpool finished as runners-up in the First Division.

Mudie again wore his goal-boots in 1956–57, when, in 38 League games, he scored 32 goals, to beat, by one, Blackpool's record for a season in Division I, set by Jimmy Hampson twenty-six years earlier. The record-breaker came, dramatically, in the last game of the season. Mudie had scored in twenty-five of his thirty-eight appearances. He steered Blackpool to three club records for the First Division: most wins, most points, most goals. Blackpool's and Mudie's records were not confined to League football. On January 26, 1957, against Fulham in the fourth round, he scored four goals, the most ever by a Blackpool player in an F.A. cup-tie. By 6-2, Fulham were dismissed: Blackpool's biggest Cup victory of all time.

For a while, it had seemed possible that Mudie might join the ranks of those who deserved, but never gained, an international cap. But this was Mudie's season. Representative honours could not be denied him. He was first chosen for Scotland at inside-right: no longer his club position, but one to which he was well accustomed. Between 1956 and 1958, Mudie made seventeen consecutive appearances for his country, and he played in all three inside-forward positions. On May 8, 1957, he scored three goals in a 4-2 win over Spain, guiding Scotland to the final series of the World Cup. That night, *Mudie* was the toast of all Scotland.

In his last years with the club, he competed for a place in the first-team forward-line with Ernie Taylor, Ray Charnley, Brian

The 1953 Cup Final. Mortensen stabs in Blackpool's second goal

The 1953 Cup Final. Mortensen equalises, daringly, from a free-kick. Blackpool and Bolton stand and stare

Peterson, the elegant South African, and Dave ("Legs Divine")[1] Durie. Mudie made his final first-team appearance for Blackpool on January 21, 1961, in a 3-1 defeat at Bolton. Peterson was about to return to the team, after a year's absence. Mudie had made his last come-back. He was sold to Stoke on March 3 for about £8,000. The next day, he scored for his new club, five minutes after the kick-off.

Of Mudie it was once said: "He's small but he's wise; a terror for his size." As versatile as he was agile, he played in every position in the Blackpool attack except outside-left. Mudie, the complete inside-forward, delighted the eye with his mid-field ball-play. As centre-forward he led his line intelligently, and at either inside-right or inside-left he made an astute general and creative genius of the attack. He favoured the first-time shot, and, despite his lack of inches, scored many goals from headers. Mudie ranked among the most persistent goal-getters in the country: in 353 League and F.A. Cup matches for Blackpool, he scored 156 goals. In seventeen internationals he scored nine, representing one in three of all Scotland's goals in those matches.

Mudie's departure signalled the end of a great line of Scots at Blackpool. Fenton, Brown, and Farm had all gone before him. Hugh Kelly alone remained, but with little prospect of regaining his first-team place.

Had it not been for that return-ticket. . . .

[1] "Legs" because he was tall and lean; his shoulders lurched from side to side as he ran. "Divine" because he was a Methodist Sunday-school teacher and a Leader of his local chapel. Despite being only a part-time professional, he was as fit as any member of the team. Durie played with relish in whatever position Blackpool chose him. No club has had a more faithful servant.

H

14

EDDIE SHIMWELL
Hard but Fair

Had it not been for English beer, Eddie Shimwell, the Derbyshire lad, might never have joined Blackpool. And had it not been for a snow-bound train, he would have made his début for his new club on the appointed day. He was travelling on a non-stop (or, rather, "non-stop") train from the midlands, and so he couldn't transfer to road: he reached St Pancras at half-time.

Sheffield United, who had already sold Jock Dodds to Blackpool, refused Shimwell permission to manage a public house, and Joe Smith, with his sharp eye for a good player, gladly paid £7,000 for him, Blackpool's first large fee of the post-war years. Dodds joined Blackpool in March 1939, and, had the war not intervened, he would have set peace-time goal-scoring records and won many caps for representing Scotland. Shimwell, luckier with his period, signed in December 1946—he at last made his début on Christmas Day— played in all three of Blackpool's Cup Finals, and won England recognition once: against Sweden in 1949. The selectors were not over-generous to him.

As a footballer and as a man, Shimwell was strong: a sturdy Englishman every inch of him. He never admitted defeat. When passed by a forward, Shimwell would always gallop back to make a second challenge. Season by season, his technique improved. He perfected the timing of his slide-tackle; and the accuracy of his kicking came to match his truly immense power of leg, right and left: never did he have to balloon the ball high into the air in order to achieve long clearances. In 1948, he became the first full-back to score in an F.A. Cup Final at Wembley. After Mortensen had been brought down, Shimwell scored the first goal of the match, in the fourteenth minute, with a cannon-ball of a penalty. Earlier in that season, in a fourth-round tie against Chester, he kicked a goal from the half-way line.

Shimwell, with his love of the traditional-English shoulder-charge, was among the last of his kind, but his occasional sorties up the field pointed the beginning of a new and more versatile rôle for the full-back. Shimwell started a dynasty of classic full-backs at Blackpool. Each, in his own way, perpetuated Shimwell's qualities. First there was Gratrix, who succeeded Shimwell at right-back and then, moving position to take over from Harry Johnston, became one of the most stylish centre-halves *never* to play for England. As well as being dominant in the air, Gratrix could, like Shimwell, kick a ball, from his own penalty-area, far into the opponents' half of the field. "There goes the big boot," the locals would shout.

When Gratrix moved to the centre, Jimmy Armfield came in at right-back. Armfield will always be remembered as the first full-back really to exploit the sprint up the field in support of his winger: the overlap, as the move has come to be called. Armfield learned from Shimwell the art of the long, low-flying ball, especially effective for free-kicks, and both players started many Blackpool attacks with a well-placed clearance. Lastly, Emlyn Hughes, who, even before he went to Liverpool for a fat fee, enjoyed, while still a teenager, a growing reputation for the nicely-timed slide-tackle, in the Shimwell manner.

A dislocated shoulder hastened the end of Shimwell's career with Blackpool. He lost his first-team place but held on to his pride in being a Blackpool player. He played as hard as ever for the reserves, and made no request for a transfer. Shimwell usually trained in Chesterfield, and Blackpool could always rely on him to be in prime condition every Saturday. In mid-January of 1957, Garrett, the left-back, was injured, and Shimwell was recalled for his only League game of the season and his last-ever for the club. "Are you 100 per cent fit for the game?" asked Joe Smith. Eddie Shimwell replied, "I'm 200 per cent fit!"

A few months later, Blackpool gave him a free transfer so that he could more easily find another club. At the end of May, he signed for Oldham of the Third Division, and a year or so afterwards he retired from football. He's an innkeeper to this day, I shouldn't wonder; probably lacking time for his hobby of breeding racing pigeons. He'll remember the time when the F.A. Cup was displayed at his inn at Clay Cross, and he'll recall having to lodge the Cup every night at the police station, only a few yards away, for safe-keeping. I hope he is enjoying his retirement from the game and the ground he graced. Bloomfield Road won't forget him.

15

EDDIE SHIMWELL
— in an Interview

I once marked Stanley Matthews in the Cup, when I was playing for Sheffield United and he for Stoke. It was in the last season the North/South leagues. The early rounds of the Cup were played on a home-and-away basis, and goal-aggregate determined the result. I was playing left-back. It was the first time I'd ever played against him. I had two fair games, and I certainly played better the second time. He had such uncanny balance and speed off the mark that, on several occasions in the first match, when I went in to tackle and thought the ball was mine, he whipped it away and was gone, and I was left high and dry. In the second match, I played off him a little, and didn't go in so rashly. I never saw any full-back master him.

The full-back didn't overlap with the winger in my day. In fact, the winger was more inclined to come back and help the defender. It depends a lot on the speed of the particular full-back. Jimmy Armfield, for example, was blessed with considerable speed for getting up the wing and then getting back into position. When the full-back goes up the wing, someone has to go back and take his place in defence. If somebody's doing that, all well and good. If not, they could be left wide open.

For a while, I was the regular penalty-taker. I relied on the power of the shot. I used to aim, usually, to the right-hand side of the goalkeeper. With my being a natural right-footer, my tendency was to pull the ball to the right of the goalkeeper (that is to say, to my left as I looked at the goal). It was prior to the 1948 Cup Final that I was asked if I would take the penalty-kicks; because one or two had been missed. Funnily enough, the first penalty I had to take was in the 1948 Cup Final.

When I scored in the 1948 cup-tie against Chester, I think I was just in my own half. I intended it as a lob, not as a shot for goal. The ground was frozen; I wasn't particularly helped by the wind.

The goalkeeper came out. The ball bounced in front of him, and over his head, and into the net. He couldn't get back again in time.

I played for England in Sweden. I didn't think I played well, and I didn't think I played badly. But we lost—it was 3-1—and I was never picked again. I was unfortunate to come into a losing team. If we had won, I think I would have played one or two more. But I wasn't playing as well then as I had been playing before, nor even as well as I played some little while after.

Any Cup Final is a special match, whether you win, lose, or draw. I think it is more of a thrill playing in a Cup Final than in any other match, including playing for England. We always had a feeling we were going to win the '53 Final. Mortensen's free-kick was the best goal he ever scored in his life—and it was the equaliser, don't forget.

In the 1951 Final, we lost a goal through playing the off-side game, but that didn't entirely cost us the match. Our forwards had chances to score, but didn't take them. When we played the off-side game, you had to have all the three defenders thinking the same; each knowing what the other was doing. It could be beneficial: if you were up against a fast centre-forward, for instance. It's very risky, playing the off-side game. I don't think it's played nearly as much nowadays. Now the emphasis is more on funnelling back into goal, and block defensive measures, or whatever they call them.

Harry Johnston was a good captain. The captain has got to be a *consistently* good player, which Harry Johnston was. And, at the same time, he was a very nice chap, on the field and off the field. He was a hard driver. But he was always driving himself as well. And he had the physical ability and the footballing ability which a captain has got to have. He was captain almost the whole time I played for Blackpool.

Joe Smith had a good set of lads, with a marvellous team-spirit. Everybody helped everybody else. If a player was having a bad patch, someone tried to make up for him; and the young players who came into the team were helped along by the older players. Joe was quite a comedian. He fostered a good spirit amongst us. He wasn't a big tactical man: he expected everybody to go out and do his best. He was a very good loser. He didn't mind you losing, if you had been trying. And he *knew* when a player was really trying, and when he wasn't.

He talked no blackboard tactics, as far as I can remember. Prior to every match, we used to have a discussion: all the players, the trainer, and Joe himself. We all had our say. We would talk about our opponents, and make plans to mark their danger men. Then we went onto the field, and played; without having to worry about conforming to this or that system.

There was such a friendly atmosphere at Blackpool. They didn't try to alter your style. They allowed you to play your natural game. They were always fair, as far as I know, to all the players. They didn't overpay you, and they didn't underpay you. You got all you were entitled to. That's what made it a good club. I used to think that Blackpool was the finest club in the country. And I still do.

The players who lived in Blackpool liked Blackpool. Half of them are still there, after all these years. The club was so good to me, personally. I never lived in Blackpool: they let me train at Chesterfield, and travel to the various matches, without any trouble and without any imposed discipline. Before some Cup matches, and particularly before the Finals, I used to go up to Blackpool and train with Blackpool. Normally, I trained with Chesterfield Football Club. And, of course, the basic training in a Third or a Second Division club was similar to that in a First Division club. After all, the only goal is peak fitness: it doesn't matter what class you're playing in. Football comes through your natural instincts.

I don't quite agree with the present wage-structure. I think there should be a maximum wage—a decent wage, mind you. It is beginning to develop in such a way that the top five or six clubs, who have got the money, are going to have the best teams because the players, who are good enough, want the top money. Some of the players sold by Blackpool in the past few years, for large fees, would never have wanted to leave the club, had they been playing in my day, before the lifting of the maximum wage. You can't blame the players. It's the system that's wrong. Footballers never made a mint of money in my day. There was a good team-spirit and club loyalty, because you knew that the chap playing next to you was getting the same as you were.

16

EWAN FENTON
Always Reliable

Ewan Fenton, Dundee-born, joined Blackpool from a junior club in 1946. He made his début in the first team in the home match against Derby on September 6, 1948, at right-half, as understudy for Harry Johnston. It was quite an ordeal for an 18-year-old débutant to have to mark Billy Steel, the Scottish-international inside-forward, then at the height of his fame, but Fenton pleased the Bloomfield Road fans.

During his National Service, Trooper Fenton distinguished himself in action (on the football field), and the day before his demob he captained the Army's Northern Command XI against Western Command. Five months later, he was playing for Blackpool against Bolton at Wembley, and it was during this season that Fenton established himself as a regular member of Blackpool's first team, equally at home in either wing-half position.

His goal-scoring in 1954–55 almost caused a sensation. Until as late as March 18, only six weeks before the end of the season, Fenton was the club's leading goal-scorer in League matches. A wing-half had scored more often than Taylor or Mortensen or Brown or Perry or Stephenson or Mudie.

In the autumn of that year, Scottish selectors were reported to be watching Fenton. He was never to play in representative football for Scotland, but his club honoured him with the captaincy, and he led Blackpool for a good portion of season 1956–57. Fenton was noted for his shrewd passes, for his thoughtful approach to the game, and for his steadiness when under pressure. Often he would move up with the attack when he could see a good opening in the opposing defence.

In the season after his captaincy, Fenton played in only eleven League games, and there were clear signs that he was coming to the end of his First Division career. A transfer request was refused early in 1958–59, but the end was near, at the age of twenty-nine.

During this his last season with Blackpool, he played in only three games, in the second of which he scored from a penalty.

His third game coincided with Blackpool's last of the season, and, shortly before the final whistle, centre-forward Ray Charnley was fouled just outside the area. The opposing defence lined up and, within a second or two, the ball was in the back of the net, kicked by Fenton. No more fitting end to his Blackpool career could have been devised; a career which spanned thirteen years and 221 appearances in the League and F.A. Cup.

In the close season, in May of 1959, he was sold for a modest fee to Wrexham of the Third Division, and was immediately made captain. In the season that followed, he suffered a serious groin injury and was told that he would never play again. But Fenton did play again and, what is more, he achieved the distinction of being the only member of Blackpool's 1953 Wembley XI, apart from Ernie Taylor, to play in the European Cup. For Limerick, in the preliminary round in August and October of 1960, Fenton played at left-half in the two-leg tie against Young Boys, Berne.

Fenton made his First Division exit all too soon. In style of play, he was reliable rather than spectacular. Ewan Fenton was part of the solid foundation upon which Blackpool's castle was built.

17

GEORGE FARM
Perfectionist

British football, in the post-war era, produced few safer goalkeepers than George Farm, of Hibernian, Blackpool, and Queen of the South. To Blackpool he gave his best years. There are those who will remember Farm for his machine-like relentless dedication, in training sessions as in matches. He was never satisfied. Day after day, he would implore his club-mates to shoot balls at him, left and right, high and low, close and from a distance. They helped to test and develop his sureness of judgement, his anticipation, his mastery of angles.

Others think of Farm as record-breaker supreme. He set Blackpool records for: most first-team appearances (508); most League games (461);[1] first-ever Blackpool goalkeeper, and first Blackpool player after the war, to make 100 consecutive appearances; most consecutive F.A. Cup matches (47); most ever-present seasons (6); first Blackpool goalkeeper to score a goal (October 29, 1955, against Preston).[2] Farm scored as centre-forward, after an injury had forced him to leave his goal. He had always teased the forwards, when they missed shots, that one day *he* would show them.

Yet others, the captious critics, will talk of his nutcracker grip. During the whole of his career with Blackpool, Farm chose to catch the ball with one hand above and one hand below; rather than the normal grip of one hand on each side of the ball. Long live the unorthodox. Long live the individual. We need more of them, in all sports. For years, the smart Alecks complained at

[1] A few years later, Jimmy Armfield broke Farm's records for most first-team appearances, and most League games.

[2] By strange coincidence, it was also against Preston, in March 1928, that a Blackpool goalkeeper scored. But, on that occasion, the goal was from a penalty, and the scorer was Benton, a wing-half, who had taken over in goal after Purdy suffered a broken nose in a collision with Roberts, the Preston centre-forward.

Zátopek's style of running. Emil Zátopek went on winning his races. And George Farm went on saving goals.

He wanted not consistency, but perfection. He used to analyse the goals scored against him. George Farm was George Farm's severest critic. He hated to be beaten. Angry were his gestures and fierce his self-disgust when he let in a ball he should have saved. At the age of thirty-four and as one of the most experienced goal-keepers in football, Farm was humble enough to say: "If ever I begin to suspect that something is going a little wrong with my game, I begin those afternoon practices again."

During eleven and a half years with Blackpool, he never missed an F.A. Cup match, and he played an important rôle in the club's 1951 and 1953 Cup campaigns. A fellow-Scot, Bob Wyllie, twice displaced Farm—each time for a very brief period—but, in all his years with Blackpool, Farm missed only a score of League games: some through injury, and some when he was playing for Scotland. Only a handful of goalkeepers have played more often, in a career, for one club. His longest run of successive first-team appearances was 188, never missing a match in League or Cup between September 18, 1948, his début, and October 11, 1952 (inclusive).

So much for the records he set. What of the man himself? Neat of movement, agile, sparing of virtuosity, proficient in his kicking of a dead ball, courageous: he never hesitated to dive at the feet of an oncoming forward. Anticipation was his middle name. A Farm foot, stuck out, often prevented a goal. I once saw him, under pressure in front of the posts, head the ball away. He developed a poised understanding with Blackpool's other long-serving defenders, such as Shimwell, Garrett, Johnston, Gratrix, and Armfield; and he would often toss the ball nonchalantly, in the Ted Ditchburn manner, to one of them. He preferred to wait at the ground, after a game, rather than face a horde of admiring fans and hunters of autographs. He was a modest virtuoso, the shy man of football.

George Farm first played for Scotland on October 18, 1952, in a 2-1 defeat of Wales. The Scottish inside-right that day, and scorer of one of the goals, was Allan Brown, another Blackpool player. Farm was awarded seven caps between 1952 and 1954, whereupon the selectors neglected him. In 1958, when thirty-four, an age that forces most players to think of retirement, the name *Farm* appeared in Scotland's shadow team. In May of 1959 he was once again chosen for his country's full-international side, and played in all three of Scotland's close-season matches, in the Indian summer of his career.

Blackpool signed him, for a give-away fee, in September 1948. Outside of Scotland, and even in Scotland, not many had heard of

George Farm. So often, and wrongly, it has been said that he was Hibernian's third- or fourth-team goalkeeper at the time of his transfer. Farm always contended that he was reserve 'keeper, and that he had played several times for the first team. Ten days after signing for Blackpool, he made his début in an away match against Bolton. One of Blackpool's full-backs was Ron Suart.

Eleven years later, Farm was to ask Suart for a transfer. Farm was still of First Division calibre, and had no dispute with the club. The soccer world was taken by surprise. He wanted to return to Scotland before his playing days were over, so that he could make plans for starting a business, or for becoming manager of a Scottish club. The directors promised to reconsider his request when Blackpool's League position had improved.

A few months later, in January 1960, they unselfishly agreed to release him. Hibernian was one of the clubs reported to be interested. Farm's last game for Blackpool was an F.A. cup-tie against Blackburn on February 3. On the following day, he decided to join Queen of the South. The transfer fee of £3,000 was more than he cost Blackpool in 1948.

Just before Blackpool's next match, Farm sent a telegram to Tony Waiters, scarcely known then, wishing him good fortune. The young Waiters was destined to become an England-international goalkeeper. He, too, was modest. He, too, trained and trained, and gave Blackpool. . . . But there! That is another and absorbing story.

18

HUGH KELLY
Mr Loyal

Hugh Kelly was eager to play for Blackpool. In his early days with the club, he used to commute from Scotland for each match. Kelly was the answer to a manager's prayer: a student of fitness, club captain, a true sportsman, a loyal long-service player who became a full international. He made 471 appearances in the first team, a total only twice surpassed in the history of the club. A nominal signing-on fee was all that he cost Blackpool.

Having joined Blackpool in May 1943 from Jeanfield Swifts, a junior club in his native Scotland, Kelly made his first-team début on February 4, 1946, in the historic marathon-Cup-replay against Middlesbrough, played at Leeds. Jim Todd could not play—he had been injured while representing Ireland in a Victory International —and so Kelly was given his chance, at left-half. The match, with its two periods of extra-time, lasted two hours and twenty minutes: a long baptism.

Kelly owes much to the unselfishness of Harry Johnston. Kelly, though normally a left-half, was first chosen for Blackpool's League side on the right flank, and Johnston risked his England chances by switching to make way for him. After little more than a score of appearances, and only a few months after gaining regular selection, Kelly played at left-half in Blackpool's 1948 Cup Final team against Manchester United. It was not long before he had established a reputation as one of the sturdiest wing-halves in football.

Hughie was an accurate kicker of penalties, and he scored from the spot ninety seconds after the start of the famous (or infamous, depending on your loyalties) 5-1 Cup defeat by West Ham in 1958. At 5ft 8½in and 11st 9lb, he had the advantage of strength, yet he was always fair in the tackle. He passed with deliberation, and the ball usually reached the intended man. He was more than adequately versed in the arts of the game. With his namesake, Jim, on the other flank, the two Kellys were considered one of the finest wing-half combinations in the game.

Hughie played in the 6-0 win over the United States, in April 1952, but never again donned the navy-blue jersey of Scotland. He succeeded Johnston as club captain at the start of 1955–56, and, under Kelly's leadership, Blackpool, by finishing second to Manchester United, attained her highest-ever position in the League Championship. Ewan Fenton took over for most of the next season, but Kelly showed that indifferent form can be an incentive to do better.

In 1957–58 he regained the left-half position and the captaincy. His club-spirit and his determination were as firm as his tackle. Although he played in the first team for the last time in April 1960, he stayed with Blackpool all through 1960–61, often as twelfth-man to the League side; on other occasions, he played in the reserves, guiding the youngsters. Kelly was placed on the transfer list at the end of the season, and he soon afterwards joined a Lancashire Combination club, Ashton United, as player-manager.

Blackpool's directors twice paid their thanks to him: in 1953, by obtaining permission from the F.A. for a special medal to be cast, as substitute for the Cup-winners' medal he would have won, but for an ankle injury; secondly, in July of 1961, when the Chairman of the club presented him with a set of cutlery, "in appreciation of eighteen years' loyal service". Today, more than ever before, football needs Hugh Kellys.

19

BILL PERRY
That Gazelle of a South African

Stanley Matthews raced down the wing, swerving past despairing defenders. The score was three-all, and only seconds of injury-time remained. This would be Blackpool's last effort. Matthews fell as he centred, accurately, for the onrushing Perry to score. That was the *coup de grâce* to May 2, 1953.

"A gazelle of a South African," was how Bill Perry used to be described; the man who "moves like a springbok and shoots with the kick of a rogue elephant". Before the knee trouble which nagged his last playing years, Perry was always splendidly fit. At his peak, there was no faster winger in the game. He could trap the ball instantly: an asset especially useful to Perry when a long crossed ball reached him from Matthews, on the other wing. How often, these days, do we see a wing-to-wing pass? How often, for that matter, does a team now have two orthodox wingers?

Always it was exhilarating to see Bill Perry loping down the left wing. He would chip the ball inside the full-back and beat him easily for speed. Then he would cross a pinpoint centre, or cut in for a "Perry Special". Some of his many goals were scored on the run, from an angle so acute that the goalkeeper, even though he ought to have known what to expect, was confidently anticipating a centre. And there was no more rousing sight than Perry, during a last-ditch effort, alert, in the middle, for a chance to score; as in the 1953 Cup Final, when, on Blackpool's day of days, his unquenchable spirit was never more welcome.

Perry was playing for Johannesburg Rangers, in the city of his birth, when Jimmy Seed, then the manager of Charlton Athletic, offered him professional terms. Young Perry had a secure job, which, at the time, he preferred to retain. Another year was to bring a more adventurous outlook and a change of heart, when Billy Butler, a Blackpool scout and coach of the Rangers, recommended Perry to Blackpool. On October 28, 1949, the *Edinburgh*

Castle docked at Southampton, and Perry, only just nineteen, signed for his new club, promptly, on board ship.

He later said: "It is a big wrench to tear up your roots in your homeland and make that first venture into English football, but, after you have once played with a club like Blackpool, the move must be easier." Whatever misgivings anyone may have had about the length of time he would take to settle down in England, let alone win a place in a leading First Division team, they were dispelled by the swift progress that his application and natural ability ensured.

He was in the second team as early as December 26, and, in the outside-left position, made his League début at Manchester United on March 18, 1950, less than five months, mark you, after his arrival. The team seemed poised to win its first Championship. Blackpool failed. But Perry held his place—being preferred several times to the well-known Willie Wardle—though he was fielded occasionally on the right wing and once at inside-left.

Perry was back in the reserves at the start of the 1950–51 season, but from September 1950, for many years to come, he was as familiar a part of the Blackpool first team as the Tower is of the Golden Mile. An outstanding inside-forward of the decade, Allan Brown, was signed from East Fife in mid-December as Perry's partner. What a combination! This left wing, of two footballers as able to create as to complete an attack, was to figure prominently in the most momentous years in Blackpool's history.

The fact that Blackpool finished third in the First Division at the end of 1950–51—the club's then-highest-ever position in the League Championship—was almost forgotten in the excitement of reaching the Cup Final. Although Perry was not a particularly frequent goal-scorer in his early days with the club, it was his goal, in the semi-final replay against Birmingham, that helped send Blackpool to Wembley in 1951. And so Bill Perry, several months short of his 21st birthday, and partnered by W. J. Slater,[1] became the first South African to play in a Cup Final at Wembley.[2] Newcastle triumphed by two clear goals, but Perry played well in a Blackpool team which, on the all-important day, concealed its best form.

In 1953, Blackpool were on the march to Wembley again. Perry scored a vital goal in the 1-1 fifth-round draw against Southamp-

[1] Slater, at that time, was an amateur player. He will probably earn a place in football history as being the last amateur ever to appear in an F.A. Cup Final.

[2] Because records are far from complete of the birth-places of many players who took part in the earlier Finals, it is not possible to establish for certain that he was the first South African to appear in any Final.

ton, and, as in 1951, scored in the semi-final. Ironically, his goal was again the first of Blackpool's two; the 2-1 score-line—this time a victory over Spurs—being identical. Allan Brown's supreme effort was a goal against Arsenal, in the sixth round, at the expense of a broken leg and a Cup medal. His place at inside-left was taken by Jackie Mudie, who proved an admirable deputy, serving Perry unselfishly. This time, Blackpool and Perry were not to be denied, by Bolton, Bell, or a 3-1 deficit.

Four years earlier, Perry had been serving an apprenticeship in South Africa, as a motor-body builder. His performance was notable for having been achieved just three years after his League début, and with short experience of English pitches: a contrast to the hard-baked ones he knew in Johannesburg. His success was shared, indirectly, by the scout Billy Butler, who had first played in a Cup Final exactly thirty years before, a colleague of Joe Smith—at Bolton, of all clubs!

1955–56 was certainly his most memorable season, during which he represented the full England team, afterwards making a triumphant return home in an F.A. summer tour. He went berserk at the beginning, scoring in successive League games against Arsenal (one goal), Burnley (two), and Portsmouth (a hat-trick); he failed to score at home to Burnley, followed with three goals in a 7-3 rout of Sunderland, did not score against Chelsea, but notched one at Aston Villa: ten goals in the first seven League games.

Perry finished the season with 20 League goals—a Blackpool record for a winger—having scored in 15 of his 40 League games. In addition, he scored one goal in one cup-tie, four in two friendlies, two in three England internationals, two in two England "B" matches, one in one appearance for the Football League, and nine in fourteen games for the F.A. XI in South Africa. His final tally was 39 goals in 63 first-class games: a notable achievement for a winger.

His irrepressible form had won the reward it so surely deserved. Perry qualified to play for England because his father was a Londoner, and, with the award of a cap against Ireland, he became one of the first South Africans to represent another country, and the first footballer since the war, from outside England, to play for the full-international side. Further caps were gained against Spain—he scored twice in a 4-1 victory—and Scotland. Blackpool's 1955–56 success—runners-up in Division I—owed much to the finest pair of wingers in the country: Perry and Matthews, who also represented England. How opposing full-backs must have shuddered at the thought of playing against Blackpool.

The 1953 Cup Final. Bill Perry (*far right*) shoots the winning goal, in the last minute of the game. The ball flashes past Mortensen (*centre*). Stanley Matthews, who fell to the ground as he made the pass, can be seen below and beyond the goalkeeper's outstretched arms

The 1953 Cup Final. Perry (*far left*) raises his arms in jubilation as he sees the ball hit the back of the net

Perry's loyalty to Blackpool was put to the test at the end of 1956, when he was temporarily out of the first team through injury. An attractive offer, of more than he was then earning, came from Johannesburg. He replied: "Blackpool are a grand club and I'm happily settled here . . . I owe everything to Blackpool . . . I expect to win back my place." He did.

Two summers later, in the prelude to Blackpool's tour of Australia, he again made the headlines: by scoring five times in the 13-2 win over a bewildered Californian team, Los Angeles All-Stars. He followed with two goals in each of the next three games, and one in each of the *next* three. Injury prevented him from adding to his total: 14 goals in half as many games, which included three "internationals" against Australia.

Perry had a cartilage operation in 1960, and knee trouble continued to beset him thereafter. The sun which had smiled propitiously for so long was now past its height and setting fast. Perry trained as often as the injury allowed, and met the frustration of spasmodic appearances in the team.

He was recalled to the Blackpool side, in January 1962, for the third-round replay against West Bromwich, but, after a brief run of success, the forward-line suffered from one of its periodic goal-famines. Dave Durie, Perry's former wing partner, was brought back at inside-left for the home match against Arsenal. Again Blackpool failed to score. After the next match—a 0-0 draw at Bolton on March 3—Perry was dropped for the last time. He had played his last game for Blackpool's first team.

To the surprise of those who thought him fitter than for some time, he was placed on the transfer list at the end of 1961-62, and, during the summer, moved to Fourth Division Southport, for a fee said to be £3,000. Nine years after the 1953 Cup victory, Perry was the last of the famous XI to leave Blackpool. And Blackpool, ever since, have missed a loyal club-man who scored 129 goals in 433 League and F.A. Cup matches. He established a Blackpool career record for most goals from a winger. His number of goals and appearances ranks among the highest for a winger in the history of English League football. . . . The man who was once reluctant to leave his homeland.

After a spell in Australia, Perry returned to Blackpool, and he can be found in his electrical goods shop, five minutes' walk from Bloomfield Road. Perry's work now absorbs most of his time, and seldom is he able to go to watch a game. He deserves a season-ticket: for life, free.

I

20

SIR STANLEY MATTHEWS
The Modest Genius

How divine the law of Nature is, which has so
connected genius with patience of industry.

JOHN RUSKIN

Stanley Matthews, the footballer and the man, dominated the post-war era, an age of personalities. He reigned not only over English football, but, as his admirers would swear, over the world of sport. In Accra he was crowned "King of Football". The Canadians, with North American directness, called him "Mr Soccer". The Swiss, just after the war, introduced him, in a programme, as "St Matthews". To the football-going public of Blackpool, he was simply "Our Stanley".

I have many memories of him: the dancing-master's delicate footwork, the quick sprint, the sway of hips. A full-back lunges at him. Matthews shows him the ball, leans one way, and goes the other. The full-back turns, and makes a second challenge. Matthews prods the ball forward with his left foot, feints to kick with his right, but steps over the ball, and kicks with his left. Down the touch-line he goes; then the centre for Mortensen, or Mudie, or Perry. Any volunteers for left-back?

On the field, Matthews could be ruthless. I once saw him batter the confidence of a Tottenham full-back. Again and again, he dribbled the ball past poor Withers. Blackpool, 2-0 down with fifteen minutes remaining, looked beaten, until Matthews, inspired, produced amazing feats of ball control. He made a 50-yard run to create the equaliser for Mortensen. One afternoon, a defender was so overawed by the advancing Matthews that he kept backing away, across half the length of the Bloomfield Road pitch, and fell over the barrier behind the kop goal.

Then there was the much-publicized day when Billy Wright switched from his usual centre-half position to left-back, in order

to mark him. Matthews made Wright wrong. Once, in an international, a Yugoslav left-back, aptly named Stankovic, rugby-
tackled Matthews. Retaliation? Argument? Never. Hand on hips,
Matthews stood, calmly, waiting until the free-kick could be
taken. Matthews the imperturbable. "Let opponents lose their
temper."

"When Matthews decides to stop haunting football defences, I
reckon they could wheel him onto the ground in a wheel-chair, and
he would still throw a scare into rival teams," wrote a sports
columnist. Age to Matthews was "only a matter of figures". Middle
age never came. He worshipped fitness. You had to be up early to
see him, on the sands of Blackpool, practising bursts of speed over
ten and twenty yards, breathing deeply, exercising, loosening up,
hardening.

Thousands of his young fans gulped with disbelief when a
magazine advertisement showed Matthews smoking a well-known
brand of cigarette. The whole sporting world knew that alcohol
and tobacco were nothing to him; self-mastery everything. Matthews
had so much to live up to, and he was equal to his reputation. All
the world wanted Matthews. In his later playing years, he found
strength, after eight months of English League football, to make
summer tours: of South Africa, Ghana, Kenya. In 1961 he played
for Toronto City. The year before, he visited Africa. And two
years before that, Australia welcomed him. Zâtopek once came
to Blackpool and asked: "Who is Matthews?" The Tower
shuddered.

Anecdotes about Matthews would fill a book. Here is one of the
choicest. Tom Finney replaced the injured Matthews, on the right
wing, in England's team. Early in the game, the Preston Plumber
crossed the ball for Mortensen to head into the net. Morty held
his head in agony. Soon after half-time, Morty again headed a
Finney centre into goal. This time, Morty fell to the ground,
doubled-up with pain. Finney rushed to him and asked what had
happened. "Thanks for your good work, Tom," said Morty, "but,
you see, Stanley centres the ball so that the lace points away from
me."

Matthews seldom headed the ball. Football, for him, was *football*. He could trap the ball with ease. A hard pass, a long-range
pass: all were brought to rest at his feet. Highly trained, he made
the most intricate manœuvre look as easy as walking down the
street. Although supremely confident of his own ability, he used to
be nervous before a game. An entertainer, he never set out, consciously, to entertain, and yet he loved the bigger grounds, especially
Highbury. Of one appearance at the Arsenal, a *Times* correspon-

dent wrote: "Highbury is champagne to him. The bubbles tickle his toes, the old magic flows out, and he becomes the heroic actor in a favourite theatre, holding an entranced worshipping public in the palm of his hand." Phew!

Not everyone admired Matthews. Some accused him of elaboration. Some said he held the ball too long. A dozen times, he was dropped from the England team. Always he came back, loving a challenge. Often he fought and beat injury. But the supreme test of a man is fame. Matthews retained his modesty, his longing for the quiet life, his desire to learn. It was never easy to tempt him to talk about his performance. A player is only as good as the support of his team-mates, as Matthews, in his humility, freely acknowledged. When, in 1957, he was awarded the C.B.E., forgetful of self he thanked his friends and his colleagues, past and present, of Stoke, Blackpool, and England.

"You play your own game, and I'll fit in with you." That was Matthews, whom Andy McCall, the neat Jackie Mudie, lion-hearted Mortensen, Taylor the tiny, and Brian Peterson, graceful South African, faithfully served. For Blackpool and for England, at inside-right and at centre-forward, Morty partnered Matthews. Matthews knew how to serve Morty, just as he knew the different needs of Mudie and Charnley, Blackpool's two other free-scoring centre-forwards of the time.

His outstanding partnership at Blackpool was with Ernie Taylor. Mention of this pair brings to mind the 1953 Final. It is one of the small tragedies of journalism that the Blackpool and Bolton match should ever have been dubbed "The Matthews Final". Give credit to Taylor, whose passes so often set Matthews on his way. Do not forget Morty, who scored three of Blackpool's four goals; nor the left wing of Mudie and Perry; nor the defence, marshalled and inspired by Harry Johnston. May 2, 1953: for majesty, for skill, for high drama, football will never know another such day.

Stanley Matthews used to score goals about as frequently as the arrival of leap-year, but he was too original a player to be judged by ordinary standards. He had not the goal-scoring urge of Meredith or Finney. But no one has excelled Matthews in his ability to feed the goal-scoring urge of others. I shall never forget one spring afternoon in London. Blackpool came south to play Chelsea, whose centre-forward was switched to left-back, and, perhaps as a bribe, made captain for the day. Matthews designed Blackpool's second goal. Chelsea drew level. Then, five minutes before the interval, Blackpool took the lead for the third time, with a goal that was worth the price of a season-ticket. Matthews received the ball just near the goal-line. In the space of a few yards, he graced his way past three defenders and centred to Perry, who scored. This was Matthews in all his glory, a great competitor; to his friends, as in his football, a giver.

Stanley Matthews was born in Hanley, Staffordshire, in February 1915, a son of Jack, barber and boxer, who taught him the four virtues: footwork, sense of balance, fair play, discipline of mind and body. From an early age, Stanley was more devoted to football than to books, and many of the good folk of Hanley, walking quietly down back-streets, would find a slight young lad practising his ball control, they being the imagined defenders. At the age of fifteen he joined Stoke City, and before another birthday came he had played in the reserves. At seventeen he signed professional forms and made his first-team début. A year later, a Second-Division-Championship medal adorned his shelf, and at nineteen he married, and scored in his first full international. He had won two of football's highest honours while still a teenager.

The war brought Matthews to Blackpool as a Royal Air Force recruit, and he accepted an invitation from Colonel William Parkinson, then the Chairman of Blackpool F.C., to be a guest player for the club. Blackpool triumphed in several of the war-time competitions, and, most notably, as Northern-cup champions, won 4-2 at Stamford Bridge a challenge match against Arsenal, champions of the South. Matthews considered that hybrid Blackpool team, of May 1943, to be the finest he had known: Savage; Pope, Hubbick; Farrow, Hayward, Johnston; Matthews, Dix, Dodds, Finan, Burbanks. Matthews was present (omnipresent) at these first of Blackpool's golden years, and his departure brought the era to an end.

Soon after the war, Matthews, who now lived in Blackpool and owned a hotel there, had a disagreement with Stoke, and asked to leave. Stoke's supporters, alarmed, remembered the days in the late thirties when they had held protest meetings, and pasted the town with signs, insisting that "Stanley Matthews Must Not Go". On May 10, 1947, the day he helped Great Britain to defeat the Rest of Europe 6-1, Matthews signed for Blackpool. Joe Smith used to enjoy telling of the negotiations. The clubs haggled over the fee, with Blackpool offering £11,000 and Stoke asking £12,000. At this point, so the story goes, the Blackpool manager produced a bottle of whisky (appropriately, for they were in Glasgow), and the clubs compromised at £11,500, a British record fee for a winger. Matthews was then thirty-two. "We didn't buy him," quipped Joe Smith, "we pinched him."

Matthews first played for Blackpool on August 23, 1947, in a

3-0 home defeat of Chelsea.[1] His team that day was: Wallace in goal; big Eddie Shimwell at right-back, partnered by Ron Suart, who, a decade later, became Blackpool's manager; a half-back line —Farrow, Hayward, and Johnston—as strong as any in the club's history; Matthews in his No. 7 tangerine jersey, the tiny busy Munro, Mortensen, George Dick, a cruiserweight boxing champion of the B.A.O.R., and McIntosh, the player who was once left out of a Cup Final team and the next week, in a League match away from home, scored five goals. The influence of Matthews was immediate and lasting.

Before his arrival, Blackpool had spent only six seasons in the First Division, and the club's longest Cup run had been to reach the quarter-finals in 1924–25. It was no coincidence that, during Matthews' fourteen years at Blackpool, they played in the Cup Final three times in six years; on two other occasions, reached the last eight; and held a place in the First Division, finishing 2nd, 3rd, 4th, 6th, and 7th, during a majestic seven-season period in the fifties. But we are leaping ahead.

In 1948, Blackpool won through to the Cup Final. On the eve of a noble defeat, by Manchester United, Matthews was saluted as Footballer of the Year, the first ever, and the other Stanley— Mortensen—who in this season scored in every round of the Cup, was voted second. The town of Blackpool found new interest in football. Three years later, General Joe Smith and Captain Harry Johnston led Blackpool to another Final, which Newcastle United won, deservedly. The fact that Blackpool finished third in the First Division, then a club record, gave only small consolation. Once again, and not for the last time, several sports-writers did but themselves confound by telling their readers: "Matthews is finished!"

In 1951, as in 1948, the citizens of Blackpool softened defeat for the players by welcoming their return home. A few months later, Matthews switched on the Illuminations, which featured the man himself, in lights, scoring a goal. "I took this as a leg-pull, because they knew I didn't score many goals." Then, in October of 1951, Joe Smith again bought wisely, bringing Ernie Taylor to Bloomfield Road. He was one of the most gifted inside-forwards of his generation, and he had played well for Newcastle *against* Blackpool in the 1951 Final. Taylor and Matthews formed a partnership in a thousand.

West Ham brought Blackpool's 1952 Cup hopes to a swift end. The next season began poorly for Matthews. For three months

[1] This match in 1947 was Matthews' first as a Blackpool player. His first-ever appearance for Blackpool was as a guest player during the war: v. Preston (A) on August 30, 1941.

a knee injury kept him out of the team, and the gossips hurled forth rumours. A transfer request was blown away by the Cup; Blackpool were due to travel to Sheffield Wednesday for a third-round tie. Matthews caused a small sensation by scoring in a 2-1 victory. A Matthews goal was always worth a headline. This time he had written the opening of the story of Blackpool's 1953 Cup campaign, whose ending, also, he was destined to write. Huddersfield, Southampton, Arsenal, and Spurs, were cast aside. And then . . . brave Bolton.

A *Daily Express* reader, in 1954, a few days after Matthews' thirty-ninth birthday, made a quite remarkable prophecy: "Football in 1964? Still being ruled by the aged . . . Stan Matthews is still our best footballer. Yes, even at the ripe old age of 49!" Who would have thought, in 1954, that nine years later Matthews would be nominated Footballer of the Year for the second time, having transformed Stoke City into a First Division side? Ten years, almost to the day, after Mr Ken Dodson made his forecast, Matthews guided Stoke City to the fifth round of the F.A. Cup.

To turn back again: his fortieth birthday was hailed with congratulations and gifts from all over the world. In the New Year Honours List of 1957, S. Matthews was awarded the C.B.E. "for services to association football", the then-highest honour ever conferred upon a British football player. "I have done nothing out of the ordinary beyond playing football." The Matthews family went to Buckingham Palace for the presentation in March, a few weeks after he had celebrated his silver jubilee: a quarter-century as a professional footballer. Billy Wright cabled: "Best wishes to a promising young lad."

Blackpool set four club records in 1956–57, but during the next ten years their chart of success was to show a steep downward curve. Towards the end of 1958, Matthews hurt his right knee, an injury that troubled him in following years. With his international career now over, he gave a number of memorable performances for Blackpool, to answer the increasing demands of his critics, whose prediction of his retirement had by now become an annual event. The years had little paled his brilliance. In 1958–59, he played in 25 out of a possible 48 first-team matches. Blackpool, in the games he graced, lost only 2, drew 11, and won 12, with a goal tally of 45–22. In the 23 games he missed, Blackpool lost 12, drew 2, and won 9; goals 29–32. Enough said?

Arthur Kaye, a gale of a player and an England Under-23 international, was signed from Barnsley for £15,000 in the summer of 1959, ostensibly as a successor to Matthews. Kaye played in the opening match of the new season, and finished with more appearances than Matthews, for whom Port Vale made an unsuccessful bid. But Kaye left Blackpool in November 1960, another fallen-one in a line of heirs apparent: Nelson, Hobson, Adams, Harris, Hill, Peterson, Gregson.

There is a story about one of Matthews' deputies. One day he knocked on the door of the manager's office, and was asked to come in and sit down.

"I've come to ask for more money, Mr Smith."

"And what makes you think you deserve more?"

"I've been with the club for six years, and I'm a regular in the reserves."

"Yes, I know."

Gaining courage, the player ventured: "And I'm Stanley Matthews' deputy."

"Well, I've got news for you! You've been playing so badly, I'm putting you in the 'A' team this Saturday. Come back again when you're a regular in the first team." He didn't come back.

Disastrous was Blackpool's play in the opening matches of 1960–61. Four points from the first thirteen games sent the club to the bottom of the Division, and the season was brightened only by the promise of Mandy Hill, deputy to Matthews. Watching young Hill, with his sudden acceleration and his fluent ball control, made you think he had been given private lessons by Matthews himself. Through all the season, Blackpool trembled in the danger of rele-gation. There were the inevitable rumours that Matthews would retire if Blackpool did descend into the Second Division. He hushed this gossip, and Blackpool, with equal speed, discouraged enquiries from several clubs; his former one, Stoke, among them.

On April 8, 1961, he was fit to return for an important game at Highbury. Defeat for Blackpool would make a desperate situation critical. Matthews prompted everywhere, but hesitant goal-attempts by his fellow-forwards allowed Arsenal to win 1-0. Blackpool glanced down nervously at the Second Division, but faithful sup-porters kept faith, saying, "While we have Stanley, we have hope." And they were right.

Blackpool, in her past, had played in many tense matches, on which promotion or relegation depended, and on April 15, against Newcastle at Bloomfield Road, there came another confrontation with history. Victory would mean virtual safety; the defeated club would be shown the door. Blackpool won 2-1, and Charnley's winning goal was schemed by Matthews. A week later, Blackpool made certain of escape by winning 2-0 at Birmingham. Matthews walked off the field weary and spattered with mud. He had given all that was in his power to give, and it was enough. His 27 League games during that season yielded 52 goals; the other 15 games yielded only 16. His appearances were worth a goal a match to Blackpool.

In the summer, Matthews, now forty-six, set out for Canada and a heavy programme of competitive matches. On his return, he played in a pre-season friendly in Ireland, but injury kept him out of the first team until the end of September. For his come-back, a youthful Chelsea side visited Blackpool, and were sent home tanned by a 4-0 defeat, three of the goals having come from Matthews' centres.[2] The national press purred with delight. A week later, when Blackpool lost dismally at Highbury, they clawed at him. Changes were announced for the next match. Dropped were Oates, Hauser, West (for the first time), and S. Matthews.

A day later Matthews publicly declared his intention to rejoin Stoke. The world of football was stunned. Local fans clamoured at the door of his house. Matthews remained outwardly at ease, while Englishmen argued in their pubs. Stoke City stood on the verge of the drop into the Third Division. The sentimentalists feared for the loss of a legend which they had helped to create. Many sportswriters decreed that he was no longer capable of playing in first-class football. Open-minded men supported Matthews in his own choice of action.

The Blackpool directors agreed to a transfer "only because Stanley said he would like to go". Albert Hindley, then the club's Chairman, told the press: "It was always entirely up to him." And so, on October 18, 1961, Matthews signed again for Stoke City, for a fee of £3,000. "21 Second Division left-backs," laughed a newspaper cartoon, "have asked for a transfer." He set about the task of helping his new-old club. His first home match was watched by a crowd four times larger than the season's average. Stoke finished eighth in the Second Division, and, in the Cup, beat, by 5-2, the previous year's finalists. Matthews continued to live in Blackpool, but there was to be no farewell match at Bloomfield Road. "We have had some great times together, Blackpool and I." The grateful town could only say a silent "Thank you".

[2] By appearing in this match, twenty-nine years and six months after his League début, Stanley Matthews broke Meredith's record for length of time as a player in League football.

21

SIR STANLEY MATTHEWS
— in an Interview

I used to be a centre-half in my schooldays. And then there was an international trial, and my headmaster suggested to the selectors that they play me at outside-right. I played in the North v. South trial, and apparently I was successful. Then I played for England v. The Rest, in another boys' match, and, a month or so after that, I was selected for England Schoolboys at outside-right against Wales, at Bournemouth. So it was from there that I took up the outside-right position. My position in the early days—when I was ten, eleven, twelve—had been centre-half, because I was apparently a big boy.

The only way to give yourself self-confidence is to know very well that you are 100 per cent fit. If you know you are fit, and you know you've got the stamina, and you know you can go for the ball, then you're all right. If you're not so fit, and you're struggling, and you can't get to the ball, your confidence goes—within seconds —and you don't *want* the ball. The man who is absolutely fit will have confidence.

If you're in a team and you're playing very well, playing good football, and you lose—that is no good. You've got to win: there is no doubt about it. Entertainment must come second. Supporters say, "Oh, what a terrible game—but they've won." It is better to play badly and win, than play well and lose.

I love the game. I love football, and I wanted to play as long as I could. I played in first-class football till I was fifty. I knew very well that I had the stamina. I could always produce a little bit of a burst, so I was always there with a chance. My mental outlook was: "I *know* I can do it." If I couldn't have run, I would have said, "Oh well, that's it." I knew I had the strength; I knew I had the quickness. I wanted to keep on and on and on. Without enthusiasm, you have no chance.

I think it's crazy to lose your temper. I had a very good concentration, and I felt that, if I wanted to argue with the referee or be naughty against the opponents, my concentration would have gone; and then I wouldn't have been able to do what I wanted. I always had good concentration. I think it was a gift. You mustn't allow anyone or anything to distract you.

I always felt that I wanted to *destroy* the left-back, as quickly as possible. The first time I had the ball, I always pushed it forward to see what strength he had; to see if he was quicker than I was. I always wanted to destroy him, because as soon as you destroy an opponent, in any sport, he loses his confidence.

A forward hasn't any chance if a player marks him very closely. If he stays with you all the time, you are shut out of the game. The only thing you can do is draw the defender out of position and hope you create an opening for your team-mates. There's a a story about Maurice Reeday. He wasn't an outstanding full-back, but he was the only one I came up against who marked me tightly, right away. Before, a full-back used to try to mark me, and I would go back to lose him, and he never used to follow. But this man followed me all over the place. He was with me, about a yard away, wherever I went. If I got the ball, I had no room. We met several times—in the League and in cup-ties—and I couldn't do a thing. Funnily enough, I met him again in a match during the war— he was playing for Burnley, and I was playing for Blackpool—and, although he was left-back, he never marked me.

Some particular moves stand out in my mind—and also the bad games! I didn't like too much praise. It embarrassed me. It was very embarrassing at times. You had your critics, and your bad notices: everyone is entitled to his opinion. But it made no difference to me.

I wanted room. I always had the left-back tagging on me, and also at times I had the outside-left coming back, so the more space I had—the bigger the ground—the better. Like almost every foot-baller, I enjoyed playing at big grounds, in front of big crowds, because there you have the atmosphere. Things always seemed to go well for me at Wembley. In London, I did well. Spurs was pretty good to me, and Arsenal, but I could never do much at West Ham. You have your lucky and your unlucky grounds. Preston wasn't a good ground for me, and I don't remember ever playing well at Sheffield United.

There was never any question that I might not have been able to play in the 1953 Final. I was rested for a match or two before the Final. Two or three days before the game, we were having a bit of a practice match, and I felt a pain in my thigh. I was rather concerned about it. The club doctor, Dr Sime, came down with us to our headquarters, just outside London, and on the Saturday morning, a few hours before the match began, he injected me with cocaine, and I never felt anything. I did feel a bit sore about a day later, but nothing much.

My father used to get me up very early in the morning, when I was about ten or eleven. When I signed amateur forms for Stoke City—I was working in the office at fifteen—I had to walk from my home-town to Stoke. It was two miles there, two miles home for lunch, two miles back after lunch, and two miles home in the afternoon: which was eight miles a day, for three years. My father would only give me bus money if it was raining or snowing.

When I first came to Blackpool, I never used to train on the beach. I used to walk on the beach—for about half an hour—after breakfast. Then I used to go straight from there to do my training at the club. It was only later on—when I got transferred to Blackpool—that I started to do my training before breakfast. I found this was more beneficial to me. Before I go out, I just have a cup of tea.

I train only on the very hard sand, so I can train hard: just as if I were on a track. I wouldn't go on the soft sand. It pulls your legs and pulls your muscles. I never practised with a ball on the beach. I used to do a lot of practising with a little rubber ball when I was at Stoke-on-Trent, when I was very young: eight or nine. After the age of forty, I didn't do much ball-practice. Too much ball-practice after a certain age can get you jaded. You've got to keep yourself fresh, all the time.

Before a big match, whether a cup-tie or a vital League game, I went through the same basic training routines: sprinting, and so on. The only time you are really 100 per cent fit is at the beginning of the season, when you've been training morning and afternoon, ready for the opening match. It is impossible to be 100 per cent fit every Saturday, but you strive for absolute fitness. Things can go badly for you on a Saturday, and you may have a worrying weekend about it. You come back on Monday for training, and then you are looking forward to the next Saturday, right away. You've got to have a goal to aim for. You've got to keep striving and striving.

I used to have—I do now—one day off food every week, usually on a Monday. I eat no food, and drink only cups of tea and fruit juices. I always felt better for it on the Saturday. If I were to eat too much food. I would feel heavy and I'd lose my keenness. When you get older, you don't need so much food. All my life, I've been a non-smoker and a teetotaller. My father was the same.

Mental preparation for a match was important to me. My mental approach was absolute. When I got up on a Saturday morning, I used to think: "This is a great day, come what may. There's a match to look forward to. There's a battle to be won." I'd have a walk on the beach after a light breakfast—not before—and then have a cold shower. I'd have a little toast about mid-day. I would always walk the mile from my home to the ground: I'd never drive down. The butterflies would start rolling at about 2 o'clock. I'd have a shower just before I went out and a little massage from Johnny Lynas, Blackpool's trainer. My main thoughts were concentrated on the idea: "It's wonderful to think there's a game to be won."

Being keyed-up was very, very important to me. If you are not keyed-up, you can't give your best. This is true of any job or profession: acting, or sport, or anything else. You've got to be keyed-up. You've got to have butterflies. As soon as I got into the dressing-room and sat down, the butterflies disappeared.

I get up early for training. I *enjoy* training. I always felt that when a club pay you, they pay you to keep yourself fit. I enjoy training now. I still go out on the beach at 7.30 every morning, and I always feel better for it. When I was getting older, I found I didn't need so much training. When I do half an hour or three-quarters of an hour, it is equivalent to a young man's hour and a half. Now, if I did an hour and a half every day, I would be jaded.

When you get older, the secret is to learn how to balance yourself. You mustn't do too much, or too little. I found that I could balance myself very well. Doing too much, at, say, 37, 38, 40, and onwards—and I mean heavy, hard training—is no good. When you get to a certain age, it is better to do half an hour in the morning and half an hour in the afternoon than to do two hours in the morning.

My reputation wasn't hard to live up to, until I reached the mid-thirties. When a player gets older—say he is 33, 34—and he has a bad match, or two bad matches on the trot, he is more or less "finished". He is "old". If you are eighteen and you play four games, and you have two bad matches and a fair match and a good match, "Oh, you're all right. You're very good." But an older player—if he has two bad matches and a fair one and a good one —No, "He's too old." This was the difficult part. When I was about 35 or 36, I had so many critics saying that I was over the hill. I knew very well I wasn't over the hill. I alone knew my condition: those reporters didn't know how I felt. It is crazy to write off anybody in sport. It is the individual who knows what he can do.

I think that all age barriers are mainly psychological. The critics

—the reporters, the journalists, and even the spectators—can drive a man into old age. They can say that a man is too old, and, before he knows where he is, he *thinks* he is too old. Mentally, he becomes unbalanced, and he thinks, "Well, I *am* getting old," and he loses some of his interest in the game. You may have three good games on the trot and then go down to London, and not play so well. Some reporters, who haven't seen you recently, will say, "He's past it."

When you get older, you tend to lose that extra bit of keenness you once had. *Not* because you have fulfilled all your ambitions. It just gets harder for you to train. You tend to say, "Oh dear, here we go again." As I've said, in order to keep going you've got to have a lot of enthusiasm, and you've got to balance yourself. At Blackpool, we used to have one day off each week. Mentally, it was very good, because we got away from it completely. And when you are jaded and tired, when you are feeling a bit stale, it is silly to keep training. You should take a day off.

I didn't feel I was very much underpaid. I love the game. Somehow, when I was playing on that field, money didn't mean a thing. You wanted to win. You wanted to play well. And you wanted the team to win. I must say I think it is marvellous that the players today are getting big money. I am very pleased that they are doing so well now. I don't know if they are any happier than players of my day. I should think they would be happy with the basic wages and the big bonuses they are getting. Players are moving about more, from club to club. They are out to make the money. There are so many incentives these days.

I don't know when we're going to see a return to a more attacking game. Sometimes it bores me to watch the ball being passed back so many times. I don't think football is as entertaining as it was in my day, in the 1950s. There seems to be more petty fouling now, and this starts off the young spectators. The players of today, when they get older, will probably say, "Football isn't as good as it was in our day."

Players are too standardized now. There are so many tactical talks, compared with our day. We had the "W" formation; today, you have your 4-2-4, 3-4-3, and so on. I think the players today are fitter than the players of our day, in the fifties. Every player in the team has to do more running now. When I signed as a professional for Stoke City, at the age of seventeen, there were little or no tactical talks.

The Blackpool team had no preference, at corner-kicks, for in-swingers or out-swingers. We didn't often rehearse set-moves— such as free-kicks—except at the very beginning of the season. We had players who could think for themselves, right on the spur of the moment. If things were going wrong, Joe Smith would have his say at half-time. He was very good, Joe was.

I always felt that if I tried to help some of the younger players, it was going against the coach. It's so, so difficult. If a younger player is pretty good, I think you've got to leave him. A young boy comes onto the ground-staff at, say, fifteen. He's got to have a bit of coaching, but let his own ability, and his own individuality, come out.

Blackpool was a very happy club. We had some good players, all nice men. There are so many I could mention and, even then, I'll probably leave one or two out. It was a friendly club. Mind you, we had a good team. When you are playing in a bad team, things are not so good. But when you have a good team, it creates more atmosphere, more friendship, and more happiness.

The forward-line was good, and so was the defence. We had George Farm in goal. I must confess that, when he first came from Hibs, we never thought he would turn out so well. In the first couple of matches he played for us, he got terribly out of position sometimes. But he turned out brilliantly. When he was beaten, he often stopped a goal by putting his foot out. Shimwell was a very nice chap, as strong as a horse. Left-back was Tommy Garrett. Tommy knew when to tackle and when not to tackle.

Harry Johnston was the right-half. He was a good supplier of the ball and an excellent captain. He knew what he was doing. I used to like to have him playing behind me. We were strong at half-back. In addition to Harry, we had Hughie Kelly, Ewan Fenton, and Eric Hayward. Eric was a centre-half. He didn't get as much praise from the press as he deserved. Then there was George Farrow, whose favourite pass was a cross-field ball, right from him to the outside-left.

Morty and I developed an almost instinctive partnership. We have always been good friends: he is a very human chap. He was always getting those quicksilver goals, and I always felt—and the rest of the team did also—that when Morty was playing we were sure of at least a draw. He was like lightning off the mark.

Ernie Taylor was a very good ball-player. He had a knack of getting into an open position. It was a gift with him that whenever you were in trouble, and wherever you looked up, he was always there. He had a sneaky little way of going over to the inside-left or left-half position to collect the ball. Wherever he went, it seemed as if the ball came to him. He had a gift of moving into the right position.

I was also partnered by Brian Peterson, whom I spotted in South

Africa, and by Alec Munro. Alec wasn't an inside-forward, really; he was more of a winger. He did well for Blackpool when he came back from the war.

Jackie Mudie was such a complete footballer. He played centre-forward quite a few times. As an inside-right he was very good, because every time you shouted for the ball he would give it to you. Sometimes I liked a through-ball, for instance if the opposing defence was struggling; but mostly I wanted the ball at my feet. I'd shout "Jackie. Quick!", and he'd give it to me. He was always ready to have a shot from just inside or just outside the box. We had a very good understanding. We carried on the partnership when I went to Stoke in 1961, and I think our partnership was more solid then. Both of us were older, with more experience.

Joe Smith was a very canny manager. He had a personality about him. Joe was a comedian. He could tell the same joke twenty times in a day, and you'd laugh every time—because of the way he told it. He didn't hold many tactical talks. He would say a few words before the match. He wanted players to keep their individuality, and yet he achieved good team-work. Joe was a good loser. I shall always remember the words he spoke when he came into our dressing-room after Newcastle had beaten us at Wembley. He didn't show any emotion. He just said: "Come on, boys. Hurry up and get into the bath. You need it."

I go back to Bloomfield Road now and then, but I don't want them to go to the trouble of providing a special ticket for me. I like to slip-in at the back so that no one will notice.

The 1953 Cup Final. *The dancing-master's delicate footwork*

The 1953 Cup Final. The captain's reward

22

ALAN BALL
Perpetual Motion

*I taught football to him not as a game, but as a
way of life.*

ALAN BALL (SENIOR)

I first saw Alan Ball in August 1962. He had graduated—from the
"A" team—direct to the first team. He was a slightly-built elf of
a winger. He could cross an accurate centre, but he was not a
difficult player to dispossess. I am ashamed to confess that I did
not, at that stage in his career, detect a future international.

The name *Ball* inspired "X"-certificate puns, from the Blackpool kop, that would embarrass even the most out-and-out
exponent of the permissive society. If James Joyce could have had
a verbal duel with a quick-witted koppite, to see who could outdo
the other in Rabelaisian humour and florid, earthy, word-play,
I would have put my money on the football fan every time.

The Bloomfield Road crowd beatified its new hero. As soon as
Ball gained a regular place in Blackpool's team, he showed sharp
reactions in the penalty-area and he dominated his forward-line.
He also, and inevitably, suffered close marking by opponents. The
more unscrupulous of them provoked his temper. And referees
were quick to penalize his slightest misdemeanour.

Shortly before Christmas 1964, Blackpool drew 3-3 in a hard,
but fair, match at Craven Cottage. In the second half, Blackpool
took a quick free-kick just outside the Fulham penalty-area. Ball
was moving forward, at high speed, to have a shot at goal, when
the referee signalled for the kick to be re-taken. Angry at this
missed chance of scoring, Alan threw the ball away and was
promptly booked. Blackpool, remember, were the attacking side,
and Ball's action was to Fulham's advantage, in allowing their
defenders more time to get into position. Four minutes later, he
scored the equalising goal for Blackpool and completed his hat-

K

trick. On the following Wednesday, he scored a goal, and was the most creative and hard-working player on the field, in the England Under-23 team's 5-0 win over Rumania. As soon as he was booked at Fulham, Alan knew he was playing under the threat of suspension. By the way he continued to concentrate on *football*, he gave the clearest possible proof of his dedication to the game.

In the 1966 World Cup Final, Alan Ball silenced his sternest critics. All through extra-time—when bigger and seemingly stronger men were wilting—Ball kept prompting his team. There was no relaxation of his output of energy, mental or physical. That day, the boy became a man.

Blackpool—although able to match the wages of a bigger club —could no longer hold him. Ball had enjoyed his spell among the world's best footballers, and he understandably wanted to play in the European Competitions. Blackpool sold him to Everton for £112,000, which at the time was a record fee between two British clubs. One Fleet Street journalist, with an eye for a headline, worked out that, based on the fee, Ball was worth four times his weight in gold. A few years later, his value in the transfer market had doubled. He was an automatic choice for England. He had learned self-discipline, and was an inspiration to his team-mates, so his manager appointed him captain of Everton, the League Champions. Now the man was becoming a leader.

Arsenal shattered all existing British transfer records by paying £220,000 for Alan Ball in December 1971 : an expensive Christmas-shopping jaunt by Arsenal manager, Bertie Mee. An interviewer asked Alan Ball if this would be a new chapter in his career; and, with typical gusto, Alan replied, "I intend to *make* it a new chapter."

23

ALAN BALL
—in an Interview

Ever since I was conceived, my father wanted me to be a footballer. For as long as I can remember, I've always had something to do with football. My father was a professional, in the lower Divisions, with clubs in Lancashire: Rochdale, Oldham, Southport. I've always been in football dressing-rooms and on football pitches. I seem to have been brought-up with this atmosphere of football around me. I didn't have a lot of time for anything else, as a boy. At three and four—as young as that—I was playing on football pitches.

I was a bright child. After the 11-plus, I went to a grammar school. I knuckled down and did some hard work for the first couple of years. When I got a little bit older, I got picked for the town schoolboys' team, and my studies went to pieces.

I went to Wolverhampton Wanderers at the age of fourteen, whilst I was still at school, and they got into a little bit of F.A. disciplinary trouble for approaching, and signing, a schoolboy—which, at that time, wasn't allowed. Now, a club can sign a boy at almost any age! The F.A. committee said to Wolverhampton Wanderers that, with my headmaster's permission, I could play for them. On Saturday mornings, I had to travel all the way to the midlands from Lancashire. In those days, the train stopped at lots of stations, and it was a three or four hour journey. I was making up all sorts of excuses about weddings and funerals and christenings, to miss playing for my school team on Saturdays.

The F.A. stepped in because I was under-age. I don't think they would have stepped in but for my headmaster going and saying that his boy's studies were being spoiled. "He's not playing for his school team. He's been making up all sorts of excuses. This club shouldn't be asking him to play and preventing him from playing for the school. He's a schoolboy, and I want him." You know what headmasters are like.

And so I had to leave Wolverhampton. They were quite adamant that, when I was sixteen or seventeen, they wanted me to go back and sign for them as a professional. I went back and played for the school team. My forms with Wolverhampton were scrapped, and then Bolton approached me. Being a young boy, I was eager to play football with a First Division club. Bolton went to my headmaster and said: "Look. We want to play him. He's near home— he's living only about ten minutes away from Bolton—and it'll not do his studies any harm." My headmaster okayed it, and I said, "Yes, I'd like to play for you." So I signed as an amateur with Bolton. Therefore I could play for my school team in the morning, and for the Bolton Wanderers "A" or "B" team in the afternoon.

I took seven G.C.E.s in my last year, and I failed every one, through sheer incompetence on my part. I played for a team called Farnworth Boys' Club, at the time, as well as training with Bolton Wanderers and playing for Bolton "B". I didn't get a game with Bolton every week, so I played for this other team as well. We had a very good team, and, at the end of this season, we had quite a lot of semi-finals and finals, and big matches in the evenings. All this football coincided with my supposed studying for the G.C.E.s, so my studies used to be put aside till the morning. You can see why I failed seven G.C.E.s. But I won a couple of football medals, which, at the time, meant a *little* bit more to me than G.C.E.s.

After I failed my exams, my father said, "What do you want to be, son?" I said, "I want to be a footballer—there's nothing else. I want to have a go." "All right," he said. "We'll go down to Bolton, and we'll ask them to sign you as an apprentice professional." So I went to Bolton, and they said I was too small, and that I wasn't going to be big enough to become an apprentice professional. I would think I was 5ft 4in then, and about 9½st. Now, I'm 5ft 7in and 10st 6lb.

I continued to play for the Bolton "B" team, but I was out of work. I was very concerned about this—not taking anything home to my mother. At that time, my father wasn't in football: he was working for a building contractor. And my mother was working in a canteen. I thought I should be earning some money for the family, but wasn't able to because I didn't want to work as a labourer, which was all I was fit for, after failing seven G.C.E.s. I used to train at night with my father, with the aim of one day becoming a footballer with Bolton.

When they shattered my dreams by saying that I wasn't going to be big enough, my father went down to Burnden Park, and asked the manager, Bill Ridding, about me. From what I could gather, Bill Ridding was rather abrupt with my father, and told him, in no uncertain manner, that I wasn't going to be a footballer, at least not with Bolton. My father, who had every confidence in me—because I had a lot of potential as a schoolboy—told Mr Ridding that he was sure I *could* become a footballer.

A week or so later, we went on our holidays. And, as a typical Lancashire family, Blackpool was our venue, year after year. We always had a good time at Blackpool, and I thoroughly enjoyed our holidays there. My father said, "Put your boots in, son. We'll do some training when we get to Blackpool." So I packed them in my case, not knowing that he had other things in mind for me.

One morning, when we got up, my father said, "Get your boots out." "Where are we going?" I asked. "Just get your boots out," he replied. It was a nice summer's day, which I'll never forget as long as I live. We got on a bus and we went to Bloomfield Road. "This is where Blackpool play, isn't it?", I asked. And my father said, "Yes. Let's go in. We're going to see a friend of mine. I used to play football against him."

We knocked on the door of the manager's office. My father, for the first time in his life, went cap-in-hand to a man, and asked him to do a favour for him and give his son a trial. Ron Suart looked at me and he said, "Certainly. I'll give him a trial. Come back to Squires Gate this evening. We're going to have a trial match for youngsters and for one or two of my amateur staff. We'll give Alan a game, and see what he can do." My father thanked Mr Suart very much, and, after an informal chat, we left Bloomfield Road. It turned out that my father didn't know Ron Suart as well as he had led me to believe. My father literally begged him to give me a trial.

We went back to the digs. All that day I was concentrating on this game. My father was talking to me and encouraging me, but I was very nervous. I wanted so much to create a good impression. I wanted—more than anything—to do well. The time came for us to leave for Squires Gate. My mother wouldn't come with us: she hates watching me play football.

On our way to the ground, my father said, "All the best, son. You've got great ability. If Blackpool turn you down, I'll take you somewhere else. You'll be a footballer because you've got terrific ability." He kept getting this through to me: that, even though Bolton had turned me down and even though everyone looked at me as being on the small side, I had lots of stamina and lots of ability. These two qualities, he said, would always pull a footballer through. His parting words were, "You are now literally fighting for your life."

So I got stripped. I was among strangers. We were all boys who wanted to become footballers. I'd been with boys like this all my life, all of us striving for this one great aim. Lots fall by the way-side. If I had failed in this trial with Blackpool, and if we couldn't find a First Division club that would sign me, my father would have taken me to clubs in the Third and Fourth Divisions. But, when I was in that dressing-room, I was treating this as my last chance.

I went out for the trial match. As fate makes footballers what they are—I believe a lot in luck and fate, because there are so many ups and downs in football—something shone upon me that evening. I couldn't do a thing wrong for 20–25 minutes. Ron Suart stopped the game and called me over, and said to my father, "I'd like to sign Alan here and now." I couldn't believe him. He said, "I've seen enough in 20 minutes." He'd never seen me play before. I knew I had been playing well, but I just couldn't believe him. I kept rolling the words over in my mind: "I'd like to sign Alan as an apprentice professional." My father said, "Well son, I've seen you play some good games, but I've never seen you play as well as you did today." The next day, Ron Suart realized that there had been a misunderstanding, and that I was still on Bolton's books. After our holiday, we went home. I got my release from Bolton, and then went back to Blackpool and signed for the club.

I'll never forget signing the forms. I kept looking at them. I was going to get £6 10s. a week, and I thought it was fantastic. "Alan Ball . . . Blackpool F.C. . . . Your basic pay will be £6 10s. a week": it was great. My father said to me. "It's entirely up to you now. You've earned this yourself. I've always told you that you've got lots of ability. Now what you've got to do is work hard and improve and improve, year by year. If you work hard and keep improving, and if you grow a little bit—by looking after yourself, and eating the right things—you'll be a great player. But never forget this man who has given you your chance. Always be faithful and loyal. Always play your heart out for him, because he has given you a chance, whereas other people haven't."

I've always remembered my father's words about Ron Suart. Ron Suart was a great man for me. I would go and play for him, with all my heart, any time. When I'm fifty, if I can still play, I'll go and play for him. He did so much for me. I still call him "boss", whenever I see him. He understood my temperament. In the begin-ning, he let me go my own way. He knew how much I wanted to be a footballer, because I told him so many times. He tolerated my temperament, to start with. Later on, he tried to knock it out of me, and he was quite right in doing so. I'll tell you more about that shortly. Let's get back to the story.

I used to catch a bus at 7 o'clock in the morning so that I'd get to Blackpool on time. The press were very kind to me in my early days at Blackpool. I was a small boy. I was an extrovert. I got into lots of trouble, but I would do things that thrilled the crowd. In my early days, I played solely and simply for myself, not for the team. That's why I got into a lot of trouble. I wanted so much for people to notice me, and I wanted to become accepted as a footballer.

I got a little bit over-exuberant at times. But slowly and surely Ronnie Suart and Eric Hayward—whom I haven't seen for a long time; he was in charge of the second team at Blackpool—knocked it out of me, and got me playing more for the team. I became more of a team-man, as the years went by. Those two had a lot—an awful lot—to do with the player that I am now, and I thank them wholeheartedly. When I sit down and think about it some evenings —late at night—I wonder, when they watch me play, if they can see any of the things in me that they tried to teach me when I was a boy. And I hope they do. Because I used to listen to them for hours and hours on end.

Even though we were often struggling to keep our place in the First Division, Blackpool was a very very happy, contented club, all the time that I was there. They were a great bunch of lads. I think we relished a fight from the bottom. When there was a crisis —and I was in a couple with Blackpool—no one was really worried. It was a happy club. We *knew* we could pull out of trouble. There were times when we did well. I enjoyed the good start we made to the 1964–65 season: we were near the top of the First Division until the end of October.

Jimmy Armfield was very very good to me. As a young lad, I was an extrovert: always talking, always wanting to learn, always asking questions about football: "Why do you do this? Why do you do that?" It may have seemed a little bit cheeky at times, but Jimmy understood me. He always had a word to say to me— always.

Ray Parry was another one. He was great. He understood me, too. Sometimes, he used to really tell me off. I can remember a day when I had just got into the first team. I should have played a ball to him, but I held it myself, and I lost it. He came screaming at me and said, "Alan, you should have given me that ball. Why didn't you give it to me?" And I said to him, "If I had the same ball again, I would do the same thing." "You wouldn't listen to my shout?" he asked. "No," I replied. "I do what *I* say." And he said to me, "Well son, don't you ever come and ask me for advice again." I'll never forget that.

Ray lived in Bolton, and I lived in Farnworth. He used to take me there, when I was a boy. He got in the car to go home. Bruce Crawford, who lived in Preston, used to travel with us. He got in the front. I got in the back. Ray never spoke to me until I took it upon myself to ask why he thought I should have given him that pass. And he told me. I realized that he was right, told him I thought he was right, and apologised profusely for the way I had spoken to him.

He turned round to me and said, "Well son, you're going to be a footballer, because you're a man who can admit when you're wrong. You're not a stubborn boy. If you're prepared to listen and learn, then you'll be a footballer. This morning, I had my doubts. But now I'm sure you will be." That's one story of an older player helping me as a boy. I still see Ray now and then, and I think of the things he said to me. He was a good friend to me in my Blackpool days. You don't think about these things until you have an interview like this, and then you remember what has happened in your life. Time passes you by, and you tend to forget these things—all too easily, I think.

That £112,000 price-tag didn't worry me. I just wanted to go out and play football. I left Blackpool simply because of ambition, pure ambition by a young boy who had played in a World Cup Final. Most of the England team had played in an F.A. Cup Final, and a number of them had been involved in an exciting League battle only a few weeks earlier. But Blackpool had just avoided relegation. I wanted to play in European football, and I couldn't see myself getting it with Blackpool. Blackpool did all they could to keep me: they offered me £100 a week and a £10,000 signing-on fee. I love Blackpool. I would love to finish my career with the club, if they would have me. They looked after the younger players exceptionally well. Blackpool, Everton, and Preston, my father's team, are the first three results I look for in the papers.

In September 1970, after Blackpool's spell in the Second Division, I played for Everton against my old club, Blackpool, at Bloomfield Road. This was the match in which Tony Green made his come-back. I wanted the Blackpool crowd to see that I had improved, that I had changed from a boy to a man: now captain of the League Champions, with another World Cup behind me, as an older player, and as a better player for having had all this experience. I didn't want to impress the Blackpool people. I just wanted to show them what sort of a player I had become; and that the lad, they once had, had become a man. And I wanted Everton to win.

When I first became captain of Everton, I treated all players alike. There were one or two quiet ones in our team. If I shouted at them and really rollocked them, they got worse and worse, and then went to pieces. Then my manager and some of the lads came to me and told me what I was doing wrong. So then I started to encourage those quiet players all the time, even if they weren't doing well. You've got to adapt what you say, and how you say it, to fit the individual, but at first I didn't do this.

I didn't know much about captaincy, but I was prepared to learn. I go out for training every Monday determined to learn something new. Once you stop learning in football, you become an empty man; and once you become an empty man, you stop being a footballer; and when you stop being a footballer—in my case, I am nothing.

I don't talk football tactics unless *I* am involved. I want to talk tactics if I'm doing something wrong, or if I think someone else is doing something wrong. I want to know why. And I want to have my say in why I think it's going wrong, and what I think we should do to put it right. I'll talk tactics with my father, and I will talk tactics all day if it concerns me or my team, Arsenal. But, other than that, I rarely talk football with anyone.

I like to think about tactics, because football is a test—you against other men. Football is a test of *thinking*, as well as a test of how you use your feet. I think much more about my game now. I can change my game during a match. If I think something is going wrong, I try and rectify it. As captain, I found myself talking to players, or I pushed them into position to plug a gap. I found myself doing this instinctively. A few years ago I couldn't have done it.

The semi-final against Portugal in the 1966 World Cup was a great game. We knew we were going to have a great game with them, because they played *football*, and that suited us down to the ground. Fortunately for us, Bobby Charlton was really on song, and one or two other players hit their top form. I'll never forget the penalty that cut our lead from 2-0 to 2-1, and put them back in the game. I thought, "Only five minutes to go. Oh, we mustn't lose it now." At times like this, I find myself praying on the pitch, because it means so much to me to win: "I don't want to lose it now. Please God, don't let us lose it now."

I was only just twenty-one when we played against West Germany in the 1966 World Cup Final. I thought to myself, "What am I doing here?" I don't think I realized the full importance of the occasion. I'll always remember Alf's words at the end of normal time: "Well boys, you'd won this game. Now you've lost it. Go out and win it again." The men who tired had given their lot. I'm just fortunate that I have so much stamina: I can carry on and on and on. Believe you me, I was tired. But I was playing for *England*.

If any boy or man in that crowd—or anywhere in England, or abroad, for that matter—could have been on that pitch, to play for England in a World Cup Final, and did not run until he dropped, and had to be carried off because of exhaustion, then, for me, he is not a true Englishman.

When we line up before a match, and I hear our national anthem being played, I know what men must have felt like, during the war, when they were fighting for their country's freedom. I follow our boxers when they go abroad: they are fighting *for England*. And when Englishmen are running in the Olympic Games, I cheer them home.

When I was out there, in the World Cup Final, I thought, "If any Englishman could come on this pitch, he would play a thousand minutes, if need be." We are such a proud little nation. We'll always produce something or someone to beat the world. *I love to win for England. I absolutely idolize England.*

England came so near to beating Brazil in the 1970 World Cup. We lost by the margin of the cross-bar, and the margin of Lady Luck's favour: she either smiles on you or she doesn't. Skill-wise, we were their equal. Endeavour-wise, we had a little bit more than they had. But luck-wise, we had nothing at all. I sincerely believe that, given luck, we would have beaten them, or at least managed a draw.

The press blamed me for a scoring-chance I missed. It was getting near the end of the game. We were pushing players forward to put Brazil under pressure. Jeff Astle headed the ball down to me. It came at me very quickly. I was at an angle to the goal, and I had to half-volley the ball. My shot beat the goalkeeper, but the ball just skimmed the top of the bar. Personally, I thought it was a hardish chance.

I still haven't got over our defeat by West Germany in the quarter-finals. I can't tell you why we lost. The game was ours. Whether it was fatigue or not, I don't know. I don't think so. The Germans gained the upper hand, and made good use of the upper hand while they had it—for the short time that they had it. If you had come to me, before the match, and said, "You're going to get beaten 3-2, after being 2-0 up", I would have bet you my house, my car, and my year's salary with Everton. And, blow me, they got one, two, three. As long as I live, I'll never forget that. I was astounded. I couldn't believe that England could be winning 2-0, and lose 3-2. It just never happens. I still don't think it happened.

When my body is getting tired, my will-power drives me on. It is so easy to give in; but I don't give in, because it is *not right*. From my point of view, it is *a sin* to give in.

There are, I suppose, three reasons for my will-to-win. It stems from fighting what seemed a losing battle with my height, all my early life, and people telling me that I wasn't good enough to become a professional footballer. It stems from wanting to earn money for my mother and father; and knowing that I couldn't do so, unless I was playing football. And it stems from knowing that football is the only thing I'm competent at.

I can talk to people now. I've been to many parts of the world, and I'm quite experienced in lots of things. But I cannot do anything except play football. And so, if I don't play football well, I can't support my wife and my two children.

I'm a very bad loser. You show me a good loser and I will show you a two-faced man. If a man can lose badly and smile, that's two-faced. His smile is two-faced because, underneath, that man is so annoyed and sick with himself. That's putting it bluntly and cruelly, but I believe you've got to be honest and show that you're annoyed. When I come home, though, I will never show my feelings. Then *I* become a two-faced man. I come through the front door, and, if I've played poorly or if we've lost, I'll smile at my older child. She'll call out, "Daddy, Daddy." She may not have seen me for two days. I can't come in and say, "What do you want? We've lost." Then *I* am a two-faced man.

Outside my home, I'll say, "I played badly, but that's forgotten now. Next week, I'll show them." You've got to be honest in football. If you come off the field and say to yourself, "Well, you did all right today", when you know you've done badly, you're kidding *yourself*. You've got to be honest and say, "Ballie, you were bad today. Well, what are you going to do about it?" On Saturday night, I'll have a couple of drinks less than usual. During the week, I'll eat carefully. I'll be in bed at 9.30 or 10 o'clock, and I'll train extra hard, and next Saturday I'll go on the field and play well.

I am a perfectionist on the field, when things are going well for me. Who isn't? I want to do things to the best of my ability, but you can't be a perfectionist when things are going badly. At times like that, if my normal game is letting me down, I make do and mend, and give sheer blood and guts and endeavour, hoping that this will get me through. You've got to roll your sleeves up and get in there, and give everything you've got. You've got to scratch, kick, or bite, so to speak, to get what you want. Sometimes you've got to throw the finer arts away, because you're playing for your living.

I brought a lot of trouble on myself, in the early days, because

I wanted to be noticed. I wanted people to see me as a firebrand, a fireball. When I was a lad, I used to fight on the pitch. Do you know what Jimmy Armfield did? He used to jump on me and pin my arms to the ground, and stop me fighting during a match. Rather than let the referee come over and book me, Jimmy would pin me down until I'd cooled off for those vital seconds that you get in trouble for. If he hadn't cared enough about me to do this, I would have got into even more trouble than I did. I don't think I was badly treated by referees: I think I brought trouble on my own head.

Nowadays, I get on very well with referees, because I don't have to be a firebrand, or anything like that, any more. I know that I am a great player. [*Alan said this without a trace of vanity. He was merely stating a fact, which the whole football world acknowledges.*—R.D.] Given luck, and the run of the ball, I know that I will go out and play well, so I don't have to fight with a referee every week. Tomorrow, I may go out, and something will upset me. Then I will have a go at the referee. But I won't swear at him, or do the things I did when I was a boy: almost deliberately looking for wrong things to do.

Referees often miss footballers' fouls: that only a former professional footballer would blow his whistle for. I don't blame the referees: *I* don't see these fouls half the time. But I see some that go unpunished, and I just look at the referee as if to say, "If I had been referee today, he wouldn't have got away with that." And the referee just looks at you: many of them don't know the "professional foul". I wish no disrespect to referees. Their standards have improved. They are trying to improve all the time. And any person who tries to improve—at anything—will always go down well with me. But I know that if I went into the boxing ring as a referee, and had never been a professional boxer, the two contestants would get away with lots of things. Not many former professional footballers want to become referees, because refereeing is not a full-time job. Once a professional, always a professional.

On the whole, I think crowds are fair. All the time I've been in football, I've found that the crowd doesn't get onto you for the way you are playing. They get onto you out of sheer frustration, knowing what you *can* do, and not seeing it on that particular day. So I wouldn't say that crowds are harsh. They know you can play football. They know you can entertain them. And when you don't, you hear frustrated OOs and AHs.

I have never seen a professional player go onto a football field and not try—never in my life. I don't think I ever will. I will never accept that a man is going to play in front of thousands of people, and not try to do well. It is the ambition of every footballer to come off the pitch, and look around at the thousands of fans he has been entertaining, and hear them shout his name and say that he is a fantastic player.

I can't do weight-training: I'm one of the worst in the club at it. I'm just lucky to have the ability to run and run and run. I believe I've got a slow heart-beat: that may have something to do with it. I keep myself fit, and I look after myself. I eat well, and I live a clean life. These are the things that preserve my stamina.

I had a business once, and I came out of it—when I first went to Everton. Therefore, it would be wrong for me to condemn other players for going into business—because, at one time, I was prepared to do the same thing. Now, I believe I must give my total involvement to football, and not let anything pinch even an hour from my football. It wouldn't be fair to the game that has given me so much.

I have one superstition. My Cup and League medals have got to be taken down from the mantelpiece when I go out to play. It would be unlucky if they were left up there.

I play crown green bowls. They say it's an old man's game, but I find it very relaxing, and I enjoy it very much. I do a bit of gardening, and I go to watch horse racing a lot. My family and I have our privacy. We used to live in a lovely little district, just outside Manchester. It's a great little place. It was *home* for me. I got lots of peace and happiness there. Now we're settling down in the south.

I get lots of fan mail: about twenty letters a day. I answer them all, myself. I leave them for a few weeks, then one afternoon I work through the lot. Mostly, they are young people wanting an autograph or a signed picture. One or two have asked for an England shirt, but I will never give a shirt or a cap to a stranger, only to a close friend or to a member of my family. I know they probably appreciate them more than I do, because I've got lots upstairs.

I have always admired Denis Law. When I was a boy, I wanted to be the same type of player. He had everything that I wanted to be. He was strong. He was fast. He wanted the ball. He scored goals. He wanted to *win*. He was a *professional* footballer. He hated every man on that pitch who was going to try to stop him from winning. I really liked him. And I liked Nat Lofthouse. As a boy, around the ages of five to ten, I used to watch him knocking in goals.

I always wanted to be a forward. I always wanted to be beating men—getting the *better* of them, with the ball. Not taking it off them—*beating* them.

24

RAY CHARNLEY
Supreme in the Air

My grandfather used to say: "An optimist looks at the doughnut; a pessimist looks at the hole." My grandad never saw a game of football, but I'm sure he would have said that a pessimist talks about the goals a centre-forward misses, whereas an optimist talks about the goals he scores. Bobby Smith, Nat Lofthouse, Bobby Charlton—they have all had their critics. So has Ray Charnley. This noble quartet of England centre-forwards answered its critics by big-heartedness and, most of all, by goals.

I yield to no man in my admiration for Charnley. It is as well that a writer and his reader should come to an early understanding on these things. He gave me many hours of pleasure, not only by his goal-scoring, but by his sportsmanship and fairness on the field. Here was a footballer with good manners. I never saw him make a gesture of defiance at a referee or at an opponent. He is a man wonderfully in control of mind and body. I admired his determination: he always chased even the tiniest chance. And I had respect for his keenness in training. In every way, he was a model for any young player or spectator.

Ray Charnley is the third-highest goal-scorer in Blackpool history. Only the two legendaries, Hampson and Mortensen, scored more often. And they played in golden eras of Blackpool football. By contrast, Charnley's years—despite his own large contributions —were among the most despairing that Blackpool have known. Hampson, Mortensen, Charnley. All three were centre-forwards and England internationals. And the strength of character of the three of them, each in his own way, has had, and will continue to have, a good influence on the course of Blackpool football.

Without any doubt, Charnley's 27 League goals in 1960–61 kept Blackpool in the First Division. He even challenged the club's goal-scoring record in that season of near-relegation. Many forwards can score when given strong backing by a successful side. Charnley so often lacked the support he deserved. But he was born to score goals. They came as naturally and as gracefully from his head and feet, as runs came fluently from the bat of Denis Compton. Charnley was always among the goals. Almost always. Once, as I left Bloomfield Road after a 6-0 win by Blackpool, I overheard a fan protest to his neighbour, "Six goals, and none from our Ray. I don't believe it!"

After several happy years with Morecambe, Charnley joined Blackpool, but he hesitated to sign as a full-time professional. Joe Smith insisted. Charnley agreed. The rest is history. You could never mistake Charnley, with his high knee action and a back straight as a Guardsman's, but more than once, in football programmes, his name was confused with that of Dave Charnley, the boxer. Opposing defenders never mistook Ray Charnley for anyone else. They marked him, and marked him closely, but he kept more or less free from injury during his Blackpool years, never once missing an F.A. cup-tie. His shots could be as sharp and as swift as an axe, and he soared high and gracefully to head the ball. What a prodigious leap! Needless to say, he liked a high centre to the far post, especially from Stanley Matthews. Every back-pass, from an opposing defender to his goalkeeper, would find Charnley in close pursuit. His interception of a back-pass, and the goal he scored, against Luton in February of 1959, brought back memories of Mudie's similar goal against Spurs, a few years earlier, also in the last minute of a cup-tie. Often, Charnley would sprint back to help his defence, when there was a corner, or when they were under pressure. Blackpool thought so highly of his value to the defence that they even chose him to play centre-half. Charnley followed in the Mortensen centre-forward tradition of cover-the-whole-field play. Do you remember the photo of Morty, in a cuptie, crouching, like a full-back, *behind* his goalkeeper?

Charnley earned the nickname "Razor". He led his club's goalscorers, in the League, in seven of his nine full seasons. Alan Ball twice took first place: in 1963–64, when he played more often than Charnley; and in 1965–66, when he had the advantage, over Charnley, of being the recognized penalty-kicker. In several seasons, Charnley netted more than double the goals of his nearest rival in the Blackpool team. On February 3, 1962, against Nottingham Forest (A), he scored his 100th League goal, in his 156th appearance. Even so prolific a goal-scorer as Harry Bedford could better Charnley's record by only a few games. Twice, Charnley came near to Mudie's Blackpool record of 32 League goals in a season in the First Division: in 1961–62, Charnley netted 30 times; and in 1960–61 27, after scoring 20 in the first half of the season.

How the fans enjoyed a Ray Charnley goal-spree, such as his five goals against V.V. Venlo, cup-holders of Holland (April 1960); his four against Wolves (January 1962); and the four against Charlton, in a Football League Cup game (September 1963). He scored dozens of goals for Blackpool in friendly matches, and scored in every one of his eight matches for the F.A. XI, on the 1961 tour of the Far East and New Zealand. I wonder how many goals Charnley remembers, and which ones? He won't have forgotten the goal against Real Madrid (August 1963), nor his 80th-minute Matthews-made winner against Newcastle (April 1961), which saved Blackpool from relegation. He left Blackpool when he was but seven short of his double-century of League goals. He came so close to election to the small band of players who have scored 200 League goals for a single club. There is no real difference between 193 and 200—only a difference of statistics. What matters more is the heart and the spirit and the effort that inspired the goals. "A pessimist looks at the hole."

I confess to having written, in April of 1962, to the Chairman of England's Selection Committee, proposing "Charnley for England". In October of that year, Alf Ramsey, soon after becoming manager of the national team, selected Charnley to play against France, in a European Nations' Cup match, with his friend and club-mate, Jim Armfield, captain of England, at right-back. The old rivals drew 1-1. Charnley had little support from an experimental forward-line. He was never given a second chance. As with Tony Waiters, he was chosen for England when he was a season or two past his peak.

Of Charnley's League matches, three remain poignant in my mind. The first memory is of Highbury, January 1958. Charnley, a fledgling of only three League games, began, this day, to establish a regular place in Blackpool's first team : a place which he was to hold, almost without interruption, for nine years. Blackpool had never won a League game at Arsenal, and when the Gunners scored twice in a minute, after about a quarter-of-an-hour, it did not look as though the spell would be broken. Charnley reduced the arrears. Then Arsenal's centre-half Dodgin scored a glorious own-goal from fully 25 yards. No more dramatic ending could have been imagined than for Matthews, prompted by Ernie Taylor, to fashion a winner for Charnley in the last seconds.

One of football's maxims claims that "a good player can perform well anywhere."[1] In September 1962, Charnley gave a masterful display at Villa Park as centre-half : Glyn James was injured after thirty minutes' play. For the last hour, Charnley defended

---

[1] There has been no finer example than Johnny Carey, Mr Play-in-all-positions.

The 1953 Cup Final. Moment of a lifetime. *Left to right:* Farm, Garrett, Johnston, Fenton, Mudie, Matthews, Mortensen

The 1953 Cup Final. Matthews with his medal

The 1953 Cup Final. "Another and another Cup". Blackpool celebrate at the Café Royal. *Left to right*: Matthews, Johnston, Mortensen

The 1953 Cup Final. The Blackpool team appears on television, in the "What's My Line?" programme. Johnston shows the Cup to the late Gilbert Harding, who identified Stanley Matthews, the mystery personality, in two questions

impeccably, in the face of constant challenge from the even-taller Dougan. Charnley's efforts ensured a draw for Blackpool. Aston Villa's supporters cheered him as he left the field.

Against Spurs, at White Hart Lane in October 1966, Charnley, at the age of thirty-one, and never fitter or faster, gave a truly heroic performance. For fifteen minutes of the second half, Charnley, brought back to help mark the Spurs' Welsh giant, Mike England, actually played the double rôle of centre-half and centre-forward. Of course it was a superhuman task, and eventually he stayed in defence, except for the last seconds of the match when he dribbled the ball half the length of the field to score his second goal and Blackpool's third. "Bottom Club Beats League Leaders" was the headline in the Sunday press. But it was the manner of the victory, and, above all, Charnley's gallantry, that will be remembered.

A year or so later, on December 7, 1967, to be precise, Charnley joined Preston. There must have been a few blushing faces at Deepdale, because he was once an amateur with the club. Nine days after joining them, he made a story-book return to Bloomfield Road, when, as Preston's captain for the day, he scored against Blackpool in the first few minutes of the game. He was also captain for his last appearance in Blackpool's colours, and, to make a fitting farewell, scored two goals in an 8-1 win over Nottingham Forest reserves. His last League match had been against Crystal Palace who at the time were challenging Blackpool for the leadership of the Second Division. Charnley steered Blackpool to a 2-0 victory, scoring once and making the other goal for Jimmy Armfield.

In his last season with Blackpool, Charnley scored three goals in four League games. Fair-haired Gerry Ingram, a buccaneer of a centre-forward, took over from Charnley after Blackpool's 4-1 home defeat by Millwall. Blackpool began a run of successive victories, and Ingram, who like Charnley was rushed straight from minor-league football to the "big-time", scored frequently. In that Millwall match, Leslie made a brilliant finger-tip save to Charnley's penalty-kick, just before half-time. Supposing Charnley had scored? This would have been his own, and Blackpool's, second goal, and would have sent his team into the second half with the score 2-2. Blackpool, given this fillip, might have won. Could Charnley then have been dropped? He might have played a leading rôle in the run of victories which followed. Thus does fate depend on small, trifling things—the length of a goalkeeper's hand.

Ray Charnley missed the chance to enjoy the good days of 1967–68, after helping Blackpool, beyond measure, through some of her darkest years. In competitive and friendly matches, Charnley

L

scored about 250 goals for Blackpool. He cost the club only
£1,000. That works out at £4 per goal! The name *Ray Charnley*
will always command a large place in Blackpool history. He can
look back with pride on a decade of service to Blackpool football.
No! on second thoughts, not pride—he is far too modest for that.
Charnley is as capable of succumbing to pride, as the Statue of
Liberty is of dropping her torch.

I watched Charnley in training at the start of his last season
with Blackpool. It was a lovely August day, and I sat alone in
the west stand. Young autograph-hunters clustered around the
players' entrance to the field. All of Blackpool's players—first-
teamers, reserves, and amateurs—were lapping the pitch. And there,
out in front, was Charnley, enjoying every stride. He had just
turned thirty-two. Age had not reduced his speed or his stamina.
I wouldn't have backed any member of the club's playing staff, of
any age, to outpace him over 50 yards. I knew, as I watched him
that morning (no! I had always known it), that there would never
be another quite like him.

25

JIMMY ARMFIELD
Captain of Blackpool, Captain of England

> When I took over Jimmy Armfield's place in the
> England team, he came up to me and said, "I
> hope you have as long a run as I had." And he
> meant it. He was the first person to congratulate
> me.
>
> GEORGE COHEN

I had the privilege of watching Jimmy Armfield throughout the
whole of his professional career. I say "privilege" because he is a
player whose name has already been inscribed on football's Roll of
Honour. Jimmy Armfield will be remembered for at least four
reasons: he pioneered the overlap—the sprint down the touch-line
in support of his winger; he was the first Blackpool player to captain
his country—he led England in fifteen international matches; he
remained loyal to his club during a dark age in Blackpool history,
and at a time when players moved from club to club, at small pro-
vocation or solely for monetary gain; and lastly, and very impor-
tantly (for, here again, he was a rarity in his generation), he is a
sportsman in the best English traditions, deserving the nickname
"Gentleman Jim".

Jimmy is not one person; he is several. Besides being a club
manager, he is a cricketer, fisherman, golfer, and F.A. staff coach;
a father; a musician; a journalist and author; a church sidesman;
and a worker for charity. He turned down the chance to go to
university and then become a teacher. I daresay, had more years
or lives been allotted to him, that he could have been a rugby
international or a social worker or a Church of England vicar.
Or, knowing him, all three.

His interests in music and in the church reveal the deeper side
of his nature. Beneath the smile and the quick wit there lies a sensi-

tive vein in his personality. He was chaired off the field after Blackpool won promotion—at Preston, in 1970—and regained First Division status. His face beamed happiness. He was pleased for his club: it was the first time during his captaincy that Blackpool had won a major honour. I spoke to him that evening. It was the first time I had ever known him to be short of words. All he could say was, "It's great, isn't it? I'll see you at White Hart Lane and Highbury." In contrast, there were the Saturday afternoons in the early sixties when Blackpool, clinging desperately to her place in the First Division, slumped to defeat after miserable defeat. And Armfield used to walk head-bowed off the field. His emotions are involved in the game, but always, always he is master of his temperament.

Many would say that his best-ever season for Blackpool was 1960–61, when the club narrowly escaped relegation. His tackles were always superbly timed (and fair), and a friend, who often used to accompany me, would greet every tackle with the claim "Attaboy Jim, you're the greatest full-back in the world." I never heard a word of disagreement from rival supporters. A year or so later, after the World Cup Finals in Chile, the host nation's press corps confirmed my friend's opinion—they voted Armfield the best right-back in the world.

It is staggering to think that, ten years after that peak season of 1960–61, he was still playing, and playing with such zest and love for the game, and still performing the overlap. At this point, a fallacy must be corrected. Armfield did not invent the overlap. He developed the move and brought it to near-perfection for club and country—in rather the same way that Haydn is nicknamed "The Father of the Symphony", although he was not the first composer to use the genre.

In April 1956, only a year or so after his League début, he played in his first representative match: for the Football League. Five years later, in a World Cup preliminary tie against Luxembourg, he captained England for the first time. He was just twenty-six. His erect stance, the assured set of the shoulders, amid the Highbury floodlights, as the national anthem was played, spoke of his self-confidence and his north-country determination.

Jimmy Armfield is a natural leader of men. He captained his school cricket team, Blackpool "A", Blackpool's first team, his regimental side, Western Command, England Under-23, F.A. XI, the Football League, and England. When he first captained England, he showed no signs of being overawed by the occasion. England had beaten Luxembourg in the first leg by 9-0. At half-time in this second match, with England leading 12-0 on aggregate,

Armfield said to his team: "There'll be no letting up, lads. I want no slacking." David Potter, a tennis coach, once gave me similar and sound advice: "When you are playing a weak opponent, it is all too easy to lose your concentration. You know you can beat him, and so you should set yourself a personal target: you must go out and try to win *every single point*."

Jimmy Armfield has earned much praise from the game: no footballer has deserved honours more, and sought them less:

1959 Young Footballer of the Year
1962 Best right-back in the world
1962–64 Best right-back in Europe
1966 Blackpool's Player of the Year

Armfield—like every other successful man—owes much to chance, fortune, timing, call it what you will. He came to Blackpool as a wing forward, an outside-right. One afternoon in 1953—while the first team was beating Spurs at Villa Park, in an F.A. Cup semi-final—Armfield was playing for Blackpool "A". He scored twice, and Blackpool led 4-1 at half-time. Then a Blackpool full-back received an injury and limped off the field. On an impulse—he still cannot find a rational reason for what he did—Armfield volunteered to deputise for the injured player. On that day, and in that way, an international full-back was born.

On the morning of December 26, 1954, Jimmy was fast asleep when Joe Smith rang. "Are you fit? Right. Pack your bags. Eddie Shimwell is injured. You're playing right-back at Portsmouth tomorrow. Good-bye." That was typical Joe Smith: quick and to the point. Thus was Armfield, on leave from National Service duty, selected to make his League début for Blackpool.

He made his England début in circumstances even more dramatic. While he was on a Continental tour with the Under-23 team, he was asked to join England's players on their tour of South America. On May 13, 1959, he played his first game for England, under a double handicap: firstly, he was selected at left-back, a position totally unfamiliar to him; secondly, England's opponents were Brazil, the world champions, on their own ground, in front of over 120,000 zealous supporters.

A year or so later, in the last minute of a match against Leicester, Armfield ran half the length of the field to score. A goal from a full-back was a rarity in those days, and Armfield's brave effort earned Blackpool a 3-3 draw. He realized the potential of this sudden surprise thrust, from deep in mid-field, and he exploited that potential with all his skill, natural speed, and willingness to learn. In the early days of Armfield's use of the move, the crowd

used to scream at him to "Get back in defence, and stay there!"
But he persisted, and crowds all over England—and abroad—
cheered their approval of the Armfield overlap, one of the most
thrilling sights to be seen on a football field, anywhere in the world,
in the 1960s.

The fifth decisive event in Jimmy Armfield's career is the most
ironic of all. Johnny Haynes[1] used to captain England. One day
in 1962, he was injured in an automobile accident—in Blackpool.
And Jimmy Armfield—sad though he was about the accident that
led to the honour—became captain of England.

One evening, some years from now, a young boy—your grand-
son, perhaps, or a nephew—will sit on your knee and ask earnestly:
"But what was he *really* like?" The name *Jimmy Armfield* will,
by then, have been added to the scroll of the most famous full-
backs in the history of English soccer: Crompton, Pennington,
Goodall, Male, Hapgood, Spencer. . . .

In case your memory dims as the years pass, I offer the following
as a sort of mental check-list. These were the principal qualities
that marked-out Armfield from his contemporaries. I make no
effort of recollection. These special talents of his come quickly to
the mind and pen: concentration, quickness on the turn, natural
speed, careful distribution, well-timed tackling, split-second decisive-
ness of action, and capacity for hard work, in training and on
match-days. Of all these, his two most precious qualities were his
speed and his gift of improvisation: he was the Satchmo, the Louis
Armstrong, of football.

Jimmy Armfield showed his versatility and team-spirit by playing for Blackpool in positions other than full-back: versatility,
in the days before substitutes were allowed, when he once took
over in goal from the injured George Farm; team-spirit, when,
three hours before a home match against Everton, he was asked,
and agreed, to play centre-forward in place of Ray Charnley who
had been injured in training.

Of all his defensive partnerships, two in particular will be
remembered: with Ray Wilson, for England; and with Roy
Gratrix, for Blackpool. From his earliest days as an amateur,
Jimmy had been willing to listen to the advice of others—managers,
coaches, and team-mates—and thus his approach to the game of
football has always been fresh and open, deep-thinking and alert.
This alertness, this quickness of mind, enabled him to continue

---

[1] Haynes was the most accurate passer of a ball I have ever seen. In a
club match at Fulham, I once counted 35 Haynes passes: every single pass
reached one of his own team-mates. And Haynes, that afternoon, was
marked by two, and sometimes three, defenders.

playing, at the highest level of competitive club-football, until well into his thirties. I vividly recall a match at Bloomfield Road against a London team. Blackpool, on the attack, were awarded a free-kick just outside the penalty-area. While the Londoners protested, Armfield seized the initiative. He ran 20 yards, carrying the ball; verified the spot for the kick; and pushed the ball to Ray Charnley, who scored an easy goal. A team does not have to wait for the referee to whistle for a kick to be taken. A wave of his hand is all that is necessary. Armfield knew the rule book.

Years after his retirement from League football, I shall still see him, with memory's keen eyes, selling the dummy as he moves the ball out of his penalty-area; sprinting down the touch-line with that long, loping stride that always seemed to have more speed in reserve; and I shall see him, at the heart of the defence, instinctively covering his goalkeeper. During his career, he made a number of dramatic saves on the line, booting the ball clear, after his goal-keeper had been beaten. In so many different situations, his uncanny tactical sense helped him to foresee and forestall impending danger.

One of Armfield's supreme qualities was his speed of recovery. Early in his career, I lost count of the number of times I saw him turn, outpace the winger, tackle him cleanly, and come away with the ball. I have seen him give a one-yard start to the fastest wingers in the game, and overtake them within 15 yards of being passed. Jimmy Armfield was the world's fastest full-back of his generation.

The Armfield memory that I cherish above all others is of the evening of his Testimonial Match at Bloomfield Road, played on his 35th birthday. Sitting in the directors' box—with Anne, his charming wife—were his two young sons, John and Duncan. When their Dad led the Blackpool team onto the field, past a guard of honour provided by the opposition (an international XI), and, later, when they heard again the Bloomfield Road slogan of the 1960s "Armfield for Eng-land", their faces shone with joy and family pride. It was a look of delight that I had seen on the faces of many young boys (and of some not-so-young boys, too) for a decade and a half, at grounds all over the country. If Jimmy Armfield ever doubted the rightness of his decision to become a professional footballer—an entertainer rather than a teacher—here was his answer. In fact, he *has* been a teacher: not of political science or economic geography or whatever the "in" subject of the day may be, but of clean living, fitness of body and mind, and fair play.

26

JIMMY ARMFIELD
— in an Interview

The three main events in football, in my twenty years in the game, have been: the abolition of the maximum wage, the winning of the World Cup, and improvements in methods of training.

The abolition of the maximum wage was the first big change. It has changed our game completely. It freed the amount of money that a club could pay to a player. In effect, this meant that clubs were going to have to spend more to keep their players. They had to prune their staffs, and consequently a lot of players were out of work, unemployed. We estimated that a few would lose their jobs. I don't think we really believed that so many players would have to leave League football. Take, for example, a club like Blackpool. When I first started—in the 1952–53 season—there were more than forty professionals. Nowadays, they have a job to get two sides for a practice match.

Some clubs have gone from strength to strength, and one or two have gone the other way. The abolition of the maximum wage has streamlined football in this country. It has affected a lot of clubs, particularly in the Second and Third Divisions. To my mind, it is the Second and Third Divisions—and not the First and Fourth— which form the backbone of League football. They can provide a decent standard of football, and at the same time they are always aspiring to reach the top. These clubs are the ones that have been hit particularly hard, and they have lost a lot of their players. About a dozen clubs are doing very nicely, and they will all probably continue to do well. For the rest, I feel rather sad. In fact, in three or four years from now, there could be a depression in English football: among the smaller clubs.

The second big change in this country resulted from our victory in the World Cup. When I first started playing, we always thought we were the best players in the world, but we had never proved it. And when we tried to prove it, we couldn't. The Hungarians came

over here and beat us in 1953, and, a few years earlier, we went to
Brazil for the World Cup. Our famous team—that included Finney,
Mortensen, Mannion, and all the great names we hear so much
about—lost to the U.S.A., a team of part-timers. That day, I expect
England went onto the field wondering how many they were going
to win by and who was going to score the first goal. Today, I don't
think England could lose to a team like that, because there is a
much more professional approach in football and more emphasis
on team-work.

The 1966 World Cup made our players believe in themselves
again. Just prior to 1966, there had been occasional good years,
such as 1961, when I was in the England team: we took everything
before us. But in the latter half of the fifties and the early part of
the sixties, the England team got a bit of a battering.

When we went to Chile in 1962 for the World Cup, I thought
we were going to win it. I think I was the only one in the team
who thought we *were* going to win it, but I really thought we were
good enough. We lost to Brazil in the quarter-finals, and we should
have licked them. If we'd beaten Brazil, we would have won the
World Cup because there was no other great side left in the
Competition. Czechoslovakia got to the Final, but they did not
have a great side.

Our win in '66 gave our players confidence, and it changed the
attitude of people in this country. They realized that they were
watching the world's best, and it brought them back to the football grounds. Television and the newspapers took a renewed
interest in football, and our teams went into Europe with confidence.
Since then, they've never looked back.

The third big chance has been in training. Training facilities are
much better today. More *thought* is put into training, and there's
a lot more emphasis on coaching. It took me ten years to become
a full-back. I started playing full-back when I was eighteen and I
first played full-back for England when I was twenty-three. I didn't
really begin to know what it was all about until I was twenty-seven
or twenty-eight. I used to make errors which, in those days, everybody accepted. There was a *laissez-faire* attitude: you just went onto
the field and, when the ball came to your feet, you did what you
thought was right. Nobody said: "Why did you do that? What
you should have done was this . . . we'll go out on the field and I'll
show you."

The gap between the First and Second Divisions is widening. I
think the big difference is that there are far more good players in
First Division sides. In the First Division side of today, there are
eight or nine really good players. When I say "really good", I mean

"useful in their particular rôle". The Second Division clubs have some good players, but there are one or two weak links in each team. There are not many weak links in First Division sides, and players have got to take more pressure in the First Division. More is expected of the individual. The gap between the two Divisions has been widening year by year. The most outstanding illustration of this is the season Queen's Park Rangers spent in the First Division. They won the Football League Cup in 1966–67, and they looked quite a good side the following season, when they won promotion. They went into the First Division and finished bottom with only 18 points. This wasn't an accident. The Rangers were short of top-class players.

Your mistakes are punished more heavily in the First Division. You can't allow opponents quite as much room. Blackpool had an example of this, a year or so ago, in a match against Arsenal. The goal we lost by began with a simple lob into the area, but Arsenal had a player of Radford's class to head the ball in. That's his forte. There are not many players in the Second Division who could have converted that lob into a goal.

Never in my career have I been able to call professional football a game of sportsmanship. I have never classed it as a game of which I could say to my sons: "Now this is what I call a sporting game." You occasionally meet teams and players who are hail-fellow-well-met—there are a few of them around—but football is a *professional* game. It is a hard game. They all play for keeps these days; they don't—as it were—take prisoners. There is more of a win-at-all-costs attitude than there used to be. But I can quote instances from my early days as a player, when I was behind Matthews, when defenders were doing their level best to slide his legs from underneath him. People talk about close marking today: well, if Matthews didn't have two players on him, he was having a birthday. There are a lot of fellows in the game who you know are out for a sporting challenge: they're after a *fair* challenge. But you'll meet some fellows who will go to any lengths to cheat and stretch the rules. Some of them disgust me.

Rugby is very much a team game. By playing rugby you learn companionship, responsibility for the rest of the team. I was a three-quarter, which helped my pace quite a lot. But I was a runner, in any case, at school: I used to be a sprinter. Rugby just sort of carried it on during the winter. Rugby helped my general fitness and taught me about team-work.

As a young boy, I used to play soccer at primary school. Then I went to Arnold, which was a rugby-playing school. During my first few years there, I used to play soccer for my church team, St

Peter's. That's the church I go to today. We formed our own team, which lasted for about three years: for me, that was between the ages of about twelve to fourteen. But then, when I got into the school rugby team, I hardly played soccer at all. If I got the chance of a game of soccer, I used to go and play, but I didn't play for an actual team. We only had kick-abouts, really. The youngsters at Blackpool Football Club wouldn't believe me when I told them that, from about fifteen to seventeen, I hardly kicked a football.

At Arnold, we played rugby from September till Christmas. In the Easter term—from January to April—we used to play hockey as a school game, but I didn't play hockey. I continued to play rugby, but we didn't have any matches. So I was free in the after-noons, and that's when I started to play for Blackpool.

George Neal, our P.T. master, said to me, "Why don't you go and have a try with Blackpool, if you fancy a game of football?" So I said, "If you fix it up, I'll go." So I went to the club, just for a bit of training. Then, at the end of one season, we were having a practice match at Bloomfield Road—I was a winger in those days. By chance, Joe Smith was there, sitting in the stand. I can see his face now, smoking a cigar. I scored three goals, and nothing impressed Joe more than a goal-scorer. "What's your name?", he asked. So I said, "Why do you want to know?" And he replied, "You're doing all right. Would you like to come and play for us next season?" "Well, yes," I said, "if I get the opportunity."

Whenever possible, when I wasn't at school playing rugby, I used to go and play in the Blackpool colts team. More often than not, I was reserve. I got a bit fed up with it, but I still turned up. I was in the sixth form at the time, and I was dashing between Blackpool Football Club, playing rugby, and doing my "A" levels. I thought to myself, "It'll be fine if I can play for Blackpool during my university course." It's just as well that I was so busy, because I would probably have got myself into trouble if I hadn't had so much to do. In those days, I was a bit of a tearaway.

I don't think I would have become an England player if I'd tried to make the grade as a winger. The skill factor—because I missed important years around 15–16–17—would have counted against me. As a defender, I had more chance to make up for the time I'd lost.

I used to play as an orthodox winger. I used to push the ball down the line, and try to get past the full-back, on the outside, and then get a cross over to my forwards. When the ball was on the other wing, I always used to be looking for goals. I'd quite often not play very well, and yet score a couple of goals. I remember one particular game I played for the "A" team at Blackburn. I hardly had a kick of the ball, and yet I scored a hat-trick.

Over the years, several big clubs wanted to sign me—Manchester United, Arsenal, Tottenham. I think I would have enjoyed playing for one of them. Being with Blackpool, I missed playing in European football. But now that I'm older, I'm probably glad I stayed with Blackpool. I've got roots in the town. I certainly would have earned more money at another club, but money doesn't mean everything to me.

Blackpool is the only club I've ever played for, apart from the church team when I was a little boy. The only other teams were when I went into the Army to do my two years' National Service. I played for the regimental team, the Western Command team, and the British Army.

Your background is the important thing in developing your sense of loyalty and your self-discipline. Your home-life is particularly important. If you were the type of child who learned respect for your mother and father, and you came from a good home, this makes for loyalty to your family and to your home. This gives you a head-start in life. Loyalty is something which is developed from childhood. You can't just get it overnight. Some chaps move from club to club; they're just out to make a fast buck. They can't have many real friends. They must have missed a lot along the way, and I feel very sorry for them. They probably make far more money than I'll ever make in football. It all depends where you pitch your ambition. Is it how well, and how long, you play? Is it all the pleasure you get from playing? Or is it money?

In addition to your home, your schooling matters a lot. In our school, the Head built up a sort of *esprit de corps*. He used to say that Arnold School was a school for the sons of gentlemen. He would often talk of pride in appearance, and he used to say that we were just that little bit better. We weren't, of course. But we used to *think* we were. This created a sense of loyalty to the school.

And you learn loyalty through respect. Players will be loyal to a club if they have respect for the manager, particularly if he's an impressive sort of fellow. Matt Busby has shown, quite clearly, that he is the type of man who can win respect. Don Revie has shown this ability, as well, by taking on a number of lads as youngsters and building them into a great side.

I think *ambition* is the most important thing for any player. If I hadn't made international class, I would have considered myself a failure. Many people say, "To some extent you've been a failure, because you've never played in a Cup Final." But these sort of things can be lucky breaks. I can think of chaps who've played in a Cup Final who wouldn't get a place in the Blackpool first team.

My ambition for Blackpool was always: to play in the First Division. If clubs like Blackpool play in the top sphere, I think they're achieving as much as they can ever hope to achieve. Even in the days of Matthews, Morty, and Johnston—even in Blackpool's great days—Bloomfield Road never had more than an average attendance of about 23,000. If that Blackpool team had been based in London or the midlands, or Manchester or Liverpool, they would have attracted a 40,000 crowd to every home match. They would have been sold-out weeks before every match.

There's a good atmosphere at Bloomfield Road: there always has been. The most important influence is the manager. He's the centre of the club, really. It's up to him to foster a good team-spirit. And I think a lot depends on where you live. If you lived in, say, Walsall or Rotherham, I don't think you'd feel quite as carefree, going down to the football ground, as you would at Blackpool, Torquay, or Bournemouth. Blackpool is a pleasant town to live in. It's nice to be by the sea. Your environment helps to mould your character: I even believe that the type of house you live in can affect you. So I think that the character of a club depends on the type of town it is in.

Even in the sixties, when we were struggling to hold our place in the First Division, the atmosphere at Bloomfield Road was pretty good. Ron Suart worked hard, and he found a good trainer in Wilf Dixon. Wilf is one of the most enthusiastic chaps I have ever met in football. When he first came, we didn't know what had hit us. We trained very hard with him. He's a real character.

I played with five good goalkeepers at Blackpool: George Farm, Gordon West, Tony Waiters, Alan Taylor, and Harry Thomson. I don't think that West and Waiters were anywhere near their best when they were at Blackpool. Waiters could have become the best of the five, because he had height and strength, and he was willing to work and train very hard. He was a good professional, a dedicated player. He didn't drink and he didn't smoke. He was just becoming a good goalkeeper when he packed in. I think Waiters would have been a terrific player.

Gordon West was rather a worrier. He was a very nervous type of person. But he adopted a very professional approach: he was tough, very tough. He had some qualities which the others didn't have. But he was another one who was only beginning to show what he was capable of when he left Blackpool.

Now Farm, on the other hand—I played with him when he was at his best. He'd got over the '53 Final: it took him quite a long time. A lot of people still talk about the soft goals he let in, in that Cup Final. But, for me, he was a good goalkeeper. He was a very *steady* goalkeeper. He didn't do anything spectacular, but he was always safe and reliable, and he had a good pair of hands. He was keen on training, and he was a clean-living fellow. He was always immaculately dressed. Pride in performance. Pride in appearance. He was everything I like in a goalkeeper.

Harry Thomson was an acrobat, a showman, an extrovert. He was small for a goalkeeper. I think his height was against him. His reflexes were very good. He was a nervous goalkeeper. A lot of goalkeepers get pretty nervous during a game.

Alan Taylor was probably the least nervous of all goalkeepers I ever played with. He had a wonderful temperament. If he made a big mistake, he'd just forget all about it. But, of the five, the goalkeeper who would have been the best—had he not stopped playing—was Waiters.

Roy Gratrix and I understood each other. He was quick, very quick. He was the best two-footed player I've ever seen. It didn't matter which foot he kicked with because he had amazing strength. He went on an England tour, but never had a game. He never made the England team. But he did very well for Blackpool. He had the potential to have been an even better player than he was. He could have been really top-class.

Dave Durie was a good player for us, a very under-rated player. He was really more of an inside-forward than a half-back. Then there was Barrie Martin who used to partner me at left-back. He was doing very well until he had an upset and left the club. And Emlyn Hughes was just becoming a good player when he left Blackpool. At first, I never thought Glyn James would make the grade. In more recent years, he's become much more steady. In our promotion season (1969–70), he played particularly well. He's a stronger player than many people give him credit for. There was a dearth of good half-backs in my time at Blackpool. We had a lot of steady half-backs, but not more than one or two of whom I could say, "He'll leave an imprint on my mind. I liked to play behind him."

Ray Charnley was one of the cleanest headers of the ball that I've ever seen. He was a clean jumper: he didn't knock anybody out of the way. He'd get you a goal out of nothing with his heading. Ray is an honest man and an honest player and I think he knew his limitations. But he had a little more skill than many people gave him credit for. I always thought he was a dangerous player. He's the kind of forward Blackpool could do with now.

We had quite a few good forwards in my time at Blackpool.

Players like Ernie Taylor: he was certainly one of the best. And then, of course, there was Matthews and Perry and Brown and Mudie. It's a pity that Blackpool had to let Alan Ball go to Everton. He's the type of player they've needed these last few years.

Joe Smith and Johnny Lynas, the trainer, helped me initially. They made me think right. You would never call Joe "a coach". You never saw him in a track-suit. He just used to talk to you about things, simple things in the game. I believe football is a simple game.

I learned a lot by playing with people like Taylor and Matthews. They didn't exactly *teach* me; I learned by watching them. They made me look a better player than I was at the time, and they gave me confidence. In those days—to be quite honest—you either learned football yourself or you fell by the wayside. There wasn't a great deal of coaching.

Eric Hayward helped me a lot. He coached the young players. He was very good. He used to spend a bit of time with us, and he was like Bill Shankly in his approach. Eric was like a kid with the ball. He would say, "Isn't it *great* when you kick it just right, and you get that feeling?" He used to make you feel as though you were enjoying it.

And Walter Winterbottom helped me—rather a lot. He started me thinking about my positioning. And then Alf Ramsey continued it. They both made me *think* more about my game. That's why I always say that it wasn't until I was twenty-seven or twenty-eight that I really started to grasp the idea of how to play full-back.

You can't generalize about when a footballer should reach his peak. It varies from player to player. People often say that forwards reach their peak at a younger age than defenders; but then you get a player like Bobby Collins. I suppose there is a physical-fitness peak, and an age when you've had some professional experience that has given you the necessary know-how: to learn the job and learn the game. If you pressed me, I'd say it was usually at about twenty-eight or twenty-nine.

Being a professional footballer has meant that I've had to sacrifice a tremendous amount. There are so many things I've always wanted to do. There are so many things I want to do—I'm not going to have time to do them all. In my Blackpool days, I'd go out and have a couple of drinks on a Saturday night, but I'd always have to drink in moderation. But that's not the sort of thing I've missed.

You have to give up so many things you would like to do. For example, it must be frustrating for your wife—the number of times she must want to go out after Wednesday. In my Blackpool days, I never went out after Wednesday. I've lost count of the number of functions we could have gone to on Thursdays and Fridays. She stopped asking me. So many times I've had to say to friends, "If you don't mind, I'd rather not go." At other times, people rang up and said. "We wanted to invite you, Jim, but we knew it was too late in the week."

There are other things I'd like to do: water ski-ing, for example. A number of my mates are water skiers, and I would have liked to have joined them, but of course I would never risk it. It wouldn't have been worth it. On Thursdays and Fridays I wouldn't even play golf, or do anything that might tire me. From Thursday onwards, my mind was occupied with what was going to happen on the Saturday. In many ways, a lot of your life goes by.

You get some players like Glyn James. He tells me he likes to get up on a Saturday morning and go and paint the car, and do this sort of thing, to help him take his mind off the match. I didn't do that. I was quite happy just to lie in bed for a while, then get up and read a book. Late in the morning, I had breakfast: my only meal, on a Saturday, before a match. Then I just took my time getting ready, and rested until the time came to leave for Bloomfield Road. "Conservation of energy" you could call it.

My speed got me out of a lot of trouble at times. I think speed is very important to a footballer. Most good players have had a bit of pace. As a manager, my ideal is to have ten fast players. And I always preferred to play alongside chaps who could travel a bit.

I preferred to play against a winger who'd take me on down the line, because of course this was my strength. The chap who comes inside is always very difficult to tackle: you just have to play him across the park. The worst wingers to play against are the chaps who don't give you a chance to tackle them. Jimmy Mullen used to be like this. He was a very dangerous winger. He never used to take you on. He just used to get the ball over. It's a very frustrating game then for a full-back.

In some ways, I was an instinctive player. I don't think I was very good at weighing up the rest of the game. I think this was one of my weaknesses. I got so wrapped up with what was going on in my team, and in my part of the field, that I didn't pay a great deal of attention—not enough attention—to the opponents; except, of course, to the chaps who were immediately around me. I often wonder whether I saw enough when I was actually playing. Sometimes, when I came off the field, somebody would say (referring

The 1953 Cup Final. "See the Conqueror mounts in triumph. . . . Riding on the clouds his chariot"

Blackpool Football Club, 1953 vintage. *Left to right.* Back row: Eddie Shimwell, Harry Johnston, George Farm, John Crosland, Cyril Robinson, Allan Brown; middle row: Joe Smith (Manager), Stanley Matthews, Ernie Taylor, Stan Mortensen, Jackie Mudie, Bill Perry, John Lynas (Trainer); front row: Ewan Fenton, George McKnight, Hugh Kelly, Tommy Garrett

to an opponent), "He played well." And I might not even have noticed him.

I can read a game all right. I think you can develop a tactical sense. Among the managers of today, there are some pretty good tacticians, even though some of them were only second-rate players. No, that's not fair: "second-rate" is the wrong word. What I mean is that they never achieved international status. And yet they are in quite good positions today. They've developed a tactical sense by learning from others: by watching and by being good listeners. They've been enthusiastic and willing to work hard.

The only booking of my career was against Norwich, in a Cup replay at Bloomfield Road. Norwich was one of Blackpool's bogey teams in the early sixties: in three successive seasons, they knocked us out of the League Cup twice, and the F.A. Cup once. Billy Punton had been in the Army at roughly the same time as I was. He was quite a good player. He was quick, very quick. He played against me two or three times, and he did pretty well every time. In this Cup replay, he went past me the first time he got the ball. The next time, I stopped him; and he went flying over the top of me. The referee said, "Look here. You're catching him on the turn." I said, "Well, if that's what you think." The next time Billy Punton got the ball, he came inside me. I put my left foot out, and he fell over the top of my foot. The referee said to me, "I won't tell you again." The next time, Billy had the ball with his back to me. I tackled from behind, trying to stop him from turning, and he went down again. The referee never cautioned me properly. He just said, "I'm booking you for that." So I said, "All right." I think I probably deserved it. But I've seen some players who have been booked very unfairly. A few of today's referees seem to think they haven't had a match unless they've booked somebody. I think they're trying to give their pencils some work.

I developed the overlap with Stanley Matthews. He used to get marked very tightly. The opposing winger often used to go back and mark him, so he had the full-back and the winger marking him. He often found himself holding-on to the ball. Then one day he said, "You could come past me." "I know that," I replied, "but I wasn't sure whether I should suggest it." And he said, "Let's try it, and see what happens." And so we did it once or twice, and it came off. Joe Smith was quite pleased with the move, but he never said a lot about it. He just said, "Make sure you get back." At that time, there was nobody taking my place, so I *had* to get back.

Once or twice in the early days, I went up the wing, and the crowd shouted, "Get back, Armfield." "What are you doing up

M

here?", they used to ask. But we pressed on with it. It's amazing how many teams got caught by the move in the early days. We probably overdid it at first. Fans used to come to Bloomfield Road and expect me to do the overlap. I felt I was obliged to do it for them. I also used to do it when we were away from home. If the local left-back clobbered me, the whole crowd used to cheer and think it was marvellous. The overlap requires a lot of physical effort. All the surprise has gone now, because so many full-backs are doing it. In the England team, Bobby Robson used to cover me, whenever I went up. He was very good.

I was captain of the school cricket team for two years. Cricket is an easier game to captain than football, but it was useful experience. I was never captain of rugger, although I played in the school side; and I was in the athletics team for three years. Many times I've thought to myself that full-back is not a good position for a captain. I always tried to encourage my team. I was never a demonstrative captain. I never went around waving my arms—like some captains do, and which a lot of spectators are taken-in by. I used to go around talking to my players, and I passed on messages, which a lot of people didn't see.

If a team is going to be any good, you should have ten or eleven captains in it: chaps who are willing to help each other. I think a captain is born. I always tried to captain by example. I know that I had shortcomings as a player—I've always known that—but never once, when I've come off the field, has someone said to me, "You didn't try your best." Whether you are 15, 25, or 35, you can only try your hardest and do what is physically your best. The chaps at Blackpool knew—or I like to think they knew—that I always tried my hardest; so they could never turn round and say, "Well, you didn't run back." I liked them to think that if I *could* have got back, I would have got back. A good captain sets an example not only on the field, but in training as well, and by the way he lives. You've got to gain the players' respect.

Being captain affected my game in the early days. I think I tried to do too much. I used to run around a lot, unnecessarily. Becoming captain definitely affects some players. I think it depends on how responsible they feel in taking the job. For example, you tell a chap off, for doing something wrong, and 30 seconds later you go and make a terrible error yourself, and you feel a bit guilty about it. You only get over that sort of thing with experience.

As captain, you have to believe in yourself and trust your own decisions: for example, when you make changes on the field. I'll tell you a story about one manager we had at Blackpool. We were losing 2-0, and I made a change on the field. We eventually lost

3-0. After the game, the manager came to me and said, "Why did you make that change?" "Well," I replied, "because I thought it was necessary." "Don't make any changes without asking me," he said. "All right," I said, "I'll resign the captaincy, and you take over the captaincy as well. Either you have a captain or you don't have a captain." Football captaincy (the part that is done on the field) is not as big a job as it used to be. At one time, you used to do a lot of things on your own initiative, but now you're always getting instructions from the dug-out.

For some players who are given the captaincy, it lifts them up right away, and they go out and do great things. But, for me, it was a bit of a burden at first. At the time, I thought I was rather an unnecessary choice. I was made captain of Blackpool in December 1960. I was twenty-five. At first, I felt I was being thrown in at the deep end, but then I thought to myself, "Crikey, you're twenty-five now. You're half-way there! If you can't take it now, you're never going to get it." So I took it. I soon found that there are a lot of sides to the captain's job. You're not just on duty on a Saturday. From Monday to Friday, problems are always cropping up. I enjoyed being captain: in some ways I did. There were other times when I wished I hadn't become captain, and I felt like throwing in my shirt. But that's part and parcel of it all. You laugh it off afterwards.

A captain is sometimes justified in shouting at a player. There are some players you've got to shout at, or they go to sleep. They tend to wander. And there are some players you've got to talk to and encourage all the time. I remember one chap we had at Blackpool: if you *didn't* get onto him, he used to just fade out of the game completely. He needed picking up all the time. He *needed* it. You've got to understand people, and you've got to treat them as individuals. There were two or three chaps in the Blackpool team a year or so ago: if I shouted at them, their game collapsed. Many lads thrive on encouragement. I used to thrive on encouragement. If people told me I was playing well, I *felt* as though I was playing well. There was one chap in our side: as soon as he did something well, I always said to him right away, "Well done". I like to feel it gave him a bit of a lift, because he was nervous at the start of a game.

I found a big difference between captaining Blackpool and captaining England. It was much easier captaining England because I had ten international-class players with me. I used to try and talk to them, and encourage them, and do what I could to get the best out of them. And, as with Blackpool, I tried to show them, by example, how much effort was required from them. But captaining England isn't a seven-day-a-week job, as club captaincy is.

My international career didn't get off to a lucky start. I went to Sheffield, in February 1956, to play for the England Under-23 team against Scotland. I had a cold when I set off. Within 24 hours, I had tonsillitis. Don Howe took my place and then had quite a long run, at right-back, in the full England team.

Season 1958–59 was action-packed for me. I began it in the Blackpool reserves and finished it in the England team. I'd been in the first team for two or three seasons. Then Ronnie Suart became manager. He put the team up for the first match, and I wasn't in. It was as simple as that. He said to me, "You're young. You'll work your way into the side." Then Jackie Wright got injured, after about six matches, and I came back into the side. In previous seasons, I'd played for the Under-23s, and I'd played well. In September 1958, I was appointed captain of the Under-23s. Within the space of ten days, I went from Central League football to the captaincy of the Under-23s and into Blackpool's first team.

I can remember my England début really well. You only have one international début, after all. We were playing against the world champions, Brazil. I was at left-back. It was a very cloudy day. Planes flew over the stadium before the match started, and dropped leaflets: it was just like snow falling. I think the leaflets were of a political nature. As many as possible were cleared off the pitch, but there were still some left when play began. I've never seen so many photographers and radio people at a match. It was murder. From the time we got on the field, it took about twenty-five minutes to get the game started. As I look back, I don't think we were really prepared for all this hubbub and excitement. That was a day I'll never forget. I don't think I'll ever forget any of my England games. I'll remember them all, because each was an individual experience.

I had one bad game at Wembley, which I can bring to mind right away, but I enjoyed most of the games I played there. I used to thrive on the atmosphere. I often look back on a World Cup qualifying game in Portugal as one of the best games I ever played for England. It was in May 1961, and we drew one-each. The temperature was very high. I don't know where I got my strength from in that heat but I played like a man inspired that day.

People always say that my best game for England was against Spain—at Wembley, in October 1960—when I was marking Gento. Another match that is often mentioned is the one against the Rest of the World, three years later, when I was marking Gento. He was my rabbit, I suppose. You get players who become your rabbits, and you get other players, who are not a patch on Gento, who'll give you a terrible afternoon. That's what happens in football.

The first time I played against Gento was in Madrid, in May 1960. We lost 3-0. I thought I'd played a blinder, when I came off the field. You know when you've played well. The little fellow hardly had a kick of the ball. I'd heard so much about him: I was very keyed-up when I went out. I used to flatter myself that I was a bit of a runner. I knew he had quite a bit of pace, but I was surprised to find that, pushing the ball past me, he gave me about five yards' start. I thought, "He's a cheeky devil." I turned round and chased the ball, and beat him to it. When I passed the ball back to the goalkeeper, Gento was still four or five yards back. From then on, his confidence went. He realized that he couldn't outrun me, and I never feared him after that.

The strange thing was that Gento and I developed a sort of subtle understanding. He was a quiet fellow. He never said anything, really. He just got on with the game. Occasionally he would mumble something in Spanish under his breath. He was a scrupulously clean player, a perfect gentleman on the field. Gento was quite a character. I had a bit of a soft spot for him, really. Even though I played well against him, I realized that he was a very good player.

I broke a toe in a match against the Football League, on the evening before the 1963 Cup Final, and I had to miss the game against Czechoslovakia a few days later. This ended my run of thirty-one consecutive games for England. I came back for the second match of the tour, against East Germany, and I played in the third match, in Switzerland, which we won 8-1.

It was in the following season that I suffered the worst injury of my career. We were at Ipswich for the last match of the season. I tore my groin open. I was running with the ball, but there was nobody near me at all. I just fell on the ground. It was the worst pain I've ever had. I felt as though I'd been shot or knifed. There I was on the ground, and the crowd were laughing. We'd only been playing for nine or ten minutes. The referee said, "Come on. Get up." I said, "I wish I could!" I was in agony, and they had to get a stretcher. Within a quarter of an hour, there was a big swelling on my hip. I couldn't dress myself. I couldn't bend down to put my shoes and socks on. One of our late directors, Dr Ken Shepherd, was with us. He gave me some pills. But for him, I would have been in agony.

Alf Ramsey was at Ipswich that day. He said, "Well, it looks as though you're snookered for the tour." We were going in about a month to South America for the "little" World Cup. He said,

"I think I'll take George Cohen then." And I replied, "I'll let you know, three weeks from now, how I feel." In the end, of course, George went. I saw a specialist, and he said, "You've had it. You're finished." I thought to myself, "Well, I'll have a go at getting fit again." I worked on it solidly for four months. I bathed in the sea; I did exercises; and I gradually got fit again. In fact, when the next season started, I played in the first match. The specialist couldn't believe it. I've still got a lump inside the groin, but it has never really affected me much.

George Cohen did quite well when he first came into the England team, and he did even better when he'd had a year or two at international level. I was a bit unlucky again in 1966. Alf recalled me for the World Cup squad. England's game in Finland, at the end of June, was to prove to be my last international. I captained the side again, and we won 3-0. The World Cup was only two weeks away. In the last minute of this game, a chap stood on my toe, and soon it was all swollen up. When we came to play in Denmark, Alf said, "How do you feel?" "I can't even put my boot on," I replied. So he put George in again. But for my injury, I must have been in with a chance of selection for the 1966 World Cup team.

In my mid-thirties, my will-to-win was as strong as ever. I still wanted Blackpool to win. I got terribly disappointed when we lost. I don't think there was any secret behind my continuing love of the game. It was just a pure and simple zest for playing football. At Blackpool, I did exactly the same training as the younger players. On a Saturday I was expected to do as much as they did, so I didn't ask for any favours during the week.

Towards the end of my Blackpool days, I had to rest more, but I've never had weight problems. In fact, I'm a bit peculiar: I've gone the other way. As the years have gone by, I've got thinner. I used to weigh 12st 13lb when I started at Blackpool; when I left the club, I was just breaking 12st. I eat less now, but that isn't by choice. I think that, as you get a little bit older, you just feel like eating less.

My boys are football fanatics—the pair of them. Duncan played his first game for the school team—the under-elevens—a year or so ago. He was only eight. I asked him what position he played, and he said, "*Right-back*." I said, "What's wrong with right-back? It's good enough for me." The younger boy, John, is more interested in the professional game: he knows all the names, and he likes to go to matches. John is mad on football. They're both very keen, but you can't tell, at this age, how they'll get on.

There are not as many comedians in football as there used to be.

I honestly think that there are fewer personalities today. The game has lost people like Jimmy Scoular, Roy Paul, Ernie Taylor, Stan Mortensen. There was *something* about them. If you think back, you can roll off names of the characters there have been in football.

The players whom I've admired the most have been older than I am. I think you always look to the older players. The best player I ever played with was Stanley Matthews, even though he was in his late thirties when I first came to Blackpool Football Club. I liked his dedication, his pace, his fitness, and his know-how. I thought he was tremendous. Few people of today realize just how good he was. You can't tell them now, because they say he'd get marked out of the game, if he was playing today. Teams tried to mark him out of the game then, but they couldn't do it. He was intelligent enough to have been able to adapt himself to present-day tactics. He was at home in the centre of the field and on the wing. Everywhere he went, he could play well. And he was *superbly* fit. I've seen him run fellows, half his age, into the ground.

Then there was Tom Finney, of course. Tom was one of the best all-round footballers I have ever seen. If somebody asked me, "What was his strength?", I'd say, "He had the lot." He had pace. His shooting was good. He could dribble. He could head the ball. He could do the lot. Tom was a player's player. As you watched him, you'd say to yourself, "I wish I could do half of what he does." He was never quite the world attraction that Matthews was: he didn't have Matthews' name or fame. Matthews was a bigger crowd-puller than Tom. What they shared—one of the great things about them both—was modesty. Modesty always gets a good mark in my book. I don't like conceited players.

The next one we go to is Di Stefano. He is possibly the greatest midfield-player-cum-striker that I've seen. His skill was beautiful to watch: it was all clean, neat. He was more of a precision player than Finney or Matthews. Without Di Stefano, Real Madrid wouldn't have been half the side it was. He didn't just rely on his own individual skill, he relied on the players around him as well; and he made other players work with him. He fed Gento, the left-winger, and he took ten years off Puskas. He made Del Sol into a world-class player.

The best all-round player of my own sort of age was Bobby Charlton. He personifies so much that is good in football: his enthusiasm to play, his shooting power, and this sort of thing. Talking now of players who are over thirty, there have been one or two other good ones in my time: Ronnie Flowers, Bobby Robson, Ray Wilson, Bryan Douglas, Dave Mackay. And, of course, Johnny Haynes and Jimmy Greaves. Jimmy was an exciting player, a great guy. These are the players I'll remember. We were all pals. A chap who could have been as good as any of them—as I look back and reflect—was the late John White. I don't think we had really seen the best of him. He was just becoming a really good player. Tottenham had a great side in those days.

Today you've got players like Best, Bremner, Colin Bell, Francis Lee, and Alan Ball. They're all good players, but I think one or two of them are just short of the flair—the *instinctive* flair—of some of the older generation of players. Some of the stars of today play like machines.

The difference between a great player and a good player is that a great player does the unexpected more often. A great player can do the impossible. And a great player *looks* different: it might be only a little thing, like pulling his shorts a little higher than anybody else. If I go and see a great player, I expect him to make mistakes, of course; but I'm looking for something which only he can do. I remember one famous occasion with Matthews at Chelsea. He limped off the field about twenty minutes from the end. We were losing 2-1, and he'd scarcely had a kick of the ball. The crowd shouted at him: "You're finished, Matthews. You're finished." He came back about five minutes later, with his leg all plastered up, and he said, "Give me the ball as soon as you get it." We gave him the ball, and one of the Chelsea full-backs kicked him. Stanley played in those last fifteen minutes as though somebody had injected him with a pile of drugs. I felt sorry for the full-back. Matthews tore him to shreds. Blackpool won in the end. Near the finish, Matthews trickled right through their defence, on his own, and scored. It was a *coup de grâce*, a finale. He silenced Chelsea, he silenced the crowd, he silenced everybody, with his own individual brilliance. A good player can do a lot of good things, but only a brilliant player can do something like that.

There have been several players who have had brilliance, but couldn't produce it regularly. I think the best example of this is Len Shackleton. On his day, you would have paid a million pounds for him—*if* you saw him on his day. There are a lot of players like that: "He would have been a good player if. . . ." And you can never say what the "if" is.

27

TONY GREEN
£150,000, and Cheap at the Price

In every walk of life, there are two types of people: there are those who think and strive and plot and plan, and are supremely conscious of what they are doing; and there are men and women of action who cannot tell you how they do this, or why they do that. Tony Green is a member of the second group. He is a naturally-gifted footballer, in an age that produces a *hundred* stereotyped players for every *one* player of individuality and character. Everything that Tony Green does on the football field reveals character: his quickness of thought and movement, his Peter-Doherty-like desire to be always in the game, his way of running, his goal-scoring.

At a time when professionals are taking themselves and their sports very seriously—some would say "too seriously"—the most striking feature of Tony Green's game is his enjoyment of it. For the whole 90 minutes, he wants to be involved. He always wants to be where the play is at its most hectic. And, despite years of brutal treatment, he shows no fear of ruthless defenders. Tony Green is a player without inhibitions. He is as likely to play half-heartedly, as a patriot is to betray his country.

Stan Mortensen brought Green to Blackpool for £15,500—one of the football bargains of the decade. Within months, Green was valued at ten times his cost price. But Morty was not in a selling mood. He once said—and he meant every word—"Even if a club offered more than £150,000, we would not be interested in selling this lad."

As long as I live, I shall not forget Tony Green's début for Blackpool. It was at Bloomfield Road, against West Bromwich Albion, in May 1967. A good second-rate player is content to submerge himself slowly into the atmosphere and first team of his new club: like the religious rite that calls for the newcomer to wade into the sea, until *eventually* he is totally immersed. But the ways of genius are swifter. Tony Green immediately dominated his forward-line. This was no début; it was a take-over.

He showed his potential as a striker, with several powerful shots at goal. His mid-field play won him an ovation at the end of the match: time and time again, he chose to try an adventurous through-ball, rather than the easier, safer cross-field pass. And his quick reflexes demoralised the opposition. During the second half, a defender, irritated by Green's elusiveness, lunged at him. Green was racing down the right wing. Seeing the impending tackle, he flicked the ball away, leapt into the air to avoid being kicked, soared gracefully back to the ground, recovered his footing, re-covered the ball, and sped down the wing. This incident takes longer in telling than in the doing. It was a masterpiece of timing, quick thinking, and self-confidence.

Within weeks of his début, he was being favourably compared to Alan Ball, and Green shares became an attractive commodity on the transfer market. Managers of most of the wealthy clubs in the country lusted after his signature.

When he was on the verge of winning his first Scottish cap, he was maimed by a torn Achilles tendon, an injury that has ended the careers of many players. He was absent from first-team foot-ball from the close season of 1969 until September 1970. He missed the whole of Blackpool's promotion season (1969–70). Just as he was returning to fitness, he had two more set-backs: a strained tendon in his right foot and a thigh-muscle injury. Some people said he was injury-prone. Many thought he would never play again. After weeks of speculation about his future, he made a splendid come-back against Everton, the League Champions. Less than five months later, he made his début for Scotland.

It is hard for anyone, who is not a professional sportsman, to appreciate the full merit of Green's recovery. He was out of first-team football for a year and a half. To a professional—primed to a high degree of fitness, by training four or five days a week—a year and a half is an eternity. To any player—especially to one who relies on pace, and quickness on the turn—the Achilles tendon is a crucial part of bodily equipment. The operation was bold and imaginative. For player, wife, surgeon, and football club —courage and patience triumphed.

Although genius can fluctuate, genius is incapable of producing the ordinary or the routine. Tony Green's goal-scoring is living proof of this truth. I have never seen him score a commonplace goal. Every single one—each in its own way—has been memorable. I vividly recall a goal at Highbury in a League Cup match. He shot from 25 yards, with an almost casual swing of the leg, and so quickly and powerfully did he strike that the goalkeeper didn't move until the ball was in the net. A year or so later, he scored another 25-yarder; this time at West Ham. I was watching Green closely. He had felt, sensed, and anticipated the goal—seconds before he actually kicked.

One of the many sad aspects of Mortensen's departure from the managership of Blackpool was the breaking of his manager-player relationship with Tony Green. They believed in each other. In July 1968, Tony Green signed a long-term contract with Black-pool. Morty handed him the contract. Tony picked up a pen and wrote his name at the bottom. "But aren't you going to read it?", asked Morty. And Tony replied, "If you say it's OK, that's enough for me. I *know* it's all right."

Off the field, Tony is the most modest of footballers. He and his charming wife, Tricia, have a well-chosen sense of values, pre-ferring harmony and family and friendship to 25in colour TV and a four-car garage.

Tony's behaviour on the field is an example to all other high-valued players: no retaliation, no arguing with referees, no friction with other members of his team. If Tony misplaces a pass—a rare occurrence—he waves to his team-mate, as if to say, "Sorry, Jock. I'll try to do better for you next time."

In a tight situation, in an era of tight defences, Tony can almost always make space for himself with a deft side-step. He has wonderfully quick reflexes, rivalling Cassius Clay—when Clay was a young man—for speed of thought, and springiness and grace of footwork.

Tony is a true professional, never allowing a problem *off* the field to interfere with his game. At the beginning of the 1971–72 season, he refused the new terms offered him and decided to stay on his existing contract. Despite this, he made week-end headlines, again and again, because of his fine performances. In October 1971, Newcastle paid £150,000 for Tony—£90,000 in cash, and a player in part-exchange—making him the most valuable Scottish player in football history And so Blackpool—town and club—lost one of her favourite adopted sons. Twenty years from now, supporters will still be talking about his brilliant last match for Blackpool: a League Cup game against Aston Villa.

In the life and career of most sportsmen, there comes a turning-point: a year, a week, or a match, in which they establish their greatness beyond any dispute. For Alan Ball—one of Blackpool's most famous exports—that turning-point came on the afternoon of the 1966 World Cup Final at Wembley. For Tony Green, the red-letter day was May 22, 1971, Scotland v. England, also at

Wembley. Many a player can stand-out in a winning side; but Scotland, that afternoon, were a well-beaten XI. Tony Green was one of the best players on the field, prompting his team-mates with enthusiasm and dozens of accurate passes. Tony looked like a world-beater. Correction: not "looked like". He *is* a world-beater.

28

HOW I SIGNED TONY GREEN
by Stan Mortensen

I first heard the name *Tony Green* not long before I signed him.
I'd heard reports about this boy, so I decided I would like to see
him. A few weeks before, I had gone to Scotland, on a recommendation from one of my scouts. I watched Cowdenbeath, and I
fancied the left-back, a lad called Henry Mowbray. He showed
plenty of determination. He had plenty of guts and spirit, and he
was prepared to run and graft. So I made an offer for him, which
was accepted after a little bit of argie-bargie. By now, I was very
anxious to see Tony Green. I decided to go and watch him, and I
picked a day when Cowdenbeath were playing Albion Rovers.
Mowbray was playing for Cowdenbeath, and Green was to play for
Albion. I was ready to sign Henry Mowbray, because I had already
agreed a fee with his club. The kick-off was in the morning. In the
afternoon, Aberdeen were to play Celtic in the Scottish Cup Final.

Harry Johnston and I went to the first match. It was *obvious*,
right from the kick-off, that Tony Green was the man Cowdenbeath feared most. A Cowdenbeath winger—I think it was—was
under instructions to follow Tony everywhere. I was intrigued by
this, and I had watched this kid for only a few minutes before I
said, "This is a great player." Something just clicked inside me
about him, and, after the match, I made an offer of £10,000. Mr
Fagan, the Albion Chairman, laughed at me. He said, "We want
more than that for this boy." We had quite a long chat, and in
the end I said, "Well, we'll leave it for now. I'll meet you at the
Cup Final."

In the afternoon, Harry Johnston and I were in the stand. I was
looking all over for Mr Fagan. Then, at last, I spotted him: he
was about four rows in front. I was so determined to get Tony
Green that I got up in the middle of the match, and walked down
the stairs. I asked the chap sitting next to Mr Fagan if I could have
his seat for a few minutes. We decided to meet in the boardroom

after the match. So I met him, and I made a further offer for
Tony Green. He said it still didn't come up to what he required.
He wanted £15,000. So I said, "Well, we'll give you £13,500. If he
plays for me a dozen-or-so times in the first team, I will give you
another £2,000." And Mr Fagan agreed to that.

Then the problem was to find Tony Green. Harry Johnston and
I had a two- or three-hour search before we eventually caught up
with him. We went to his home and he wasn't there. We made a
few phone calls to various places, and eventually we did meet
Tony in the evening. I talked to him. I wanted him to come to
Blackpool, and have a good look round. I suggested that he, and
his mother and father, and his girl friend, should come to Blackpool. Blackpool speaks wonders to everybody who comes. It's a
fabulous place. I was so confident in Blackpool: I think it's a
great thing to fetch people here and let them look for themselves.
So they came, and they had a wonderful week in Blackpool. They
stayed in the digs where I said I would put Tony when he came
to live in Blackpool. He was going to be living in very good digs:
his mother and father knew that he was going to be well looked
after. He signed-on for Blackpool without any problem.

I brought that kid to Blackpool, and I put him in the first team
straight away, in his first week at the club. We were playing West
Brom. His début was fantastic. He had come from a Second
Division team in Scotland, and he walked into Blackpool's first
team. We were beaten 3-1, but Tony got a standing ovation as he
left the field. From that very moment, the Blackpool public took
to Tony Green. I think he is a great player, this boy. I particularly
like the spirit and heart he shows in every game. And the guts.
He never stops trying. He will run and run and run, for you, till
he drops. He gives everything he's got to the game.

Harry Johnston agreed with me, fully, regarding Tony Green.
I may watch a fellow who I think is not playing very well; but he
may still show qualities which interest me. I could see a player
have a real stinker of a game—never kick the ball—and yet I
could still want to see him again. But I am not a fellow who wants
to see a player six or seven times. I like to see players and make
up my mind quickly about them. When I was manager of Blackpool—provided we had the money, and provided we needed to
fill a position in the team—if I saw a player I liked, I'd say, "We'll
have him." Even if this was the first time I'd seen him play.

I've heard that a Fulham scout had been to watch Tony Green
week after week—before Tony joined Blackpool. And Tony had
trials with Blackburn Rovers a few weeks before he came to us.
And so did Tommy Hutchison and Henry Mowbray, funnily

enough—at the same club. The three players I bought from Scotland! I didn't know about this until they had been on the staff at Blackpool for quite a long time. When I learned about it, I was quite shocked.

I recommended Alan Skirton to Blackpool when he was at Bath City, but Blackpool didn't buy him. He went to Arsenal. Then, a few years later, Blackpool paid £30,000 for him. Another player I recommended to Blackpool Football Club was a lad called Tony Book. He was playing for Bath City at the same time. Later, he became a Manchester City full-back. He won League and F.A. Cup honours with City. Actually, I stuck my neck out when I signed Tony Green; because there had been a report from two Blackpool directors that he wasn't good enough. So you can understand the risk I took.

Tony is such a natural player. While I was manager, I always tried to help players to make full use of their own individual ability. Today, too many set ideas are thrust at players. They are given set jobs to do; they are not supposed to get into *this* position or *that* position. I think this is ridiculous.

A player like Tony Green has got to be encouraged to use *every bit* of his individual ability. He has to be given the freedom to do the unexpected: so many games are won just off the cuff, by a fellow who shows a sudden flash of brilliance. If we try to produce stereotyped players, this flair will never be seen.

A team needs flair in its attack, but it also needs discipline in defence. One of my strict rules to full-backs was "*Never ever* attempt to beat a man with the ball". The full-back must either kick the ball clear, or pass it to a team-mate who is unmarked. To try and get a full-back to beat a wing man is asking for a lot of trouble, because, if the winger takes the ball away from the full-back, he may get a clear run to goal. If the full-backs ever took big risks, I used to come down on them heavily.

Many, many great players of the past had little or no coaching in their younger days. They just came into the game, and they were natural ball-players. Tony Green is like them. He is one of the most natural ball-players I have ever seen in my life. What a wonderful come-back this kid has made, after having that terrible injury. I think it is a personal triumph for Tony. Since his return, he has done so much in such a short time.

Jimmy Armfield used to come to me and say, "Don't let Tony play in the practice match. He might get injured." This is how the players themselves feel about the lad. When Tony was in the Blackpool team, and if he was performing well—if he was on song —he gave confidence to the players around him.

I would tell Tony to try out a particular move in a game, and he would try his utmost to do what he was asked. We had lots of sessions with Tony, and, in particular, we wanted to brush-up on his shooting. We didn't really have to do anything else with this lad. In fact, he hits a very good ball. He has been very unfortunate at times: some good chances he has made for himself have just not gone into the net.

I think Tony would make a tremendous winger. I always thought that would be his best position, because, whenever he gets the ball, he carries it thirty or forty yards. When he is playing as a mid-field man, he picks the ball up in his own penalty-area and, before you know what has happened, he has carried it right up-field. He is so quick with the ball.

We've had some good players in the Blackpool team in the last few years, but, if Tony had been in a better team, he might have been even better than he is now. On the other hand, he mightn't have been as good as he is now. It's a problematical issue. He had a lot of work thrust upon him at Blackpool, and he thrives on work. If he had been in a team with a lot of fine players, he mightn't have shown up as well as he did in the Blackpool team. He has so much natural talent, this boy. You could play Tony in any position, and he would play well.

"It's almost Blackpool v. Hungary", said the *Daily Mirror*. Four Blackpool players represent England in November 1953. *Left to right*. Back row: Ramsey, Wright, Merrick, Johnston (Blackpool), Dickinson, Eckersley; front row: Matthews (Blackpool), Taylor (Blackpool), Mortensen (Blackpool), Sewell, Robb

Roy Gratrix, an England centre-half whom England never chose

29

TONY GREEN
— in an Interview

I had a very good friend at school. Peter went on to university, and I went to technical college. He's living in a great big multi-storey block of flats. He's had umpteen jobs. We have a laugh together: he says, "If you didn't play football, you'd be in the same position as me."

I can only vaguely remember the first house I lived in. I was the youngest of three brothers. We three, and my mother and father, all lived in the same room. In Glasgow, they call it "a single end". It was a bedroom and a kitchen—all in one wee room. The next place we moved to had two rooms: one bedroom and a kitchen. Then we moved to a new housing estate. We were miles away from my Dad's work. He's a docker. He worked on the other side of Glasgow, and he used to have to get up at about 6 o'clock. But we had two bedrooms: my mother and father moved house for the sake of my two brothers and me. That was the first house I can really remember. I lived there from when I was seven until my signing for Blackpool.

I think of those days, and then I think of when I got married. I told Morty I was getting married. He took us around Blackpool, and we picked a house. Blackpool F.C. had the house wallpapered. They got it all ready, and all we had to do was move in. We had three bedrooms. When I compare this with what my mother and father once had, I can't fail to appreciate how lucky I am.

There have been no sportsmen in my family. I've never been good at golf or swimming or athletics, or any other sport apart from football. I've been helped at every club I've played for. So many people helped me in my early days. I could name six or seven who were great, but it is hard to single out any particular person. When you're a schoolboy, you usually have a different manager every year.

I was almost eight when we moved to the new housing estate.

N

They were still building when we came, and so there were a lot of wide-open spaces. Boys from one street would play against a team from another street. I can't remember how many players there were on each side. Sometimes, there'd be only one pair of boots between two players: one boy would have a boot on his right foot and a gym shoe on the left; and another boy would have a boot on his left foot and a gym shoe on the right. There used to be big arguments if a team borrowed a good player from another street.

I used to play football every day. Everywhere I went, with my brothers John and Thomas, we always had a ball. When we went shopping, I would go on one side of the street, and one of my brothers would go on the other. It was a miniature dual-carriage-way. There were trees right down the middle of the street, so we could pass to each other between the trees. I never did anything to make myself a better player. I've never done anything consciously. Quick reflexes and good ball-control are qualities you've either got or you haven't got.

Brother Eustace was very good to me. He was a teacher at a Roman Catholic school in Glasgow. He helped me when I was about eleven. That is the very first organised football I can remember. I did quite well in school football. I scored quite a few goals, but I was never top scorer. I was usually an inside-forward; but, if I played in a team with older lads, they'd put me on the wing because I was too wee for inside-forward. I was almost always the smallest on the field, but it didn't worry me. In fact it may have helped me: because I *had* to play the ball. If you're big for your age—in school football—you can often get away with brute strength.

I was a part-timer with Albion Rovers. I was at a technical college studying for a degree in maths and science. But I always wanted to be full-time player. I always had fabulous encouragement at home. My Dad used to come to most of my matches, and sometimes my mother used to come as well. But she used to get too excited, so she stopped coming. They were over the moon when I signed for Blackpool.

I learned later that Blackpool were said to have been interested in me some months before I joined them, but nothing happened. The first I knew was after a match. The Albion Chairman called me in, and introduced me to Stan Mortensen. We had a 12 o'clock kick-off, because it was the day of the Scottish Cup Final. We just said "Hello", and went to watch the Final.

I went back to my girl friend's house after the match, and Morty was there with Harry Johnston. It was exactly a year since Tricia

and I had started courting. Morty didn't have to sell me the idea
of joining Blackpool. I was dying to go to Blackpool. It was a
chance for me to better myself. I jumped at the offer.

Before that day, I hadn't even heard rumours that Blackpool
were interested in me. I heard whispers about other clubs—but
not about Blackpool. I think Fulham had watched me quite a bit,
and I heard that Dunfermline were interested in me. But you only
hear rumours: you never hear anything official.

I used to play inside-forward in my Albion days. I trained two
or three nights a week with Albion. Sometimes, it was Tuesday,
Wednesday, Thursday; at other times, it was just Tuesday and
Thursday. I was earning only £8 10s. a week. The £15,000 fee that
Blackpool paid for me was a lot of money for a Scottish Second
Division club. We used to have gates of 500. Probably the lowest
crowd during my Albion days was the last game I played for the
club—against Cowdenbeath. It was Cup Final day, and there were
only about 200 at the match.

My début for Blackpool was just like any other game. I'm
always excited before every match. I suppose I was a wee bit more
excited than usual. There were 10,000 people at Bloomfield Road
that day. To me, it was a helluva crowd. I thought it was like
Wembley. There was nothing at stake: we had been relegated, so
there was not a lot of kicking. I was quite surprised at this, because
when I used to watch First Division football on TV, there was
always somebody getting walloped. When I signed for Blackpool,
I thought it might take me a season to win a place in the first
team. And here I was—playing in my first week. I think I did quite
well in this match. You know in yourself if you've played well and
if you're happy with your game. I got a good press the next day.
If we've lost, or if I've played badly, I don't want to read any of
the Sunday papers; but if we've done well, then I buy the lot!

I enjoyed the atmosphere at Bloomfield Road. Everyone was
very friendly. It was like a new life. Jimmy Armfield and Gordon
Milne were very good to me. Jimmy is a good lad. He was always
there, if you wanted advice. You could always go and talk to him.
He was always ready to help anybody.

I found the English Second Division completely different from
the Scottish Second Division. They're as different as day and night.
In Scotland, we were part-timers; but here in England you're
playing for your living. In England, there's a lot more kicking.
It's rougher. It's faster. Players take the game a lot more seriously.
In the first part of my first season with Blackpool, I used to come
in at half-time exhausted. I used to feel sick. It was murder. But
I got stronger as the season went on.

Morty helped me a lot. I used to come back in the afternoons, and he used to help me with my shooting. You always knew, after a match, if he was pleased with you. If he didn't say, "Well done", you'd start thinking. He didn't like to get beaten, but he wasn't a bad loser. He was always the same: he was not the type who goes away and sulks. Morty was the sort of manager that everybody always tries hard for. If you did well, you were pleased for *him*.

I liked Morty, as a person and as a manager. He was fabulous . . . terrific. He always used the personal touch. When Tricia and I were looking for a house, Morty took us all over Blackpool. Then he took us around the shops to see what furniture we wanted, and he advised us. We'd walk into a shop and look around, and he'd say, "Not bad". Then he'd ask what discount we'd get. We got very good discounts, because everybody knew him.

And Morty's wife, Jean, also used to take a great interest in me. She used to tell Tricia, "Give him steaks. Keep him well." Tricia and I were out shopping one day. There was snow on the ground. We walked past the football ground. I was carrying a couple of bags. Jean came out, and said to Tricia, "Couldn't you carry one of the bags?" "Are you all right, Tony?", Jean asked. "Mind you don't slip. Do you want a lift home?"

When I got married, Morty used to pick me up in the morning. He lived just around the corner. One day he didn't come and so I went on the bus. I heard a car-horn tooting. I turned round, and there was Morty following the bus. I jumped off, without paying the fare, and he took me to the ground.

I think everybody likes Morty. It's *impossible* not to like him. He was a manager you could go and talk to, at any time. There was always a good atmosphere about the club. Everybody gave 100 per cent effort. You always ran hard, because you knew he'd be chuffed if we won.

When I first came to Blackpool, I was called "the new Alan Ball". It was just because we play in the same position; and we are both small, and we run about a lot. When Brian Kidd started playing for Manchester United, he was called "the new Denis Law". And when Gerry Ingram was knocking them in for Blackpool, he was called "the new Stan Mortensen". This sort of publicity dies down. I never feel outside pressures, either from the press or from the fans. I never think about it. Every week is the same to me. I've got my own standards. I always want to do well.

I don't think there are a lot of similarities between me and Alan Ball—in the way we play. He does a lot *off* the ball. He gets it, and he gives it, and he gets it back again. You don't so often see him go up the wing, and lick two men. He's got the ability to do it, mind you. He's a wee bit more experienced than I am. He's a good player.

One game that stands-out in my mind is the game at Huddersfield, at the end of 1967–68, the season when we almost won promotion. We were a bit unlucky that year. That is probably the most exciting League game I ever played in for Blackpool. But I can't say which was the best game I ever played for Blackpool. No particular match comes to mind.

My injury was in July 1969. My ankle had been giving me a bit of trouble, and then one day we were training. I hadn't trained for a couple of days, because my tendon had been feeling sore. I thought it would be OK. We were due to play Liverpool the next day, in a pre-season friendly. I ran past John McPhee, and the tendon must have just snapped. I looked up at John and said, "Did you kick me?" And he thought I was taking the mickey. He was nowhere near me. I was just sprinting past him. The tendon must have been ready to tear, because it had been giving me a bit of pain.

Mr Keith Barnes, a surgeon at Wrightington Hospital, performed the operation. And then, every time I went to the hospital, he was the one who gave me instructions. He always said, "So far, so good. Keep your fingers crossed." He was a really friendly fellow. Deep down, I always fancied my chances of making a come-back. Every report I got from Mr Barnes was good.

A number of people put doubts in my mind. While I was still hobbling about with a walking-stick, I got into a taxi. The driver, who obviously hadn't recognized me, said, "Have you got a bad leg? Tony Green has a bad leg, and he won't play again. He's finished." This happened several times.

I heard so many stories about somebody who knew somebody who had said that I would never play again. I got a bit fed up with it all. People used to come up to me in the street and say, "Will you ever play again?" And I would think to myself, "Well that's a *nice* question to ask." Newspaper reporters used to ask me the same question, and I would say under my breath, "Well, you've got a cheek. How do *I* know if I'll ever play again?" I now realize that these reporters were just doing their job. There were so many rumours going around, about me.

When I was injured, I thought that people were being cruel in saying that I would never play again. But I now realize that this is a natural reaction by people—when a player is out of the game for a long time. Since my injury, I've heard people say the same thing about Mike England and Terry Hennessey.

The most depressing time for me was early in 1970. I had hoped

to be playing again by this time. But, with more than half the
season gone, my come-back was away out on the horizon. My
plaster had been taken off, and I was using a walking-stick instead
of crutches, but I had no idea when I would be allowed to play
again.

Vin Conboy, the club's physiotherapist, helped me a lot. I spent
a lot of time with him until the end of season 1969–70. And, once
I was told I could start training again, I was never left on my own.
As soon as we had won promotion, there was somebody with me
every day. Les Shannon, Jimmy Meadows, and Len Graham: they
each took turns with me. I had to train all through the close
season of 1970.

Gordon Masson, a young wing-half who had broken his leg,
trained with me. For quite a while, we were on a par: we both
seemed to be recovering at the same rate. I got back into the
Blackpool team, but he was told that his career was finished. I felt
very sorry for him: we'd spent a lot of time together. Gordon's
bad luck made me all the more grateful that I was able to play
again.

I'll never forget the day when the specialist said, "Everything
is going well. You can start kicking a ball again." Those were the
most exciting words I'd ever heard. So I went to Bloomfield Road
with Vin Conboy, who had been such a good friend to me during
all the time that I was out of the game. When we got to Bloomfield Road, we found that it was all locked up! So we got the keys,
and went in. I got changed, put my boots on, and went onto the
pitch. It was great to be able to kick a ball again. It was something
I hadn't done for about a year. Vinny can remember the day of
the week and the exact time—almost to the second!—when I took
that first joyful kick at the ball.

I wouldn't exactly call it an exciting time, as my return to first-
team football came nearer. It was tough. It was harder than anything I'd known before. I couldn't run a lap at first, but everyone
at Bloomfield Road gave me plenty of encouragement. And people
like Harry Johnston and the secretary, Des McBain, were very
good to me. Blackpool looked after me well during my time out of
the game.

I was quite patient during most of my injury year: there was
nothing else I could be. I was always thinking about getting back
into Blackpool's first team. Everything was in stages. I didn't
worry about heavy tackling, or losing my speed, or things like that,
but, naturally, these questions were always at the back of my mind.
I just got fit, and got on with the game. When I came back from
injury, it was like starting all over again. At first, I struggled to

recover my strength and speed: I had to pace my game. Then, in the New Year (1971), I began to feel physically stronger.

In my first game back—against Everton—the pace was fantastic to start with. Everyone seemed to be buzzing around me. It was like being in the middle of twenty-one madmen, all running! I didn't know what was happening. In the second half, I felt a wee bit better. It's when you're not involved in a game that you start thinking, "Have I made a mistake? Have I come back too early?" I was still feeling the effects of a pulled muscle. I kept wondering if I'd done the right thing.

In my year out of the game, I couldn't train; and I lost weight. After I came back, I went up to 11st 5lb. So, for the first time in my life, I had to watch my weight. The only food I don't like is vegetables. I love steak and fish.

I don't smoke. I have a drink on a Saturday, but I don't drink to excess. A lot of people seem to think that footballers shouldn't drink. Now, a businessman has a few drinks, and the next morning he has a hangover—and he can't face work. But a player can have a couple of drinks on a Saturday, have a rest on Sunday, and feel fine. Unlike the businessman, the player has been training all week.

We have a lot of spare time, some weeks. But it evens itself out. A lot of times, we go away on a Friday and we're not back till Sunday morning. And sometimes the club takes us away for a few days before a match. Players, who don't own a business, have quite a lot of spare time. But if we trained every morning and every afternoon, we'd soon get fed up. There's got to be a happy medium.

We didn't do a lot of weight-training at Blackpool; at Newcastle, we do one afternoon a week. When Blackpool were training with Joe Lancaster, the athletics coach, it was agony for me. But it was nothing to my pal, Tommy Hutchison. Big Hutchie can run all day. I don't particularly enjoy running. I'll do it—because it gets me fit—but, if we run for a long stretch, I'll always find myself at the back.

I enjoy short sprints: anything that's short and sharp. I enjoy training when there's a ball involved. And I enjoy the spirit of things. There's always a laugh with the lads.

I start feeling excited on Friday night: I get a bit irritable. I always feel excited right up to kick-off time. Usually, it takes me a wee bit of time to fall asleep on a Friday night. But I take a hot drink, and, when I get to sleep, I sleep soundly. On a Saturday, I usually get up at about 10.30. I don't have any breakfast—just a cup of tea. I used to have a steak for lunch, but, when Brian Doyle came to Blackpool, he advised all the players not to have a steak before a match, because it takes quite a long time to digest. So nowadays I just have scrambled eggs and some toast at about 12 o'clock. Then we go for a game of snooker. It's just a way of passing the time before a game. It's either snooker or television.

I'll tell you a funny story about something that happened just before the start of a match. Bob Stokoe had told Dennis Booth that his job in the team was to win the ball, and then give it either to me or Alan Suddick. We were waiting in the tunnel, before going onto the field, and I heard Boothie mumbling: "Win it and give it. Win it and give it. Win it and give it." He seemed to be hypnotizing himself!

I don't have any real superstitions. At Blackpool, I sometimes liked to go out fourth: the captain, the goalkeeper, Henry Mowbray, and myself. But if I came out last, I didn't go onto the park feeling upset. It didn't bother me.

I found it hard to get keyed-up before my début for Scotland—against Belgium, early in 1971. I was a substitute; I didn't expect to be playing. It took me by surprise. Until half-time, I didn't know for sure that I would be playing. When I went on, we were 1-0 down. I played up front, alongside John O'Hare. Then, after ten minutes, they made it 2-0. They were well in front. They were playing before their home crowd. We were never in the game.

My first fully-fledged appearance for Scotland was in the 1971 Home International Championship. In two previous internationals, I'd come on as a substitute. The match against Ireland was on a Tuesday night. I was told on the Tuesday afternoon that I was going to play. It came as a complete surprise to me, because I didn't think I had a chance of being selected. There was a pool of about sixteen players, but one or two were injured.

I was one of the two mid-field men, playing very deep. We were playing 4-2-4, and we had to stick pretty rigidly to the formation, so there was little chance to go up front. I was afraid to wander, because I might have had to get back quickly. I was virtually playing right-half, which was completely different to what I was used to. We were beaten 1-0.

The match against England was on the Saturday. This time, all the Scottish players were fit, and I didn't know if I would be selected. I heard on the Friday—at a training session—that I would be in the team. I was really pleased, because they had the whole pool of players to choose from.

Against England, we had three men in mid-field, with one playing deep. This gave me, and Billy Bremner, opportunities to go up front. I really enjoyed this game, although, of course, you're always sorry when your team gets beaten. The atmosphere at Wembley was out of this world. The Scottish roar was terrific: it sounded like a million Scottish supporters. The only time you heard the English supporters was when their team scored, and even then it was not as loud a cheer as the Scottish one. This was the first time that I had ever *seen* Wembley, let alone played there.

I didn't think I would be playing in the game against Ireland. The season had finished, and I had been training on my own. In the last quarter of an hour of the Irish game I got cramp pretty badly, but I felt OK on the Wednesday, Thursday, and Friday. At the end of the England game, I felt a slight cramp, and so I rolled my socks down. The lads on the bench signalled that a substitute was going to be sent on. I was taken off, with only about seven minutes to go. I could have played for the rest of the match. Scotland's manager, Bobby Brown, probably thought he was doing me a favour. He said he was pleased with the way I'd played.

Sometimes, when I was walking down the street in Blackpool, people would stop me every few minutes. At other times, people never noticed me. I don't mind people coming up to me. The time to worry is when people ignore you. My family and I had quite a lot of privacy, because we lived in a quiet part of Blackpool.

I like playing with my little kiddie, Thomas. I don't have a lot of interests outside football. I don't read a lot. I like a game of snooker, and I like records. My favourite singers are Andy Williams, Jack Jones, Johnny Mathis, and the Beatles.

I believe in living for the present. I'd like to make as much money as I can: I suppose everybody would. But we didn't even have a car until we moved to Newcastle: to a little village a few miles outside the city. I'm not interested in status symbols. I just live my life the way I *want* to live my life.

Because of my injury, I played only a handful of games for Les Shannon. Bob Stokoe made quite a big impression when he came to Blackpool. He's a good manager. He's a completely different character from Morty. Bob Stokoe keeps himself to himself, whereas Morty is more extrovert. Both of them win your respect —but in different ways.

The fans at Bloomfield Road? I used to wish that the crowds would be bigger, but the Blackpool fans were always fair to me. I really enjoy playing in front of big crowds. It makes a big difference. I'd rather go to Liverpool, and play in front of the kop, than go to Oxford and play in front of 10,000.

I don't hear the crowd. Sometimes people say "The crowd was good" or "The crowd was bad", and I don't know what the crowd was like. But I do feel atmosphere. I know if it's good or bad. I get lifted if there's a good atmosphere.

I don't think about my game while I'm on the field. I just go out and play for an hour and a half. I do things automatically. If I can't lick somebody one way, I suppose I try other ways. I don't know if I concentrate, or what I do: I just get *involved*. I never think, "I'm going to do this." I just do it; and if it comes off, it comes off. I play by instinct. Journalists often ask me, "What went through your mind just before you scored?" Or "What were you thinking about when you were taking the ball down the right wing?" And I can't tell them. I just don't know.

I'm not particularly keen on talking tactics. Every week, we have a tactical talk: about how we've played, how our next opponents play, and about football in general. I *try* to listen. I *try* to get involved.

I watched a game a year or so ago. Bob Stokoe said "So-and-so did this" and "So-and-so did that"; but I would never notice these things in a million years. When I'm watching, I can notice things a bit better than when I'm playing; but I can't pinpoint things the way someone like Bob Stokoe can. I know if I've played well or not, but I can't go through my team, after a match, and say, "He had a good game, but *he* didn't." After a match, I can come into the dressing-room and say, "So-and-so played well", and everybody will contradict me.

In Britain, you have to get used to all types of grounds. I don't really mind heavy grounds, but I suppose they suit the bigger chaps better. Until recently, I wasn't sure what my favourite position was. It depended on how well I was playing. It depended on how my team was doing. Sometimes I preferred to play up front. Bob Stokoe used to encourage me to create more chances up front, and to look for goals. If I play inside-forward, I'll play inside-right or inside-left. I don't mind which.

If you play mid-field, you have to chase back a lot: you're involved with the play, but you haven't always got the ball at your feet. At Blackpool, I sometimes played with a No. 7 on my back, but I wasn't playing as a true winger. I don't like playing as a wing man. You're not in the game as much. You've got to rely on other people. Nowadays, I'm happiest when I'm playing in mid-field.

Sometimes I wear shin pads. Then I get fed up with them. I don't wear them for a while, until I get a few whacks on my shins. Then I start wearing them again. Then I take them off. And so on. I always wear one layer of bandage on my ankles. It's for support: to stop my feet from curling under me.

In some games, you can keep getting kicked, and yet never really get hurt. If you're running at full speed and somebody trips you up, you land on your face. It looks bad to the crowd, but you're not really hurt. The time when you do get hurt is when you go for a 50-50 ball. If you get there first, you often get whacked —but it isn't necessarily a foul.

Fouling is all part of the game. Sometimes I get annoyed; sometimes I don't. I suppose it depends on who does it. I used to get a wee bit more annoyed—than I'd ever done before—in the season when I returned from injury. Maybe that's because I had to sit out for a year. You wonder before a match who's going to be rough. Sometimes you think somebody is going to be really dirty, and he's not; at other times, somebody you've never heard of keeps having a whack at you.

I've never played against anybody who has punched me or done sly fouls that the referee couldn't see. Usually, you just get tripped, or a player "goes over the top". All the fouling has been open. A year or so ago, I went for a ball, and the ball was cleared. A player ran up and kicked me in the back of the leg. But this is rare.

Referees vary. You get away with something one week, and you may get caught for it the next week. Sometimes, I've come off after a match, and people have said, "That referee gave the other team everything." And I've never noticed it.

My appetite for the game? There's no secret about it. I just feel that the more running you do, and the more you're in the game, the more chance you have of doing well. I can read the game a wee bit better now, than when I first came to Blackpool; but I never sit down and think, "Well, I couldn't do that last year, and I can do it now." I never really sit down and think about my game. I just try and improve in every match.

I'd like to improve my heading, because I'm not very good in the air. An inside-forward can get away without heading the ball once in the whole of a match. I'd like to score more goals. I'm right-footed, and I shoot better with that foot. When I first came to Blackpool, I wasn't really bothered about scoring: if a goal came, it came. But now I'm looking for goals.

The most exciting event, in my career with Blackpool, was the Anglo-Italian Competition in 1971. At home, we'd drawn with Verona and lost to Roma. As well as the usual two points for a win, and one for a draw, you get a point for every goal. After the two home matches, Blackpool had five points and Swindon had nine. At that stage, I wasn't particularly keen on going to Italy. We thought we'd just play the two games out there, and come straight back. We didn't think we'd get to the final. As it turned out, we were in Italy for a fortnight.

I was injured in the home match against Verona. I couldn't put my weight on my heel; but it cleared up in time for the matches in Italy. Glyn James, our centre-half, was also injured in the Verona match, at Bloomfield Road, and he didn't come with us to Italy. We all felt sorry for Glyn.

We left on a Monday. There was a good spirit among the lads, and the directors were in good form. We started to call Mr Frank Dickinson, Blackpool's Chairman, "Tricky Dicky". He just used to laugh. At the end of the trip, he was calling himself "Tricky Dicky".

Before the return game against Verona, our manager, Bob Stokoe, said: "This is your big chance. If you knock a few in, you'll be back among the leaders." They had one terrific player— Clerici, their centre-forward—but we knew we had a good chance of beating them. We were winning 1-0, and they made it 1-1. Then we got three goals—just like that. So we scored six points, just from that one game.

All the lads were keyed-up before the Roma match. We knew we were only one game away from the final. We played really well that night, and we won 2-1. Italian crowds aren't noted for being kind to visiting teams, but the Roma supporters cheered us as if *we* were the home side. This was a pleasant surprise. They obviously liked our attacking style of play.

Tommy Hutchison, Alan Suddick, and I, were the mid-field trio. All three of us are forwards, remember. In English soccer, a team usually has at least one defensive player in mid-field, but, in this Competition, it's goals that win the Cup. We threw caution to the wind, and played attacking football. On paper, our line-up was 4-3-3; but, in practice, it was more like 4-6! : the back four; three attacking mid-field players; and three strikers. We were going all-out for goals, but we had to be careful not to get carried away. The back four got hoarse, shouting at us to come back and do a bit of defensive work. All our tactical plans seemed to click.

The secret of our popularity with the Italian crowds was the briefing Bob Stokoe gave us. We were warned not to argue with the referees. We were told to play fairly. The Italians are not particularly dirty players, but they tend to be emotional . . . temperamental. It's easy to get annoyed at them—especially if they spit at you! We were told not to get involved—and we didn't.

We took a number of Blackpool F.C. badges and pennants with us, and we threw them to the crowd before each match. The crowds loved this: they thought it was great. The Italians are fervent supporters of their own teams, but they were very fair to Blackpool.

We played Roma on a Friday, and we had to wait until the following day to see if we'd be in the final. Swindon had one more match to play. The second half of their match was on TV, but I couldn't bring myself to watch it. Swindon won 2-1, and finished one point behind us in the league table of English clubs. I was out shopping with Hutchie and Johnny Craven. We asked an Italian what the result was, and he told us in sign-language. We were very excited at having got to the final.

We stayed in Montecatini until the day before the final. Our hotel was terrific. There was no special menu: we just ordered what we wanted, within reason. There was very little drinking. We had a big game to look forward to, and we all did what we were told. No one complained. If we were told to be back at the hotel at a certain time, we made sure that we were back on time.

One day, I went with Big Hutchie to buy a pair of trousers. The man in the shop threw his arms in the air, when he saw Hutchie, and said: "Oooo. *Mamma mia*. Biggum leggums!"

Brian Doyle, our new coach, settled down very quickly: he had just joined Blackpool. He's a very enthusiastic coach. We had a whole week to prepare for the final. We trained every afternoon at about 4 o'clock—the same time of day as the final was to be—so that we would be prepared for the heat. We knew exactly what conditions to expect in the final, and we were ready for them.

Bob Stokoe didn't give us any special advice before the final. He just told us to carry on where we had left off in the previous two games. Bologna were one of the top teams in Italy. They'd finished fifth in their national league. We had the same line-up for the final, but, at the start, Johnny Craven was brought back to plug any holes in mid-field, because, once the Italians get a one-goal lead, they close-up the game.

Before the games against Verona and Roma, they played only the English and Italian national anthems. Before the final, Hutchie said to me, "We'll give our pennants and badges to the group of disabled people in three-wheeler cars." They played the English national anthem, then the Italian national anthem. Then we ran towards the crowd. Johnny Johnston and Dennis Wann came with us. We were throwing our souvenirs into the crowd, and handing them to the disabled people. Then we heard a lot of whistling. I was saying to myself, "That's funny. They usually clap when we hand out our gifts." When we turned round, we saw that everybody was still standing to attention. They were playing a *third* national anthem—in honour of the referee and his linesmen. I think they were Austrians. All the other players were still lined-up in front of the main stand. We were miles away. So we stood to attention, as well. We were giggling to each other, wondering if the TV cameras had spotted us.

We could see the group of Blackpool supporters who had come to cheer us on. There were quite a lot of them, considering what short notice they had that we were going to be in the final. We couldn't hear them, of course, because they were outnumbered by all the Bologna supporters, but we were pleased to see those familiar tangerine-and-white scarves.

Bologna were the first to score. We were so busy playing that we didn't have time to weigh up our chances. Thinking about it after the match, I realize that Bologna must have been favourites at that stage: 1-0 up, in front of their own supporters. On paper, they were the better side: we had just been relegated to the Second Division, and they were one of the top teams in Italy. We just kept plugging away, and we seemed to get the breaks when we needed them. We were all working for each other. We'd been together for a fortnight, and we'd built-up a terrific team-spirit. If you don't get on with someone off the field, and you make a mistake during a game, you don't feel too worried. But we all liked each other, and we were all pulling for each other.

Then we went to extra-time. Johnny Craven had to come off, because of cramp. Alan Ainscow came off. Hutchie and I had cramp: most of us did. Johnny Johnston and Dennis Wann came on, as substitutes, and they ran and ran. In those last minutes, we kept pushing the ball to them. They did a wonderful job.

It was great when Mickey Burns got the winning goal. It was a terrific feeling to win the final, especially since it had been tele-vised, live, to everyone back home. When the final was over, the Bologna fans gave us a great ovation. We ran around the pitch, with the Anglo-Italian Cup, and they clapped and cheered and waved their flags at us. We wouldn't have been any happier if we'd won the F.A. Cup.

After we'd beaten Bologna, we went to a night-club to celebrate. Most of the lads came back at 4.30 a.m. in a special bus. I left early (at 3.45!) because I was jiggered. At 6.30 we were up again, to leave for home, so some of the lads didn't get much sleep that night—or, rather, that morning!

There can be nothing worse than a team playing for, say, £300 each; and the lads, sitting in the dug-out, only getting a fiver. The directors gave out £X to the thirteen players who appeared in the final, but what we did with the money was up to us. We shared the money with the lads who didn't play. We simply divided the whole amount by sixteen so that everybody got the same. That shows you how good Blackpool's team-spirit was—and still is.

John Burridge—we call him "Budgie"—had just joined us. He

had a terrific game in the final. I think he'll be a great goalkeeper. And Alan Suddick did really well out in Italy. All his good points showed up. In every game, he played consistently well.

When we got back to Blackpool, we had no idea that there would be a reception for us. We were laughing and joking when we arrived in Blackpool. We were so happy about winning and about the great time we'd had. It was about 2 o'clock on a Sunday afternoon and it was pouring with rain: we didn't think anybody would come out of doors to see us return. We were saying to each other: "Look at all the *crowds*. There are so many *people*; our coach can't move." But, in fact, there was nobody in sight.

When we got to the football ground, there were hundreds of fans waiting for us. It was only then that we were told that our next stop was the Town Hall. There were a lot of people on the Promenade, and, when we got to the Town Hall, we were mobbed. We couldn't believe it. This terrific reception we were given was especially good because we hadn't expected it.

Bob Battersby, Blackpool's Publicity Director, interviewed a few of us: our captain Johnny Craven, Mickey Burns, Alan Suddick, and myself. We were enjoying ourselves. I was clowning a bit, when Bob Battersby asked me questions. I kept saying, "Get this parrot off my shoulder." "This parrot" was Dave Hatton. I'd travelled back from Italy along with Dave.

It was a terrific experience to win the Cup, after being relegated. It helped us to believe in ourselves again. I was sorry that Jimmy Armfield missed the final. He left Blackpool without ever winning a cup medal. He was very good to me. I would have liked to have seen him share in our success.

The press speculation about me began in the spring: "If Blackpool are relegated, will they sell Tony Green?" We won the Anglo-Italian Competition in June. During the Competition, there was a lot of talk about a possible transfer to Newcastle. When we got home, the deal seemed to have fallen through. Apparently, the two clubs couldn't, at that stage, agree on terms. I *tried* not to let all the "will he go?" talk bother me, but it was obviously very unsettling. In July—just before the start of the season—I was offered a new contract by Blackpool, who were now back in Division II. I refused to sign it.

Ambition. That was my main reason for wanting to leave Blackpool. I'd hate to have any regrets when I finish my playing career. I don't want to have to say, "Well, if only I'd. . . ." I'd put in a transfer request in 1969, but Blackpool turned it down. Then Morty got the sack, and in the close season I got my injury.

My long spell of injury taught me how a footballer feels when his playing days are over. When you're out of the game, nobody wants to know you. I also learned the importance of money, as security for my family. I became determined to make the most of my best years as a player. I left Blackpool when I was in my mid-twenties—which was the right age to make a move. It isn't so easy to move *up* the ladder when you're in your late-twenties. Nowadays, when a player reaches twenty-eight or twenty-nine, people begin calling him "a veteran".

I'd had a taste of First Division football in 1970–71, the season in which I returned after injury. For the first part of that season, I was finding my feet again. Now—a year later—I was 100 per cent fit, and keen to have another crack at First Division football. I like to play in front of big crowds every week—like most players, I thrive on big-match atmosphere—and I wanted the chance of playing in European football.

I signed for Newcastle in October 1971. Although Newcastle were struggling when I came, I knew they were better than their League position showed. There was obviously a lot of talent in the team. The first couple of weeks at a new club are murder! You have to move your family. You are a stranger in a new town. You have to fit into a new team. For the first couple of weeks, you hardly know what is going on. But I soon got in the swing of things. I soon felt 100 per cent Newcastle. This area is soccer-mad: everybody wants to talk football. Newcastle have a very good set of supporters, and they made me feel welcome, right from the start.

I always want to do well—in every match. The £150,000 price-tag didn't worry me. Because Newcastle were in a rather desperate position, I couldn't go onto the field thinking: "I must prove I'm worth £150,000." I went onto the field thinking: "We're at the bottom of the First Division. We've got to win today." Everybody in the team was grafting. Every player was prepared to run himself into the ground. Right from the start, I felt involved in the need to help Newcastle.

When I look at the football results in the Sunday papers, I look to see what Bolton have done—because my old Blackpool team-mates, Henry Mowbray and Jimmy Armfield, are at Bolton. I also look for Celtic's score. As a boy, Celtic was my favourite club. I still have a high regard for Celtic. But the first result I look for is Blackpool's, because Blackpool gave me my first big chance in English football.

I liked Blackpool. I liked the part of the town we lived in: it was nice and quiet. We made a lot of good friends. And I'm sure that, in the whole country, there is no friendlier football club than Blackpool. It's a *happy* club. I sometimes read that some clubs

Tony Waiters, a courageous and agile goalkeeper who once displaced
Gordon Banks from the England team

Blackpool's rival to the Concorde: the airborne Ray Charnley. Dave Durie (*far left*) appears to have lost sight of his high-leaping team-mate

are split into this camp and that camp. Some clubs have cliques. At some clubs, there is a lot of petty gossip: other players talk behind your back. There was none of this at Blackpool.

At Bloomfield Road, there's terrific friendliness among the players; and the wives all get on well together. After a game, you'd go somewhere for a drink, and, whoever you were with, you felt you were among friends. Jimmy Armfield is a perfect example of someone who gets on well with everybody.

It's a great help to a club to have a set of players who get on well with each other *off* the field, as well as *on* the field. Blackpool Football Club has something that money can't buy.

30

THE SEARCH FOR TALENT
A Cat-and-Mouse Game

For clubs of Blackpool's size, it is becoming increasingly important that they should find and develop their own players. A strong scouting system is essential to survival. But even when a club has found a promising youngster, there is no guarantee that he will stay. A few years ago, Blackpool were nurturing an unusually talented lad. "We did everything," a director told me, "but tie his shoe-laces and take him to the toilet." He won schoolboy honours in Blackpool, and was keen to join his local club. One day his father came to Bloomfield Road and announced: "My son has just signed for ————." And he drove away in a new Ford.

Bill Stewart, Blackpool's chief scout in Scotland, spoke to me about the search for talent:

I'm daft about the game, and I'm lucky enough to be paid to watch it. With the advent of floodlights, I see two or three matches a week. I'll go anywhere at a minute's notice. Even though I may go to a match with a particular lad in mind, I watch all twenty-two players. You never know what you might see. In the old days of 3-3-4, I might go to see an inside-forward. The first thing I'd do would be to look at the man playing behind him. A half-back might be working like a slave, murdering himself, to give the ball to his team-mate in the forward-line. You don't get so much of that now, with systems. Numbers don't mean much any more.

I played centre-half for Galston, a non-League club, just before the war. I was there two seasons, and in the second season we won the Scottish Qualifying Cup. After that, I was in the Services, and I captained the R.A.F. in Scotland on two occasions. I played full-back with Bobby Ancell. Later on, he became manager of Motherwell. He discovered Ian St John. His forward-line was very good, and his team was called "Ancell's Babes". I got John McPhee from that team: he was one of the first lads I helped Blackpool to sign. Pat Quinn was another member of that team, and he eventually went to Blackpool as well. Pat was a beautiful player, a lovely player. I never saw Ernie Taylor, but he must have been very similar to Pat.

After the war, I took the Scottish F.A. training course—the coaching course. I was a scout for Stirling Albion for seven or eight seasons, and then I had one year with Charlie Mitten, when he was manager at Newcastle. I'd played with Mitten when we were in the R.A.F. He was an outside-left. He was a grand type.

I've been with Blackpool for more than ten years. Over all this time, I have built up a tremendous number of connections. These laddies of mine often save me going to watch a player the first time. If he sounds good. I'll follow up the recommendation. I go to hardly a single game without seeing someone I know.

I don't represent any other club besides Blackpool. I, personally, am paid by a retainer. On top of that, I've had a bonus now and then. Not many scouts have contracts: only the top men, the ex-professionals, who are full-time scouts. For people like myself, it's a part-time job, a job-cum-hobby. Scouts come and go. If a manager leaves a club, the scouts usually go too.

I can go just about anywhere in Scotland without any trouble. I can go to the north-east—Aberdeen, Forfar, or Montrose—and be back in Glasgow the same night. There are hundreds of juvenile clubs around Ayrshire and Lanarkshire. And there's Edinburgh, of course. But Scottish football is chiefly around Glasgow and the west. I'm not being unfair in saying that. Football in Scotland *is* Glasgow.

When Blackpool got pipped for promotion, under Stan Mortensen, there were five Scots in the team—Henry Mowbray, John McPhee, Tony Green, Tommy Hutchison, and Tommy White. I helped bring four of them to Blackpool: all except for White.

I had heard of Green's prowess with Albion Rovers, and first checked on him myself on October 1, 1966. I was favourably impressed and sent a report to Ron Suart, Blackpool's manager. Two weeks later I sent one of my aids, who also reported favourably. On October 22, I watched Green in a hard game, away from home, when his team was beaten 2-1 by Morton. I again sent in a good report, but we were trying to make do with our existing staff, and nothing was done at the time. Then Stan Mortensen replaced Ron. I met Stan, for the first time, in March 1967, and the quest was on again for new players.

The famous Tony Green deal was finalized on the day that Aberdeen played Celtic in the Final of the Scottish Cup in 1967. Cowdenbeath were due to play Albion Rovers (Green's team) on that same Saturday. Tommy Fagan—the Albion Rovers manager

. . . director . . . he *is* Albion Rovers—changed the kick-off time to 12 o'clock, instead of postponing the game because of the Cup Final. When Morty saw Green, he said, "I have no one like that on my books." Those were his exact words. It took Stan only ten minutes to decide. And, of course, Harry Johnston agreed. Then they went to the Final, and I, putting duty first, went to watch a junior game in Ayrshire.

Green used to fall out of a game quite often; and, when I made enquiries about him, people told me that he was studying. I used to hear all sorts of alibis about why he didn't last for a whole game. Tony would often drift to the left wing. But I liked him from the start. He's a natural. He's got such good control. He's so quick in himself. He's got a beautiful shot. I don't know why he doesn't score more goals. He used to score quite regularly with Albion Rovers. They were good shots, often from 18–20 yards.

A lot of clubs were looking at Green. A scout from a London club was reported to have watched him *nine* times. I hadn't seen him before that season. The Cup Final day was, I think, the fourth time. Up in Scotland, if a boy shows anything at all—in the Second Division, particularly—everybody knows about it. It's very difficult —I'd say it's impossible—to get a player who's completely unknown. In the Second Division, everything must be done through the club: you're not supposed to make direct contact with the players. It's different with the juniors or the juveniles or the amateurs.

I don't very often have time to go and see Blackpool play. If I see them twice in a year, I'm lucky. I try and go down when one of the junior teams has an early kick-off. I can see the youngsters, and then go and see the first team. When I see the junior team— the boys of 16, 17, 18—I compare them with the Scottish boys I'm looking at.

I have a reporter friend in Glasgow. He sometimes sends me Blackpool's local paper. It's not difficult to keep in touch with what's happening at Bloomfield Road. I ask on the telephone how boys, whom I've found for Blackpool, are getting on. I have to go by hearsay. Then I have to visualize how a player is doing.

I communicate with Blackpool in all possible ways: telephone; letter; you name the method, and I bet I use it. If I'm not reporting on a particular match, I just send a general letter, which I usually write on a Sunday morning. If I'm really interested in a boy, I fill in a report, and give details of height, weight, age, and so on. At Blackpool, they sift through reports from all the scouts. These reports will be read and then filed. Blackpool can refer back, if they want to. They may say, "Five weeks ago, you were at so-and-so, and you mentioned so-and-so. Go and have another look at him."

At times, the club will instruct all scouts that a mid-field man, for example, is needed. Blackpool may say, "We've got to get a left-half." A ready-made first-team player is needed. Everything else has to be sacrificed. For the time being, we have to forget the youngsters and our routine search for talent.

When watching young players, I look for ability in the basic skills—good use of the ball, with both feet; heading; firm and accurate tackling—plus the will-to-win. Height is an asset, but lack of height is not necessarily a disadvantage. Good physique is essential—particularly the legs. I get quite excited when I come across a lad who measures up to my requirements. I can *usually* assess this in the first forty-five minutes. I then check that his character and other personal matters are OK.

The man on the terrace, who is a dyed-in-the-wool supporter of his team, would not be a success as a scout. Fans seldom see any good players in the opposing side. I have tested this out, by asking supporters about a particular player who had played against their team. Often, they can never recollect even *seeing* him. This applies to supporters *and* officials, in all grades of soccer.

Everybody wants to be a scout. All sorts of people ring Blackpool—with the best will in the world—and recommend a player. If the player is Scottish, nine times out of ten I've already seen him; often, the recommended player is on the point of signing for another club. This type of recommendation seldom comes up with someone from scratch: someone we don't already know about.

If I go to a Second Division match, I usually go on the terracing. You learn far more gen there than you ever get in the pavilion: what you hear in the pavilion is always wrong! It's amazing how much you learn just standing beside a relative. I'll be standing, watching a game, and I'll say to the laddie next to me, "That's not a bad left-half." "Aye, that's his brother down there." Then I'll go and stand next to the brother. "They tell me that's your brother who's playing left-half." And before you know where you are, you've got his birthday, the name of his grandmother—the lot.

In a young player, I first look for skill. I put courage next. There are not so many late-developers these days. Boys are so much better fed nowadays! I'm inclined to think that many modern players are *manufactured*—that gives a clue to my age. Years ago, they were either footballers or they weren't. They were either hard men or they weren't. Now, there are lads playing who are better trained. Perhaps even at the lower levels—juniors and amateurs—they have been better trained. But, with 4-3-3 or 4-2-4,

I think there are players in the game now who wouldn't have been in it had they been playing some years ago.

To get to the top, a young player needs a lot of persistence. The club that signs him has to take that gamble. If I'm interested in a boy of about seventeen, the first thing I do is to go to his home. If his mother is going to break down at the mere mention of her son crossing the border, I wish them the very best of luck and depart, and I don't waste Blackpool's money and my time. A lot of people—some schoolteachers become involved in this—are inclined to push a boy. They send him down to England at sixteen and less. His parents never see him for months, and go off their heads with worry. So many of these young boys come back, not having made the grade. If Blackpool get a young local laddie, he can play for one of the club's junior teams, and keep up his studying or his work. But to take a boy miles away from home—that's something different.

I don't have regular contacts with headmasters. I could if I wanted to. I know two or three sports-masters, but I don't go out of my way to make these contacts. I don't bother with the schools, unduly, until they've got their trials sorted out. I've never taken a schoolboy down to Blackpool. The youngest players I watch are about seventeen. There's a League in Glasgow and the west of Scotland called the Under-Age League. To play in that League, a boy can't be over eighteen at a certain date. At about seventeen or eighteen, a boy has been broken in. Some of your work has been done for you. There is a competition for the Under-Age teams, and two or three hundred teams play in it. So the teams that get to the final stages have come through quite a lot.

The wealthier clubs can afford to watch the really young boys. Some managers like to boast that they are watching eleven- and twelve-year-olds. A big club can take a young boy on an apprentice form, and, if he doesn't do well, can forget him. But, at Blackpool, we need a fairly quick return for our investments. We can't have boys of thirteen and fourteen hanging around the place.

Up here in Scotland, we have what is called a provisional form. You and I can go to a game. Say I'm scouting for Blackpool, and you're scouting for Motherwell. We've both been after a boy for some time. We both fancy him. You can sign this boy for £150, and leave him with his club. You now have him on a provisional form. Quite a lot of clubs take this gamble. You can do this in August, September, October, and leave the boy to play with his club. His club gets £150, and, on top of that, you're probably paying him £2 or £3 a week. You go back and see him: either in April or May—when the clubs are playing in their semi-finals or finals—or when your boss says to you, "Go and check up on this boy." If he's improved, so much the better: your club might call upon him for the next season. If he's gone back, you scrub him.

Any boy, who plays at all well, will be chased. There'll be scouts at every game. But I don't think any boy benefits from knowing that he's being watched. He's bound to be worried a wee bit if he knows there's something in the offing. I never tell a secretary of a club that I'm coming to see so-and-so. I'll go to a match. I'll go to see a particular boy: perhaps he's been mentioned to me by some of my connections. "Not bad," I say to myself. So I go back and see him again. But I don't tell the club that I'm coming back. If I feel the boy has possibilities, I enquire about him. I go to the secretary and I say, "Now, look. I'm asking you this boy's age, and his weight. Is he at school? Is he working? Is he an apprentice? When I go through that door, don't you go to the phone and tell the press." Because that boy will see it in the papers, and he'll be sitting, waiting every night for the Blackpool scout to come to the door. I might never go near that boy again. I'm only asking for some data to keep by me. A leak to the press can be very disheartening for a lot of laddies. People in Blackpool say to me: "There's a bit in the paper claiming that you were impressed by so-and-so last night." Sometimes, I've not even been to the game!

A scout can't talk terms with a boy, but you can give him an idea of what wages he can expect to earn. Often, that's the first thing a boy wants to know. I tell them that we are not a wealthy club, but that we have an excellent ground, which is kept spotless. I tell them that all their gear will be first class, and that the players are taken to the best hotels. I plug two of Blackpool's big attractions. Firstly, most people have been there for a holiday or a week-end, and have enjoyed themselves. Secondly, I point out to the father that, if he's got a car, he can come down to Blackpool, and can be with his son in four hours. As well as being a scout, I have to be something of a salesman.

When I've decided that I'll send a lad down to Blackpool for a trial, the first thing I do is get permission from his club: usually, they're only too willing. I get the boy's home address, and I see his parents. I ask: "If he is successful in his trials, and if he likes the place, have you any objection to him staying in Blackpool?" If I don't go with a boy to Blackpool, I put him on the train. Sometimes, the secretary of his club wants to go with him. This is just a wee bit of Scottish canniness: some secretaries fear that, when a boy goes south, a club will put pressure on him to sign forms.

I buy two return-tickets from Glasgow to Blackpool. I either see that they are met at Blackpool or I tell them to take a taxi. I give them money to have a meal on the train. I tell them to claim all the expenses that are due to them. I don't want any complaints. I've never had a boy come back dissatisfied.

Blackpool may want to play a lad in one of the junior teams, but it depends on what grade of football he comes from in Scotland. The amateurs, the juveniles, the Under-Age boys, can play for a junior team, but you are not allowed to field a Scottish Second Division player in one of these matches. This is one of the underhand things a club can do.

If the boy is at school, he'll have to be back for the Monday. If he is a working type—a joiner, a plumber, or a bricky—I usually leave his return-date open. Sometimes, I've got to contact the boy's firm. Firms get a bit fed up if a boy is away for a trial, every few weeks: one week to Blackpool, one week to Birmingham, and so on. If he's a labouring type, and he plays fairly well, the Blackpool officials may ask him to stay for a few days, or they may fix another date for him to come down.

There used to be a joke about a Scottish scout, of a famous northern club (it wasn't Blackpool!), who used to make a point of sending at least one boy, for a trial, every week. That's mad. That's daft. I've got to be pretty sure about a lad before recommending him for a trial. I don't send very many lads down to Blackpool.

I'll tell you how Blackpool signed a player, a few years ago. The manager and I went to see a right-back. He was quite good, but he was twenty-six or twenty-seven. His partner, the left-back, was a young laddie. He was running like a train. He wasn't overlapping, as such; he was just flying up the wing. He was very enthusiastic. The manager said, "I like the look of this boy." In the second half, he was even better. He was only about nineteen: you can do so much with a laddie of that age. You may not get an international, but, if he's a keen type, you'll get a good team-man. The manager said, "Go and find out what you can about him." I saw him walking out with one of his pals. So I said to the manager, "You just wait here. I'll go and speak to this boy." He was standing outside. I went up to him and said, "You did quite well today." "Do you think so?" he replied. "Do you fancy being a full-time football player?", I asked. If you begin like this, you can quickly tell if a boy is interested. I don't know if he was a miner, but all around that area there are a lot of mining types. Anyway, my question was enough. He would have come with us on the spot. And I hadn't even told him what club we represented!

I go into a home, and I see what sort of a place it is. I can tell right away if I'm going to have a chance. I don't wish to be snobbish about this, but if it is a good working-class home, and the laddie is working, he's not always so keen to come south. But if you go into a poorer-class home, sometimes you'll find that the boy can't get away quick enough. I made one major signing like that. I was told by one of my contacts about a boy playing in the Glasgow Corporation Youth League. It was a very good recommendation. I went to watch him on the Saturday. The teams were stripping in an old railway carriage. They came straggling out, in twos and threes. I was waiting for the No. 10. He was the last man to come out. He came down the steps. I didn't know the bloke from Adam, but I said to myself, "That's him. He'll do." I could tell right away. He hadn't even kicked a ball. It was just the way he came out. I can see him now. One look, and I *knew*.

He was a real gallus member. [*This is Glaswegian. It means "cheeky", "confident".*—R.D.] He was miles ahead of the other twenty-one blokes on the field. They were all the same age—about seventeen—but he was old in the head. To give myself another chance to see him play, I spoke to a friend of mine, secretary of a club in the junior grade—that's the next grade up. This secretary was in a bad way. He was short of a man for his team. I said to him, "Look. There's a laddie playing in a Glasgow Youth team. I saw him the other day. He's quite good. You can play this boy, but don't get his address. Don't touch him!"

He played in this game, and he scored *four* goals. They nearly went frantic to try and sign him. I had a bit of fun, because I knew the secretary, and I said, "Oh, you've had it." They nearly went daft. I asked the Blackpool manager to come up. The boy lived in a very ordinary home. He was working as a storeman, not far from Central Station. It was too easy.

As I gained experience as a scout, I found I could cut my work in half. My perception quickened up. But I must never become complacent. You can't be hard and fast about how many games it takes before you're sure about a young player. It all depends. For someone like the boy I've just told you about, I needed only a game or two. I don't know why, but I liked the way he trotted down the steps and walked across to the park. I said to myself, "If he can play at all, he'll do." And that was it.

I'll tell you a funny story. I had my plans all set for one Saturday. I got an urgent phone message, late on the Friday night, that I should go to see a junior game the next day in Fife. The centre-forward *had* to be seen—immediately. He was a six-footer, aged nineteen. He'd got everything. I went with a friend to the game. We went to the little village, a colliery. We got to the miners' club at about 2 o'clock and had a beer. We spoke to a couple of people at the bar. "How's your team doing this year?", I asked. "I hear you've got a good centre-forward." "Aye, very good." "That's fine," I replied.

We went out for the 3 o'clock kick-off. We watched the teams coming out. I was waiting to see the No. 9. He was neatly and beautifully made. His whole body was well proportioned and he had good legs. But he was only 5ft 4in! During the game, he got a knock, and they carted him to the touch-line, near where we were standing. I had a look at him, and I said, "That boy's not nineteen." The game finished—I forget the score—and we went back to the miners' club. The players all came there after the game. In walked two sailors: one big one and one wee one. The wee one was the centre-forward. Do you know what age he was? Twenty-seven! His girl-friend's father had phoned Blackpool and given them the tip-off. A scout gets a lot of bum steers like this.

All the time I've been with Blackpool, I've found that they always keep strictly to the rules. They don't do anything underhand. If a club wants to cheat the system, they put a boy's father on the payroll as a scout. A parent or a relative can be taken-on as a scout, and never go near a match. He just gets the money. I don't think it's wise to try to bind a boy to your club by paying his parents or his relatives. Often it's not in the boy's best interests. You may pay a regular sum to his father for a couple of years. If a Scottish club were to come and want to sign the boy on the spot, your payments would embarrass the family. They would say to themselves, "Well, what do we do? We've been taking money from a club for two years." I don't think it's worth it. If you do things through the back door, people are frightened to deal with you: because you will soon get a reputation for doing things underhand. I always like to be able to go back to any home, or any club, or any secretary. I can go into any ground in Scotland and know that I'm trusted.

I know quite a few scouts of other clubs, and they know me. We always acknowledge one another, but we go our separate ways. It's every man for himself. Once, I was at a boy's home. Another scout arrived soon after I did, so I adjourned into the greenhouse until he went away.

If I go to an Under-Age game—they are usually played on an open field—I look around, and I often see a scout I know. I'm friendly with one or two. There's no harm in speaking to them, but you're wary. I say, "I'm going for that full-back," when, in fact, I'm watching the centre-half. And he says, "That right winger is terrific," when, in fact, he couldn't care less about him. It's a cat-and-mouse game, all taken in good part.

31

THE SECRETARY
All-hearing, All-seeing

More and more clubs are struggling to make a profit. And there are ever more frequent changes of top personnel: in the boardroom and in the manager's office. These two facts make an efficient and far-sighted secretary increasingly valuable to the League club of the seventies.

Des McBain is one of the younger generation of club secretaries. He was born in Sunderland, but his family moved to Blackpool when he was about six months old. He went to school in Blackpool. So he can almost be called a "sand-grown 'un". He worked in industry and in the Civil Service before joining Blackpool F.C. in December 1966. He took up his present appointment in February 1967.

Here is what Des McBain told me about Blackpool and Lancashire football, and the rewards and responsibilities of being secretary of Blackpool Football Club:

When I became secretary of the club in February 1967, Blackpool were doing very badly in the First Division and were virtually certain to be relegated. But, strangely enough, the atmosphere at the club was quite good. There wasn't the feeling of complete failure that you would expect at a club that had won only four games by the end of the year. What is the reason for this good club-spirit that we have at Blackpool? I think it is something that's in the four walls of the club.

During our three-year spell in the Second Division (1967–1970), the clubs we played against were still of the opinion that we were Blackpool Football Club, the First Division club. They felt we were trespassers in the Second Division; that we weren't in our rightful place. This was very flattering, but in fact you're only as good as the Division you're in.

The war years, when we played such good football, helped our reputation a tremendous amount. We had many great players guesting at Blackpool. Everybody looked at Blackpool as the Mecca of football in the north. Since then, the public has looked to Blackpool to produce star players. When we got promotion in 1970, we received many many telegrams and letters of congratulations saying, "You're back in your rightful place in the First Division." We had success for so many years that we had become an institution in the First Division.

Blackpool is proud of having achieved more success in football than any other seaside resort in Britain. We are the only one ever to have played in the First Division of the Football League. The reason for this is partly geographical. Bournemouth, for instance, is out on a limb. Torquay is out on a limb. Those areas of the country aren't soccer crazy, and never have been. But Lancashire has always been soccer crazy, and, since transport is so much more mobile these days, people are coming from farther afield to watch matches. They will come, particularly if you're turning on some good football. We have supporters coming fifty, sixty, eighty miles, to every home match. They've taken a liking to Blackpool, and I think some of this interest stems from the Matthews-Mortensen-Johnston era. We had a great side in the forties and fifties, and the public took notice of Blackpool. Blackpool was always in the headlines as being a wonderful footballing side, always turning on the skills. People still look at Blackpool and expect a high standard of entertainment from the team.

Publicity is tremendously important, and we get a great deal of help from our local press, who give us invaluable free advertising. Every time the club is mentioned—whether it be a player signed, or a player sold, or a match played—it's free advertising for Blackpool.

We have to feed our local reporters with as much information as possible, but we must be very careful. Like all other clubs, we've got to be secretive at the time of a possible transfer. Another club may be interested in the same player. If the word gets out, the transfer deal suddenly becomes an auction, and the price spirals.

We often have to take the local reporters into our confidence. This is very important. If you do this—whether it's a major issue or a minor issue—and they don't leak the information in their columns, it seals the relationship between the local press and the club. In Blackpool, we have a very good relationship with the local press. We also have a close liaison with the nationals.

At Blackpool, the manager gives all quotes and statements to the press with regard to the team and the players. Anything outside that is the responsibility of the secretary: for example, the financial position and publicising matches. On anything regarding club policy, and on anything which is very controversial, the Chairman will normally give the statement. If the press approach the Chairman, and he doesn't feel he'd like to give a quote, then he will refer them to the manager or to the secretary, depending on which aspect of the club is in question.

Normally, none of the other directors will give quotes to the press. It is an unwritten law at the club that only the Chairman, manager, or secretary—or a person delegated by one of those three —will make official statements to the press. My assistant, for example, has given many quotes to the press regarding the sale of tickets for a big match. He's done this with my full authority.

The population of Blackpool is about 150,000. The population of Blackpool and the Fylde is over 300,000. And yet, even in Blackpool's golden years after the war, the home gates averaged only 20–25,000. A vast number of people living in Blackpool are of senior-citizen age. A lot of people, from all over the country, come to retire in Blackpool. We have no heavy industry that can employ large numbers of working people. Young people are growing up, and wanting to find work—the north-west isn't noted for its opportunities of employment—and they're moving out of Blackpool. In their place come the pensioners. There is a steady flow of people in and out of the town. Blackpool isn't keeping in the town what we call "sand-grown 'uns", and therefore many of the people who come to Bloomfield Road have no allegiance to Blackpool Football Club. At our home matches, quite a large percentage of the crowd are supporting the opposition because it is the team from their home-town. They still have affection towards the town they were born in and lived in.

In my opinion, pre-match entertainment would only be a success in a fully-enclosed stadium; in other words, if matches were played indoors, with the cold and rain shut out. The public won't come and sit, or stand, in inclement weather, half an hour or an hour before a match, to watch entertainment—when they can sit at home a little bit longer, before making their way to the ground. I can foresee something like the Astrodome in Texas. When we have this sort of stadium in England, you will have a full evening's entertainment. The pre-match entertainment would start at about 6 o'clock, and the match would begin at about 9.30. By the time the public were drifting away, at about 11.15, they would have had a full night's entertainment. The scope is so vast. Blackpool is the top entertainment centre in the country. It is one of the best in the world—if not *the* best in the world—and there are no limits to what the football club could provide in the way of entertainment.

The supporters' club has a first-class committee who are 100 per cent behind Blackpool Football Club. They're not out to boost their own names, nor to tell Blackpool F.C. what to do. They make an annual subscription to the Development Association, which is always very welcome, and they run various efforts during the year for the benefit of the football club. For example, they sell our Golden Shot tickets on the ground at every home match. They do this voluntarily, and we keep the proceeds. If there is something they want to do which is over and above the normal activities of the supporters' club, they first approach the Board of directors. They have had this close association with us for as long as there has been a supporters' club in Blackpool. In fact, Blackpool was one of the first clubs in the country to have a supporters' club.

At Blackpool, we have a good record for crowd behaviour. We have a police station on the ground, which is available to the police on match-days. They operate from this station and they have an external telephone: in other words, a direct line of communication to the police headquarters. The police patrol around the ground, and internally. They are a tremendous help to us. I put it down to the vast experience that the Blackpool police have in handling misbehavers and crowds in the town itself. Some young people come to Blackpool, in gangs, to have a good time. The Blackpool police know how to handle these sort of people. Police in lots of towns have never had this experience. The amount of publicity that has been given to trouble-makers by the press and TV, over the last few years, has, in my view, helped to increase the misbehaviour of football crowds. I think the publicity has given them more ideas. But, at Blackpool, the police have been trained in handling masses of people. Millions visit Blackpool during the year and, amongst them, there are many disreputable characters.

The police are in constant contact with me. They will say, "So-and-so are coming to Bloomfield Road in a month's time. They are known to have some rowdy 'followers'. What precautions shall we take?" One of the Chief Inspectors and I will discuss it. We draw up a plan of campaign—that I won't disclose, for obvious reasons—and we say, "Right. We know what's going to happen on the day, and we'll be ready for it." We have an agreement that whatever is necessary is done. We leave it like that. It's a very loose thing. I don't say to the police: "We want fifty policemen." I say to them: "We shall be getting an approximate gate of 17,000 people on Saturday. I've been in touch with the club, and they don't have much trouble at their home matches. Therefore we won't be expecting trouble." And they say: "Right. In that case, X number of policemen will be sufficient." And this works admirably. Of course, the police forces in various parts of the country are always in touch with each other, and, if there are trains carrying supporters, the police carry out spot checks on the way. There's a nation-wide network of police forces and football clubs combining to try and reduce hooliganism.

I'm very pleased that I didn't come into football until I did; although there are times when I wish I'd been secretary when it was easier financially for Blackpool—when it wasn't such a burden. I had a really good grounding in industry and in the Civil Service before I came into football. I have introduced ideas into the club which I wouldn't have known about, had I not had these previous positions. I think that a football-club secretary needs some experience of outside industry and outside organization before he comes in.

The secretary is the hub of a football club. Briefly going through the duties of a secretary, you start with the condition of the ground : this is the groundsman's job, but everything that he does and buys has to be channelled through the secretary's office. The general-maintenance staff are also attached to the secretary. It's the secretary's responsibility to make sure that the ground is safe for spectators, that it's clean, tidy, and fresh. He is in charge of the administration of the ground on a Saturday, and sees that all the turnstiles are working correctly, and that the police are there, and so on. The secretary has overall responsibility for the ticket office, that is to say the producing of tickets for each match, the selling of these tickets, and the advertising of matches. The secretary is the liaison officer between the Board and all the staff at the ground.

General administration of finance comes under the secretary; and problems the players have with regard to finance and contracts : this is done along with the manager. The secretary attends all Board meetings, and takes the minutes and gives advice at the meetings.

I am responsible for the production of the programme, but this is delegated, and in the last few years the assistant-secretary has done most of the work. I am responsible for all advertising on the ground and in the programme. All advertising media come under my jurisdiction. We don't sub-let the advertising to an agent. We handle it all ourselves.

All booking of accommodation, the directors' travel rota—they take it in turns to go with the team—the booking of coaches: all this comes under my jurisdiction. I don't do it all. Much of it is delegated. But it all has to come through me for approval. We'll go to a hotel for a number of years, and then have a change. It helps to impress on the hotel, we have been using, that it isn't the only hotel in the town. And it helps to improve the service if, eventually, we go back: they're that little bit keener to look after us and make sure that everything is spot-on. The arranging of a club tour—and all that that entails—is also my responsibility.

I'll tell you an amusing story about a club holiday. We went to Majorca in 1968, and at that time Stan Mortensen was manager. We took a number of players. When we arrived at Gatwick Airport, a chappie tagged himself on to us. He had a transistor tape recorder, and he said he was a script-writer for Bob Monkhouse and various other big names in show business. He was going to the same place we were—a Pontin's camp. He was going to have a fortnight out there, and he said he would be compèring the talent contest and one or two of the evening shows. He hung on to us all the way over to Majorca, and in the camp he trailed us about.

One night in the camp he was saying what a great script-writer he was, and that he'd written for a great number of well-known people. Morty said that for every joke this chap told, he would tell two. They made it into a challenge match. The manager of the camp said, "OK, we'll put it on tomorrow night." There was tremendous publicity about the match. They got up on the stage and had their contest, and, sure enough, Morty won the day in his inimitable style. For every joke this chap told, Morty told two. He peeled them off, just like peeling bananas. You couldn't stop him once he got going. This is the sort of manager Morty was. He injected tremendous enthusiasm and enjoyment into everything he did.

One of the major jobs of the secretary is the liaison with the F.A. and the Football League. This is solely the secretary's responsibility. We are members of the Football League and, as such, it is our governing body. We don't contact the F.A. anywhere near as often as we do the Football League. We're on the phone to the League at least three or four times a week; sometimes three or four times a day. It depends on what matters we're dealing with.

And, nowadays, correspondence to and from the Football League is almost daily. There is too much paper-work at the moment, but the whole country has this problem. The League bring in new ideas. To put these ideas into force, they have to have more staff. As soon as they have more staff, they must have more information from the clubs. Therefore they're writing more often to the clubs. Therefore the clubs are having to write back more often. And so on. It's a vicious circle.

We are fortunate in being on the doorstep of the League's headquarters. We can register a new player in a matter of minutes, whereas other clubs often have to fly a helicopter or send a fast car

Gordon West, a Blackpool discovery who joined Everton in 1962 and
became an England international

Alan Ball, Mr Perpetual Motion, one of the world's most valuable players

to get to the registration office on time: forty-eight hours must elapse after the registration of a player—at the Football League headquarters—before he is allowed to play for his new club. We often get visits from managers and secretaries of other League clubs. They just bob in for a few minutes to have a chat. They've either been to the Football League to register a player, or they're on their way to register one. In this way, we meet quite a number of the officials of the other ninety-one clubs.

The secretary must have a tight hold on all aspects of the club. Some clubs have a general manager or an admin. manager-cum-secretary. It doesn't matter what title you give him, but there must be one person at the centre of the club's activities. Everything must come through his office. A club needs a secure and stable person as secretary. Look at what's happened at Blackpool in the period I've been here. We've had several different managers and a number of new directors. Some of the directors who have retired or lost their positions were very experienced in football matters. So a club needs somebody who is holding everything at his finger-tips.

Whatever the manager does—and this is fairly general through-out the country, I would think—the secretary hears about it. What-ever the directors decide to do, is done through the secretary. Whatever the Chairman feels should be done, the secretary is delegated to do it. The secretary has got to have competent staff around him, dealing with all these intricate pieces, so that, in the end, they all culminate into one smooth system.

Take the scouting system, for example. Although the secretary doesn't hear all that's going on, he knows the scouts, he's met them, and he knows where they are. He knows how, at a minute's notice, he can contact them. He must be able to contact anyone who is in any way connected with the club in, say, an hour.

As secretary, I've got to have a competent staff around me, so that I can delegate a lot of my work. I am the liaison between the directors and the club. I have to be available at any time for the Chairman or any director who wants to see me or speak to me on the telephone.

At Blackpool, we have various committees. A committee which the manager can call upon if he wants to discuss the strengthening of the team. He may want to discuss the scouting system and recommend that we should take on more scouts. We have a finance committee. They deal with all aspects of finance: players' wages, staff, overheads, possible renewals to machinery, possible re-design-ing of various parts of the ground, refreshment bars, buying land which could be built on in later years to make, say, a social club.

All this comes under the finance committee. Then we have what we call the legal committee, which discusses legal aspects of rulings of the Football League and the Football Association. We also have a Development Association committee. In all these committees, the directors take an active part, and they're always available, if possible, for Board meetings, which we normally hold once a fortnight. It is to these meetings that sub-committee work is submitted for ratification.

I have to be available for all these meetings, and I have to try to produce, out of *all* these meetings, a concise detailed report available for whenever the directors may wish to talk about any one aspect of the club's policy. In other words, we produce a coherent club policy from all these various committees. The main thing, for me, is to be available whenever I'm needed: so the club has to tick away, on its own, for much of the week. A match-day is different. I like to be at the ground for a first-team match, and I'm there from 9 o'clock in the morning till about 6 or 7 at night. I don't leave the ground during the day. I even have lunch at the ground.

During the week, there are routine jobs to be done, but, at the same time, many things crop up which have never happened before. I may have to go to a special meeting called by the Football League or the Football Association. New things come up all the time, all through the year. The F.A. may suddenly decide to hold a meeting in London. Well, I just pack my bags and go to the meeting, and usually a director accompanies me. I have to be available, at all times, for these matters. One thing that is really enjoyable about being club secretary is that it's not a routine job.

There has to be co-ordination and co-operation between the three most important people in a football club: the Chairman, the manager, and the secretary. These three must be like brothers. They must be all-hearing and all-seeing, and they must tell each other exactly what is going on. They are the entrepreneurs, the decision-makers. The Board of directors meet every week or every fortnight, and they decide the policies of the club. They have the final word. But a lot can happen in a week, at a football club, and somebody has to make decisions. A good Board of directors, of a well-run club, will delegate responsibilities to the Chairman, the manager, and the secretary. This is the general routine at Blackpool. Everything, except for major decisions, will be decided by these three persons, and then backed by the Board at their next meeting, when reports are put to them of all the happenings of the previous week or fortnight.

Whatever a club does—even including its match programme—

must be a financial success. I don't mean that we must make a large profit, because the majority of a club's profit goes in tax anyway. So all we want to do is to make sure that we're running at a reasonable profit. This is one of the secretary's problems. He has to try and estimate what it will cost to run the club for twelve months ahead, and this includes three months when there are no matches, and therefore no receipts. He has to estimate what sort of gates the club will have, work out the amount of cash to be taken at the turnstiles and from the sale of season-tickets, set this against wages and expenses and overheads, and then come to an answer which says either you're going to make an annual loss of X pounds or a profit of X pounds.

These figures don't take into account the buying and selling of players. With fees being so inflated, this can be a big item. All the secretary can do, is to give the club an annual budget based on estimated receipts and running expenses. There's no other way of doing it. Unfortunately, you can be so far out—either way. The club could start off the season with three home wins, and you find you've added 5,000 people, at every home match, to your expected gate, Or the team could lose the first half-dozen matches, and you find you've lost £1,000 a week, in cash, on your gate—therefore your budget has gone to pot.

If we have a good run in the League Cup or the F.A. Cup, this is extra money for us. In my pre-season budgeting, I don't include possible receipts from these two competitions. This can be our cream. But it may be only one-off. We may be knocked out in the first round. Of course, it depends on what club we're drawn against. We can be drawn against a top club or we can meet a small club. For example, we met Newport at home in the League Cup in 1970. We had a very poor gate. We met Bristol City in the next round, again at home, and had another poor gate. We could have done with an Arsenal or an Everton or a Manchester City to really boost our coffers.

Every good club has always had its control over expenses. But nowadays it's most involved. Years ago, you would find that when a player was transferred for X-thousand pounds, the club he was joining would pay out the money there and then. Write a cheque. And that's it. Finish. Nowadays, there are very few clubs who can write a cheque for £100,000 on the spot. Most clubs have to pay on terms, for the transfer of a player's registration: so much down, and so much every month; or so much at the end of the year.

Normally, you'll find that, within twelve months, the whole transaction is paid for. Clubs are having to do this because transfer fees have spiralled so greatly, and receipts haven't increased in proportion. So, if you read in the press that a player has gone for £150,000, it's odds-on that the transfer fee will be on a terms basis, unless he is going to one of the clubs that has made a big profit that year.

During our conversation, I've sometimes used the words "buy" and "sell". I've done this because they are quick to say. But let me put it right. You don't "sell" a player: you "transfer his registration". Clubs don't like the press, or anyone, to say: "Blackpool Football Club bought Joe Bloggs for £10,000 today." We're not buying and selling cattle. We would rather hear people say that this or that club has "transferred the registration of Joe Bloggs for a fee of X-thousand pounds".

At Blackpool, the secretary is in charge of finance. I don't know of any other club that uses our type of financial control. We make use of a firm of accountants who work for us all twelve months of the year. I liaise with the accountants almost every day. Within a few hours, I can have a balance sheet produced by them which gives us an up-to-date financial picture of the club. I produce a draft statement for every Board meeting: this is the approximate state of affairs at the time of the meeting. If the Board want an absolutely spot-on report on the finances of the club, ready for the next meeting, I usually give the accountants a couple of days to do it.

On a match-day, we have 100–150 people working for us. But our permanent staff numbers no more than twenty. Of that number, quite a few are ground-staff who have to clean up the ground and get it ready for each match. We have a groundsman and his assistant who prepare the pitch at the ground and also at the training ground. And we have about eight office staff. It wouldn't pay the club to hire people, on a permanent basis, to deal with accounts, and wages and salaries, and this sort of thing. It's easier to put it all out to a firm that has staff who can do other work as well. The club is charged for the number of hours spent on our work. We've found this to be a first-class system.

We have an organiser for our Development Association. A final decision on any matters regarding finance or design of various money-raising schemes is made by a small sub-committee of directors, of which I am secretary. The organiser and I make decisions on less important matters. For anything major, the sub-committee is brought in. At Blackpool, the Development Association is for the redevelopment of the club. The Association is not used to subsidise the running of the club. At our club, it exists solely to redevelop the ground. For example, we have a stand on the west side which is forty years old. It will have to be replaced. At some time in the future, we shall have to build a new stand.

We need money for that, and the only way to raise money week by week is through the Development Association. We can't dig into our general income, to make improvements to the ground. We therefore have a separate organization running the Development Association, though it is controlled by the directors and the club secretary.

The town clubs of Lancashire are going through a difficult patch. The biggest challenge at the moment is that we will have to produce more home-grown juniors than we've been producing recently. The public mustn't expect us to buy big-name players, because we just don't have the money. We have an average gate of 16–20,000, and this doesn't bring in sufficient money to allow the club to buy many players. We can't afford to pay £100,000-plus for a player.

We can't expect the public to pay a lot of money to come and watch a football match. We can't charge more than the city clubs do. We must be on a par with them. They command the bigger gates, so they will always have more money. Their overheads are often larger than ours, but not so much more, than ours, as you might think. It is only the players' wages and bonuses which are significantly greater than at our club. It doesn't make a lot of difference whether it is Manchester United or Blackpool—or the Workingtons, Newports, and Rochdales of the League—the overheads are still tremendously high. We each have a ground to maintain. We each have ground-staff to pay. We each have match-day staff to pay. We each have the basic commitments of a Football League club.

The only answer for the town club is to produce its own players and keep the majority of them. Every year, many of the small clubs have to sell one or two of their star players. We have to be very careful that we don't finish up with all the town clubs producing youngsters to sell, and only a very few clubs who can afford to pay the transfer fees. The town club would then be unable to sell some of its star players, and, therefore, be unable to raise enough money to survive.

How long is it since people began saying that the smaller clubs would go out of existence? People have been talking like this for thirty years, and most of the small clubs are still playing. The big club is using the small club as a nursery for players. The small club is grooming players for the big club to buy one day, so the big club doesn't want to lose the small club. The big clubs can't afford to pay a wage each week to, say, 1,000 players; but 1,000 players can be paid by Third and Fourth Division clubs. The big club can then come along and say, "He is a good player—I want him," and pay for the transfer. Instead of letting the Government take all the profits in tax, the big club will plough the money back into football. It will go back into football, somewhere, to strengthen this brotherhood of clubs which is the Football League.

The smaller the club, the more it feels it has to give hospitality, and we're met—every time we've gone to places like Newport and Workington—tremendous hospitality. A little while ago, we went to Chorley, a non-League club, for a Lancashire Senior Cup match, which for Blackpool is a reserve-team game and for Chorley would be a first-team game. We played there under floodlights, and the match resulted in a draw. They were thrilled to bits that a League club was coming to Chorley, and their hospitality was absolutely tremendous. I think this is true of football throughout the country. The majority of clubs treat each other as brothers—off the field! —and they help each other where they can. This is one more reason why I don't think any of the larger clubs want to see any of the little clubs go out of the League. They all feel part of a brother-hood. There are only 92 League clubs, and 92, spread through the whole country, isn't many. We don't want any less. We want it to stay at 92.

We have a Development Office in the stadium itself, with a shop front. The Development Office and shop deals with all requests for programmes, autographs, and photos. People write to us from all over the world. We sometimes get requests from people who are trying to trace an ancestor. We had one recently from New York. This chappie's friend's uncle was a player at Blackpool at one time. They're trying to trace where he lives now, and what happened to him when he left Blackpool. Of course, this takes some doing. We have records, but they don't always go back as far as some of these people wish. So what we normally do, if we can't trace it, is to pass the query to the local press who have cuttings going back to the year dot.

We get some strange requests. We had one a year or so ago from a scout troop in Bispham. The scout leader wrote to say that he had approximately forty scouts in his troop and they idolized Harry Thomson, the goalkeeper. They were having a fête and a show, and they wondered whether, during the show, Harry would like to sit on a chair in the middle of the stage, while they sang some scout songs. Poor Harry would have to sit there and keep a face of responsibility and elegance about him. These are the sort of requests we get for a player who is the idol of the crowd. If a player has a gimmick, the youngsters love it. These are the players the crowd likes, and they're always having to turn out to do jobs.

I feel deeply involved in the success and failure of the team. You have to try and avoid feeling involved, but you can't help it. Every person has his own idea of what is a good team, who is a good player, what would make a good combination of players, and so on; and I have my own ideas. But I would never voice them to the manager, or to anyone else, unless asked for my opinion. But I feel these things, tremendously.

The main personal reward for me is success. I want the club to be successful. I also take pride in the presentation of the club to the public. This is a major thing for me. I want to hear the public say, "Oh, it's Blackpool Football Club, *the* Blackpool Football Club." We aren't the biggest club in the country. We can't possibly be. We know this. But we can be the smartest club, the tidiest club. I like to hear spectators say: "My word, what a clean ground." "What a smart-looking place." "What efficient staff." This is what matters to me—that everything about the club should be good. It gives me great pride to feel that Blackpool Football Club is doing what it has set out to do—and that is to impress everybody, from the public to the press. I don't want the club in disrepute for any reason whatever. Everything I have control over I like to think is being done to the benefit of Blackpool Football Club.

32

THE CHAIRMAN
Umpire or Dictator ?

Frank Dickinson is—so far as he knows—the first architect to be
Chairman of a Football League club. He has been a director of
Blackpool F.C. since 1964, and he became Chairman in October
1970. 1970 was a challenging year for a new Chairman, because
the club was being tormented by problems: in the boardroom, in
the manager's office, and on the field of play. Under Mr Dickinson's
Chairmanship, the club has steered a much more steady course.

He was born in Balby, a suburb of Doncaster, but has lived in
Blackpool since he was one year old. He has been watching Blackpool football for half a century: "Although I'm Yorkshire-born,
I like to consider myself a true 'Seasider'." He manages—even *he*
doesn't know how—to serve his family, Blackpool Football Club,
and Mackeith, Dickinson & Partners, the Blackpool-based firm of
architects, of which he is the senior partner. Over to Mr Dickinson:

There is a tendency in some clubs for one man to believe that he
is the club, the dictator of the club. No doubt these men have the
very best of intentions. I could quote you several examples—
I'm thinking particularly of one or two big clubs in the north—
where a wealthy Chairman has helped to put a club right on the
map.

I see my job, as Chairman, as being that of an impartial man
in the boardroom. There are nine directors—not just one. My rôle
is to get as much as I can—in the interests of Blackpool Football
Club—out of the other members of the Board. Every member of
our Board has a part to play, and every member must be allowed to
play it. We have a number of sub-committees—all of which I serve
on—and, by this method, every director has a specific job to do.
The sub-committees meet, and then report-back to the main Board.
The sub-committees have not got the power to act, unless they
have been given a specific authority from the main Board. Unless

we have this system of reporting-back, a few directors might attempt to take charge, and run the whole outfit.

Blackpool went through a period of discord, and it has been my wish to bring harmony to the club, and have everybody working as a team. Football is a team game, and it is team-spirit—in the boardroom, as well as on the field—that keeps a club going.

Chairmanship is a human-relations job. I let every director have his say. I very seldom rap the table. Occasionally I have to, because talk can go on and on. No subject is more contentious than football. I don't hesitate to call for a vote. If it's 6 to 3, then the "ayes" carry the day. The "noes" have had their say, and they've lost. Nobody falls out over a vote.

The Chairman has a seven-day-a-week job. And it's a day-and-night job. I'm inundated with phone calls from the press, at all hours. Reporters always want to speak to the Chairman. It would be helpful if they confined their calls to normal office hours—unless the circumstances were really exceptional. Looking at it with hindsight, I doubt if I would have taken on this job. Almost daily, there's some important point to be settled. I just couldn't do the job without the co-operation of my two partners, my four associates, and the staff. They've all rallied round.

Luckily, I've got a very good Vice-Chairman, Clifford Sagar. He takes more than his share of the responsibilities, and, although we have different personalities, we work well together, in the interests of Blackpool Football Club. Fortunately, one of his businesses is within 300 yards of Bloomfield Road, and so he can visit the club almost every day.

My first year was the hardest. We had a temporary manager for a while: Jimmy Meadows, under difficult circumstances, did a grand job and got the best out of the players. Then I had quite a tussle—over a number of weeks—to get Bob Stokoe as our manager.

I've tried hard. I've really done my best. I'd be a hypocrite if I said I hadn't enjoyed it. My job shouldn't be quite as arduous from now on. We have more harmony in the boardroom. We have first-class officials: a fine manager, experienced coaching staff, and a secretary (Des McBain) who is growing in stature all the time. When you've got a good manager, and good staff, a football club is similar to any other business: you have to control it, and make sure that there are no loop-holes and that everything is running smoothly. The main difference—between running a normal business and running a football club—is that, at a football club, you are not under pressure to show a profit for the shareholders:

firstly, because the directors themselves usually hold the majority of shares; secondly, because not very many clubs pay a dividend to their shareholders. You therefore have to ensure that this does not lull you into a false sense of security.

At Blackpool, the position of Chairman comes up for renewal each year. My personal feeling is that the Chairman should relinquish his post after about three to five years. He should hand over, preferably, to the Vice-Chairman, who will have had a few years to learn about everything that goes on in the club. I don't believe that someone should be Chairman for a number of years, but this depends on your having a director who is willing to accept the responsibilities of being Chairman.

The first qualifications, for becoming a Blackpool director, are that you should love the game and have at least twenty-five shares! I'm convinced that a love of the game is still vital, but I can see that things are changing. The abolition of the maximum wage brought about big changes in football.

In days past, a director was mainly required to give of his time. Since the abolition of the maximum wage, the directors of town clubs have had to put their hands in their pockets and lend money to their clubs. This obviously limits the number of people—however willing, and enthusiastic about football, they may be—who can now become directors. Right through the history of Blackpool Football Club, you'll find that we've managed to sell more players than we've had to buy, and therefore we've balanced the books. But, in recent years, this has not been the case. We've spent far more—on players—than we've recouped.

In our Articles of Association, the maximum number of directors is nine. Every year, three directors retire, and, if they wish to stand again offer themselves for re-election. They have to compete with any nominees there may be from the ranks of the shareholders. My personal view is that nine is too many. Five would be a good number; at the most, seven. I think you'll find that only half-a-dozen League clubs have as many as nine directors. Most clubs have five or six.

I didn't play football after I left school, but several Blackpool directors did. Mr Parr played at right-back for Accrington Stanley. Tom Lane, a right-half or inside-right, was prominent in Fylde amateur football for many years, and at one time he was on Blackpool's books as an amateur.

Derek Lewin was an England amateur international inside-forward, and he represented Great Britain in the Melbourne Olympics of 1956. He was a member of the Bishop Auckland team that won the Amateur Cup in 1955, 1956, and 1957. The 1956

Final went to a replay, making four Cup Final matches in three years. Derek Lewin scored five goals in those four games.

Wally Lines played wing-half/inside-forward, and he was awarded a county cap at schoolboy level. Watford wanted him to sign professional forms, but his father didn't want him to become a footballer. A year or so ago, the Blackpool team went to Watford, accompanied, as usual, by several directors. Before the game, Mr Lines was speaking to a Watford director. "What is your name?", he was asked. "Lines." "Lines? We once had a good player here by the name of Lines." "That's right," came the reply. "Me."

In the past, I've often thought that more ex-professional footballers should be co-opted onto the Boards of League clubs. They wouldn't necessarily have to be big shareholders, but they could give clubs the benefit of their advice. A perfect example of what I have in mind is Sir Matt Busby, a very distinguished player and manager, who was recently elected to the Board of Manchester United.

Nowadays, the tendency is to pay higher salaries to managers. The standard of managers has never been as high as it is now. They are more truly professional than ever before. Today, they are better paid, they are better coaches, and they have better business brains. They have less job-security, than before, and this makes the competition for jobs very keen.

How much do directors know about the playing side of the game? That, of course, is the $64,000 question. Football is a game of contention. If each director picked the first-team for next Saturday's match, you wouldn't get two teams alike. Everyone who watches football has his or her own ideas, and surely this is one of the joys of the game? You can curse the referee, you can shout at the players, you can cheer the players, you can jeer at the players. You can even curse the Chairman! If you took all that away, there wouldn't be much left. To a lot of people, football is an outlet for their emotions.

I never played in senior football, but I contend that my appreciation of the game is as good as most people's. I have not got Mr Stokoe's *finer* judgement of what players do, because he was a good player, and he can see moves and subtle things in a game which I, to be honest, miss—but this doesn't detract from my enjoyment.

Many football-club directors think they are quite capable of watching junior football and picking out good players. I question that. I don't think many of them have that qualification. It's merely a bit of ego. I, personally, wouldn't put myself forward as the man to go out and find the boy of seventeen who will be a star at twenty-two. But I don't think that, these days, that's one of the prime qualifications of a football-club director. More of that—directors giving opinions on young players—used to take place in previous years. Today, what a club director needs is clear thinking and a good business-sense. Generally, you'll find that directors are men who have been successful in their own businesses. This enables them to have the time to spend on the affairs of the club, to travel with the team, and to attend Board meetings. And, if they've been successful in their own field of business, they often have money to put into the football club.

Where else do you get a more varied selection of people than in a football-club boardroom?

Clifford Sagar, the Vice-Chairman, is a director of several companies, with interests in the motor trade, wholesale textiles, and warehouse discount houses. He's a very live-wire businessman and a keen negotiator. People are *born* with this flair, and he has it in abundance.

Ismail Gibrail is a director on the board of management of several hotels, and he is the managing director of a company that whole-sales and retails tea and coffee.

Alderman Albert Stuart is a former Mayor of Blackpool. He has been a town councillor and alderman for many years, and a company director associated with the licensing trade and provisions. He is the President of the South Shore Cricket Club, and has been the backbone in the development of Blackpool Football Club, and many other sporting activities in the town.

Tom Lane's business interests have centred on Blackpool's amusements and entertainments industry. He is a former Chairman of the South Pier Company.

Derek Lewin is Chairman of a company that imports foodstuffs. He gave a lot of help and support to Manchester United after the Munich crash.

Wally Lines is a director of a catering-equipment company. He was a co-founder of the Blackpool Football Supporters' Club in 1925: it was one of the first supporters' clubs in the country. He was responsible for the formation of the Lancashire Football League in 1936, and has been President ever since. This League provides age-for-age football for amateurs and apprentice professionals of Football League clubs in Lancashire.

Dick Seed is a former company-director. He was hon. secretary of Blackpool Football Club from 1940 until 1962, and was awarded the League Long-Service Medal. In his long association with the club—as secretary and as Chairman—Mr Seed has seen many changes. During the club's fluctuations of fortune, over the years, he has always been a calm and steadying influence.

Stanley Parr is the managing director of a firm of painting contractors. One of his grandfathers was Tom Parr, a Blackpool half-back who played in the club's first-ever season, 1887–88. Harry Parr, Blackpool's captain in the club's first-ever League match (1896), was Tom's brother and, therefore, Stanley's great-uncle.

I'm an architect. The day I left school, I went to work as an articled pupil. On the Monday morning—I was sixteen at the time —my very first job was at Blackpool Football Club. There was some work to do on the ground: to provide a cover on the east side (affectionately known as "The Scratching Shed"). From that day onwards, I have always been associated with the club's architects.

Some directors travel on the coach to a match, and seldom even speak to the players. The directors have very little contact—formal or informal—with the players. Contact between directors and players is not a thing to be encouraged. The big danger in fraternization is that some players would think that they were favoured. That would be bad for dressing-room discipline.

I don't believe in an excess of fraternization with the players, but a genuine interest in their welfare, and in the welfare of their families, is desirable—in the interests of promoting a happy club.

Directors don't know a lot about the working relationship between the manager and his players. A director would only know about this if he were familiar with a player, to a point where the player could confide in him. I don't find that players are often disloyal to a manager, even though they may be at odds with him. In other words, the club captain doesn't come knocking at my door to say: "We've asked for something. The manager has refused point-blank. Will you please take action." I, personally, would resent this and rebut it. If things were really difficult at the club, and the captain came to me with a very serious matter, then I would have to listen. But I would never encourage this sort of liaison.

The players have to get permission from the manager if they want to give a quote in the press, or on radio or TV: whether they want to talk about Blackpool or about football in general. In some cases, I should think the manager may want to know about the content, or see the actual text, before he says "Yes".

The directors watch what happens on the field of play and in practice matches: these are our main sources of information about the relationship between the manager and his players. You can see whether or not the players are running for each other. If

there is any disharmony, you can sense it. This is one of the responsibilities of being a director. You may not know the cause of the
trouble, at that stage, but you can feel that something is wrong. A
football-club director has to know a lot about life and a lot about
people; he doesn't need an Oxford degree, or a brilliant brain, or a
"first" in economics.

A number of directors—in all clubs—like to watch the younger
players develop. Apart from watching the first team, a director
can learn a lot from travelling with the reserves. Some players,
who are left out of the first team, do tend—and they're only human
—to let it be seen by their play that they feel a bit half-hearted
about Central League football. They think they're above reserve-
team football, and, if he's a senior man, it takes a jolly good
player to buckle down and help the youngsters. A moment of truth
comes in every player's career, when he realizes that he is no
longer an automatic selection for the first team.

And take a first-team player who has been injured. Usually, he'll
play a game in the reserves to prove that he's back to match fitness.
I would expect him to be as keen as mustard to show his paces.
But just supposing the first team has struck a good patch, and the
manager doesn't want to change a winning side. The player, after
three or four games with the reserves, may say to himself, "Well,
I've had enough of this." This is understandable. A footballer has
a short career. If a player is at the top, he wants to stay there as
long as he can. This is an example of the sort of problem that can
occur in the reserve team of a club of Blackpool's size.

The city clubs, by contrast, have benefited from the advent of
the no-maximum wage—to such an extent that they have each
formed a strong pool of first-team players, some of whom have to
play in the reserves. But they remain on first-team wages.

Blackpool had a long settled period under the Chairmanships of
Harry Evans and Dick Seed. As I see it, every club has cycles of
good times and bad times. We'd had a smooth time. The *end* of that
cycle coincided with the removal of the maximum wage. We seemed
to be fighting an eternal battle against relegation from the First
Division. In recent years, a lot of shares have changed hands, and
we have had a spate of managerial changes and new faces in the
boardroom.

I've tried, in every way possible, to bring harmony and unity
to the club: by giving every director something to do, and by
listening attentively at Board meetings. I've tried to set an example
by being unstinting in whatever I've done for Blackpool Football
Club, and I've encouraged my co-directors to do the same. Is there
any more practical way in which a Chairman can fulfil his rôle?

Blackpool's trip to Italy in 1971—for the Anglo-Italian Competition—did me a lot of good. Our manager and our secretary came back to Blackpool for a few days—in the middle of the trip—and so for a while I was in charge of the touring party. It was quite an education.

I've toured all over Europe for the past twenty-five years, and I've become familiar with the customs of the various countries. Italy, in particular, enjoys an afternoon siesta. Occasionally, the Blackpool party would arrive at a hotel in mid-afternoon and be frustrated by *apparent* lack of service. I took it upon myself to help the hotel management in every way possible, always explaining that the players' needs should receive priority—because, without the players, there would have been no Italian trip. And, after all, the players had training schedules to keep.

At one hotel, the wives in our party responded to the example I was trying to set. Realizing that the hotel management were in difficulties, during a siesta period, the wives set to work: they cleared the tables and did the washing-up. That is a true story.

For me, the most pleasing thing about the whole trip—apart from our splendid victory in the final—was the behaviour of the Blackpool players, on and off the field. They were terrific. They really were. Here they were—young lads, most of them—hundreds of miles away from their wives and sweethearts. They fully enjoyed themselves, and, at the same time, they behaved well and were a credit to Blackpool Football Club.

We had a barnstormer of an evening after the lads had beaten Verona. We had an impromptu get-together in the hotel. We sang some songs: one of the most popular was *We all play in a shirt of tangerine* to the tune of the Beatles' song *Yellow Submarine*.

Now, do you see the difference between fraternizing—which we spoke about earlier—and being in a party of people away from home? I feel that this particular evening won me a lot of respect from the players. Until then, they must have thought I was a bit stodgy. We really let our hair down: that was a special situation in which I could do so. I remembered all sorts of longish limericks and songs à la Billy Bennett. They are risqué, without being dirty. I noticed that some of the younger players looked amazed at this repertoire of humour which they obviously had never heard before. I have a good memory for this sort of thing. In fact, it appals me!

Our trip did a lot for the town of Blackpool, as well as for the football club. The night before we played Roma, a reporter asked: "How would you describe the Roma Football Club?" I replied, "I regard Roma as the Arsenal of Italy." Arsenal, of course, had just done "The Double". It made banner headlines: "President of Blackpool regards Roma. . . . " The Italians don't understand the word "Chairman"; they use the word "President". The President of an Italian club is an overlord. He runs the whole outfit, unlike the Chairman of a British club.

The press regarded us as a family. They described us as "The Blackpool family". You see, the Blackpool directors brought their wives. This is absolutely unknown in Italy. Very few directors' wives go to matches over there. The press were delighted to see us—the directors and our wives—travelling with the team, as a family. It seemed to strike the right note: the Catholics are very family-minded. The reception we were given in Montecatini is a typical example. The local club offered us every facility. In return, I presented a little pennant to every member of a youth team. I gave their President a bigger pennant, and there were badges for every member of his Committee. We went to endless trouble to have good relationships with everybody we met.

We won thousands of friends when the players threw Blackpool badges to the crowd before each match. The Italians thought this was fantastic. I think we took four gross. We should have taken ten gross. Perhaps the local council could help us with this, another time. The Italians go mad over the tiniest souvenir.

When we came out of the Roma stadium, our coach went up a ramp. There must have been at least 100 soldiers—with tear gas and tommy guns—lining the Olympic Way. It's a big broad avenue, similar to Wembley's Olympic Way. There were some armoured cars and a huge crowd of people. A few days earlier, another English club had been there, and there was a riot. It was rather frightening. I was sitting in the front of the coach, wishing I was in an armoured car. We'd just beaten Roma, remember. When we got to the top of the ramp, we realized what the crowd had come for. They had come to cheer us. "Viva Blackpool! Viva Black-pool!", they shouted. We opened the windows of the coach. We threw to the crowd every souvenir we could find—I threw them my tie—and they went frantic.

Before the home matches in this Competition, we gave a lot of thought to public relations. One of our best inspirations was to take seven interpreters to Manchester Airport, to meet Verona and Roma: four to be with the squad of players, and three to be with the visiting directors. The touring party was never left on its own. We took them to the night-clubs, and they thought it was marvel-lous. Blackpool is a publicity-minded town. We're used to entertain-ing people. We're used to being the hosts. Even after Roma had beaten us, we went back to their hotel and took them out.

Jimmy Armfield, captain of Blackpool and captain of England, one of the
fastest full-backs of all time

Emlyn Hughes, a stylish and crisp-tackling player who became Britain's most expensive teenage footballer when he joined Liverpool in 1967

The Italian hospitality *before* a match was impeccable. Till the end of my days, I'll never forget the meal we had in the Leonardo da Vinci Hotel in Rome. It was owned by the President of the football club. Every waiter wore white gloves. The cutlery and linen were beautiful. I don't suppose that royalty dine in more sumptuous surroundings or are ever served a more exquisitely cooked meal.

Now let's get back to our discussion on Blackpool Football Club. It's hard to over-estimate the importance of having a first-class manager. He is the key man at a club. He needs so many qualities: tact, coaching ability, leadership. I think that the directors of a club should give a manager a *minimum* period of three years to make his mark. I don't think it's fair to a manager to give him a contract for less than a three-year period.

At Blackpool we've had two recent cases of a former player becoming manager: Ron Suart and Stan Mortensen. I wonder if a former player commands as much respect as a stranger? I think a man cannot be a prophet in his own country. Of course, success is what counts, whether you are a local man or not. If Ronnie Suart had taken us to the Cup Final once or twice, he would have been hailed as one of the best managers we've ever had. Morty was wonderful with the players. He was enthusiastic, a born P.R.O.

We were very keen to have Bob Stokoe as our manager. He'd been with Bury, and he made a success of that job. He really made his mark at Carlisle. They were "in the red" when he came to the club, and they were "in the black" when he left. He pruned the staff to about sixteen professionals, in order to cut down expenses. He was one of the first managers to do away with a reserve side.

A manager *must* have certain qualities. He can't hope to control his players or guide them or stimulate them, unless he has the right qualities. And, in the same way, it's important for players to have the right qualities. We'd had discipline problems at Blackpool before Mr Stokoe came. You will never get me to recommend the signing-on of one of these reputed bad-lads. It would kill the good name of the club. It's too high a price to pay.

There was no doubt about Mr Stokoe's ability as a manager—he had a fine record. Having satisfied ourselves that he had—in addition—the right personal qualities, we strove to get him. And Carlisle strove to keep him! We handled it from Chairman to Chairman, which is the correct way. At first, Mr Sheffield, Carlisle's Chairman, said he wasn't interested. He would not even permit me to interview Bob Stokoe. That wasn't good enough, because, in my opinion, every man is entitled to influence his own destiny.

We felt we could offer Mr Stokoe better chances at Blackpool than he would have at Carlisle. Mr Stokoe was prepared for a move. He felt he'd done as much as he could at Carlisle.

He was working with only about sixteen players, so his reserve players seldom got a game. If the team was playing well, he had five surplus players on his hands. All they could do was play football amongst themselves. Every manager has ambition. They all want to run a First Division set-up—which we have at Blackpool—with a first team, a Central League team, and one or two junior teams. In the same way, I would rather manage an office of sixty architects, than an office of only six. There's more work. There's more *challenge*.

After a lot of negotiations, we finally got permission to see Mr Stokoe. We agreed terms that suited both clubs. There's a happy ending to the story. Carlisle had been trying, for several years, to arrange a testimonial match for Dick Young, their trainer/coach. Blackpool promised—through our new manager, Mr Stokoe—to help Carlisle. We took our team there for the testimonial match. I met Mr Sheffield, and my wife met his wife, and we were all friends. I saw him again at the Cup Final. I'm happy to say that there is no animosity at all between our two clubs.

I'm sure that the move to Blackpool has suited Mr Stokoe. This is a nice coast to live on. The air is good. The sand is good. Blackpool is Britain's premier resort, simply because it has a lot to offer. Over the years, the town of Blackpool has helped to attract a number of players to the club. But Blackpool is a two-edged sword for a football club. It's a gay place. There are a lot of nightclubs, and a lot of temptations for players.

The longer Bob Stokoe is with us, the more my faith in him is justified. He's a clean-living man: he doesn't smoke, and he drinks very rarely. He's a very good golfer. He is dedicated to football—almost to the point of fanaticism. He's a perfectionist. His dedication to his work is unbelievable. I wouldn't have thought it possible.

The manager, the Chairman, and the Vice-Chairman, of a football club work very closely together: more closely, I would say, than in a normal business, in which a general manager seldom goes to his Chairman to discuss day-to-day affairs.

Mr Stokoe is a disciplinarian—which we needed at Blackpool. A few years ago, Blackpool had the finest and cleanest record of any club in the League. Then our club discipline—on and off the field—gradually deteriorated.

Mr Stokoe would normally mention a disciplinary measure, before carrying it out. He would mention it to the Board, or possibly to me in an informal way—depending on the seriousness of the offence. He deals with some offences entirely on his own.

Mr Stokoe has sole responsibility for all team matters: team selection, and so on. This is normal at most League clubs. Some Chairmen, in years past, have thought that they were very knowledgeable about football. Perhaps they were. We had a Chairman at Blackpool called Harry Evans, a great character. He knew his football backwards. I daresay Joe Smith, Blackpool's manager at that time, would discuss team selection with Harry. But I'm quite sure that—even in those days—the manager would have the final word.

All directors obviously have their own views on team selection, and they can be raised with the manager at a Board meeting. The manager attends every Board meeting and he submits a report. We usually meet on a Tuesday afternoon, from 2.30 until 4 o'clock, or sometimes later. The manager doesn't attend the whole of the meeting. His report is normally the first item, because he usually wants to go to a training session.

He is never asked to submit his team for the *next* match, but what he does do is to submit a report on the previous week's games. That's his first item. Then he goes through his list of injuries. Then he might talk about possible transfers, buying or selling. He'll raise any problems concerning specific players. A player may have said that he'd like to buy a club house. One of the scouts may be asking for more money: could we give him another 1p-a-mile on his travel allowance? And so on. When the manager has finished making his report, I always say to the directors, "Have you any questions to ask the manager?" A perfectly fair question would be, "Why do you play so-and-so instead of so-and-so?" The manager would then give his reasons. This sort of question isn't a subtle way of telling the manager what to do. I know of no Blackpool director who has ever said, "It should be *obvious* to you that 'X' is better than 'Y'. Well, for God's sake, don't mess about. Put 'X' in the team." This doesn't happen. By asking a question about team selection, a director is, in fact, being *fair* to the manager. This sort of question can clear up a possible misunderstanding, and it also gives the manager a chance to justify his decisions. And, after a discussion, some managers are big enough to say, "Well, it would appear that I've made a mistake." No one is infallible.

I've been watching Blackpool football for fifty years, since I was nine or ten. I feel terrifically involved when I'm watching a match. I "kick" every ball. My heart beats faster. I smoke more. I have a difficult job trying to stop myself from shouting. You're not supposed to shout if you're in a directors' box. You must never criticize one of your own players, because you may want to sell that player to a visiting director, who will be listening. You've got to be tactful.

When Blackpool score a goal, I jump up and I wave my arms. I can't help it, I'm sorry! I'm very much involved. There have been times when I've had to leave before the end. Sometimes a match is just too tense, and I can't stick it any longer. When I used to stand on the kop or in the paddocks—those were the years when I most enjoyed my football. There, you can shout and have a jolly good argument, if you want to.

My fellow-directors also enjoy their football. There's quite a lot of chit-chat between us. Mr Seed is rather taciturn. He doesn't *look* to be emotionally involved, but I'm sure he's churning inside. Mr Gibrail is the man to be careful of. He's forever kicking you. If you sit next to him, your legs will be black and blue! So, as you can see, the atmosphere in a directors' box is similar to that in other seated parts of the ground. If anything, the atmosphere is a bit more controlled—with one or two exceptions!—because of possible transfer deals.

Football is an art as well as a science: it's difficult to proportion it. But football is definitely becoming more scientific—not always to the betterment of the game. The natural ball-player represents the "art" side of football. He has superb co-ordination between eye, brain, and feet. People are *born* with this ability—I'm convinced of it. You can improve a footballer's skill, just as you can improve a singer's voice. But, if you haven't been *born* with a singing voice, no amount of training will produce a *good* voice. The same applies to football. An ordinary player can be improved by training, but he'll never have natural flair.

From a mile away, you can spot the naturals, the artists of the game: the Tony Greens, the Bests, the Bobby Charltons. One of the best-ever Blackpool players—with natural flair—was little Ernie Taylor. He is a diminutive little chap, but he could dictate a game: slow it down; quicken it up. What a player! Peter Doherty was another Blackpool player who could control a game. Alan Suddick is yet another who can control a game, when he's on top form. He's *made* that way. He's got that *something* extra. You can improve ability, but you can't *create* genius.

Sometimes, though, a club *buys* genius. I'll give you an outline of how a player is bought. A League club has a number of scouts. Each manager seems to have his own particular brand of scout, who knows the types of players the boss is looking for. A player is watched for 3, 4, 5, 6 games, and, if the need arises for this player, you approach his club. You must always approach the club first:

Chairman to Chairman, or manager to manager. You mustn't approach the player first. That's unforgivable.

Before an approach is made, the manager would come to a full Board meeting—not a sub-committee meeting—and say, "I have a player in mind who would strengthen the team, but he would cost us £40,000." Then the directors would have a discussion with the manager. The manager might add, "This is the man I want. I've had an offer of £25,000 for one of our players. If you can find £15,000—or if £15,000 is already available—we can go into the market."

A transfer involving a large fee is a high-level decision. I doubt if any manager has the power to negotiate a major transfer, by himself. But all things are relative. If a manager came and said, "I've just bought a player for £5,000, and I'm sure this is a bargain," he probably wouldn't get any severe criticism from the Board. He may have had to make a quick buy. But there is a limit to what you would permit a manager to spend without the Board's sanction. After all, it is the directors—at most clubs—who own the majority of the shares. They obviously have to protect their own money.

It isn't always the manager who recommends that the club should obtain a new player. Depending on who the directors are, and how much they know about football, a suggestion may come from a member of the Board. He may have had a player recommended to him by a friend, or he may have seen a player while away on holiday. The manager, in turn, would ask his scouts to give an opinion. A transfer could start in this way.

I would always prefer a director's recommendation to be made at a Board meeting. Nothing starts more trouble in a boardroom than an individual director persistently hob-nobbing with the manager. Every director has a right to know what is going on. Every director should make his contribution to the work of the club *as the member of a team*. Some directors have discovered really top-class players. But, nowadays, directors tend to leave talent-spotting to the professionals: the manager and his scouts.

The other side of the coin is the selling of a player. There are several reasons that may make you want to sell a player. First of all, you have a player who is dissatisfied with the size of his wage packet. We may value one of our players at £120,000 in the transfer market, but on the field of play he is only one of eleven players, and only as good as his contribution to the success of the *team*. I suggest that there is a difference in the two values. For example, we may have over-valued him because we want to retain his services.

Although this player may be getting more than any other member of the team, he is still likely to say, "If I'm worth £120,000, surely I'm worth £X a week?"

Transfer talk sometimes starts after a player has been on international duty for the first time. He meets players from other clubs who boast: "I've got a 4.2 Jag. I get £100 a week basic; and £50 appearance money." He comes back to his club and he thinks, "Well, I should be getting more money." This is understandable. These days, a player has a League career lasting ten to fifteen years. In that period, he has, possibly, five years right at the top. It's natural for players to want to make the most of their ability, under the no-maximum wage. I don't blame them.

Players are after their 5 per cent share of the transfer fee. They don't get anything if *they* ask for a transfer. *The club* must put a player on the transfer list for him to qualify for the 5 per cent. But if a player really wanted to leave Blackpool, I wouldn't stand in his way. After all, you can't force a person to work for you, against his will. A disgruntled player can apply to the League. He can write and say, "My club value me at £X-thousand, but they're only paying me £Y. I think this is unfair. I should have £Z a week." Then his case goes for arbitration at a tribunal: with the Players' Union, on one side; the League Management—representing the club—on the other side; and a neutral person as Chairman. So the players are not slaves, and the clubs are not free to dictate to their players. Each side is protected.

The main time for selling is at the end of a season, when the club compiles its retain-and-transfer list. The manager says to the Board, "I can do without these four. They're not playing to the standard I want." Then you notify other clubs that these men are available, and you invite offers.

Another time, when you may want to sell, is if a club fancies one of your reserve players. If you haven't room in your first team for the player, and the fee is right, you'll probably sell him. A number of Lancashire clubs—the Boltons, the Burnleys, and the rest—have kept going by rearing promising young players and then selling them to the city clubs.

Some players—who are deputising for a first-team man, who is only slightly better—get reserve-minded. I've seen it happen so often. They may then develop business interests outside football. Some managers don't agree with this. They are so dedicated to the game that they think every player should live, eat, and sleep, football. I admire a manager like that, but I think a boy should be encouraged to have another string to his bow—no matter how good a player he is. A player should provide for middle age and old age: he has many years to live after he is thirty-five, when his playing days are over.

I believe it is of incalculable value for a top-ranking seaside resort like Blackpool to have a First or a Second Division football club. We bring thousands of people into the town during the winter —when money is tight in Blackpool—and they almost all spend something. We are determined to regain and maintain a place in the First Division. Not so many people will come to see us play Portsmouth, but they'll come from far and near to see us play Manchester United.

Blackpool Football Club is an important part of the town's entertainment business. We help to get a lot of publicity for the town. Take our victory in the 1971 Anglo-Italian Competition: the name of Blackpool was being praised all over Europe. I think the Town Council, in return, should help us as much as possible. At the present time, we are getting fair treatment. They've recently made a car park available to us—for nothing—for our season-ticket holders.

We own Bloomfield Road, but not every club owns its ground: some are owned by the local Council. But I don't know of any town where there is a nominee, from the Council, on a football-club Board. I would strenuously oppose a Town Council that wanted to take part in the running of a club, but I do firmly believe that a Town Council and a League club should work closely together, as partners, in the good interests of the town.

Blackpool Football Club has had a distinguished history— especially since the mid-thirties. I see this glorious past as being a help to Blackpool F.C. in the seventies: we have a fine tradition behind us. Some people think there is a danger in having a glorious past "because the present team is always being compared with great teams of the past". I don't agree with this argument. The comparing of teams of different eras is all part of the contention in football. It's all part of the scene. Thousands of people in Blackpool—and in every town that has a League club—have fun taking part in heated discussions. Which was the best-ever Blackpool team? Who has been the best Blackpool player in each of the eleven positions? You know the sort of thing.

What we *are* suffering from at Blackpool is that we did not take full advantage of our success. I'm thinking particularly of ground improvements. There comes a time, in every club's history, when certain things have to be done. In the post-war years, the Blackpool team—with such great players as Matthews, Mortensen, and Johnston—was picking itself, week after week. I suppose that building costs always seem high, but, compared to what they are today, they were cheap in those days. The directors should have had the courage to say, "Right. That stand comes down. Up with the new one." It is unfortunate that Blackpool missed that chance. At one or two clubs that have built new stands, the spectators have gone wild because their team hasn't been doing too well. The job of the directors is to strike a balance between the money spent on new players and money spent on ground improvements. A good Board thinks long-term. Every club must improve its facilities. The day has come when quality of comfort counts for more and more. A League club has got to offer first-class refreshments—tea, soup, a bar. And women have to be looked after. As an architect, I won't be satisfied until there is a lot more seated accommodation—not only at Bloomfield Road, but at all football stadiums.

We are ambitious at Blackpool. Ambition is a must. We want to regain our place in the First Division. I'm quite sure we can. We've got a good manager. He wants to do well. It's his living as well, don't forget. And we've got some good young players in the pipeline. I feel that we are now building on solid foundations. I'm confident about Blackpool's future—but not over-confident. I don't go about shouting the odds: that's tempting fate. Football is such a chancy game. Supposing we have two or three injuries early in the season. Then we promote "Jimmy Jones" from the reserves, and he breaks a leg. What are our chances then. Even a Manchester United can't cater for that sort of run of bad luck.

Clubs of Blackpool's size have been facing two big problems in the last few years: the removal of the maximum wage, and the difficulty of borrowing money from the banks. Blackpool F.C. has been rather heavily in debt in the last few years. We've had to fight to keep going, to survive. *Of course* major ground improvements would help to attract more people to our matches. But where can a club like Blackpool get the money? It's back to the old question: Which comes first? The chicken or the egg?

Team-building has to take priority at Blackpool, at the present time; but I would love to see a new west stand. Our west stand is very vulnerable: it is constructed mainly of timber. We have it well insured, and we take all the necessary fire precautions, but, when the old steam trains used to shunt up and down at the back of it, the risk was tremendous. There were sparks flying out of the funnels. But the old stand never went up in flames. [*Mr Dickinson said this with sadness in his voice!*—R.D.]

In my view, the future—for the town clubs of Lancashire—isn't particularly bright, I'm sorry to say. People talk about changing the off-side rule, having more regional matches, and so on. But football seems loath to change, which is a pity. Let's try out new ideas.

I think that a Super League would kill football. Once the odds become too long—against a club like Bury getting into the First Division—a lot of interest in football will die. Bury might get relegated after one season, but at least they will have played against Everton and Manchester United, and had a taste of glory. Why has the F.A. Cup always been so popular? Because a little club will occasionally do the unexpected, and get into the semi-final.

In some countries you just couldn't play football in the summer: it gets too hot. But we don't have the sort of summers that would prohibit football. I think that summer football, played on Sundays, is the ultimate solution. Sunday is the one day of the week when the whole family has time to spare. If you're a churchman, you can still go to church: football wouldn't interfere with that. If we had summer football, there could be a break in August, when so many people are away on holiday. I do think that March–July and September–November are the months when football should be played. The close season would be December–February. You could even send your players abroad for a holiday in the sun.

At Blackpool, we have a nucleus of 10–12,000 hard-core spectators. Considering the size of the Fylde area, you'd think we would do better. But there are a lot of retired people in Blackpool, and a lot of people who were not born in Blackpool. Supposing a man was born in Birmingham, and he comes to live in Blackpool. He'll come to Bloomfield Road to watch Blackpool play Birmingham, but we have a tough job to persuade him to buy a season-ticket.

Television doesn't exactly help to boost our gates. In the middle of February, when it's icy cold, what do you do when you have a nice Saturday lunch inside you? Go out into the cold, or put your feet up and watch your colour TV? I'd like to see stricter control on the amount of football shown on TV. And I'd like to see clubs that are featured on TV paid more money. If you really want me to go to town, let me add that Football League clubs should get a far larger share of the thousands of pounds—not thousands, but millions—being made out of our fixture list. If only we could get more money from this source, we could make more ground improvements, and it would be a wonderful thing for the game. Ground improvements would stop a lot of hooliganism: people aren't so inclined to fight and brawl if they're sitting down.

Money spent on ground improvements—and here I'm thinking of enlarging the capacity of grounds—would help to minimise the dangers to human life. Recent disasters at football stadiums have proved that—in spite of the precautions being taken—there are still many vulnerable spots that are only revealed when maximum-crowd-capacity is reached. And it is the ambition of all clubs to reach maximum-crowd-capacity.

We'd also like to spend more money developing our youth policy, which is so vital to a club of our size. You'd be amazed if you knew how much a youth policy costs—even on our limited scale. We've got to pay for coaching, kit, expenses, travel. A few hundred pounds a week goes *just like that*.

Some people say we should have a new share issue. It's a one-off job. It's not a cheap affair, and it carries no guarantee of success. I don't think things have come to that yet. The present directors have loaned the club tens of thousands of pounds, in an effort to strengthen the team.

I should think that at least three-quarters of the shares are held by members of the Board. This proportion is quite normal at a Football League club, and I don't regard it as being too high. If a club is not successful, everybody knows about it. Everybody! Not just the shareholders. Look what happened at Aston Villa a few years ago. They were doing badly, and a number of directors lost their places on the Board. I'm pretty sure that, at the time, they held most of the shares. But the spectators turned against these men, and public opinion turned against them. You can't fight public opinion. If people jeered at me, every time I drove away from Bloomfield Road, I wouldn't stick it for long. I'd say: "All right. We're not doing well. Let somebody else have a go."

I don't think that the public at large, nor the spectators at football matches, really appreciate how devoted directors are to their club. We give of our time, and, particularly at a club like Blackpool, we give of our money. And what is our reward? We get a cup of tea at half-time, and a drink at the end of the match. We get a lot of satisfaction in helping to run the club. But let's face it, the *real* beneficiaries are the players and their families, and the spectators. If only the spectators realized the worries we have to bear, on behalf of our club. We don't mind criticism, as long as the public comes and supports the club.

I think some clubs pay a dividend to their shareholders—because the bigger clubs own property and other things—but we don't pay a dividend at Blackpool. If Blackpool F.C. ever made big profits, we'd spend a lot of money on the club—on ground improvements, comfort and new amenities for the spectators—long before we would ever think of paying a dividend. I sometimes wonder if the relationship between the directors and the spectators is a tiny bit

one-sided. All we ask for is *support*—at all times—as a reward for
the time and money we put into the club.

There are few *material* rewards in being a Blackpool director.
Take, for example, those of us who went on the Italian trip in
1971—we all paid our own fares and hotel expenses. For League
games, we have a travel rota: two or three directors go to every
away match. But, to save money, we mostly travel by coach these
days; not by train, first class. We stay at a nice hotel, but not at
one of the top ones. We don't stay at the Hilton or the Savoy,
believe me!

It's nice to get away. You're in pleasant company, and the
hospitality of home clubs is amazing. They welcome you, and there
is a lot of *bonhomie*. In our relegation years, other clubs used to
say to us, genuinely, "We're sorry."

And we do our part, when *we* are at home. Blackpool F.C. is
noted for its hospitality. When you change Divisions, you meet old
friends again. You make a lot of friendships in football. Despite
the very severe competition within the League, we keep on very
good terms with the directors of other clubs. If we go to an away
match, and we win, it would be very rare for the directors of the
home club not to come over to us and say, "Well played. Come and
have a drink."

I am proud to have been appointed Chairman of Blackpool
Football Club. I hope that the club will prosper, regain its right-
ful place in the First Division, and continue to be a credit to
Blackpool, the premier seaside resort of the British Isles.

33

THE MANAGER
Football: 25-hours-a-day

Bob Stokoe is a much-respected name in English football. He was with Newcastle from 1947 to 1961—a wonderfully successful era in the club's history. He made his League début at centre-forward, on Christmas Day 1950, and scored a goal that afternoon. After playing in a number of different positions for five or six years, he finally settled-in at centre-half.

In the mid-fifties, he was on the fringe of the England team, but Billy Wright was an automatic selection for England's No. 5 shirt, and Bob Stokoe had to be content with one appearance for the Football League. He won a Cup-winners' medal in the 1955 Final, in which Newcastle beat Manchester City 3-1. Don Revie was City's centre-forward, and Newcastle had an outstanding inside-forward trio in Jackie Milburn, Vic Keeble, and George Hannah.

Milburn and Keeble used to dominate the headlines Sunday by Sunday, because of their goal-scoring feats (feets?). George Hannah, by contrast, was a member of that select company of artist-footballers who remind us that football is not only a game of speed, fitness, and muscle, but a game also of delicacy and imagination. The fifties and sixties also presented for our visual—and vocal!—pleasure: Ernie Taylor, John White, George Eastham, and Tommy ("The Charmer") Harmer. They were all small in stature and light-boned, and their passes and movements across the field, *their* brush-strokes, were memorable for grace and swift penetration.

Bob Stokoe was a member of a fine team, in a famous period of Newcastle United history. In February 1961 he was transferred to Bury, in part-exchange for John McGrath. From the day of Stokoe's début, until the end of the season, Bury did not lose a single League game: Bury finished 1960–61 as Division III Champions with 68 points, the third-highest points-total in Division III history.

Within a year of his arrival at Bury, Bob Stokoe became player-manager. In the season in which Bury were promoted to Division II,

Newcastle—his former club—were relegated to Division II. He had the pleasure of leading Bury to victory at St James' Park in four consecutive seasons.

He became manager of Charlton in 1965, and was relieved of his duties a couple of years later. He spent a year at Rochdale, and then two years at Carlisle, before being appointed manager of Blackpool at the end of December 1970. I now leave it to Bob Stokoe to take up the story, and to make, along the way, many wise comments about the game of football:

When Blackpool first approached me, I didn't want to come. This was before Les Shannon became Blackpool's manager. I had just moved to Carlisle, and, at that stage, I had no intention of leaving them: I'd done a fair bit of moving around over the previous ten years.

When Les Shannon left Blackpool, they came for me again. They made about four approaches. They were really persistent. The first couple of times, I wasn't particularly interested. Things were going well at Carlisle. I was given a lot of authority. We had quite a good team—which I had worked hard, for two years, to re-build—and we'd just missed getting to the 1970 League Cup Final. I was quite enjoying it at Carlisle, and, when I felt they were ready, I was looking forward to taking them into the First Division.

But Blackpool persisted and persisted. I think they'd make up their minds that I could be the salvation of the club. They felt that I was the one to lead them. This influenced me more than anything: the fact that I was wanted so much. I started to waver. In addition, they offered me quite a nice contract. Eventually I said, "If Carlisle are prepared to release me from my contract, I'll join you." Everything was sorted out by the two Chairmen.

On my first day as manager, I felt I was a Blackpool man—and I looked upon the players as "my" players. I went home that night with a list of my players, and details of their backgrounds. Already I was searching: I wanted to know what was going on in the club, and what the players could do. It was a case of total involvement—right from the start. Being a manager is my *life*, and I've got to make a success of it. I am *totally* and *completely* involved with my club. I put the other 91 into the background.

Instead of sitting nicely, near the top of the Second Division— Carlisle had the F.A. Cup to look forward to, as well as the promotion race—I went to Blackpool, who were right bang at the bottom of the First Division. Blackpool were in serious trouble. The club was over-staffed with players, and there were discipline problems. Blackpool had been rather lucky to get promotion the previous

season, and didn't have money in the kitty to strengthen the playing staff during the summer. As an outsider (at the time), I didn't
think Blackpool were well equipped to survive in the First Division.
I was proved right, because they got off to a very poor start.
Blackpool lost the first match of the season, but at least it was an
away match. I always feel it's a tragedy if you start the season with
a home defeat.

Some teams are going to win their first three or four games, and
find themselves at the top. If you make a bad start, you find yourself down at the bottom, looking up the League table. If you find
yourself five or six points behind a team—once the mid-week games
are over—you've got to win three games in three weeks, and they've
got to lose three games in three weeks, before you can catch up.
It takes such a long time to overtake teams that are above you:
that's why a good start is so important.

When I first came to Blackpool, the worst thing possible
happened. We beat West Ham in the Cup 4-0, and everybody was
shouting and jumping about and saying, "Well, this is it. This is
the turning-point." What I tried to say was "Let's not shout too
much—yet." I couldn't believe that First Division defences would
be as easy to beat as West Ham's was that day. We took full
advantage of ground conditions and Tony Green's brilliance. Tony
scored a couple of goals, but he didn't knock in another one until
the very last match of the season.

After beating West Ham, we went to Liverpool and drew 2-2,
after being 2-1 up with eight minutes to go. On the following
Saturday, we got off to a great start against Manchester City at
home. We were leading 3-1 until the last fifteen minutes. The game
ended in a 3-3 draw. If the game had gone on for another five
minutes, City would have beaten us. When things started to go
wrong, Blackpool just used to crumble.

When I came to Blackpool, two players were out of favour:
goalkeeper Harry Thomson and Fred Pickering, the centre-forward.
They'd had problems with the club: they'd been disciplined and
fined. And yet these were the two players who *might* have been
our salvation. I'd always had a lot of respect for Fred Pickering,
as a player. I brought him back in the Liverpool match, and he
scored a goal. The next week, he scored twice against Manchester
City. If only he could have kept it up, it might have given us a
chance to find our feet.

Blackpool had problems with the goalkeeping position. I had
to bring Harry Thomson back, in the hope that he would hang on
until I could find another goalkeeper. I brought Harry back into
the side for the vital match at Ipswich. We were drawing 1-1 until

the last ten minutes, and then Ipswich got the winner from a corner-kick. That was the end for Harry. I bought Neil Ramsbottom from Bury, but I wanted to give him a little time to acclimatise himself. He came into the side a week or so later, but, by then, it was far too late: Blackpool were in real trouble at the bottom of the First Division.

One of the most cruel blows of the season was our defeat by Wolverhampton, early in February. We outplayed them for well over an hour, and it was 0-0 until the last five minutes. We lost 2-0, which was a sad blow. It destroyed a lot of things we'd been working for. Blackpool obviously had some problems in defence, and I've worked very hard to re-build this department.

Only a miracle could have saved Blackpool from relegation. Possibly in lower Divisions, it is a little bit easier to get out of trouble. I managed to do a rescue operation at Carlisle when they were right at the bottom—but that wasn't in the premier Division. You can't go and pinch points at Arsenal and Chelsea, and other clubs of their standard—although we nearly *did* at times.

We went nineteen League games without a win. This sad run was sad in many ways, because, in some of those games, we thoroughly deserved to get better results. But the breaks wouldn't go for us. One of the cruel parts of this game is that you've got to learn to accept bad breaks—because, once the game is over, you can't do anything about them. The unfortunate thing is that the same thing can happen in the *next* game: again you may play well, and still the breaks don't go for you. You keep hoping for better luck in the next game. After a while, your players start to lose heart. The only thing that can help a manager, as he tries to build a new side, is to get results.

When I came to Blackpool, the club was grossly over-staffed. There was a lot of dead wood, which had to be drastically pruned. We have to make Blackpool Football Club a paying proposition. This club couldn't possibly pay its way, with the type of playing staff it had. So I had to do a sorting-out job as quickly and as effectively as possible. It *had* to be done.

A manager can become very unpopular over some of the decisions he makes concerning players, but I was determined that the atmosphere in the dressing-room should be put right: a player's *character* is as important to me as his ability on the field. We wanted to stay in the First Division—but not at all costs. If we'd avoided relegation, we would have had to face another difficult season in the First Division. If you're not good enough to be in a Division, then it's no good being there. With the playing staff we had at the time, we couldn't produce the consistency to keep our

place in Division I. There wasn't anything left in the kitty, because
the club had spent a lot of money on players during the previous
three or four years. So I had to do a lot of trading, a lot of weed-
ing out.

Don't get me wrong. We want to re-establish ourselves as a First
Division club. But we want to re-enter the First Division from a
position of strength. We want to have a good chance of staying up,
and we want to *enjoy life* in the First Division—and not always
have to look over our shoulders to count how many places we are
from the bottom. It's no good going up for just one season: all
the champagne you drink, at the end of your promotion year, can
turn sour very, very quickly. This can happen—all too easily—
unless you are sure that your playing staff is strong enough.

I was quite pleased with several plucky performances from the
lads, late in the season. At that stage, we were almost certain to
be relegated. We were playing simply to satisfy our own pride-in-
performance and peace of mind. I can't stand a cheater. A cheater—
in my terms—is a player who will go onto the field and not *enjoy
himself*. Enjoying yourself means getting involved in the game. And
getting involved means *working*. Nothing upsets me more—regard-
less of what team it is—than to see a player who is not working.
Because life has to go on, and there *will* be a turning-point, no
matter how black the present may seem. If you *believe in yourself*
—that what you're trying to do is right—then you have the hope
that the little spark you're looking for, the little turning-point, will
come. We searched and searched for this, in the first six months of
1971, and then we won the Anglo-Italian Competition. That victory
gave us some of our confidence back.

Before I came to Blackpool, the club had declared its interest in
playing in this Competition. When Derby County pulled out, Blackpool were then committed to take part. At that time, it looked
as though we were going to be relegated. I felt quite strongly that,
if we were relegated, the important thing to do was to forget about
football. My plans for the end of the season were: "Let's have a
break from football. I'll do what sorting-out has to be done with
our playing staff. Then we'll get down to pre-season training." But
Blackpool had committed themselves, so that was it: we had to
play. The season ended; we gave the players a couple of weeks'
break; and then I brought back what I felt would be the nucleus
of the coming season's team. We didn't make a very impressive
start in the Competition. In the two home matches, we drew with
Verona and lost to Roma. And so we went to Italy for the return
games, with seemingly no chances at all.

This Competition gives points for goals. Before the home game

Harry Thomson: goalkeeper, acrobat, and a favourite of the Bloomfield
Road kop

Tommy Hutchison, skilful outside-left, one of Mortensen's bargain-buys
from Scotland

against Roma, I said I didn't mind if they got three goals; so long as we got four. I didn't mind if they got five goals!—so long as we got six. We fielded only three defenders that day and we created a lot of goal-chances: but we didn't knock them into the net. Roma kept breaking away and scoring, and we finished-up losing 3-1.

We kept our policy to go for goals, even when we played away from home. The turning-point for Blackpool came in the second half at Verona. The kick-off was at 9 o'clock, and there was a nice, quick type of surface. It was 1-0 to us at half-time. Then Tony Green and Tommy Hutchison began to buzz, and we won 4-1. The lads played magnificently in the second half. We got six points from that match. The next morning, when we saw the results of the other matches, we realized that we had crept into the reckoning: we had a chance, a slim chance, of qualifying for the final.

And so we went to play Roma on the Friday night. Stoke City had pinched a 1-0 victory against them on the Tuesday, thanks mainly to the brilliance of Gordon Banks, but we knew Roma had some very good players. It was 0-0 at half-time, and we scored two fine goals in the second half. Roma got a consolation goal in the last kick of the game, and so we won 2-1, which meant another four points. We'd collected ten points from our two games in Italy, giving us 15 altogether. We had to wait until the following afternoon, when Swindon were playing, to see which of us would qualify for the final.

The Swindon game was on TV, but I don't think any of us were brave enough to watch it. We went into Rome to do some shopping on the Saturday afternoon, and many of the stores we went into were showing the game on TV, so we saw flashes of the game.

The whole Blackpool party had dispersed, and we were going to meet-up at St Peter's Square at 6.45. Brian Doyle, Len Graham, and I, were together. It was Alan Taylor, our reserve goalkeeper, who told us the happy news: Swindon had only won 2-1. They hadn't scored enough goals, and so we were through to the final against Bologna.

The kick-off time for the final was 5 o'clock, and it was a very hot day. Heat hadn't been a problem in our previous games in Italy, because they were played in the evening. We didn't make a very good start, and we conceded a goal in the first half. Because of the heat, we couldn't run as freely as we would have liked, and it was obviously going to take a pretty big effort in the second half for us to win. The game started to swing our way after the interval, and John Craven's equaliser gave us new-found life.

I thought we were going to win in normal time, but it was still 1-1 at the end of 90 minutes. Mickey Burns got the winner during

R

extra-time. It was a very good goal indeed, a goal that was worthy of winning a cup. Extra-time added to the drama of the match, and it certainly proved our fitness. We'd pulled-off a fine victory, in a Competition in which, at one time, we weren't really interested.

I don't know if we went into the Competition—in the home matches—as wholeheartedly as we should have done. We'd just been relegated, and there'd been a major sort-out of the playing staff. There were several players on the transfer list whom I didn't want to involve in the Competition. I wanted to try out some of our younger players, to see what they could do. In Italy, we began to find a little *blend*, and we developed it quickly. And the strong character and temperament of our players began to show through.

In my view, we beat Bologna because our team-work was more thorough. I have the highest respect for Italian players—as individuals—but they wouldn't do particularly well in English football, because of their temperament and the way they're brought up. The Italians, with all their natural talent, would be *great* players in English football if they came over here as youngsters and were brought-up in our environment.

I played against the Italians in my own playing days, and I soon learned that they can flare-up at the smallest thing. Their temperament is against them. This, I feel, is where Blackpool triumphed. Bologna began to lose heart, when things started to go wrong for them. Blackpool showed more character in the face of difficulty. When we were trailing, we kept going.

A team can score a couple of goals in a couple of minutes, and this can change the whole picture of a game. So you've got to keep going, and *believe* that it can happen. You may get this break in the last five minutes of a game, so you've got to keep working.

Our Chairman, Mr Dickinson, did a very good public-relations job: for the club and for the town of Blackpool. We gained a lot of new friends in Italy. We'd had quite a lot of players "booked" in our relegation season, and the last thing we wanted was any sort of trouble in the Anglo-Italian Competition. We had no real trouble. We had a couple of bookings in the final, but they were for minor offences: one player was accused of time-wasting, and the other of playing-on after the whistle was blown. In Italy, many whistles come from the crowd, and I told my team to play-on until they were sure that it was the referee's whistle which had been blown.

I gave detailed instructions to the players about their behaviour on the field. There was to be no tackling-from-behind. I have always felt very strongly about this: you mustn't—in fact you *can't* —kick through a player in order to get the ball.

Charging goalkeepers was *definitely* out. Goalkeepers are given more freedom in Italy, than in England, and we wanted to play it the Italian way. We avoided doing anything that might niggle the Italian players. We were determined not to have a riot at one of our matches. We got a wonderful reception from the Bologna supporters, after we had beaten their team, on their own ground; and this proved that all the things we tried to do were right. The lads behaved themselves *off* the field, as well.

When we got back to Manchester, it was pouring down; and it rained hard during our journey to Blackpool. When we got to Bloomfield Road, there was quite a large crowd there to cheer us. We could hardly believe it—we'd just been relegated, don't forget. We drove down to the Pleasure Beach and then, right along the Promenade, to the Town Hall. We were amazed. Our win in Italy obviously gave our supporters a boost, and their great reception, on our return, did us a power of good. The Anglo-Italian Competition had helped to re-build relations between team and public.

Last season (1971–72) was a mixture of joy to begin with, then frustration, and then a little more joy. The main objective for me was to continue the work I started when I first came to Blackpool: to build a first-class squad of players, about sixteen or seventeen, as skilful as possible, but also as reliable as possible, so that we can have a go at achieving promotion.

We got off to a good start, thanks to the confidence we gained by winning the Anglo-Italian Competition. Then came the transfers of two key players—Johnny Craven to Crystal Palace and Tony Green to Newcastle. I signed several players, such as Keith Dyson, Dave Lennard, and Chris Simpkin. These were players who I was sure would come into the team, and be good enough to stay in. The newcomers had to be blended into the existing first-team squad, and our tactical plans had to be slightly re-shaped.

In the League, we got eight points in our first five games. It took us another fifteen games to get the next eight points. Then came the turning-point which I had been waiting for—for a whole year, ever since I came to Blackpool. It was at Charlton last December. We were 2-0 down at half-time. Then, after the interval, everything started to go right for us and we won 3-2.

If we had lost at Charlton—and the odds were stacked against us at half-time—we would have been only three points above the club in 21st place; and that club had a game in hand. But, as fate would have it, we won. And we began to string together some good results in the New Year. That gives you some idea of the sharpness of the knife-edge that hangs over the manager of every football club.

A manager can never relax. He can never say to himself, "Well everything is going all right now. I can take things a bit easier for a while." When you're losing, you're fighting all the time to hit a winning streak. When you strike success, you've got to work hard to keep up the momentum. Believe me, a manager has worries even when his club is in the middle of a winning run. However your club is doing, you always know there is room for improvement.

A manager sometimes has to put football before his family life. If you had been driving on the dual carriageway on the way to Scotland, last Christmas Day, you would have seen me sitting at the road-side, having a picnic lunch. I was on my way to see a couple of matches. The first one had a 2 o'clock kick-off. I saw the first half, and then I went to another game, which had a 3 o'clock kick-off.

Although we've started to show more consistency, it doesn't mean that I've found the perfect answer or a perfect team. There's always room for team-strengthening: to create more competition for places, to keep players on their toes. In the next year or so, we want to be high-up in Division II, challenging for promotion to the First Division.

In the early part of last season, we used to play a "blinder" one Saturday, and score a hatful of goals, and then give a mediocre performance the following week. We haven't "arrived" yet, but the confidence, the work-rate, and the skill, are beginning to show through. There's a lot of satisfaction in seeing tactics you've worked on—and individual players you've tried to help and encourage—*come right* on the field.

It is very important to me to have a set of players that I can *trust*. I want to have players at Bloomfield Road whom I can work happily with, and share football's ups and downs with. This is the feeling I've got at the present time. I've got a lot of confidence in my players.

By "trust" I mean: that I know the players look after themselves when they're away from Bloomfield Road; that they do their training with enthusiasm; that they give of their best at all times; that they want success for the club, and want to be part of a good team; that Blackpool Football Club means a lot to them. If a team has that sort of spirit, it will always be able to pull out of a bad patch. And, when things are going well, the players will never get complacent.

1971 was a good year for Blackpool in cup football, with our 4-0 win over West Ham in the F.A. Cup, the victory in the Anglo-Italian Competition, and getting to the quarter-finals of the Football League Cup.

We enjoyed our League Cup run. We went to Bournemouth and won convincingly, and then had two big home wins—against Colchester and Aston Villa. We went to Tottenham with a depleted side, and lost 2-0. Tony Green, one of our key players, had gone to Newcastle. Two players that I'd signed—Dyson and Lennard—were cup-tied. Bill Bentley was injured and Alan Suddick was down with flu.

Tottenham's first goal was a rather scrappy one in the early part of the game—which was the *last* thing we wanted—but their second goal was a tremendous header by Martin Chivers. Terry Alcock, one of our centre-backs, was right up with Martin, and his forehead was probably only six inches away from Martin's. We knew we couldn't leave Chivers unmarked—not even for a split second. The free-kick was low and accurate, and Chivers "read" it slightly quicker than Terry Alcock did. Although Chivers only flicked the ball with his head—he didn't dive: it was all done from the neck—the ball went into the net like a rocket. Our goalkeeper didn't have a chance.

We had one very good period in the second half. Until that great goal by Chivers, we looked to be in with a chance of a draw. I thought it was a bit harsh to lose 2-0: 1-0 would have been a fairer result. Considering that we didn't have our full team on view, we gave a good account of ourselves; and we were glad to have got into the last eight.

Our 1972 F.A. Cup run came to an early halt, with our home defeat by Chelsea. The draw was cruel to us: we couldn't have picked more difficult opposition. Chelsea have a very strong pool of players, and they're a well-organised side. We needed the encouragement of an early goal, but it didn't come. We gave Chelsea a good match, but they always seemed to have the edge over us.

In June 1972, Blackpool played again in the Anglo-Italian Competition, this time as holders. At the end of the League programme, I gave my players a fortnight's rest, and then I brought them back for training. Their enthusiasm to play again very quickly returned: we've got a very good spirit in the club.

We'd learned a lot from playing in the 1971 Competition. We had learned how to play against Italian teams. Our players were well prepared physically and mentally.

We went to Italy for the first series of matches, and started off with a 4-1 win over Sampdoria. We really enjoyed ourselves in the first half, and we scored four goals. Blackpool were playing as well and as attractively as at any time during the League season. Mick Hill, on loan to us from Ipswich, was playing in his first game for

Blackpool. He scored two goals from two close-in chances in the first twenty-five minutes.

Players like Alan Suddick and Tommy Hutchison did well: they were given a lot of room to move in the middle of the field because the Italians by nature funnel back when they lose possession. We missed an absolute "sitter" at the start of the second half, after the home fans had thrown cushions at their own team. Sampdoria crept back into the game, but our victory was never in doubt, and we went straight to the top of the table of English clubs in the Competition.

Then we went to Vicenza and beat Lanerossi 2-0. It was a very humid night, and our players took a few minutes to get into their stride. Mickey Burns opened the scoring towards the end of the first half. If you get the first goal against the Italians, you're half-way there. We scored another goal—this time through Alan Suddick —and we could have had a few more.

We'd given two very confident and competent performances against two Italian First Division sides, but we felt that our two home matches might be more difficult. By religion, the Italians are defensive-minded, especially away from home. We played some delightful football in the first hour, in the return match with Sampdoria, but somehow their 'keeper managed to keep his goal intact. Then Burns and Hill scored. Instead of two goals, we could have had five or six.

We thought the Lanerossi game, at Bloomfield Road, would be a difficult one, because they'd had two close games against Birmingham. We were still leading the English clubs, but Carlisle were only two points behind us, and they had an easy final fixture. We got the sort of start that every manager dreams about: two goals in the first two minutes. This really upset the Italians. We went on to win 10-0, a peace-time record score by Blackpool. Hutchie had a field-day, often beating three or four defenders, and he put over some magnificent crosses. Lanerossi didn't know what was hitting them. Some of them were genuinely trying, but they were on their knees with tiredness. It was our day. It was the game we'd been waiting for—a game when most of our goal-chances went in.

While giving full credit to Roma for their victory in the final, our biggest obstacle was the weather. After a long, hard season, the Blackpool team had to play a final in Rome in a temperature that had soared to the high 80s. We didn't pace our game particularly well. If we'd been a bit more forceful in the first hour, we might have taken the lead and gone on to win. It is so important to get the first goal against the Italians. In the first half, Keith Dyson was very unlucky with a fine header that went just wide.

Roma made it 1-0 just after half-time. The ball cannoned off Davie Hatton and broke well for a Roma player to score. Glyn James came close with a diving header, and Mickey Burns almost scored with a scissors-kick. But Roma had six men back in defence by this time, and we just couldn't break through. Roma finished with two well-taken goals, and then Terry Alcock got one for us.

We didn't play as well as we can do, but the 3-1 score-line didn't do us full justice. We went into the match with the intention of playing attacking football, but we didn't set out to win *at all costs*. The conduct of all the Blackpool players was of the highest order, both on and off the field. The Italian officials and the British newspaper reporters said that Blackpool's conduct had helped to restore dignity to this Competition. So, although we lost the match, we won in other ways. It was nice to hear so many people say that Blackpool are a credit to English football.

1971–72 will always be remembered as the season of the clamp-down on discipline. It certainly helped skilful forwards—such as Blackpool's Suddick, Burns, and Hutchison—by giving them a little more room to work: they were able to do more "on" the ball than before. The clamp-down was just about 100 per cent early on, but, later in season, I saw niggling little things begin to creep back into the game—possibly more in cup-ties than in League matches.

I could quote you many many instances of inconsistency in bookings last season. Mickey Burns, for example, got booked at Cardiff for showing dissent—it was a very harsh decision. A few days later I went to watch a Cup replay, and I saw some diabolical goings-on. The referee warned one particular player at least five times for fouling—there was a two-footed tackle, a late tackle, a trip—but the player wasn't booked. Each time, he just looked at the referee, as if to say, "I'm sorry, Dad. I didn't really mean to do it." And then he'd go and do it again.

The contrast between these two situations makes a manager want to do everything he can to defend one of his players who has been booked for a mild disagreement with a referee. Here is what happened, over and over again, last season: the referee warns a player; the player says he didn't do anything wrong; the referee says, "It *was* a foul"; the player denies it again, and gets booked. And this player is given the same punishment—a booking—as a player who has been fouling. This is very unfair.

I think there should be clear-cut categories of misbehaviour. To say that three bookings for dissent is equal to three bookings for fouling—in both cases the player has to appear before the Disciplinary Committee—is nonsense. A player is *bound* to react if an opponent has kicked him. It's easy to say, "Just walk away".

But let the man, who says that, go out onto the field and try to do it. It takes a lot of courage and super-human self-control.

Football will never be free of fouling—because no player likes to lose. All managers are concerned about the tackle from behind, the over-the-top tackle, and the two-footed tackle. But the late tackle will never disappear. For example, a forward will sometimes see an opportunity a little bit quicker than a defender does. The defender has already committed himself to a tackle on forward "X", but "X" lets the ball go past to fellow-forward "Y". The defender, more often than not, will get the blame, but the late tackle was due to "Y's" quickness. Nine times out of ten, this sort of tackle *looks* worse than it really is.

For certain defenders, in certain situations, it is by natural instinct that he stops the man rather than the ball. A defender's job is to stop, to destroy, an attack. English football has always had a reputation for strong defenders. A good tackle is as important to me as a good pass. By all means let's clamp-down on tackling from behind. By all means let's give forwards more room and more freedom. But I would hate it if a purge by referees took the physical element out of the game.

The honest shoulder-charge, the race for a 50-50 ball, the forward who tries to force his way through a packed defence: these situations are part and parcel of English football. And yet some referees of today punish any hint of physical contact. This saddens me. I don't want football to become an old-woman's game.

I suppose the biggest single event for Blackpool F.C. last season was the transfer of Tony Green. I was very sorry to see him go, but if a player knows he can better himself—and get higher wages at a bigger club—do you think a manager should block his progress?

In the summer we said to Tony, "If a club is prepared to pay what we consider to be a good fee, then we will let you go." This promise was made, and this promise was kept. Obviously, I miss a player of Tony's ability. Everyone in Blackpool would have liked him to stay. But only two or three clubs outside the First Division —the ones that get consistently good home gates—can hope to hold-on to a player of Tony's ability. A club like Blackpool—with an average gate of about 15,000—has to buy and sell, in an effort to make ends meet.

In the end, I felt that the press sold Tony Green. We didn't! I shall never forget the press comments on the morning of the day he was transferred. We'd beaten Aston Villa in the League Cup, and Tony had played a superb game, one of his best ever. The newspaper reports were not at all concerned about the game or about Blackpool's convincing victory. They were speculating on how many managers would be queuing outside my office that morning, and how soon it would be before Blackpool sold Tony. The newspapers proved to be right. Newcastle stepped in, and the deal was completed in an hour and a half.

The press often instigate—or at least accelerate—a transfer. They latch on to a possible transfer and they don't let go until the transfer is completed. After Tony Green left, I had peace! We hadn't been doing too well in the League, and the only thing reporters could think of to write about Blackpool F.C. was Tony Green. Every week, a reporter would stir it up.

The press is important to the game, but sometimes reporters go a little too far. They pester players at home, probing their feelings. These reporters know it's wrong for players to talk to the press without permission, but the only thing the reporters are interested in is getting a big-headline story. I'll give you an example: one which made me very upset. Just before John Craven left us, there was a story on the back page of one of the nationals. It wasn't an interview with John; it was an interview with his wife, speaking about John and Blackpool Football Club. I'm glad to say that many reporters—including our local pressmen in Blackpool—have too much integrity to do something like that.

So much for last season. Now I'd like to give you a run-down on my first-team players, and tell you how I think they'll do in the next two or three years.

When I was manager of Carlisle, I saw John Burridge play for Workington. I always thought he had a lot of potential. At the end of our relegation season, Neil Ramsbottom, whom we'd just bought from Bury, broke an arm. We needed another goalkeeper rather urgently, and I persuaded Workington to let John come to Blackpool on a month's trial. We sent him to Goodison Park for his first match. We drew 0-0, and he had a fantastic game. It was sad for him, in a way, because he may never play like that again. No one could have made a finer début in First Division football. At times, John seemed to be holding Everton at bay, on his own. And he made three or four great saves. He made one save from Alan Ball that was out-of-this-world. Alan just dropped to his knees: he couldn't believe it.

John did very well against Bologna in the Anglo-Italian final last year. He can produce wonderful displays like this, but his job is to be *consistent*. More than anyone else in the team, a goalkeeper *cannot* afford to make mistakes. He must aim to be perfect.

John is still young and he's got a lot to learn, but he's very dedicated and he's got a fine temperament. He's a very keen and enthusiastic goalkeeper, the kind of boy every manager likes to work on. We'll just have to wait and see how he develops. He lacks an inch or two in height. On his goal-line, he has as much agility as any goalkeeper; but he can't always cut out crosses from the wing. His future will depend a lot on his attitude to the game. You find a lot of small people—in every walk of life—who want to prove the world wrong: by trying to do things that most people think they're not able to do.

We've recently signed George Wood from Scotland. He's another goalkeeper who only cost us a few thousand pounds. We call him "Wee Georgie Wood" because he's 6ft 2in. He's about 14st at the moment, but we hope to get him down to 13st 7lb. Like John, he has a lot of potential.

Our No. 1 right-back is Dave Hatton, who was signed from Bolton a few years ago as a "sweeper". He moved to full-back in order to make way for Peter Suddaby. Dave is a very able player. He has settled down very well in his new position, and he enjoys his rôle in the team.

Competing for Dave's position is Peter Hardcastle, who is a more recent signing. He joined us in his early twenties. He's a former amateur player who, having a teaching degree under his belt, wanted to have a crack at being a professional footballer. Peter wrote to Blackpool for a trial: he knew Peter Suddaby and Mickey Burns. Knowing how well these two had done—they also came to us after getting a teaching degree—we were pleased to have a look at Peter. I liked him very much. I liked his attitude to the game.

Peter Hardcastle came to us as a mid-field player, but we thought he might do better at full-back. For ten consecutive games in the reserves last season, he never had a bad report. We gave him a few matches in the first team, and he did very well. I think we could have a winner in this lad.

A few years ago, I wouldn't have been keen to sign a player of around twenty-two. But I've been very encouraged by the success of Suddaby and Burns. Now I open my arms to this type of player: he's got experience; he's intelligent; his attitude to the game is right. What really interests me is that, even though a lad with this type of background could make a career as a teacher, he loves football and he wants to see if he can make the grade. For what little it costs the club—with players being bought and sold, these days, for fantastic fees—we're prepared to take a gamble.

Our left-back is Bill Bentley, who was signed from Stoke by Stan Mortensen. He was plagued by injury last season, but has re-established himself in the team. He's a good club-man. Bill is quite an aggressive player: he's the type of full-back we need in our particular line-up. He enjoys going forward. Thanks to the pioneering-work of Jimmy Armfield, the overlapping full-back has added a new dimension to the game. The days are long past when full-backs used to stay at the back, and pump long balls up the field. In some matches nowadays, the full-backs actually make more crosses than the forwards!

We've got a good young full-back in Stevie Harrison, a local boy. He had a spell in the first team last season, when Bill Bentley was injured, and he did well. I like his character. I like his attitude. He's got one or two little weaknesses that we've got to work on. We've got to give him as much Central League and first-team experience as possible, because I'm sure he can make the grade.

Paul Fuschillo is like Peter Hardcastle in that we've switched his position. Paul came to us as a full-back, and we've developed him into a middle-of-the-back-four player. He has settled down well in his new rôle, and has been producing very consistent performances in our Central League side. He's a good user of the ball—which is something I like in a player—but he needs to improve his tackling and heading. We'll see how he shapes-up in the next season or two. He's another player who could get into our first team.

Peter Suddaby and Glyn James, our skipper, have teamed up very well together in the middle of the back four. I put Peter into the first team just after Christmas 1970. Blackpool were in a hopeless position at the bottom of the First Division, and this was my opportunity to give Peter experience of first-team football. He didn't let the side down, but he tended to make vital mistakes that cost us goals. I put this down to his lack of experience. I kept saying to myself: "He's got to learn the hard way." Being in the middle of the back four, he's got a vital position in the team. If he makes a mistake, he's only got the goalkeeper to help him.

Peter wasn't costly last season: he made only the occasional vital slip in the penalty-area. He's a player who is improving all the time. He's strong in the air, and he's a good tackler. If he can add a little culture to his game—I'd like to see a little better "touch" in his passing—he'll be very good indeed. It's beginning to show-through in practice sessions. He's using the ball with more confidence and more accuracy. Peter is well on the way to becoming a top-class player.

Peter has a very sound player alongside him in Glyn James, who is a Welsh international. Glyn is a good, reliable player and a very loyal servant of Blackpool Football Club. The *best* part of his career is *past* him, but I don't think he's *past* his *best*! He played superbly in the 1971 Home International Championship. He's playing as well as ever. His experience is invaluable to the team. Glyn and Peter made a vital contribution to Blackpool's improvement in the second half of last season.

Terry Alcock, another centre-back, is a bit of a mixture. He played some very good games for Blackpool last season. I particularly remember the League Cup game against Aston Villa, when Terry was marking Andy Lochhead. I don't think that Andy —in his whole career—has had such a quiet game. Terry can really knuckle down at times, and produce a very, very good performance; at other times, he can be too easy-going, and allow forwards to dictate to him. This is why he's never fully established himself in the Blackpool first team. He's got such a lot of ability, but he doesn't always show enough aggressiveness.

Chris Simpkin is in his middle twenties. I bought him from Hull last season, and I bought experience. He's going to give Blackpool several very good years. Chris has been a consistent performer for a number of seasons. He's been used to playing with two very good forwards at Hull, Chris Chilton and Ken Wagstaff, and he developed a type of game that fitted in with those two. This has made it a little bit harder for him to settle in at Bloomfield Road, because we haven't got two such strong strikers.

Blackpool will soon reap the benefit of having Chris in the team. He's popular with the other players. He really enjoys watching and talking about football, as well as enjoying the playing side. He's a very good professional, a good trainer, and a good competitor.

Another recent signing is Dave Lennard. A few years ago, he was given a free transfer by Bolton: a lot of people can't understand how this happened. But I could name several players like Davie, who are playing better at the age of twenty-seven or twenty-eight than they've ever done before.

He's settled in very quickly at Blackpool. He likes the club. He's very appreciative of this opportunity to get back into top-grade football. He's got a lot of skill and ability, and he's a good team-player. He's a manager's player: a player who can adjust his game to the needs of the team. You don't have to tell Davie what to do. If a Blackpool player gets injured during a game, Davie will take over in no time. He slots-in to the new rôle, and we send out a substitute to take over his original position. Except perhaps for in goal, we know that Davie can fill in for an injured player in any position on the field. He's an invaluable member of the team.

Our other mid-field player—along with Chris Simpkin and Dave Lennard—is Alan Suddick. Alan has a most vital rôle in the team— especially since we lost Tony Green. Alan has a certain flair that every team needs. He has many qualities: skill with the ball;

superb passing; the ability to size-up a situation quickly. He also has a lot of good shooting ability, but we don't see as much of this as we might do.

I've tried so hard to make Alan see the importance of his rôle in the team: not just once in three games, but every week. I want him to be pegging away every Saturday, and doing justice not only to the team, but to himself. He's a great trainer. No player in the club is faster; no player in the club has more stamina. This might sound rather surprising to those who watch him on Saturday afternoons, but we've proved it in training sessions. One of these days the penny is going to drop, and Alan will show himself to be what we know he is—a top-class player. I firmly believe that his best is still to come.

Our three front-runners—Burns, Dyson, and Hutchison—are beginning to play really well together. Mickey Burns has a lot of natural talent. He's a very quick little player. He's now beginning to improve on his all-round team-work. In the past, Mickey has been a little too easy-going. Goals always came very easily to him in amateur football. His attitude to the professional game has been similar: "If I score, I score. And if I miss, I miss." I've worked hard at him to increase his contribution to the team: to run and chase harder; to fight harder to get the ball.

He's only in his mid-twenties, and he's got such a lot to give to the game. He's got Jimmy Greaves' flair for getting into goal-scoring positions: the natural instinct of being on-the-spot when the goal-keeper drops the ball, or when the ball cannons off a defender. It's impossible to teach this. It's just something that's in him. Mickey has a little built-in radar that guides him to the ball in and around the penalty-box. What we've had to work on is his willingness to work for the team outside the box. I think we're winning.

Keith Dyson came to Blackpool in part-exchange for Tony Green. Keith is settling down well at Bloomfield Road. At Newcastle, he was in and out of the first team. When he came to Blackpool, I assured him that I wouldn't drop him after one bad game. He has the responsibility of leading the Blackpool forward-line. Provided he's giving of his best, I'm prepared to stand by him.

Keith had some lean spells last season, but you must remember that he's got a very difficult job. Having been a centre-half in my playing days, I know how difficult life is for a striker. He's got a defender on his back all the time. He has to take a lot of stick. But Keith can take it. He's a strong lad, and he has an excellent temperament. He can take punishment without turning round and retaliating. He's only a young lad, and he'll continue to improve for some years yet.

Tommy Hutchison is a great lad, a pleasure to work with, a pleasure to have in the club. He's got a good character, he looks after himself, is always well dressed, and is a very gifted player. He probably doesn't know how gifted he really is. He can take defenders on—and go past them—as well as any player I know. But he doesn't always put an end-product to his work. It's easy for people to say, "Well, why doesn't he?" If we knew the answer, we'd put it right. *If* he could put crosses onto the end of his runs, and *if* he could put in a shot after beating a couple of defenders in the box, Tommy would be one of the most wanted players in the country. He's still learning a lot about football, and I hope he can tie up the loose ends in his game. I'm sure his best is still to come.

There is so much talent in the present Blackpool side. My big task now is to get all this talent to function consistently. Several times, towards the end of last season, we were beginning to move really well. The defenders were covering each other, we were getting splendid through-balls from Alan Suddick, Mickey Burns was running well—on and off the ball—and Hutchie was taking-on defenders and beating them. On that form, we're a match for any team in the League. But we've got to produce this form more consistently.

In the second half of last season, we began to show more signs of consistency, because the team—after a lot of buying and selling of players—was more settled. 1971 was a year of many changes at Bloomfield Road, but 1971 is behind us now, and I'm hoping for better things in the future. I'm trying to build a promotion team, and a promotion team is a settled team: a team that has played together for at least a couple of years. This is very important.

Although I want a settled team, it's useful to have two or three good youngsters competing for places in the side. We have several promising young players at Bloomfield Road at the present time. Prominent among them is Alan Ainscow, who played in the first team a few times last season. I've often named him as substitute, so that he could gain experience of travelling with the first team, get the feel of big-match atmosphere, and learn about team tactics. We're working on young Alan to improve certain ball-skills. But he's only a teenager, and he's a fine prospect. He has a natural flair for driving in hard towards goal.

We've got a little Scots lad called Billy McGrotty, who has had a few matches in the first team. He's another good prospect, and, like Alan Ainscow, he's got a flair for goals. Billy has been doing well in the reserves, and I want to give him as much Central League experience as I can. He shows a lot of flair in and around the box. He's got a bit of a mean streak in him. But, physically, he's not strong enough yet. He needs sharpening up. He needs strengthening. If we can achieve this, he could be a match-winner.

There have been quite a few new faces in the Blackpool team since I became manager. There are still a lot of ideas I want to try out at Blackpool, a lot of things I want to do. When you come to a new club, you've got to set your priorities. The first thing I wanted to do was to get the playing side put right. It's difficult to say how long a manager needs at a club before it is fair to judge his work. When I first went to Carlisle, everything started with a bang: the team played well; we had a settled side; and few injuries. I think every manager would like to have a five-year contract, and be given that sort of period in which to re-build his club.

I hope that I'm going to be at Blackpool for at least five years, and be given the opportunity to re-build the side into an established First Division outfit. But it's very difficult for a manager to plan too far ahead nowadays: he can never be sure how much time he will be given. It depends on so many things: what happens in his first two or three seasons; how much faith his Board of directors has in him; and so on. I want to take Blackpool back into the First Division, but I can't be sure how long it will take. Look at Frank O'Farrell. He went to Leicester in circumstances similar to those that brought me to Blackpool. He couldn't save Leicester, and they were relegated from the First Division. It took them a couple of seasons to get back. Now look where he is—manager of Manchester United.

One of a manager's main responsibilities is to supervise the scouting. Our youth-team manager and Mr Lewin, who is a member of the Board, are very much involved on the junior scouting side, on which the future of every clubs depends. It's a long, hard job looking after the players who are coming through the pipeline: the apprentices who are coming up, from the "B" team, into the Central League team, and are then being prepared for the first team.

Our youth-team manager and the Blackpool scouts have one of the toughest jobs in football: that of finding these little rough diamonds. Every week, there are always thousands of kids playing football—at schoolboy level, youth-team level, and so on. We go out searching: looking for a little diamond we can work on. Scouting for young footballers is like being a prospector for gold in the old west. You find a little nugget, and then you polish it up: it's either worth nothing or else it's worth a fortune.

We are reorganising Blackpool's scouting system, trying to make it more efficient. We've decided that we can't continue to try and cover the whole of England, Scotland, Wales, and Ireland, because we haven't got the time or the money or the people to do it properly. To start with, we shall concentrate on, say, Lancashire, the north-east, and southern Scotland.

The Fylde is a fairly good area—but by no means the best—for finding football talent. This is a *holiday* area. It's not a *hard* area, such as a mining or a manufacturing area. I can only talk from my own experience about the hunger to want to do well. I am the son of a miner, and I was brought-up in a mining village. Life was pretty tough. There was never very much money about, and the opportunity to play professional football was something that many youngsters wanted—more than anything else. Today, life seems to be a little bit easier for young boys.

A year or so ago, we managed to pick up Jimmy Gordon, a schoolboy-international goalkeeper. We're all looking for the cream, but the best youngsters usually go to the big clubs. A promising young player will get the opportunity to go to several clubs—to have a look at their set-up, their facilities, and so on— and going to Leeds or Liverpool or Everton will leave him a little bit more starry-eyed than going to Bloomfield Road. All we can do to encourage him to join us is to say that—if he turns out to be good enough—he will probably have an earlier opportunity to play first-team football. At one of the city clubs, he would pro- bably have to serve a longer apprenticeship, because of the calibre of first-team player that these clubs require.

Even if we manage to sign a promising youngster, scouts from the big clubs will be hovering around Bloomfield Road as soon as he begins to show his paces in our first team. It is disheartening to lose a player you've developed, but every club has to pay its way: either by getting enough money through the turnstiles or by selling its assets. Every club would prefer to do the former, but it's not always possible: bills and wages have got to be paid.

The directors of Blackpool F.C. have carried quite a lot of responsibility, over the last few years, by putting money into the club; but a club can't go on making a loss, year after year. If I had a successful business and was making a lot of money, I wouldn't put any of my money into a football club *unless* I could see some daylight, some return for my generosity. Unless a club is getting big enough crowds, there comes a time when it *has* to sell—and it may have to sell one of its best players. This is a sad fact of life that a manager simply has to accept, because of the circumstances of the club he's with.

I don't believe that a manager should treat his top stars any differently from the rest of his players. The top stars are part of a

Everything that Tony Green does on the football field reveals character: his quickness of thought and movement, his Peter-Doherty-like desire to be always in the game, his way of running. . . .

April 13, 1970. The promotion team and club officials celebrate in the dressing-room after the game at Deepdale. Blackpool beat Preston 3–0, thanks to a hat-trick from Fred Pickering. *Left to right.* Back row: J. Murray, J. McPhee, D. Hatton, M. Burns, H. Thomson, J. Craven, F. Pickering; middle row: J. Meadows (2nd-team Trainer/Coach), W. Cartmell (Chairman), J. Armfield (Captain), T. Hutchison, H. Mowbray; front row: H. Glossop (Dressing-room attendant), L. Shannon (Manager), G. James, S. Parr (Director), A. Suddick, W. Bentley, V. Conboy (Physiotherapist), L. Graham (1st-team Trainer/Coach)

team: it is very important to remember this. I would never do more for a top star than I would for any other player. You can't run a club for the benefit of two or three well-known players. I do, of course, have sympathy for a big-name player if the press are continually putting a high valuation on his worth in the transfer market. This can put a lot of pressure on a player—to ask for higher wages, or even to ask for a move—when, in fact, he may be quite content with his present club.

I try to gain respect from my players by being honest and by being as fair as I possibly can. I don't think there's been a manager in the history of football who has been able to keep *all* his players happy. A manager can only field eleven first-team players, and one substitute, each week. There are bound to be several players who think they should be in the first team.

I aim to get respect: by giving players, who are trying to do their best, a fair crack of the whip; by showing that I know what I'm talking about; by trying to convince them that what I'm searching for is right; by building up a mutual understanding that I won't *be* cheated *by* them, and that *I* won't cheat *them*; by telling them, frankly, if I don't think they match up to what I want—in these cases, I'll find them clubs where I feel they can do themselves justice.

I keep an eye on the little things: for example, I fine players if they're late. It is the little things that I worry about more than anything else, because, if I can kill them when they're small, they won't grow into big problems.

I've stopped the players from going into night-clubs after a Monday night, and I've stopped them from drinking after a Tuesday. I don't suppose these rules have been popular with one or two players, but I've made these rules because I believe them to be right: right for the players, as individuals, and right for the club. I want the players to understand that all I'm interested in is their welfare, and success for Blackpool Football Club. The two go together: if the *club* is successful, it follows that the *players* will be successful, and be rewarded. If we can build on these ideas and all pull together, having gained each other's respect, we'll be a happy club and a successful club.

A career in football today offers really big financial rewards. What the Arsenal players earned in the season they did "The Double" made the salaries of some club managers look small. A young player who is good enough—if he's sensible, and is prepared to dedicate himself to the game, and is lucky enough to be with a successful club—can have ten years at the top, and finish up with quite a bit of money in the bank. Football today can provide

s

a good standard of living, and a healthy way of life, for the young man who's got ability.

In the past few years, football has established itself as a socially-acceptable profession, and we're beginning to attract young men who have a degree or a teaching diploma. We've got several lads at Blackpool, at the present time, who have one or other of these qualifications. They fit in perfectly well with the other players. They're only in the club and in the team because they're good enough—not because of their intelligence. In fact, their football intelligence may not be greater than that of the players who don't have degrees—so they're probably all on about the same level as far as that's concerned.

My sole interest is on the football side, and I look upon my players primarily as *footballers*. If a player has a degree, and can do a crossword puzzle a lot quicker than any of the other lads, that's fine; but it doesn't make any difference to me as club manager. If he wants to go to a college in the afternoon and teach French or English, that's fine; but he can only do this if he's not needed for training. Football must come first. But they know this, and so we don't have any problems. A player with a degree is just one of the lads, the same as anybody else.

I think appearance is important: I like to see my players looking smart. I'm not one of the it's-OK-if-they-wear-their-hair-down-to-their-feet brigade, but, if I ask a player to have his hair cut, I'm thinking of his health as much as of his appearance. It does a player no good at all to be persistently perspiring in training, and then to leave the ground—particularly in cold weather—with his hair not properly dried.

Another unwritten rule concerns smoking. If I see a player who I think is smoking too much, I'll have a word with him. I admit that I played with some quite heavy smokers, such as Jackie Milburn and Joe Harvey: they would often have a cigarette. But there is a right time and a right place to have a cigarette.

I have more control—than you might think—over discipline away from the football ground. If a player has misbehaved, or has had a late night out, word usually gets back to me. I have fined players for misbehaviour: I've brought them into my office, and we've sorted it out.

Blackpool is a holiday town. I feel for the players. There are so many attractions in Blackpool: it is understandable that a fit, healthy, young lad should want to get involved. I don't want to stop players from having their fun—because life passes very quickly —but I've *got* to stamp down on certain things.

Dedication is the key word. If a player wants to do well in football, he *must* look after himself, and work hard. When his playing days are over, he can do what he likes: he can stay out all night if he wants to. But if a player starts over-indulging in certain things, then he's only cheating himself. He's cutting his own throat, damaging his own career.

I place great importance on the *type of person* I bring into the club. Before a possible transfer, a manager gets to know quite a lot about a player. Before signing a player, a manager has to get the answers to all sorts of questions. Will the player be able to settle-in at a new club? Is his wife happy about moving to another part of the country? Is he a good team-man? How good is his behaviour off the field? And so on.

I know what players I'd *like* to be able to buy, but I'm manager of Blackpool—not manager of Tottenham Hotspur—and I can't spend a fortune on new players. Ever since I came to Blackpool, I have continually searched for the right blend. A manager has got to build a *pattern* into his team. An individual can *win* a game for you, but good team-work can *prevent* you from losing. I encourage individual flair, but insist that it is harnessed to the overall need for team-work. Each player has his part to play, and it's my job to blend, and make the best use of, my assets. If I can build a team that has enough winners of the ball, enough good users of the ball (creative players), and enough strikers—and couple this right blend with good spirit, good morale, and good team-work—then Blackpool will be successful. We must continually strive to get closer to this ideal.

The difference between a *good* and a *great* player is to be found in the mind. You can go to a Fourth Division game and see some fine-looking athletes. Then, the next Saturday, you can go to a First Division game and see some wee scrappy-looking blokes playing really well. They're in the First Division because of the way they read situations. They respond to certain situations *much quicker* than players in lower Divisions. The First Division player has greater skills, almost certainly, but the key difference is that he always knows what he's going to do: he's quick-thinking. When lads in lower Divisions get the ball, you can almost *see* them thinking what they should do, who they should pass to. It's all in the mind.

You can go some way to correcting a player's weaknesses. I like to think that we're *thorough*. Sometimes, certain things are revealed on the field that make spectators say, "They must have been working on that during the week." It does a manager a power of good to hear that sort of comment, but the fact is that we are *always* striving for improvement. We're always working on basic skills, helping players to overcome their weaknesses, and giving them practice, as individuals and in groups. This is all we—the manager and the coach—can do. We can give players shooting practice, but during a match they've got to create shooting positions for themselves. We can train them, but we can't *play* for them.

In addition to ball-skills, practice matches, and so on, the players have to do quite a lot of body-work. By "body-work", I mean circuit-training, weight-training, or medicine-ball training. We work, for example, on the thigh muscles and on the stomach muscles (we call this area of the body "the engine room").

I attend almost every first-team training session. I see reporters from the local press at pre-arranged times. I do my mail and make telephone calls, as soon as I get to the office in the morning, and then I'm off to be with my players.

Tactics and training are planned much more thoroughly than they were fifteen to twenty years ago. This may not be to the entire benefit of football. Many people fear that individuality is being squeezed out of the game. I, personally, never seek to kill individual flair: I want to blend it into my team. This is important to me.

I often think back to the days when I was a young player. Although I was with a very successful club, I could have been helped, a lot more than I was, to overcome certain weaknesses in my game. Nowadays, if a club wants to be successful, it has got to be thorough. The players have to be well trained, and their team-work has to be very sound.

My coaches and I have introduced a number of new ideas into the training routines at Blackpool. Mid-week matches, in the early part of the season, interrupt the training schedule, so I'll give you an outline of a typical week at Blackpool F.C., once the mid-week games are over.

As soon as possible after Saturday's game—as soon as we can get the whole team together—we have a post-mortem: to talk about what we did right, and what we did wrong, and how we can do better.

Players must report to the ground on Sunday morning if they need treatment for any knocks or bruises or strains, or anything like that.

On a Monday morning, we take the first-team squad of players to the Derby Baths, which also has a gymnasium. First, the players do exercises to loosen-up. Then we go to a steam bath or a sauna bath, and cool down by doing a little bit of swimming. One or two players may need a light massage.

On Tuesday we do a hard morning's work. If we're not satisfied with the way things are going—if, for example, we need to tightenup on our team-work—we'll have a practice match on Tuesday morning. Selected players will come back in the afternoon for individual work: running, basic skills, shooting, or whatever is needed.

If things are ticking over fairly nicely, the first-team squad might have a day's golf on Wednesday. It depends, of course, on the weather, and it depends on how things are going. If things are going well, our training can keep a nice tidy pattern. If things are not going so well, then we do more work on certain things: we push the players harder. As you can see, the players—by the results they achieve: on training-days as well as on match-days—set the pattern of their own training.

We work hard on a Thursday morning, and come back in the afternoon to do a bit more: perhaps some sprinting. Then, on Friday morning, we just loosen-up and we go through certain things in preparation for Saturday's game. In other words, we have a team talk and, if necessary, we go onto the pitch and practise set-moves, or defensive ploys, or whatever is needed.

I try never to over-worry players with problems or ideas or advice. If we're at home on the Saturday, we'll have a chat about tactics, but our main plan will be to go *at* the opposition. If we're *away* from home, we tend to plan our tactics in more detail. We always have a team meeting at our hotel on a Saturday, before we leave for the ground. We have a thorough pre-match talk, and we make sure that certain things are *fresh* in their minds. Saturday is a day-off for most people, but, for us, it is the most important day of the week.

I'd like to make one more comment about our mid-week training schedule. I never want my players to be able to say, "We *know* what's happening next week." I do my best to see that they can never anticipate what they're going to do. A training schedule must never become boring: it must never become a *routine*. For example, Wednesday—instead of being a golf day—can be a full day's training. Tuesday *and* Wednesday can both be hard training days, with the work-load easing-off on Thursday and Friday, if the lads have done well early in the week. If the training has gone well on Monday and Tuesday, we may give the lads a complete break on the Wednesday.

We have no facilities for training at Bloomfield Road, so we go to Stanley Park, to our training-ground at Squires Gate, and to the Derby Baths with its gymnasium. In the past, the Bloomfield Road pitch was often used for training. I've cut this down, because I want my players to have the best possible pitch for their match on the Saturday.

Some people think that professional footballers have too much spare time. I'd like to give you my views on this. You can only hammer away at the body for so long. Last season (1971–72), we began our training in the middle of July, and we went right through to the end of the Anglo-Italian Competition the following June. So we've had to prepare our players for eleven months of football. We work them hard, but we've got to be careful not to work them too hard. They get a fair bit of spare time—three, sometimes four, afternoons a week—plus the occasional complete day of rest.

Most players are sensible about the way they use their spare time. At the present moment, we've got a handful of players at Bloomfield Road who have teaching diplomas. They obviously want to keep in touch with their particular field. One or two others go to evening classes. Quite a number have taken up golf. Others enjoy a game of snooker. And so on. But the body can only take a limited amount of wear and tear. Football has *got* to be No. 1. My players know that I will never allow any outside involvement— whether it be a sporting activity or a business interest—to interfere with their football.

We've covered training pretty thoroughly. Now let's talk about a match-day. Before home matches, the Blackpool players used to go to a local hotel for lunch. But they really didn't enjoy it, and so we don't do this any more. They'd rather stay in their own beds—till mid-morning, if they want to—then get up, go for a walk, and prepare for the match in their own way. We trust them to have had only a light lunch: they know that *they* will be the sufferers if they over-eat before a match. They report to Bloomfield Road at 2 o'clock, an hour before the kick-off. They get changed. We have our final little chat. And then they're ready to go onto the field.

If our match is away from home, we find it's safer to travel on the Friday, and stay in a hotel that night. If we travelled on the Saturday, our coach might have a breakdown, or we might be delayed by heavy traffic, and therefore we'd risk being late for the match.

There's more tension before an away game. The rules are the same; you're still playing on the same sort of pitch; you're fielding the same eleven players. But, for an away game, the match-day is quite different from when you're playing at home. For a start, you miss the support of your own home crowd. You miss the familiar routine and familiar surroundings of your own home. The central heating at a hotel can cause drowsiness among the players, and at a hotel they may be tempted to over-eat.

We let the players lie-in till mid-morning. Then we usually go for a walk together, and come back to the hotel for a light lunch. Depending on what time we have to leave, we may watch *Grandstand* in the hotel. We try to keep their minds occupied until kick-off time, but, in fact, we all start thinking about the match as soon as we wake up on the Saturday morning. The tension rises as 3 o'clock comes closer, and it doesn't ease off until the players get out on the field. The players can lose their tension in the hurly-burly of the match. It's much harder for me. I have to sit on a bench and watch. All of our work during the past week is settled— one way or the other—in those 90 minutes. All our work may be undone by a bad refereeing decision or by an unlucky bounce of the ball. These are the puppet-strings that are tied to a manager's back. They clutch at you pretty hard at times.

I always like my team to get the first goal. The next five minutes, after you've scored, are vital: you've got to hold on tightly, because the other team now has nothing to lose and will therefore attack you hard. I've seen so many games which have been 0-0 until well into the second half. Then team "A" scores, and they think, "Well, that's it. We've won the game." They lose their concentration, and, before they know it, team "B" goes straight up the field and scores an equaliser.

If Blackpool score first in a match, we aim to play really hard in the next five minutes. Once the hustle-and-bustle is over, the game steadies down again. We then try to build up from there, doing all that we can to go to 2-0, before they go to 1-1. The team that scores first, by drawing out the other team in their gamble to get the equaliser, must exploit the bigger gaps in defence. When people ask me if I feel happy when Blackpool get a 2-0 lead, I say, "No. I begin to enjoy a match when Blackpool have got their *third* goal."

Touch-line coaching isn't strictly legal. But touch-line *coaching* isn't a very accurate term, so far as I'm concerned. I've had the whole week to do my coaching—along with the trainer—and I've given the lads a pre-match talk, so I'm not going to blare away from the bench for the whole 90 minutes. My main rôle is to try to *encourage* my players: to keep them going, if they are flagging or looking down-hearted. I certainly don't believe a manager can make major tactical changes from the touch-line. I may tell a player to drop back into another position, or I may urge the players to put more pressure on the opposition, but nothing more involved than that. No matter what I say from the touch-line, mistakes will still happen. Once a player has made a mistake, it's too late to do anything about it. Football is a game that is full of mistakes. A manager's job is to try to see that his team doesn't make as many mistakes as the opponents do. But *both* managers can't be right. We can't both win!

Quite a bit of thought goes into the selection of the substitute. There are several possibilities. We may select someone who plays in a particular position. Or we may select a jack-of-all-trades, a utility player. Or, if we have a utility player in, say, the right-half position, we select a right-half as substitute. Then, if there is an injury during the match, the utility player takes over from the injured man, and the substitute comes in at right-half. We don't make a change unless it is really necessary.

The choosing of the captain is something else that needs a lot of thought. The *individual* is more important to me than the *position* he plays. I like to think that, in their own way, all the players should be little captains on the field. They each have a part to play. *Drive* has got to come from *all* positions, if a team is going to be successful. The captain has the added responsibility of having to make the more important decisions during the course of a match.

A club captain has a job to do *off* the field as well, and, if you bear in mind what I said about the importance of the individual, you'll understand why I've had no hesitation in the past in selecting a centre-forward to be captain, if I thought he was the right man for the job. I did it at Carlisle with Hughie McIlmoyle. He was a player who I felt would do better if he was given the added responsibility of being captain. And he responded. When I came to Blackpool, I made John Craven captain. He, too, was playing in the No. 9 shirt at the time, and he was another player who I hoped would respond to more responsibility. He did a very good job as captain—both on and off the field—in the 1971 Anglo-Italian Competition. Glyn James (in our first team) and Fred Kemp (in the reserves) are two other players, in a No. 9 shirt, whom I've made captain. As far as I'm concerned, the captain's team-position is just coincidence. I go for the man I want to be captain; the number on his shirt doesn't really matter to me.

Discipline on the field of play is one of the most controversial talking-points in football. It is very difficult to say just how much control a manager has over the behaviour of his players. No matter how much I may warn players—about not tackling from behind, about not arguing with the referee, and so on—situations will arise that no one can anticipate. Supposing you're in the middle of a tense match. What would *you* do if somebody kicked you up in the air? What would *you* do if the referee or a linesman gave a diabolical decision? A match-winner, for example, will always come in for more physical punishment than an ordinary player. What would *you* do if a defender tight-marked you for the whole of a game, followed you all over the field, and always tackled you the moment you got the ball? This can be very, very frustrating.

The "professional foul" is—and always will be—a very difficult subject to give a clear-cut answer to. I would never encourage a player of mine to commit a "professional foul", but how can I say how every player will react in every circumstance? After all, many "professional fouls" are committed not in cold blood, but in the heat of the moment. These days, so much prestige and money hang on the result of certain matches. Players are very keyed-up. They want to win, and they want their team to win. They're very deeply involved—physically and mentally—in a big match. What would *you* do? Would you risk getting booked, if the foul you committed helped your side to win an important match? I wonder.

I was always regarded as a *hard* player. I didn't get on *badly* with referees, but there was a certain *respect* between us. I tell my players before every game: "Let the referee get on with his job. And remember—he can make a mistake, just the same as you can." Players have got to learn to accept a referee's decision: once he has made a decision, he won't go back on it unless a linesman's flag is up, to signal for an infringement which the referee didn't see. Most referees will then go and consult the linesman.

I have great respect for referees: they have a very difficult job to do. I very much doubt whether professional referees would make a lot of difference to the standard of refereeing. They might be a little fitter than the present referees, but they would still make the same sort of mistakes.

One of the biggest talking-points of today is the lack of goals in League football. The scoring-rate has been getting lower and lower. I believe that the answer is in the hands of the managers, and how they *allow* their teams to play. It's a lot easier to stop goals being scored than to score them. And so a manager has to strike a balance between the *gamble* of trying to score goals and the *danger* of leaving the gate open at the back.

If team "A" plays a heavily defensive formation, team "B" may be tempted to attack hard and thus over-expose its defence. In this sort of situation, team "A" will often manage to steal away out of defence and pinch a goal, and win 1-0—even though team "B" has had 90 per cent of the play. Blackpool have suffered in this way in a number of matches during the last couple of years.

A negative attitude has crept into football, and it now seems to be the accepted thing. I have never shared this attitude. I've always liked my teams to play with *flair*. I like to be *proud* of the way my team plays. I don't like to pinch a result, and hear all the fans say, "You were lucky."

The *manner* of victory is important to me. When I was at Carlisle, I criticized a very well-known manager for the negative way his team played. I said that I would rather sweep the roads than manage a team that had "fear" written all over it. I don't believe that any team should go out onto the field and try to strangle and destroy a game in order to get a result.

People often ask me if giving entertainment to the fans is high on my list of priorities. "Yes," I reply. "But I want Blackpool to give *winning* entertainment." I can't afford to say to the lads: "Go out and entertain. As long as you play well and excite the crowd, it doesn't matter whether you win or not." I can't say that. My team has got to go out and *win*. My job is to blend the players I have, in order to produce the best that we, as a club, can achieve. If we can get the right blend—with flair in attack, and tightness in defence—then we shall have a successful side.

One of the sad and cruel things about football is that not every team can be successful. Supposing Liverpool are drawn to play Manchester United in the third round of the F.A. Cup. They might be joint-favourites to win the Competition, but one of the two has to get beaten. So one set of supporters will be happy, and the other set will be sad. Even if there were twenty-two clubs like Liverpool in the First Division, and twenty-two managers like Bill Shankly, two teams would have to be relegated at the end of the season—no matter how good they were.

There's got to be teams at the bottom as well as at the top. The crowds will flock to see the teams that are doing well. The fans will have loads of enthusiasm, and there won't be enough matches for them. If their team had three or four matches a week, the home ground would be full every time. It all depends on how the team is doing. Who wants to see a team that is at the bottom? The fans of the bottom clubs say to themselves, "Oh, there's too much football." So the successful clubs become more successful, and the poorer clubs get poorer.

Success has its problems. I am a great believer in the importance of confidence, but *over*-confidence is something which can creep in when things are going well. There is a very thin dividing-line between confidence and over-confidence. If a team is in the middle of a winning run of matches, the manager must constantly remind his players where they got their confidence from. He must remind them of the sort of things they've done to achieve their confidence: the part each has played, the hard work in training sessions, and so on. If the team is going to continue to be successful, the players have got to continue to do the right sort of things. This is where individual character begins to show: in the willingness to keep working at the simple things.

Like every manager, I get letters from the club's supporters, telling me how to do my job! These people tell me that certain players are useless; that there are certain players I mustn't sell; that I have no idea about tactics; and so on. I just have a little chuckle to myself, and then put these letters straight into the waste-paper basket. A manager will always get this type of letter—and letters will appear in the local press—especially when the team is not doing so well. People like to get on the bandwagon and have a go at the manager.

A manager needs to have a strong belief in himself and in his own ability. I do things the way *I* think they should be done. I won't be influenced at all. I'll listen to other people—I'm always interested to know what other people feel about things—but I won't let them influence me. I'll make my own decisions, and, if they turn out to be wrong, then I'll hold my hand up, and say, "It was me." I'll never be able to turn round and say, "Well, so-and-so suggested it, and I thought I'd take his advice."

It is obviously very important for a manager to have the backing of his club's directors. I look to them for financial support if I want to buy a player. In day-to-day affairs, I simply want their backing. I want them to let me get on with the training, and all other team matters, in my own way. The Blackpool F.C. Chairman and his Board of directors have been tremendous in that respect. Even in our relegation year (1971), they didn't interfere at all. If they have that sort of confidence in me, and if they know that I'm working honestly and conscientiously for them, then we have as good an understanding as any manager can hope for.

A manager can have a very strong influence over the future of a football club. Look at Bill Shankly. I have tremendous respect for him, not only for his ability, but for his *enthusiasm* for his club and for his players. He *lives* for Liverpool F.C., and his attitude is reflected throughout the club. All his players are *great* players, as far as he is concerned, and they all have tremendous respect for him. He talks a bit of blarney at times—by now, he probably believes it to be true!—but the result is that his team plays with the greatest of enthusiasm. And he's got a big, enthusiastic crowd behind him.

It is much easier, in many ways, to manage a big club, because you have a big ground, a big home crowd, and big financial backing. A good manager can stay many years at that sort of club: it pays the highest wages and it therefore gets the best players. But all credit to the managers and directors who have built up these clubs, and kept them at the top.

There are a lot of pressures on managers these days, and some men don't survive. I feel very realistic about my job. I think it probably does a manager good to be sacked once during his career: it makes him fight that little bit harder to stay in football. After all, there are only ninety-two managers in the League. Over the last few years, there have been *thousands* of people who would have liked to have a crack at the job.

I can only talk about myself, because I don't know what other managers feel, deep down. Managers respond differently to problems and situations. I can't ever relax. I can't get away from football. Not so long ago, after Blackpool had won an important home match, and had pleased everyone (from the directors to the supporters), I was out after midnight walking with my dog. I had a restless night. I was up at 7 o'clock the next morning and went out with the dog again. And we'd won the game! Whether we're doing well or doing badly, I'm *totally* and *completely* involved in my job at Bloomfield Road: with the big things and the small things. I don't intend to change, unless my health starts to be affected. I have a medical before the start of every season, and the doctor always says I'm in A1 condition.

I'm only in my early forties, which isn't old for the job of club manager. I think I handle situations after a game very well at times. At other times, I may say something which, on reflection, was better left unsaid. But I'm sure that players, when they sit back and think about it, understand their manager and his problems and his frustrations—particularly if what has upset him is something that he'd hammered away at so much that he was entitled to hope it would never happen in a match. Football can be a very cruel game. For example, there was a vital match in my first season at Blackpool. We were fighting like hell to stay in the First Division. Blackpool had had a good game. We'd missed two or three great chances of scoring. Then, all of a sudden, the defence let in two "soft" goals. I felt I wanted to snap something. But, with experience, you learn to respond to these sort of situations a little bit better. I'm not perfect. I'm still learning, still gaining experience. But I never want to mellow. I want to stay totally involved in the game.

I'm very pleased to be a manager. I'm doing something I want to do. I've been completely involved in football since I first went to Newcastle, at the age of about sixteen. Football is my life. I read the sports page in the newspaper; I leave politics and the business world to other people.

I am very ambitious to do well. If I can carry on for another twelve to fifteen years as a manager—till I'm about 55—I think I will have done well. When I think of all the people who are now out of football, and unable to get back in, I realize how fortunate I am. I've always tried to be realistic and stay down-to-earth, and be grateful for what I've got, and *fight like hell* to keep it.

34

BLACKPOOL, BY GEORGE
by Eric Todd

(*The Guardian*)

It is an interesting rather than a significant fact that no seaside club
has ever won the Championship of the Football League. You can,
of course, get a whiff of sea air at Portsmouth and Sunderland,
but none of the accredited watering places, Blackpool excepted, has
finished in the top three in the First Division. Still, you can't have
everything; and such places as Bournemouth, Torquay, Brighton,
Southport, and Southend, do very nicely without having to rely on
their football clubs to attract visitors.

Blackpool, too, could argue quite reasonably that over the years
the Illuminations, the Golden Mile, and Reginald Dixon, to say
nothing of its sands and superb air, were sufficient to lure the
millions to that part of the Fylde coast. And it may well be that
some of those millions have never heard of Bloomfield Road and
what it stands for. But mention the F.A. Challenge Cup Final of
1953, and talk about Stanley Matthews, Stanley Mortensen, Harry
Johnston, Peter Doherty, Jimmy Hampson, Joe Smith, and a few
more, and you'll soon find that there are plenty of people to whom
Blackpool is a place noted for something other than fresh air and
fun.

Few clubs have experienced more changes of fortune than
Blackpool since they took their first hesitant steps in the Lancashire
League way back in the 1880s. They won the Championship of
that League in 1894, were elected to the Second Division of the
Football League in 1896, went back to the Lancashire League in
1899, back to the Second Division in 1900, and in 1908–1909,
when they finished at the foot of the Second Division, they were
allowed to retain their status. And they lived to show their gratitude
to their town and country.

The dawn of the new century heralded a new era for Blackpool, and never again were they out of the League. There were some well-known names in those distant days including "Gyp" Cookson; Dorrington; R. B. Middleton, the club's secretary about the time Blackpool moved from Raikes Hall Gardens to the Athletic Grounds, and thence to Bloomfield Road after the amalgamation with South Shore; and a schoolboy who was known as "Jubba". This bright young man turned out to be Harold Hardman who stayed with Blackpool until 1903, moved on to Everton, played for England, and subsequently became the highly respected and much loved Chairman of Manchester United.

In 1922, Blackpool narrowly escaped relegation to the Third Division. They survived by completing an unexpected double against West Ham United who were challenging strongly for promotion. It did Blackpool good, and it taught them a salutary lesson. In 1930 they won the Championship of the Second Division in which Oldham Athletic, Bradford, and Bury were among their pursuers! Cinderella had gone to the ball at last, thanks in great measure—although he himself never would have agreed—to Jimmy Hampson, one of the truly great centre-forwards of all time. He was signed in the manager's office at a Nelson cinema in 1927. He was drowned during a fishing expedition off Fleetwood in January 1938, and the football world mourned his passing.

In 1931 and again in 1932, Blackpool finished in 20th position in the First Division, and in 22nd in 1933—Cinderella was not having such an enjoyable time after all—but they won promotion in 1937 by which time the incomparable Joe Smith had taken over the managership, and Peter Doherty had moved to Manchester City. Sir Lindsay Parkinson, for so long a big name in Blackpool, had died and had been succeeded by his brother, Colonel W. Parkinson. Another era was in the making.

In the years immediately preceding the war, Blackpool's League position was secure without being impregnable, and in one six-month period they consolidated it by spending the (then!) huge sum of £30,000 on buying Jock Dodds (Sheffield United), Dai Astley (Derby County), George Eastham (Brentford), Tom Lewis (Bradford), and Hugh O'Donnell (Preston North End). They also recouped nearly £20,000 by selling Frank O'Donnell, Louis Cardwell, T. W. Jones, and Tom Lyon. The club's overdraft had soared to nearly £30,000, but they picked up three "bargains": Harry Johnston, snapped up under Manchester City's noses; Jimmy Blair; and a thin, pale-faced boy from South Shields who had come to Blackpool to play for a Shields' school team. Stanley Mortensen no less.

During the war, Blackpool was one of the R.A.F.'s chief training centres, and nearly every famous footballer was drafted there at one time or another. Among them was Stanley Matthews—then with Stoke City—and Blackpool persuaded him that it would be very nice to live and play by the seaside. It is not known generally, by the way, that Manchester City went to "spy" on Matthews in his formative years and decided that he was not the material they wanted. Ah well! You can't win 'em all! In the years ahead, when Blackpool at last really meant something in the world of football, Matthews, like Hampson before him, used to say "No man ever made a team on his own. There must be ten others." Those who saw the Cup Final of 1953 might take leave to challenge Matthews' modesty.

In 1956, Blackpool finished second to Manchester United who won the Championship with a margin of eleven points. Blackpool were fourth in 1957, seventh in 1958, eighth in 1959, eleventh in 1960, 20th in 1961, and at last in 1967 the brakes failed, and Blackpool went down with Aston Villa. Blackpool fought their way back again in 1970, but in 1971 they were relegated once more, with only 23 points to show for their efforts.

So Blackpool over the years have shown themselves to be just an ordinary team, almost an unfashionable team, yet one capable of days of unsurpassed brilliance, and one to which traditions mean more than they do to most clubs. The place does not seem the same since Joe Smith lost his gallant fight against ill health, and since "Percy", that most vociferous, hypercritical, and exasperated supporter, shouted "For Heaven's sake pull your bloody socks up, Blackpool" for the last time. But as always Blackpool have a happy blend of youth and experience, and as always, when the mood takes them, they are quite capable of providing the high quality of entertainment for which the town is famous.

Yes, indeed, Bloomfield Road Ground is well worth a visit. It is only a few minutes' walk from the Promenade, and, whichever road you take, you are left in no doubt that this is a seaside resort. The names of the hotels and boarding-houses or guest-houses are those you can find from Torquay to Tynemouth, and from Bridlington to Bideford. In the depths of winter when the holiday crowds have gone home, you can peer through the windows and see the spotless tablecloths, the shining cruets, and the bottles of brown sauce, all conspiring to assure the casual visitor that when the notice says "Vacancies", it means at the table as well as in the bedrooms. Colour television is another lure for long-distance football supporters who can afford the time and the money to stay overnight. Not only in the Welsh hillsides do they keep a welcome.

Jimmy Hampson (Blackpool: 1927–1938). 251 Cup and League goals in 371 games

Jock Dodds (Blackpool: 1939–1946). More than 200 goals in matches during World War II

Stan Mortensen (Blackpool: 1938–1955). 226 Cup and League goals in 349 games

Ray Charnley (Blackpool: 1957–1967). 203 F.A. Cup and League goals in 384 games

A "welcome home" for the Blackpool team, after beating Bologna in the final of the 1971 Anglo-Italian Inter-League Clubs Competition. *Left to right:* Peter Suddaby, Tony Green, John Craven (Blackpool's captain)

Inside the ground, the pitch is a credit to the staff, and the club make you as welcome as they can, whether you stand or sit down. The press reach their nest by means of a long staircase at the back of the main stand, and on arrival they are met and greeted, as they have been for years, by "George", whose love of the game, his fellow men, and Blackpool in particular, have fitted him admirably for the post of press steward. A pity there are not more like him.

He directs you to your seat, hands you a programme with an assurance that he will give you the team changes as soon as he can get them, and presents you finally with a small ticket which will admit you to the Refreshment Room after the game. This used to be the boardroom and at a pinch would accommodate the directors, secretary, and manager, in comfort. Now it is a haven for Distinguished Visitors—including the press—while the directors and their intimates have another room which is not much bigger but at least is more select.

At half-time, however, the press and the photographers squeeze into what formerly was the secretary's office—you can see the cupboard where the safe was housed—on the walls of which are massive photographs of some of Blackpool's greatest footballers and their achievements. And they are all looking a bit faded now. Here the ubiquitous George helps to dispense the refreshments whose quality and quantity depend to a great extent on Blackpool's League position. Since they returned to the Second Division, there are more biscuits and fewer cakes. If Blackpool descend into the Third Division, the press presumably would be advised to take their own sustenance!

Everywhere below stairs is congested at Bloomfield Road, and the rush for some of the conveniences makes it necessary to adjust your dress *after* leaving and not before. Otherwise, those waiting for admission would not have time to satisfy Nature before the whistle went for the start of the second half.

More than once it has been said that Bloomfield Road is the most uncomfortable ground in the country—which is far removed from the truth—and this false rumour may explain why attendances there have been so small in recent years. Even allowing for the "floating" population in the holiday months and during "The Lights", the average attendance at home League matches has seldom been likely to gladden the heart of the club's Minister of Finance.

If you haven't the money, then you cannot expand or improve, and over the years there have been few major structural changes at Bloomfield Road. Like many clubs these days, Blackpool exist

T

on the proverbial shoe-string, and, like many clubs, they wonder whether the future can hold as many triumphs and produce as many star players as did the past. There is in fact a touch of defiance about Blackpool's letter heading which shows that, apart from the Anglo-Italian Cup, no major trophy has found its way to Bloomfield Road for nearly twenty years.

But what do they know of football who only Tottenham Hotspur, Arsenal, Manchester United, Liverpool, and Leeds United, know? Blackpool are nothing if not optimistic and determined, so who can tell? There may yet be three varieties of sandwich, and cakes with real cream, at half-time. Then George himself will realize that Blackpool once more are back where they belong.

35

A CLUB OF CHARACTER
by Stanley Whittaker
(*Lancashire Evening Post*)

There is a progressive air at Bloomfield Road these days. With one hand, Blackpool Football Club is waving farewell to a glorious past—all our yesterdays; with the other hand, the club is summoning a successful future—all our tomorrows.

As the Seasiders strive to live in the competitive soccer world of the seventies, their past achievements should not be allowed to fade from memory. This has been averted thanks to Robin Daniels who has written this up-to-date history of Blackpool Football Club. In systematically documenting the old glories, not forgetting some saddening defeats, he has undertaken a praiseworthy task. Blackpool can look back on many "yesterdays" that were epics. *Blackpool Football* will serve as a valuable and lasting record.

Working in the press box, my frequent pleasure, and periodic disappointment, has been to report on Blackpool's changing fortunes during more than three decades. Once, when recalling his own climb to fame, the imperishable Sir Stanley Matthews, "Wizard of Dribble", indirectly summarized the Seasiders' many ups and downs: "The road to the top is hard—but it is even harder when you get there. So much is then expected of you by the public. Without let-up."

Blackpool's finest hour was undoubtedly the 1953 F.A. Cup Final victory over Bolton Wanderers. This being so, I imagine that the most critical few minutes in the club's history must surely have been those that ticked away, earlier that day, some miles from Wembley. For there was *nearly* no historic "Matthews Final".

At the Elstree Country Club, where the Blackpool team stayed before the big match, serious last-minute doubts cropped up as to whether Matthews would be fit. What had been kept a closely-guarded secret was the fact that the Maestro's chances of playing were as slender as a thread, because of a pulled-muscle injury.

Blackpool's Cup Final quandary never became publicly known. Behind closed doors, Matthews had his injury treated, with a pain-killing injection, by a club medical officer and trainer Johnny Lynas. Afterwards, as Blackpool rejoiced and the sporting world hailed Stan for his superlative exhibition, his admirers remained in the dark that he had played with one leg almost numb from the treatment necessary to ease his pain.

Joe Smith, Blackpool's most renowned manager of all time, rightly qualifies for a chapter to himself in this book. Long before he contemplated a managerial job, he was famed as one of the greatest inside-forwards ever to play for Bolton Wanderers and England. Joe was man-at-the-helm with Blackpool for twenty-three years.

Joe was splendidly rewarded by the Seasiders' directors for his outstanding service. They provided him with a rent-free house for the remainder of his days, presented him with a generous "golden handshake", offered him hospitality and an ever-open door to their boardroom, and allocated him a special seat in the grand-stand for every home match. Joe lived to attain his 82nd year, and died in hospital on August 11, 1971. In body and in personality, he was as rough-hewn as a chunk of granite.

His tremendous sense of humour is affectionately remembered by all who knew him. Among the many many anecdotes about good old Joe, the one I like best is of a wearisome cricket match at Blackpool's Stanley Park. Few runs had been scored and *even fewer* seemed likely to be scored, as one batsman after another doggedly refused to have a go at the equally lack-lustre bowling. Unable to control his boredom any longer, Joe turned to a companion and remarked: "I'm off home! Sitting watching this stuff is worse than sitting in the garden—watching celery grow."

Photographs in the Bloomfield Road boardroom are constant reminders of a long line of players, directors, and officials, who have rendered the club devoted service. For example, Mr Richard Seed, a former Chairman, has been a director since the thirties. Richard Seed (his grandfather), Leonard Seed (his uncle), and Fred Seed (his father), all gave many years of service to the cause of football in Blackpool. In the early sixties, his noteworthy contri-bution to the game—particularly his many years as Blackpool's hon. secretary—gained him the award of the Football League Long-Service Medal.

In one way or another, an indelible mark has been left upon Bloomfield Road by a succession of post-World-War-II Chairmen;

as, indeed, by others before them. One recalls such personalities as Col. William Parkinson, the forthright and warmly-regarded Harry Evans who was a walking encyclopaedia on soccer, Albert Hindley who died while on a tour with the team in Spain, Richard Seed, Charles Gaulter, William Cartmell, and, latterly, the widely-respected Frank Dickinson.

In the managerial seat, Joe Smith was succeeded, in May 1958, by Ronnie Suart. Suart, in fact, was returning to the scene where he earlier had reached the top flight as a player. A sterling full-back/centre-half, he played for Blackpool for ten years until being transferred to Blackburn Rovers in 1949. He was manager of Blackpool for nine seasons, and then became assistant-manager at Chelsea.

One of the most popular players ever to have worn Blackpool's famous tangerine jersey was Suart's successor. Ex-international Stan Mortensen can always proudly claim that, after a distinguished career on the field, he only missed leading the Seasiders back into the First Division by a fraction of goal-average in 1967–68, his first full season as a manager.

Morty left Bloomfield Road in the following season and was succeeded by Les Shannon, under whose managership the Seasiders finally climbed back to Division I, in April 1970. Team problems and other pressures created many difficulties for Mr Shannon during Blackpool's short-lived renewed membership of the First Division. He resigned not much more than a year after taking over from Mortensen, and shortly afterwards took up a managerial appointment abroad.

Bob Stokoe, previously with Carlisle United, became Blackpool's next choice as manager. His long-term strategy has been to re-build the team, pending a further determined bid for promotion. Stokoe arrived under no illusions as to the size of his task, but he could not have wished for a better start: the Seasiders won the Anglo-Italian Competition of 1971, in his first year as manager of Blackpool.

Change is as inevitable in the press box as elsewhere on the football front. One remembers many friendly faces that are seen no more. They have been followed, of course, by other accomplished sports journalists. Down the years, the reporters who have covered Blackpool football have included Clifford Greenwood, "Spectator" of the Blackpool *Evening Gazette*, George Hunter and Jack Ingham of the Preston *Evening Post*, Cuthbert Collinge and Cyril Middleton of the Blackburn *Telegraph*, Jack Barnes of the now-defunct Manchester *Evening Chronicle*, and Hartley Bracewell, a free-lance. Other well-remembered names come to mind, such as Tom Duxbury and Harry Hall of the Blackpool *Gazette & Herald*; more recently, Don Creedy and Phil McEntee of the Blackpool *Evening Gazette*, and free-lancers Roy Watson and Peter Tinsley.

And Blackpool football would have lost a lot of colour without generations of supporters, many of them *characters*. Mr Knowles Thompson, for example, an octogenarian, cherishes memories that date back almost to the very beginnings of Blackpool Football Club. He recalls directors of yesteryear, such as Charles Ramsden and Sam Butterworth, long-serving secretary Tom Barcroft, and winger Harold Hardman, who went to Everton and ultimately became Chairman of Manchester United. Mr Thompson talks enthusiastically of the skills of players such as Georgie Mee, Jack Cox, and Joe Dorrington. One has to trace back many years in the record books to read of the exploits of these players.

But—I want to stress—not all the notabilities of Blackpool football have been on the field. In fair weather and foul, the Seasiders have had the support of many grand personalities. At one time, these included the names of Eli Percival and "Parson" Evans, Hughie Cunliffe; and, in more recent times, Sam Bailey, Syd Bevers with his Atomic Boys, and such Supporters Club stalwarts as Jack Pickard, Harry and Walter Alker, Cath Barrett, and Jean Crabtree.

All in all, Bloomfield Road has provided a sporting panorama as fascinating as can be found anywhere. And maybe the best days have still to come.

36

THE YEARS OF SPLENDOUR
by Alan Hoby

(*Sunday Express*)

They stretched—Blackpool's years of splendour—from the first seasons of World War II until the mid-fifties. During that brilliant span, Blackpool's greatest-ever team lit up England's football scene with their tangerine magic. Watching them, in the early days of food rationing and clothing coupons, the pulse ran faster and the heart was miraculously lifted.

The Blackpool teams of those years were—in the total sum of all their talents—an enchantment, a visual delight. Wherever they played, the crowds poured towards the ground in an eager flood, and the traffic choked the streets.

As the fans squeezed through the turnstiles, orderly and non-violent, only their bright eyes and aura of suppressed excitement betrayed the fever which gripped them. Once in their seats, or standing on the packed terraces, they waited in fidgeting impatience until the game began. Then their pent-up emotions erupted into a roar of welcome for one of the gayest, cheekiest bunch of characters English football has ever produced.

Yet, even amid the mounting tumult, something was missing. The Wizard, the greatest ball-juggler of his time (probably of *all* time) was not yet involved. In the opening stages of the game, the ball, by some infuriating whim of the gods, seemed to be constantly on the left flank or in the middle of the field. Or was it a deliberate Blackpool ploy to ignore, in those preliminary skirmishes, the greatest player of all? Were Blackpool trying to lull the opposition into a false feeling of security?

The spectators began to squirm with frustration as the two teams tore into each other, while, alone on the right touch-line—as remote as a man on a desert island—the star player, who was called "The Maestro" even by his fellow-professionals, looked on.

Then, suddenly, rising from the throats of those rapt watchers, came an ear-blasting bawl. For at last, with a swift, stealthy pass, the ball reached that familiar stoop-shouldered figure with the No. 7 on his back.

It was a spontaneous tribute to genius. It was also an expression of affection—almost of *awe*—for a talent which defied analysis. For the man they were watching was England's most beloved footballer, the demi-god whose unique hip-waggle and expressionless, poker face were as familiar to the nation as Sir Winston Churchill's cigar.

STANLEY MATTHEWS. What a player! Will there ever be anyone quite like him again? "The Wizard", "The Prince of Dribblers", "The Sorcerer": all these labels had been pinned on him. Not one of these nicknames was extravagant. *Anyone* who saw him at his best will assure you of that.

Searching for words to describe Matthews, the star of those halcyon times, when the game—less grim and dour than now, and far more fun—was dominated by personalities and characters, I can only repeat what I once wrote about soccer's supreme illusionist: "As fastidious as a Siamese cat stepping over puddles, as elusive as an eel, as strung-up as a ballet dancer, and as skilful as a conjuror, he destroyed his enemies by ability, by the extraordinary quality of his footwork."

There was the famous full-back who, totally frustrated by the hopeless job of trying to cope with The Maestro's dance of destruction, suddenly stepped aside, with a theatrical bow, and waved Stanley on. Imagine that happening today!

There was the full-back who, at a mere shrug of Stan's shoulders, fell flat on his face, his features an astounded gargoyle of surprise.

There was the full-back who had the temerity to bounce the great man on his bottom with a tackle of blatant illegality. Off, for instant repairs, hobbled the victim—to return, a few minutes later, with his leg spectacularly bandaged.

Immediately, he signalled that he wanted the ball, and his command was obeyed within seconds. Then the Stanley Strut, the Matthews Waltz, began. A choking gush of emotion welled-up in the crowd as Stanley teased and tormented the full-back until the poor chap was falling over himself with alarm.

The alarm turned to terror, as Matthews and Blackpool—hitherto rather disinterested—piled on the goals and the agony. The back, a big man, was torn inside out. As the game moved into the second half, his morale collapsed, and he was reduced to kicking at shadows.

As Matthews, having beaten him yet again, waited implacably

for a second challenge, his tortured prey thought he saw his big chance. Hurtling forward, he launched himself into a frenzied tackle. The crowd hushed. But something extraordinary happened. The full-back kicked the *corner-flag*. One moment, Stanley was there, the ball tantalizingly at his feet; in the next moment, miraculously, he had gone. The full-back looked utterly astonished —as if he had just seen a ghost. It was humiliation, bitter and abject.

He was one of many backs who tried to rough-up Stanley Matthews and lived to rue their folly. For Stan never forgot. . . .

"He was utterly ruthless on the field," says his old skipper, Harry Johnston, the former England wing-half. "He would beat the full-back at will. He used to paralyse the opposing team in the second half, when he was in the mood.

"He was exceptionally fit—a fitness fanatic, you might say— and, once he got his opponents down, he murdered them. He was like a boxer delivering the knock-out punch. All we had to do was give him the ball straight to his feet, and he would do the rest. He was the complete professional.

"Stan did not like dirty players. He always played cleanly, and he expected others to do the same. There was one back, I remember, who had treated him roughly in the last game of the season.

"The following week, Old England met Young England, a fixture that is no longer in the calendar. By coincidence, the same back was playing for Young England, and Stan couldn't wait to get at him. Stan trampled all over him. He beat him again and again. He would take the ball right up to him, and tease him with that marvellous swerve and body-balance. When Stan was in the mood, he was unbeatable.

"He gave this same treatment, at one time or another, to several full-backs who had tried to foul him. He remembered them. He punished them. Oh yes, Stan had the killer instinct all right. But it was all done by skill.

"You can't keep skill or genius down: Stan Matthews would have been great in any era. The more people he had in front of him—in other words, the bigger the challenge—the happier he was. The one thing he didn't like was being tackled from behind. Well, there are many forwards today who don't like it either."

Matthews played in first-class football until he was fifty. Of course the game by which he will always be remembered —although it probably was not his *best*—was the unbelievable Wembley Cup Final of 1953.

Twenty minutes from the end of this historic match, Bolton were leading 3-1, an apparently unassailable lead. Once again, it seemed, the 'Pool—and Stan—were to be denied the victory they craved more than any other. Twice before—in 1948 and 1951—the Seasiders had reached Wembley, and twice they went down: 2-4 to Manchester United, and 0-2 to Newcastle.

Now, at their third attempt, there seemed no way they could win. It was, apparently, all over. Then the pint-sized Ernie Taylor, Blackpool's inside-right with the size-4 boots, pushed the ball out to Matthews, for seemingly the 100th time.

Few had any inkling of the soccer miracle to come. Yet a sudden shiver of intuition shot through me as Matthews dribbled down the touch-line, stopping, accelerating, pausing again, and then darting off on his mazy course. With another wiggle, he left one of Bolton's backs, Ralph Banks, stranded and lost. The great winger had got through the Bolton defence. The way to goal was as open as the sea. Looking up, he scanned the goal-mouth, and then, as he had done a myriad of times before, he swept the ball over. It rose into the air. . . . The crowd's roar swelled.

Tommy Lawton, one of the finest centre-forwards ever to wear an England shirt, used to say: "Stan could plop the ball right onto your head, and all you had to do was nod the ball in." It was this knack of centring the ball—so accurate did Matthews become that, in practice, he would drop the ball, nine times out of ten, into a chalked circle by the far post—which now transformed Wembley into an inferno.

The ball, at the apex of its flight, seemed to hang in space. This was yet another illustration of the Matthews control. For any goalkeeper, harassed by hungry forwards, this sort of cross was sheer hell to judge. Bolton's 'keeper, Stanley Hanson, was no exception. He waited. We all waited. Then, taking flight, Hanson flung himself upwards to grab the ball. But, somehow, it slid through his fingers like a slippery fish. Down it fell—the whole of Wembley Stadium was a pit of noise. And there was the *other* Stan—Stan Mortensen, the guy who never knew when he was beaten—right on the spot, sliding down on one knee and prodding the ball into the net before he crashed into a post. 3-2.

Poor Bolton. As the crowd raved and roared, as grown men behaved like crazed kids, as the whole arena became gripped by a strange rapture, Bolton, their lead cut from beneath them, must have felt that their luck was ebbing away. Eric Bell had pulled a muscle and was limping on the left wing. Harold Hassall, the inside-left, had fallen back into defence. Even so, with two minutes 40 seconds left, it still looked as if only an act of Nature, an earthquake or a freak storm, could save Blackpool from their third Wembley defeat.

Then, with time running out, with the near-hysterical crowd hanging on every Blackpool move, Jackie Mudie, their Scottish inside-left, was fouled a yard outside the Bolton box. A free-kick. Wembley was frozen into an eerie silence. Like puppets pulled back on invisible strings, the tired Bolton defenders grouped to defend their goal—and their narrow lead.

It was then that Morty—"I've always been a gambler"—turned to Ernie Taylor and said, "I'm going to have a go." "But," Taylor replied, "there's no gap." "Gap or no gap," Mortensen retorted, "*I'm going to have a go.*"

With the eyes of 100,000 spectators watching him, Mortensen walked back to take the kick. His shot blasted straight into the net. Talking about that theatrical late equaliser, long after the cheers and tears were only a memory, Morty told me: "I've always impressed on people that if you have a go—if you have the deter-mination and power, and the *will* to graft and really do your best —the impossible will sometimes come off. And this, of course, applies to all walks of life. One split-second decision can turn success into failure, or failure into success."

How many footballers would have been so cool, so cheeky, and so damned *optimistic*, with the score at 3-2 against them and less than a minute to go? Perhaps, more than anyone, Stanley Mortensen, with his pale face and unusual high-stepping action, his limitless courage and willingness to take half-chances, illustrated the irrepressible *spirit* of that great Blackpool side.

As Bolton kicked-off, I glanced at my watch: *40 seconds to go.* 3-3. The game—but this was something *more* than a game—was in the balance. On this day of magic, I felt that the great conjuror's last trick had still to be played. And there, down on that smooth green carpet, the ball was suddenly laid, as if on a butler's salver, at the Master's feet.

Away he dribbled, shimmying with exquisite finesse. In front of him was the Bolton defence, mesmerized and nervous. But they could not be blamed for their helplessness. Nobody, in those moments of rapture, could have stopped Stanley Matthews. He was like a ghost. He glided inside one defender. He slid outside another. He cut in; he cut out. He was there. He was not there. Then, with the spectators' scream rasping on the ears, he was behind the whole Bolton defence, almost on the goal-line, measuring his final, vital pass.

In desperation, Malcolm Barrass, the Bolton centre-half, came over to challenge. But he might as well have been tackling a phantom. For, bent half over, like a sapling caught in the wind, Stanley feinted Barrass one way, before slipping the ball coolly and cleanly across goal. It was a lovely, low pass. The ball rolled inexorably towards Mortensen, with the Bolton defenders as transfixed as a group of statues. Morty appeared to be shaping for a shot, but Bill Perry, Blackpool's South African left winger, had already called for the ball, and, sizing up the situation in a fraction of time, Morty let it run on.

Fever gripped us all. 100,000 people were yelling. Bolton's goalkeeper Hanson was on his knees. John Ball, his right-back, thrust out a leg, in a frenzied bid to stop the unstoppable. But the ball, as fate had long before decreed, eluded poor Ball, and moved irrevocably across the line and into the left-hand corner of the net. 4-3. Blackpool had done it!

As Perry stood with arms stretched wide in triumph, the cheers swelled up and up. Everyone, as if yanked from the seats by some vast invisible hand, was standing. Near me, a man was weeping. In the press box, hardened newspapermen were surreptitiously wiping away tears of emotion. One little band of Blackpool supporters were so overcome that they had actually thrown away their overcoats.

The gangways of the press box were a messy shambles of paper and notes—scattered and lost for ever, mine amongst them—in those final crazy seconds of release. Surely it could not be true that Blackpool—and Matthews—had won. Yet it *was* true.

I had a lump in my throat as Stanley Matthews, architect of the last wondrous master-move, climbed the steps to receive his long-awaited Cup-winners' medal from the Queen. Never before or since have there been such scenes at a sporting event. It was all summed up by Joe Davis, the snooker king and, like Matthews, a son of Staffordshire, when he said: "It was absolutely marvellous. I shall never forget Stanley Matthews' exhibition as long as I live."

What was The Maestro's secret? Well, what is the secret of genius? Answer that, and you will discover only *part* of the secret. For, in sport, even genius will wither, if the body is not constantly geared to a peak of fitness.

Matthews is a non-smoker and teetotaller. His father was a boxer. When Stanley was a boy, Matthews senior made him do deep-breathing exercises every morning in front of an open window. He also made him walk to and from the Stoke ground. Years later, when he was at Blackpool and at the height of his fame, Matthews still walked from his house to Bloomfield Road. Along the way, he would breathe deeply in order to clear his lungs.

He is an out-and-out believer in a balanced diet. Like the old-time boxers, he ate only two main meals a day—breakfast and a late supper. On match-days, it would be commonplace for Stan to play football after having no more than a light salad and one cup of tea. This was his only sustenance before the Blackpool-Bolton Cup Final.

If Blackpool were lucky in the star forwards they could call on —Matthews, Mortensen, Taylor, Mudie, and Perry—they were equally fortunate in their skipper, Harry Johnston. Harry was a genial type off-field. But, once he removed his teeth before the match, he became the born battle-commander, a natural leader, a hard driver. In his common-sense, his lack of pettiness, his know-ledge of human nature, Johnston was a splendid skipper. Few could resist his warmth of heart, his dry humour, and his enthusiasm. After one away game, in which Mortensen had been so badly injured that he was unable to walk, Johnston simply picked him up and carried him on his shoulders to the waiting coach.

There was—remarkably—no envy, no jealousy, in the Blackpool team, from goalkeeper George Farm to the lithe, long-striding Perry on the left flank. Practical leg-pullers to a man, they were a bunch of genuine fellows and good friends. When the pressure was really on, and there was a match to be won, they all played for each other.

They fully realized that, in Matthews, they had an "original" no rules or pre-match planning could shackle. Stanley, on his day, in his own unique way, was ready to take anyone on: an art which is fast disappearing.

If Matthews was the Wizard, Mortensen was the Lionheart. In fact the greatest game I saw Morty play was not for Blackpool. It was for England against Italy on May 16, 1948, in Turin. This was one of the finest England teams I have ever seen. It was captained by the late Frank Swift, and when I bracket Swifty with Gordon Banks, right at the top of the goalkeeping hierarchy —although they had vastly different styles—you can see how highly I regarded him.

But it was Morty who inscribed his greatness on the Italian consciousness with a super-goal when the game was barely two minutes old. What Mortensen had, above all, was a remarkable instinct for the open space, an ability to accelerate and change pace, plus a drunkard's thirst for goals. But his fame—*before* this match against Italy—was mostly confined to England. On the Continent he was practically unknown. Lawton, at centre-forward, the foreigners knew and feared. Matthews was hailed—as he was in Britain—as "Maestro". "But this Mortensen. How could he

be an *international*? Why, he doesn't even look like a *footballer*."
The Turin crowd were soon to be enlightened.

The Italian team of that time was the most formidable in
Europe. They were commanded by Commendatore Pozzo, one of
the great names in European football, a manager of endless guile
and ability. They had players who could volley the ball to each
other, first time, at incredible angles. They *oozed* talent. And they
thought they were going to destroy the mother country of football.

Until Mortensen took the game by the scruff of its neck, in that
utterly incredible second minute, the huge crowd, which had come
from every part of Italy, by car, plane, donkey-cart, cycle, and on
foot, seethed in a white-heat of expectation—the expectation of
victory.

But the fever died down when Billy Wright broke up a smooth,
silky attack, and slipped the ball to Matthews on the right.
Mortensen, lurking at inside-right, was instantly alert. For that
Wright pass to Matthews meant just one thing . . . a Matthews-
stamped pass straight into the unmarked area ahead. It was the
famous two-Stans Blackpool move they had often rehearsed at
home.

And so Morty took off, running in his odd, high-stepping style
like a trotting pony, knees flashing up and down like white pistons.
The Italians, totally committed to attack, realized the threat—
too late. As Morty ran on to the ball and sprinted clear, one man
turned and began to lope after him with long, raking strides. It was
Parola, Italy's swarthy centre-half.

We watched dry-mouthed. Gradually, Parola closed the gap.
Suddenly Mortensen slowed and it looked as if Parola would catch
the human hare in front of him. But, just when it seemed that
Morty's chance had gone, he accelerated again. It had been a feint
to try and put Parola in two minds.

Now Morty was almost on the by-line, 15 to 20 yards to the
right of the Italian goal. Bacigalupo, the goalkeeper, an acrobatic
figure in a jockey-cap, came out, expecting a cross. Simultaneously,
another blue-vested Italian defender came charging across, in a
frenzied attempt to stop Mortensen. But, as the defender flung
himself into a desperate tackle from behind, Mortensen shot. It
was a fantastic drive, hit from an equally fantastic angle, split
seconds before the England star fell. Amazed, we watched the
ball fly up like a big brown bomb and explode into the *near* top
corner of the net.

For long, lingering, palpitating seconds there was a vast silence.
That Latin crowd, with its mushroom clusters of black umbrellas,
the women's dresses bright daubs of colour, the multitude of

confetti-dot faces staring stupefied at the Italian goal, was like a scene from some French Impressionist painter.

They could not believe the evidence of their eyes. They could not believe that a shot could defy all known angles, all *apparent* laws of gravity, and spin into the net inside the *near* post. If the ball had flashed across goal, they could have believed it. It might even have been possible for the ball to have veered into the far corner of the net. But this goal, this piece of outrageous luck (was it luck?), what can you do. . . ?

Behind me, a little man leapt to his feet, his arms raised to the skies. It was too much. Yet this was only the overture to a truly extraordinary international. For the Italians, inflamed by such a bolt of sheer misfortune, swept back into attack. The wing-halves linking perfectly with the forwards, they advanced in a series of menacing assaults on the England goal.

It was beautiful football arrogantly executed, and the English defence was engulfed by a remorseless blue tide. Twice, Frank Swift caught blistering point-blank-range shots, his huge hands plucking the ball from the air as if the ball was an orange. Swift stood 6ft 4ins, a genial giant. He had never played better, or shown more resource and courage, than during this Italian cannonade.

Twice in the first half-hour, the Italians got the ball into the net, only for the Spanish referee, Pedro Escartin, to signal off-side. An ear-splitting whistle screeched from the stands and terraces. I thought the stadium would erupt with fury. Behind me, the thin fanatic I had noticed earlier was not content just to whistle his anger. His features twisted in rage, he flung off his coat and stamped on it. He sobbed and ranted at the gross injustice being meted out on his team, on his country, and—most of all—on *him*.

But—hardly had he sat down, as the game resumed—England, against all the play, scored again. Once again, that Blackpool Matthews-Mortensen one-two opened the way. Once again, Mortensen pelted down the Italian flank to reach the box. But this time Morty cut the ball back, across the bumpy turf, to Tommy Lawton following up. And Tommy, catching the ball full on the instep, hit it first time: a low scorching shot which hit the back of the net with Bacigalupo utterly helpless. In fact, if the goal-keeper had got in the way, he would have been in imminent danger of decapitation.

That did it. A grave-like stillness greeted this goal. Behind me, the infuriated fan began to wrestle with his collar, as tears streamed down his face. I thought that at any moment he would give us a strip-tease, so unrestrained was his anguish.

The rest is history. At half-time the Englishmen sipped lemon tea, while the weary Italians were sprayed, from siphons, with iced water. Then back to the clinging humidity of the Turin stadium. Swift made another tremendous save from Gabetto, and the Italian centre-forward pummelled the ground in frustration.

After that, the Italians were finished, and two goals by Tom Finney (from passes by Wilf Mannion and Mortensen) completed an English victory which Frank Swift and Stan Mortensen had done so much to earn. No wonder Morty used to be called "The Electric Eel", "The Jet-Propelled Dynamo", and "The India-Rubber Man". In Italy, for years after this match, he was known also as "Mortensen il magnifico" and "Il fantastico Mortensen".

These then—the 1953 Cup Final and the 1948 England v. Italy international—were two unforgettable games from Blackpool's years of splendour. The two Stans were wearing the white shirts of England in the 1948 match, but their wonderful understanding had long before been fashioned, and their vintage magic distilled, in innumerable club games when they were wearing Blackpool's tangerine.

Matthews, Mortensen, Johnston, and the rest of that great Blackpool team ... who, of all those who saw them, will ever forget their monumental contribution to the true glory of football? If I had to write their epitaph, it would be: "THEY PLAYED FOOTBALL BECAUSE THEY LOVED THE GAME. THEY PLAYED FOR EACH OTHER."

Blackpool Football Club 1972. *Left to right.* Back row: John Burridge, Keith Dyson, Bill Bentley, Tommy Hutchison, Alan Suddick, Terry Alcock, Glyn James (Captain), Peter Suddaby, George Wood; middle row: Peter Hardcastle, Dave Hatton, Bob Stokoe (Manager), Frank Dickinson (Chairman), Des McBain (Secretary), Mickey Burns, Chris Simpkin; front row: Alan Ainscow, Dave Lennard

Blackpool Football Club's Board of Directors. *Left to right*. Back row:
G. S. Parr, Ald. A. E. Stuart, R. Seed, D. J. Lewin; front row: T. H. Lane,
I. Gibrail, F. M. Dickinson (Chairman), C. A. Sagar (Vice-Chairman),
W. S. Lines

37

ITALIAN INTERLUDE
by Philip McEntee

(West Lancashire Evening Gazette)

Before the month of May, 1971, the Anglo-Italian Inter-League
Clubs Competition meant little to anyone who follows the fortunes
of Blackpool Football Club. Born the previous year of a temporary
marriage of the Football League and the Italian League, and
fathered out of ambition to bring English and Italian football into
somewhat happier accord, the new Competition had almost choked
at birth—from an overdose of violence and misunderstanding on
the field in its unhappy 1970 inauguration.

News, in Blackpool F.C.'s dark winter of 1970–71, that the club,
who were fighting a desperate battle against relegation, had accepted
an invitation to participate in the 1971 Anglo-Italian Competition,
caused only the mildest ripple of interest.

At the time, Blackpool fans were understandably more concerned
to see the preservation of First Division football in the town. The
harsh realities of a northern winter seemed light-years away from
the fiesta atmosphere of an Italian summer.

Even Blackpool's new manager, Bob Stokoe, had reservations
about entering a Competition notorious for the bad blood it had
created among the teams of the two countries. With one eye on the
future, Bob Stokoe doubted the wisdom of taking part in a
potentially punishing Competition in the summer, for fear of its
effect on the team's build-up for the following season. His reservations were understandable.

But the Blackpool Board of directors had responded to the
challenge the Competition seemed to offer: to make a name for
the club in Europe, the wider theatre that had opened its doors
too late for the great Blackpool teams, of the early post-war years,
to benefit.

After years of bread-and-butter football, the Blackpool directors

o

wanted a little of the glamour of the European soccer scene for the club's supporters . . . and if the Competition made a little cash for the club, so much the better.

What happened is now a proud chapter in Blackpool history. Blackpool not only entered the Competition but went on to win it; and, in the process, became what Football League secretary Alan Hardaker described as "England's finest football ambassadors". Blackpool earned this accolade by the sporting manner in which they played, and by their emphasis on attractive, attacking football—something approaching heresy, to Italian fans fed on a stolid, unchanging diet of defensive tactics.

As things turned out, the directors' decision to enter the Anglo-Italian Competition could not have been more clearly vindicated. After the sadness of the club's relegation at the end of 1970–71 —after only one season back in the top flight—the Competition brought some *joy* back into Blackpool football.

The streets were lined with cheering, chanting fans, as Blackpool's proud players returned home to the seaside, bringing the gold trophy with them. On that rainy Sunday, after the 2-1 triumph in Bologna, Talbot Square was crammed with excited supporters. The victors made speeches and displayed their trophy from the steps of the Town Hall. The triumph in Italy had taken the sting out of relegation.

But—even more important—to win a European Competition gave the Bloomfield Road club new status and width and maturity. It was a new maturity eloquently expressed in the vital field of international relations.

The seaside club, relatively inexperienced in playing host to foreign teams, excelled in this sphere. The club's popular Chairman, Mr Frank Dickinson, and secretary Des McBain did a particularly masterly job. The Italians were received cordially and quartered comfortably; their every need was seen-to by their solicitous hosts. It did the trick in cementing international relations, and, when it was Blackpool's turn to play in Italy, the Italians reciprocated.

I write this because I want to stress that it was no *accident* that, out in Italy, Blackpool was the most popular of the six English clubs who took part in the Competition. The Blackpool players set out to *enjoy* their football, and the club officials gave the very true impression that they enjoyed meeting their Italian opposite-numbers in a co-operative venture to further the good of the game. Blackpool's players and officials were not only ambassadors of football, they were couriers of goodwill for Britain.

As the 1971 Competition got under way in England, there were warnings, in the press, of squalls: because of differences in interpreting the rules of the game, the Italians' dislike of physical contact, and the temperamental Latin character. The sports-writers of the two countries had their notebooks and pencils poised for trouble, and indeed there *was* trouble in some parts of the country, as Huddersfield Town, Stoke City, Swindon, Crystal Palace, West Brom, and Blackpool, did battle—in three groups of four teams —against Bologna, Roma, Inter Milan, Cagliari, Verona, and Sampdoria.

But Blackpool had done their homework well. Bob Stokoe had warned his players that some of the tackling that passed as commonplace in English soccer would not be tolerated by the Italian referees who were to officiate in the matches to be played in England. Mr Stokoe's players heeded the warning, and, in the opening game, against Verona at Bloomfield Road, the emphasis was much more on football than feuding. The game ended in a 3-3 draw, and was remarkable mainly for two things: Blackpool's goal of the year, scored in the first half by an inspired Alan Suddick, and the outstanding personality of the huge Italian referee, who made a big hit with the crowd.

After their first game, Blackpool were fairly optimistic. Their point for a draw, plus three points for three goals, put them in second place among the English teams. The club wanted the team to do well in their first European Competition, so they were paying the players good bonuses for every goal they scored.

There seemed even more reason for optimism when Mickey Burns scored for Blackpool after only four minutes of their second home game: against fashionable A. S. Roma, who featured several big names in their side. But hopes of a big home win against the cultured Romans were dispelled when the Italians fought back strongly in the second half to storm to a 3-1 win. Roma gave Blackpool a lesson in chance-taking.

This left the Seasiders well down the field at the half-way stage, with three English teams ahead of them in points, and Swindon, the 1970 winners, looking likely to reach the final again. Without a win from their two home games, it had been a disappointing Competition so far for Blackpool, and it seemed that their task in Italy was well-nigh hopeless. Strange to reflect that, at this stage, it seemed that Blackpool had almost wasted their time in entering the Competition.

But, as so often has been the case throughout their history, Blackpool rose to the occasion when the chips were down. In the return match in Verona, a competent team-performance, and goals by Terry Alcock, Peter Suddaby, Dennis Wann, and Tommy

Hutchison, gave them a 4-1 victory—the Italian fans had scarcely ever seen so many goals in one match!—and raised their hopes of qualifying for the final after all.

Three days later, in the vast Olympic Stadium in Rome, Blackpool brought their total of points to 15 by beating Roma 2-1, thanks to goals by Bill Bentley and Hutchison. This points-total proved sufficient to take Blackpool to the final. Blackpool had a week of preparation in the Italian sun before the great day dawned when, at the Stadio Communale in Bologna, the Lancashire team was to carry the hopes of all England.

Blackpool's opponents, Bologna, one of Italy's leading clubs, were no doubt confident of victory. After all, hadn't they—unlike the English side—already sampled the strictures of European competition? And weren't they due to play in front of 30–40,000 of their own fanatical fans, in a familiar climate, and on their own pitch? On the other hand, the favourites—in *any* encounter—usually have more pressure on them.

Apart from in goal—a few weeks earlier, John Burridge had been playing for Workington's reserves in the obscurity of the Northern Alliance—and in mid-field—where the promising young Alan Ainscow was about to play the most important game of his life—Blackpool had plenty of experience to pit against the greater individual skills of the Italians.

Would the occasion prove too much for the two young Blackpool players? Would the heat prove a decisive factor in Bologna's favour? It seemed, in the first half, that it would be the Italians, and not Blackpool, who would be celebrating at the finish. The blue-and-red banners of Bologna were waved wildly over the tiered terracings of the sun-baked stadium when the dangerous striker Pace gave Burridge no chance with a well-hit shot in the 32nd minute.

A small group of Blackpool supporters had flown over the Alps in two charter flights in order to watch and to cheer-on their team. They, in their tangerine and white, on the high terracing opposite the main grandstand, were almost swallowed up, as the Italian fans saluted their heroes. But the glee of the citizens of Bologna was to be short-lived.

Italian football seems—to the observer from outside—to carry its own death-wish. From the very start, in true Italian tradition, the home side had adopted a cautious attitude, filling their own half of the field with players, and relying on flying breaks out of defence to win the match.

The speed and ferocity of these lightning attacks could not be doubted. Could Blackpool hold the Italian attacks in check, and then make use of the mid-field space that Bologna were prepared to surrender (in order to build a *catenaccio* defence around their own penalty-area)? After a rather disappointing first half for the Seasiders, this was no doubt the question Bob Stokoe was asking his players during the interval.

On the re-start, Blackpool set-to with a will. Tony Green, the Scottish-international star who later became Blackpool's first £150,000 sale, kept bustling forward, using his speed and acceleration, from tight situations, to upset the Italians. Alan Suddick, not originally included in the Anglo-Italian squad but a player gifted enough to delight the Italian purists, sprayed passes of precision from mid-field. And, taking a leaf from Tommy Gemmell's 1967-European-Cup-Final book, Bill Bentley, a player of more basic construction, kept moving forward to add his weight to the attack.

Bentley's sense of adventure paid off in the 62nd minute, exactly half an hour after Bologna's goal. Bill, one of several fine players Blackpool have obtained over the years from the Potteries, picked up a pass mid-way inside the Bologna half. He looked up and saw John Craven running into a space the Italians had left, momentarily dropping their guard. Bentley quickly shoved the ball into the path of Craven, the burly Blackpool skipper and centre-forward, who scored the equaliser by crashing a great shot into the net from just inside the penalty-area.

At that moment, one could almost *feel* the initiative draining away from the Italians. There were no more goals in normal time, but it was Blackpool, who had dominated most of the second half, who were in the ascendant. And Blackpool's will-to-win was more apparent, even though cramp pulled at tired legs: Blackpool's coach, Brian Doyle, was on the field more than once to massage aching muscles.

The winning goal was worthy of winning *any* match. Nine minutes into extra-time, substitute Dennis Wann (brought on for the exhausted Ainscow) pushed an accurate 25-yard pass towards Mickey Burns. Burns, a player with rare talent for opportunism, took the ball, as the Italians hurriedly grouped, pushed it to his left, and cracked it into the net. It was a typical Burns goal. Although there was still 21 minutes of extra-time to play, the Italians never looked like recovering—and they didn't.

Members of the younger generation in Blackpool, who never had the chance to watch Matthews, Mortensen, Johnston and company, are almost weary of forever being told by their elders about the famous Blackpool combination of seaside troubadours who used to light up the land with their immense talents.

Comparisons between Blackpool's great post-war team, and other teams who have worn the famous tangerine since then, are not entirely valid—no comparisons ever are—in the light of the vastly changed circumstances of modern-day football. I am reminded of the agonies suffered by successive generations of Arsenal players who were always being compared with Herbert Chapman's mighty pre-war team. At last, in 1971, Bertie Mee's "Double"-winning team broke the Chapman spell for ever.

Blackpool will suffer similar comparisons—for Herbert Chapman, substitute Joe Smith—until they write themselves a new tradition, built on fresh glory. Until then, I am grateful—in my own reporting experience—for the considerable highlights modern-day Blackpool players have provided over the past few years.

One memory that stands out vividly in my mind is Blackpool's valiant but unsuccessful attempt to gain promotion in season 1967–68, under the cheerful and ebullient leadership of Stan Mortensen. Their promotion chances seemed to be on the wane when they lost at Blackburn on April 3. But, in a glorious run of success, Blackpool won all of their last seven matches, beating Cardiff, Charlton, Blackburn (H), Norwich, Portsmouth, Derby, and Huddersfield.

Alas, Blackpool were kept in third place by a tiny fraction of goal-average, and became the only Second Division side ever to obtain 58 points and not win promotion. But what Blackpool supporter will ever forget the tense atmosphere of that match at Huddersfield? With the exception of John Craven at right-half in place of Graham Rowe, in the last two matches of the season, the Blackpool team that so nearly clinched promotion, after only one season back in Division II, was: Taylor; Armfield, Mowbray; Rowe, James, McPhee; Skirton, Green, White, Suddick, Hutchison.

Another vivid highlight of Blackpool's recent years was the 3-0 triumph in the last-but-one game of season 1969–70, which *did* ensure promotion after that narrow failure two years previously. This 1970 highlight was probably all the sweeter for Blackpool supporters because promotion was achieved against local rivals Preston. Centre-forward Fred Pickering, who had performed yeoman service with Blackburn, Everton, Birmingham, and England, sealed Blackpool's elevation with three excellently-taken goals. That night, Deepdale belonged to Blackpool. But success was tinged with sadness, because Blackpool's win helped to push Preston down into the Third Division.

I remember other days when Blackpool Football Club has brought special credit to the town, but my favourite memory of the recent past was that sunny evening in Bologna, when Blackpool triumphed at their first attempt in European competition. As the white-shirted Blackpool players ran a lap of honour with the trophy, and as the Italians applauded their skills, the supreme status-symbol in the Stadio Communale was to be *from Blackpool*. Even the tall cypress trees, on a hill overlooking the giant bowl of a stadium, seemed to stand in tribute to Blackpool.

My biggest hope is that this memorable occasion will be the start of a new Blackpool tradition, which will add a new future to enhance a glorious past.

38

FUN AND GAMES AT BLACKPOOL
by Alistair Cooke

I don't know when I first became aware that my mother's morning battle with her bronchia was abnormal: that people do not usually bark away like a pack of wolves on getting up in the morning. It was a frightening sound to strangers but, being a small boy and therefore accepting almost everything about our family life as normal, I took it for granted, just as I took for granted the endless dark mornings, the blanket of smog, the slippery veil of mud on the streets, which only later did I discover were not typical of life on this globe but only of life in Manchester.

"It was her cough that carried her off," my mother's friends would chant, with that peculiar cheerful grimness of Lancashire people. Happily, it took quite some time. She bore it for 86 years. But it was her cough that first took us from Salford to Blackpool. Towards the end of 1916, after a particularly harrowing bout, the doctor told us that the Manchester climate was not meant for her (the implication that it was meant for *anybody* is another interesting facet of Lancashire phlegm; and phlegm, I think, is the right word). He solemnly announced that she should move to either of two places: to Blackpool or Egypt! Since my father, an artist in copper work (who fashioned the flagship on the mast of the Town Hall), had gone into an airplane factory by way of doing his wartime bit, Egypt was not on; or, as the politicians would say, it was not "a viable option".

So we moved to Blackpool, in March 1917. And in spite of the War, and the fierce rationing (also normal), and the dark nights, and the sight of every other housewife wearing widow's weeds, it was for me the entry into paradise. For Blackpool was a luxury granted only once a year to the ordinary mortals of Lancashire. It was now to be my daily circus. Sand castles, and the sea, and the Pleasure Beach, and laying down lines on the sands at night for catching plaice, and ducking the high tides on the lower Promenade.

A little later on, and in the crowded summertime, there was a special Sunday-evening pleasure, all the more intense for being at once sinful and delayed. In those years, the Wesleyan Methodists held an overflow evening service in the Grand Theatre. By then, I was old enough to be an usher and hymn-book dispenser, a duty that relieved me from the compulsion to stay sitting through an interminable sermon. It was possible to hang around in the foyer and not even hear the man droning on with his promise of life eternal—for mill workers earning a pound a week. Such sociological ironies never crossed my mind in those callow youthful years, but I'm pretty sure that the younger bloods in the congregation were as impatient as I was for the blessed sound of the benediction, which was like a starting gun that sent two or three of us out along the Promenade and towards the sandhills (there were big rolling dunes then, both at the Squires Gate end and the North Shore) where you could get an eyeful of the promenading, and sometimes reclining, birds.

A Freudian item occurs to me here which may explain my later affection for all games both indoor and out. It was noticed by some concerned parson that as a small boy I played only with girls. (After adolescence it was, of course, big girls.) So at some point, care was taken that I should meet and play, for a change, with little boys. I took to marbles, then to flipping cigarette cards against the pavement, and then, when we moved to Blackpool, to fishing and cricket on the sands. And then to bagatelle. My father bought me a table for Christmas, a splendid thing of mahogany and green baize that I would gladly buy back today at its no doubt ruinously inflated price.

After that, though notorious from an early age for my addiction to books, I never felt any conflict between work and play. And so, in the course of time, and with my father's encouragement, I went on to play soccer, rugby, and cricket for the school; ping-pong, badminton, squash, tennis, you name it. But, for a happy period, between I should say the ages of eleven and fifteen, my particular mania was gymnastics. Next to the public library was the town gymnasium, and, since I lived up the road, I came at a tender age under the sharp eye and expert instruction of one H. Gregory, father of Alfred Gregory, the Alpinist. By the time I moved to the Secondary School, as it then was, I was pretty good on the horizontal and parallel bars and had gone through the whole genteel gamut of country and folk dancing. During my years in the second and third forms, I must have been an odious figure to the giants of the Sixth. We had at the time a regular master who, until the sensible importation of H. Gregory himself, "took" us at gym.

He knew a few Swedish exercises and what he could recall of the army's routines. He was chronically fatigued and was always making excuses to skip his sessions with the Sixth. So he would get permission of the headmaster, a small bouncing figure of Roman imperiousness named J. Turral, to fork me out of class (any class) in order to take the Sixth at gym. It must have been galling for those seventeen- and eighteen-year-olds, already sprouting the down of the first moustache, to have to obey the hip-hup instructions of a twelve-year-old, who now recalls with relish the mean pleasure of showing some hairy giant how to vault the pommel horse, perform hand-stands and cart wheels, not to mention the hopeless attempts to give them the elements of doing up-starts and "hocks off" on the horizontal bar. I realized very much later why, for a time, I came in for a delinquent's share of "lines" from the prefects, smarting under the helpless giggles of their contemporaries every time they demonstrated their ineptitude at climbing a rope or crashing from a hand-stand.

Football, anyone? It took quite a while to get around to it, didn't it? But then it took me quite a while too. I had picked up from Hal Gregory a firm prejudice about the distinction between athletics and gymnastics. Athletics were for gorillas; gymnastics appealed to a subtler breed that appreciated grace and timing. After I had spent long Saturday afternoons at the gym, my father would come home from Bloomfield Road, and pretty soon I was converted by his ravings about the speed of little Mee, the walloping defensive tactics of Tulloch, and the hair's-breadth retrieves of Mingay. I began to skip Saturday afternoons at the gym, except when we were in training with "the girls" for the folk dancing division of the Lytham Festival. (Of all those enchantresses I recall only one, because she was a knock-out and was the first girl to knock me flat. As old H. L. Mencken put it: "A man always remembers his first girl; after that he tends to bunch 'em." Her name was Mamie Woods, and down the vale of fifty years I salute her. If she is still around, all she has to do is whistle.)

So I became, with my father, a regular Bloomfield Roader. Of that 1920 team, I remember only Mee at outside-left, then Heathcote (who bore a surprising resemblance to Henry Edwards, the reigning British silent-screen star), Barrass with his curls, and Benton. The name of Donnachie has been suggested to me, but if he was there in my time he must have been on the injured list throughout the season. Robin Daniels also informs me that Blackpool had a goalkeeper, around this time, by the name of Richardson. I am sorry to say he has left no impression on me. Mingay was *the one*, alternately the hero and the butt of the Bloomfield Road crowd. He was a glum little man with ping-pong-ball eyes, and lids as heavy as Sherlock Holmes got up as a Limehouse lascar. His regular expression was one of gloomy contempt for the game and the crowd. No footballer I remember, except possibly Harry Bedford, lurched so unpredictably, from one week to the next, between brilliance and bathos. One Saturday he fumbled everything; the next he slithered, darted, plunged, leapt, in a series of jagged but wonderful recoveries.

Bedford, of the permanently furrowed brow and the prison hair-cut, came to us, I guess, in 1921. He was, after Cecil Parkin, my sporting hero. And I watched him till the dizzy day he played for England. After that, the "regulars" became hypercritical of him, as Lancashire people will of anybody who has acquired an extra-local reputation and might begin to put on airs, which Bedford never did. I don't know if it's true of Lancashire crowds in general but the Bloomfield Road mob never lost its head over any idol. Either he was a "reet champion" or he was "disgoostin' ".

I'm afraid my memories of Blackpool football fade after that, along with my enthusiasm. I played for the Secondary School and cannot truthfully say I was crazy about standing between the goal-posts on witheringly dank afternoons. Then the inimitable J. Turral, who was a terrible snob but an absolutely Dickensian original, decided that soccer was gross, fit only for cave-dwellers. So the school changed over to rugby, and I didn't enjoy that much either, breaking my back and weaning arthritis in the mud on other shivery Saturdays, as I heeled the ball out to Ken Jones or Norman Hinton.

When I went to Cambridge, I swore never to play football again, and I never did. There was, astoundingly, no gymnasium at Cambridge, so for a brief spell I turned to long-jumping. I had the honour of jumping for Jesus (the college, not the Superstar) but, since sport was no longer compulsory, I gave it up, what with the humid-steaming Fen country, and the jolt to the system of thudding your heels in the sand-pit twice a week.

Years later, by the time I'd become the New Yorker guide-in-residence to visiting Englishmen, I would incite them to watch American football because it was, and is, such a fascinating com-bination of chess and armored warfare. But I always warned them that they might take understandable offence at the nauseating American habit of using substitutes every time a man bruised an ankle; and the even more odious custom of bounding to embrace each other after every touchdown. Well, two years ago, I saw my first English soccer match in decades and, sure enough, the players had followed the usual English procedure of first ridiculing an

American fashion and then adopting and exaggerating it. To watch any soccer player in the moment after he has socked the ball into the net would give a man from Mars the impression that he was seeing a film clip of V-E Day or the arrival of Lindbergh at Le Bourget.

Since my family died, I have not been back to Blackpool. But on the last trips, I had a regular sensation, as the train wheeled around the coastline, and the Tower came into view, that I had never known in all the years I lived in Blackpool or travelled there. In the interval between the Bloomfield Road days and my last few visits to my ageing mother, I had taken up golf in the most maniacal way. Being still incapable of keeping books and sport apart, I read everything I could find on the game. And now, some years later, I regard myself as having earned a creditable Master's degree in the history of golf. On the last visits, when the train gave the lurch that takes it alongside the green undulations of Royal Lytham St Annes, I got up and dropped the window and peered out. This was the very place where Robert Tyre Jones Jr, the immortal one (and all the more immortal now that he is dead), fired his devastating iron shot from a bunker or sandy swale on the 17th to win the British Open of 1926 and obliterate Al Watrous. On that very day, I was four miles away, playing cricket amid the yeasty odours of the abattoir that adjoined the Secondary School field. How dull, blind, and insensitive can a boy be?!

There is, they tell me, a plaque in the bunker today to commemorate the feat. I have never seen it. I have never played Lytham St Annes. One day, I hope to. And, if the weather is right, maybe I shall drop in again at Bloomfield Road and see if Mingay is still at it.

39

EPILOGUE:
Selector For a Day

If I were asked to select a Blackpool XI to take on an all-time XI from, say, Everton, Arsenal, or Manchester United, I would select Blackpool's '53 Cup Final team—every player from Farm, the goalkeeper, to Perry at outside-left—and be fully confident of my team's success. But, if the rational overpowered the sentimental in me, I should have to cast my selectorial net into the first five decades of Blackpool's League life.

By inviting myself to look back upon the whole history of Blackpool football, I set out on a major task: far more taxing than the season-by-season job of those who choose teams of contemporaries. I am faced with different eras of the game, entailing different tactics, different training methods, different financial incentives, and different styles of play. Finally, I must select players on the basis of their attainments while they were with Blackpool.

I am forced to exclude, from my dream XI, England internationals such as Jack Cox, an outside-left, who joined Liverpool in 1898 and played in their League Championship team of 1900–01, and also in the Liverpool side that topped Division II in 1904–05; Harold "Jubba" Hardman, also an outside-left, who was discovered by Blackpool F.C. at a local high school, and, after joining Everton in 1903, played in two successive Cup Finals—1905–06 and 1906–07; George Wilson, who captained England in the 1920s while he was with Sheffield Wednesday; and, of much more recent vintage, Bill Slater, Footballer of the Year in his Wolverhampton days, Gordon West, a Cup Final victor with Everton in 1966, and Em Hughes, who became an England international while with Liverpool. These players reached maturity, in age and as footballers, after leaving Bloomfield Road. It may (or it may not!) be a consolation to Blackpool supporters to be reminded that, as long ago as the 1890s, the bigger clubs were abducting Blackpool's best players.

I shall spare you a description of the agonies I suffered in choosing my team. After all, isn't the definition of a selector "someone beyond—and above—criticism, who never condescends to justify his decisions"? I am comforted by two thoughts: that I am a committee of one—the best number for decision-making without rancour; and that no computer programme has yet been written to prove me wrong. Here, then, is my ideal Blackpool XI:

Ball	Doherty	Hampson	Mortensen	Matthews
(England)	(Ireland)	(England)	(England)	(England)

	Johnston	Gratrix	Farrow	
	(England)			

	Garrett		Armfield	
	(England)		(England)	

Farm
(Scotland)

And my reserve team is:

Perry	Mudie	Dodds	Finan	Green
(England)	(Scotland)	(Scotland—war-time)	(Scotland—war-time)	(Scotland)

	S. Jones	Hayward	Benton	
	(Ireland)			

	H. Jones		Shimwell	
	(England)		(England)	

Waiters
(England)

I blush as I contemplate my Blackpool XIs. I am ashamed that I have not found a place for two priceless inside-forwards: Brown (Scotland) and Taylor (England). And where are the two stalwart centre-halves, Tremelling and Watson (Scotland)? And what about Hughie Kelly (Scotland), a wonderfully consistent half-back, and George Mee, outside-left of the 1920s? And, probably most damning of all, I have had to leave on the side-lines four centre-forwards, whose combined value—if they could come, in their prime, onto today's transfer market—would be beyond the powers of the most modern adding-machine: Lane, Bedford (England), O'Donnell (Scotland), and Charnley (England).

I have selected Billy Benton to captain the reserves, but who should captain the first team? Armfield or Johnston? Both captained Blackpool for a decade, and both would feature in many people's best England XI of the post-war years. I have mused over this for hours, and cannot reach a decision. So much for the committee of one! I would, therefore, ask Johnston (being the senior of the two) to act as captain in the first half, and Jimmy Armfield in the second. English diplomacy wins again.

APPENDICES

These records are complete to the end of the 1971–72 season.

Unless stated otherwise, records for appearances do not include substitutions.

For biggest-ever wins and biggest-ever defeats, the records are determined by the winning team's score; not by goal-difference or goal-average.

BLACKPOOL F.C. RECORDS
INDEX

1   CENTRAL LEAGUE

Blackpool have been Central League Champions on two occasions:

	Played	Won	Drew	Lost	Goals For	Goals Against	Points
1919–20	42	28	2	12	94	51	58
1949–50	42	24	12	6	82	36	60

2   COLOURS

Until 1967, a club—with permission from the Football League—could change its colours in mid-season. Now, except to avoid a colour clash between two competing teams, no club is allowed to change the registered colours, or combination of colours, in mid-season. A list follows, giving Blackpool's official beginning-of-season colour changes (shirts only) since entering the Football League:

1896–97	Blue and white stripes
1902–03	Red or white
1903–04	Red and white
1904–05	Red
1915–16	Red, yellow, and black
1918–19	White
1923–24	Tangerine
1934–35	Dark- and light-blue stripes
1939–40	Tangerine

F.A. CUP

3 List of Matches in the Competition Proper

Season	Round	Opponents	Venue	Score
		(And their Football League Division at the time the match was played. Non-L = Non-League)	*(*Denotes Blackpool sold ground rights)*	*(Blackpool's score given first. A.E.T. = After extra-time)*
1891–92	1	Sheffield United (Non-L)	H	0-3
1892–93	1	Sheffield United (2)	H	1-3
1895–96	1	Burton Swifts (2)	H	4-1
	2	Bolton (1)	H	0-2
1905–06	1	Crystal Palace (Non-L)	H	1-1
	Replay		A	1-1 A.E.T.
	2nd replay		Villa Park	1-0
	2	Sheffield United (1)	A*	2-1
	3	Newcastle (1)	A	0-5
1906–07	1	West Ham (Non-L)	A*	1-2
1907–08	1	Manchester United (1)	A	1-3
1908–09	1	Hastings & St Leonards (Non-L)	H	2-0
	2	Newcastle (1)	A	1-2
1909–10	1	Barnsley (2)	H	1-1
	Replay		A	0-6
1910–11	1	Manchester United (1)	A*	1-2
1911–12	1	Crewe (Non-L)	A	1-1
	Replay		H	2-0[1]
			H	2-2 A.E.T.
	2nd replay		Hyde Road, Manchester	2-1
	2	Bolton (1)	A	0-1
1912–13	1	Tottenham (1)	A	1-1
	Replay		A*	1-6
1913–14	1	Gillingham (Non-L)	A	0-1
1914–15	1	Sheffield United (1)	H	1-2
1919–20	1	Derby (1)	H	0-0
	Replay		A	4-1
	2	Preston (1)	A	1-2

[1] This match—played in a blizzard—was abandoned after 61 minutes.

x

Season	Round	Opponents	Venue	Score
1920–21	1	Darlington (Non-L)	A	2-2
	Replay		H	2-1
	2	Southend (3 S.)	A	0-1
1921–22	1	Watford (3 S.)	H	1-2
1922–23	1	Derby (2)	A	0-2
1923–24	1	Sheffield United (1)	H	1-0
	2	Southampton (2)	A	1-3
1924–25	1	Barrow (3N.)	H	0-0
	Replay		A	2-0
	2	Bradford P.A. (3N.)	A	1-1
	Replay		H	2-1
	3	West Ham (1)	A	1-1
	Replay		H	3-0
	Quarter-final	Blackburn (1)	A	0-1
1925–26	3	Swansea (2)	H	0-2
1926–27	3	Bolton (1)	H	1-3
1927–28	3	Oldham (2)	H	1-4
1928–29	3	Plymouth (3 S.)	A	0-3
1929–30	3	Stockport (3 N.)	H	2-1
	4	Hull (2)	A	1-3
1930–31	3	Hull (3 N.)	A	2-1
	4	Southport (3 N.)	A	1-2
1931–32	3	Newcastle (1)	H	1-1
	Replay		A	0-1
1932–33	3	Port Vale (2)	H	2-1
	4	Huddersfield (1)	H	2-0
	5	Sunderland (1)	A	0-1
1933–34	3	Cheltenham Town (Non-L)	A	3-1
	4	Stoke (1)	A	0-3
1934–35	3	Leicester (1)	A	1-2
1935–36	3	Margate (Non-L)	H	3-1
	4	Fulham (2)	A	2-5
1936–37	3	Luton (3 S.)	A	3-3
	Replay		H	1-2
1937–38	3	Birmingham (1)	A	1-0
	4	Aston Villa (2)	A	0-4
1938–39	3	Sheffield United (2)	H	1-2
1945–46	3	Wrexham (3 N.)	A	4-1
	2nd leg		H	4-1[1]
	4	Middlesbrough (1)	H	3-2
	2nd leg		A	2-3 A.E.T.[2]
	Replay		Elland Road	0-1 A.E.T.[3]
1946–47	3	Sheffield Wednesday (2)	A	1-4

[1] Blackpool won the round on aggregate, 8-2.
[2] There were 2 half-hour periods of extra-time.
[3] The teams were still level after half an hour of extra-time. The referee ruled that the next team to score would win the match. Middlesbrough scored after a further 20 minutes' play, and won the round on aggregate, 6-5.

Season	Round	Opponents	Venue	Score
1947–48	3	Leeds (2)	H	4-0
	4	Chester (3 N.)	H	4-0
	5	Colchester (Non-L)	H	5-0
	Quarter-final	Fulham (2)	A	2-0
	Semi-final	Tottenham (2)	Villa Park	3-1 A.E.T.
	Final	Manchester United (1)	Wembley	2-4
1948–49	3	Barnsley (2)	A	1-0
	4	Stoke (1)	A	1-1 A.E.T.
	Replay		H	0-1
1949–50	3	Southend (3 S.)	H	4-0
	4	Doncaster (3 N.)	H	2-1
	5	Wolverhampton (1)	A	0-0
	Replay		H	1-0
	Quarter-final	Liverpool (1)	A	1-2
1950–51	3	Charlton (1)	A	2-2
	Replay		H	3-0
	4	Stockport (3 N.)	H	2-1
	5	Mansfield (3 N.)	H	2-0
	Quarter-final	Fulham (1)	H	1-0
	Semi-final	Birmingham (2)	Maine Road	0-0
	Replay		Goodison Park	2-1
	Final	Newcastle (1)	Wembley	0-2
1951–52	3	West Ham (2)	A	1-2
1952–53	3	Sheffield Wednesday (1)	A	2-1
	4	Huddersfield (2)	H	1-0
	5	Southampton (2)	H	1-1
	Replay		A	2-1
	Quarter-final	Arsenal (1)	A	2-1
	Semi-final	Tottenham (1)	Villa Park	2-1
	Final	Bolton (1)	Wembley	4-3[1]
1953–54	3	Luton (2)	H	1-1
	Replay		A	0-0 A.E.T.
	2nd replay		Villa Park	1-1 A.E.T.
	3rd replay		Molineux	2-0
	4	West Ham (2)	A	1-1
	Replay		H	3-1
	5	Port Vale (3 N.)	A	0-2
1954–55	3	York (3 N.)	H	0-2
1955–56	3	Manchester City (1)	A	1-1[2]
			A	1-2
1956–57	3	Bolton (1)	A	3-2
	4	Fulham (2)	H	6-2
	5	W.B.A. (1)	H	0-0
	Replay		A	1-2

[1] In the Charity Shield match—at Highbury on October 12, 1953—Blackpool lost 3-1 to Arsenal, the League Champions.
[2] Abandoned after 56 minutes, because of fog.

Season	Round	Opponents	Venue	Score
1957–58	3	West Ham (2)	A	1-5
1958–59	3	Southampton (3)	A	2-1
	4	Bristol City (2)	A	1-1
	Replay		H	1-0
	5	W. B. A. (1)	H	3-1
	Quarter-final	Luton (1)	H	1-1
	Replay		A	0-1
1959–60	3	Mansfield (3)	H	3-0
	4	Blackburn (1)	A	1-1
	Replay		H	0-3
1960–61	3	Scunthorpe (2)	A	2-6
1961–62	3	W. B. A. (1)	H	0-0
	Replay		A	1-2
1962–63	3	Norwich (2)	A	1-1
	Replay		H	1-3 A.E.T.
1963–64	3	W. B. A. (1)	A	2-2
	Replay		H	0-1
1964–65	3	Stoke (1)	A	1-4
1965–66	3	Manchester City (2)	H	1-1
	Replay		A	1-3
1966–67	3	Birmingham (2)	A	1-2
1967–68	3	Chesterfield (4)	H	2-1
	4	Sheffield United (1)	A	1-2
1968–69	3	Coventry (1)	A	1-3
1969–70	3	Arsenal (1)	A	1-1
	Replay		H	3-2
	4	Mansfield (3)	H	0-2
1970–71	3	West Ham (1)	H	4-0
	4	Hull (2)	A	0-2
1971–72	3	Chelsea (1)	H	0-1

4 Match Records

Biggest win: 6-2, v. Fulham (H), 26-1-57.

Biggest defeat: 0-6, v. Barnsley (A), 20-1-10.

Longest match: 2½ hours, v. Middlesbrough (A), 30-1-46. There were two
½-hour periods of extra-time. The three matches—that it took to settle this
round—lasted a total of 6 hours and 20 miniutes.

5 Goal-scoring

Most goals in a match: 4, J. Mudie, v. Fulham (H), 26-1-57.

Most goals in a season: 10, S. Mortensen, 1947–48.

Most goals in a career: 29, S. Mortensen, in 34 matches between January 1946 and
January 1955.

Scored in every round: S. Mortensen, 1947–48. This feat has been achieved by only
a handful of players in the whole history of the F.A. Cup.

Quickest goal: 13 seconds after the kick-off, E. Taylor, v. Manchester City (A), 7-1-56. This record is only semi-official: the match was abandoned because of fog. Taylor had missed the previous three first-team games because of injury.

Goals in consecutive matches: S. Mortensen scored in 9 consecutive matches: Sheffield Wednesday (A) in January 1947 to Stoke (A) in January 1949 (inclusive). A national record.

Goals in consecutive rounds: S. Mortensen scored in 12 consecutive rounds: Wrexham in January 1946 to Southend in January 1950 (inclusive). A national record.

Most goals in a Cup Final: 3 (a hat-trick), S. Mortensen, 1953. Mortensen is the only player in the 20th century, and only the third of all time, to score 3 goals in an F.A. Cup Final.

Most goals in Cup Finals: 4, S. Mortensen: 1 in 1948; 3 in 1953.

6   Appearances

Most appearances in a career: 49, S. Matthews, between January 1948 and January 1961.

Most consecutive appearances: 47, G. Farm. Farm, who never missed a Cup match during his career with Blackpool, played in all the Cup campaigns from 1948–49 to 1959–60 (inclusive).

Most Cup Final appearances: 3. This record is shared by E. Shimwell, S. Matthews, S. Mortensen, and H. Johnston. H Johnston was Blackpool's captain on all three occasions.

7   General

Best seasons: Winners: 1953; Runners-up: 1948, 1951; Quarter-finalists: 1925, 1950, 1959.

Most consecutive wins: Between January 1953 and February 1954, Blackpool won 8 consecutive Cup rounds, beating Sheffield Wednesday, Huddersfield, Southampton, Arsenal, Tottenham, Bolton, Luton, and West Ham.

Most consecutive defeats: Following the third-round victory over Mansfield in January 1960, Blackpool did not win another Cup match until January 1968. In those eight barren years, Blackpool played 13 F.A. Cup matches, drawing 5 and losing 8.

Longest round: Third round v. Luton, 1953–54. Blackpool won 2-0 in the fourth meeting, after playing for a total of 7 hours. Blackpool and Crewe met four times in the first round of the 1911–12 season, but the second of the four matches was abandoned.

Most postponements: The third-round match against Norwich, in 1963, was postponed 11 times because of bad weather. The original date was 5th January. The match was finally played on 4th March.

8   Cup Finals

1948: v. Manchester United, 24-4-48.

The Blackpool team was: J. Robinson; E. Shimwell, J. Crosland; H. Johnston, E. Hayward, H. Kelly; S. Matthews, A. Munro, S. Mortensen, G. Dick, W. Rickett.

Blackpool became the first seaside-resort club to appear in an F.A. Cup Final.

This was Johnny Crosland's first-ever F.A. Cup appearance for Blackpool.

When Eddie Shimwell scored from a penalty in the 14th minute, he became the first full-back to score in a Wembley Cup Final.

Blackpool were only the third team in F.A. Cup history to score two goals in the Final and yet lose. (Excluding the year that Sheffield United drew 2-2, and then lost the replay.)

1951: v. Newcastle, 28-4-51.

The Blackpool team was: G. Farm; E. Shimwell, T. Garrett; H. Johnston, E. Hayward, H. Kelly; S. Matthews, J. Mudie, S. Mortensen, W. Slater, W. Perry.

Bill Perry was the first South African to play in a Wembley Cup Final.

Bill Slater was the second amateur to play in a post-war Cup Final. He will probably earn a place in football history as being the last amateur ever to play in an F.A. Cup Final.

1953: v. Bolton, 2-5-53.

The Blackpool team was: G. Farm; E. Shimwell, T. Garrett; E. Fenton, H. Johnston, C. Robinson; S. Matthews, E. Taylor, S. Mortensen, J. Mudie, W. Perry.

1953 was Coronation year. The Queen attended the match and presented the awards.

Bill Perry became the first South African to score in, and gain a winners' medal from, a Cup Final at Wembley.

The receipts (£49,900) were the then-highest ever taken at a football match in Britain.

The total of seven goals equalled the most ever in a Cup Final.

This was the first Cup Final to finish 4-3.

Blackpool's four goals equalled the most scored by one team in a Wembley Final.

Before 1953, no team had lost in a Cup Final after scoring three goals.

Blackpool became the second team to win a Wembley Final after twice being a goal down. The first team to achieve this feat was Manchester United—in their 1948 victory over Blackpool.

Until 1953, no team had won a Wembley Final after being two goals behind.

Blackpool fielded nine men who had previously played in a Cup Final. One of them, Ernie Taylor, had played for Newcastle in 1951, in their Cup Final win over Blackpool. One of the forwards who helped Bolton, in the 1920s, to set the all-time[1] record—ten players with Cup Final experience—was Joe Smith, Blackpool's manager at the time of the '53 Final.

Blackpool became the first seaside-resort club to win the F.A. Cup.

---

[1] Bolton's record was beaten by Leeds in the 1972 Final: all eleven Leeds players had Cup Final experience.

FOOTBALL LEAGUE

9 Season-by-season Records

Season	Division	Position	Points	Played	Home Matches Won	Drew	Lost	Goals For	Goals Against	Points	Away Matches Won	Drew	Lost	Goals For	Goals Against	Points
1896-97	2	8	31	30	11	3	1	39	16	25	2	2	11	20	40	6
1897-98	2	11	25	30	8	4	3	32	15	20	2	1	12	17	46	5
1898-99	2	16	20	34	6	3	8	35	30	15	2	1	14	14	60	5
1899-1900	Blackpool played in the Lancashire League															
1900-01	2	12	31	34	11	6	4	20	11	20	5	1	11	13	47	11
1901-02	2	12	29	34	9	3	5	27	21	21	2	4	11	13	35	8
1902-03	2	14	28	34	7	5	5	32	24	19	2	5	10	12	35	9
1903-04	2	15	27	34	8	2	7	25	27	18	3	3	11	15	40	9
1904-05	2	15	28	34	8	5	4	26	15	21	1	5	11	10	33	7
1905-06	2	14	29	38	8	3	8	22	21	19	2	6	11	15	41	10
1906-07	2	13	33	38	9	4	6	25	19	22	2	7	10	8	32	11
1907-08	2	15	31	38	11	3	5	33	19	25	0	6	13	18	39	6
1908-09	2	20	29	38	9	6	4	30	22	24	0	5	14	16	46	5
1909-10	2	12	36	38	7	7	5	24	18	21	7	1	11	26	34	15
1910-11	2	7	42	38	10	5	4	29	15	25	6	5	8	20	23	17
1911-12	2	14	34	38	12	4	3	24	12	28	1	4	14	8	40	6
1912-13	2	20	26	38	8	4	7	22	22	20	1	4	14	17	47	6
1913-14	2	16	32	38	6	10	3	24	19	22	3	4	12	9	25	10
1914-15	2	10	39	38	11	3	5	40	22	25	6	2	11	18	35	14
World War I—No official competitions																
1919-20	2	4	52	42	13	4	4	40	18	30	8	6	7	25	29	22
1920-21	2	4	50	42	12	3	6	32	19	27	8	7	6	22	23	23
1921-22	2	19	35	42	11	1	9	33	27	23	4	4	13	11	30	12
1922-23	2	5	47	42	12	4	5	37	14	28	6	7	8	23	29	19
1923-24	2	4	49	42	13	7	1	43	12	33	5	6	10	29	35	16
1924-25	2	17	37	42	8	5	8	37	26	21	6	4	11	28	35	16
1925-26	2	6	45	42	12	6	3	41	16	30	5	5	11	35	53	15
1926-27	2	9	44	42	13	5	3	65	26	31	5	3	13	30	54	13
1927-28	2	19	34	42	11	3	7	55	43	25	2	5	14	28	58	9
1928-29	2	8	45	42	13	4	4	49	18	30	6	3	12	43	58	15
1929-30	2	1	58	42	17	1	3	63	22	35	10	3	8	35	45	23
1930-31	1	20	32	42	8	7	6	41	44	23	3	3	15	30	81	9
1931-32	1	20	33	42	9	4	8	42	40	22	3	5	13	23	62	11

Season	Division	Position	Points	Played	Home Matches						Away Matches					
					Won	Drew	Lost	For	Against	Points	Won	Drew	Lost	For	Against	Points
								Goals						Goals		
1932–33	1	22	33	42	11	2	8	44	35	24	3	3	15	25	50	9
1933–34	2	11	43	42	10	8	3	39	27	28	5	5	11	23	37	15
1934–35	2	4	53	42	16	4	1	46	18	36	5	7	9	33	39	17
1935–36	2	10	43	42	14	3	4	64	34	31	4	4	13	29	38	12
1936–37	2	2	55	42	13	4	4	49	19	30	11	3	7	39	34	25
1937–38	1	12	40	42	10	5	6	33	26	25	6	3	12	28	40	15
1938–39	1	15	38	42	9	8	4	37	26	26	3	6	12	19	42	12
World War II—No official competitions																
1946–47	1	5	50	42	14	1	6	38	32	29	8	5	8	33	38	21
1947–48	1	9	44	42	13	4	4	37	14	30	4	6	11	20	27	14
1948–49	1	16	38	42	8	8	5	24	25	24	3	8	10	30	42	14
1949–50	1	7	49	42	10	8	3	29	14	28	7	7	7	17	21	21
1950–51	1	3	50	42	12	6	3	43	19	30	8	4	9	36	34	20
1951–52	1	9	45	42	12	5	4	40	27	29	6	4	11	24	37	16
1952–53	1	7	47	42	13	5	3	45	22	31	6	4	11	26	48	16
1953–54	1	6	48	42	13	6	2	43	19	32	6	4	11	37	50	16
1954–55	1	19	38	42	8	6	7	33	26	22	6	4	11	27	38	16
1955–56	1	2	49	42	13	4	4	56	27	30	7	5	9	30	35	19
1956–57	1	4	53	42	14	3	4	55	26	31	8	6	7	38	39	22
1957–58	1	7	44	42	11	2	8	47	35	24	8	4	9	33	32	20
1958–59	1	8	47	42	12	7	2	39	13	31	6	4	11	27	36	16
1959–60	1	11	40	42	9	6	6	32	32	24	6	4	11	27	39	16
1960–61	1	20	33	42	9	3	9	44	34	21	3	6	12	24	39	12
1961–62	1	13	41	42	10	4	7	41	30	24	5	7	9	29	45	17
1962–63	1	13	40	42	8	7	6	34	27	23	5	7	9	24	37	17
1963–64	1	18	35	42	8	6	7	26	29	22	5	3	13	26	44	13
1964–65	1	17	35	42	9	5	7	41	28	23	3	4	14	26	50	10
1965–66	1	13	37	42	9	5	7	36	29	23	5	4	12	19	36	14
1966–67	1	22	21	42	1	5	15	18	36	7	5	4	12	23	40	14
1967–68	2	3	58	42	12	6	3	33	16	30	12	4	5	38	27	28
1968–69	2	8	43	42	9	8	4	33	20	26	5	7	9	18	21	17
1969–70	2	2	53	42	10	9	2	25	16	29	10	4	7	31	29	24
1970–71	1	22	23	42	3	9	9	22	31	15	1	6	14	12	35	8
1971–72	2	6	47	42	12	6	3	43	16	30	8	1	12	27	34	17

10 Match Records

Biggest home win: 8-4, v. Charlton, Division I, 27-9-52.

Biggest away win: 7-0, v. Preston, Division I, 1-5-48.

Biggest home defeat: 3-7, v. Leeds, Division I, 20-9-30.

Biggest away defeat: 1-10, v. Small Heath, Division II, 2-3-01; 1-10, v. Huddersfield, Division I, 13-12-30.

Highest attendance at a home match: 38,098, v. Wolverhampton, Division I, 17-9-55.

Highest receipts at a home match: £10,615, v. Everton, Division I, 19-9-70.

11 Goal-scoring

Most goals in a match: 5, J. Hampson, v. Reading (H), Division II, 10-11-28; 5, J. McIntosh, v. Preston (A), Division I, 1-5-48. McIntosh had been dropped from Blackpool's 1948 Cup Final team. He equalled this club record on the Saturday after the Cup Final. He had previously played for Preston.

Most goals in a season: 45, J. Hampson, in 41 matches, 1929–30, Division II. Blackpool's Division I record is held by J. Mudie, who scored 32 goals in 38 games, in 1956–57.

Most goals in a career: 247, J. Hampson, in 360 matches between October 1927 and January 1938.
197, S. Mortensen, in 315 matches.
193, R. Charnley, in 363 matches.

Most goals in a season—by a winger: 20, W. Perry (OL), in 40 matches, 1955–56, Division I. In 1955–56, Perry scored 39 goals in 63 first-class matches.

Most goals in a career—by a winger: 119, W. Perry, in 394 matches between March 1950 and March 1962.

Quickest goal: 11 seconds after the kick-off, W. Slater, v. Stoke (H), Division I, 10-12-49. This was Slater's first-ever goal for Blackpool's first-team.

Fastest hat-trick: $3\frac{3}{4}$ minutes, G. McKnight, v. Fulham (H), Division I, 4-9-50. This was McKnight's first League match of the season. He was a reserve-team wing-half, playing as an understudy centre-forward. He never scored again for Blackpool's first-team.

Most goals on début: 3 (a hat-trick), A. Withers, v. Huddersfield (H), Division I, 18-11-50.

Goals in consecutive matches: S. Mortensen scored in 11 consecutive Division I matches, from February 3, 1951 to April 7, 1951 (inclusive).

Goals in consecutive appearances: S. Mortensen scored in 15 consecutive Division I appearances, from December 23, 1950 to April 21, 1951 (inclusive).

Fastest century of goals: J. Hampson, in 97 matches between October 15, 1927 and January 4, 1930 (inclusive). This is a Division II record. Hampson celebrated his century with a first-half hat-trick against Southampton (H). His second goal was his 100th in League matches for Blackpool.

Most seasons as top scorer: 9, S. Mortensen, from 1946–47 to 1954–55 (inclusive). In one of the nine seasons—1952–53—Mortensen was joint leading-goalscorer.

Division's top scorer:

Division	Player	Season	Goals
II	H. Bedford	1922–23	32
II	H. Bedford	1923–24	34
II	J. Hampson	1928–29	40
II	J. Hampson	1929–30	45
II	R. Finan	1935–36	34
I	S. Mortensen	1950–51	30

H. Bedford was the League's top scorer in 1922–23 and in 1923–24. Since then, only one player has been the League's (outright) top scorer in consecutive seasons.

J. Hampson was the League's top scorer in 1929–30.

In 1935–36, R. Finan shared the title—top goal-scorer in Division II—with E. Dodds. Dodds, who was then a Sheffield United player, joined Blackpool a few years later.

No goals: R. Gratrix (CH) never scored for Blackpool in his 400 League appearances for the club.

One Blackpool forward played for more than five years without scoring a League goal. S. Matthews scored once v. Tottenham (H) on September 3, 1956. It was his last League goal for Blackpool. He left in October 1961, without scoring in his last 110 League matches.

12 Appearances

Most appearances in a career: 568, J. Armfield, between December 1954 and May 1971. This is a Football League record: most appearances for one club by a right-back. While he was with Blackpool, J. Armfield played in 690 first-class matches. This total includes representative matches (for England: 43; the Football League: 12; and England Under-23: 9) as well as his appearances for Blackpool (in League: 568; F.A. Cup: 33; and Football League Cup: 25).

Most consecutive appearances: 195, G. Mee, between December 1920 and September 1925.

171, G. Farm, between September 1948 and October 1952.

Most ever-present seasons: 6, G. Farm: 1949–50, 1950–51, 1951–52, 1955–56, 1956–57, 1958–59.

13 General

Best seasons:

Division I	Runners-up: 1955–56.
	3rd place: 1950–51.
Division II	Champions: 1929–30.
	Runners-up: 1936–37, 1969–70.
	3rd place: 1967–68.

All-time records: Blackpool hold (unwillingly) the following records:

Football League (all Divisions)

1. Fewest wins in a 42-match (or more) season: 4, 1970–71 (equals the Football League record).
2. Fewest home wins in a 42-match (or more) season: 1, 1966–67.[1]
3. Fewest home points in a 42-match (or more) season: 7, 1966–67.

[1] In 1966–67, Blackpool won more League matches in *Liverpool* than in Blackpool. By an amazing paradox, that single home victory—6-0 against Newcastle—was the second highest of the season in Division I.

4. Most home defeats in a season: 15, 1966–67 (equals the Football League record).
5. Most home games without a win: 16, 1966–67/1967–68 (equals the Football League record).

First Division
1. Most goals conceded in a season: 125, 1930–31.

Youngest player: 17 years—98 days, A. Ball, v. Liverpool (A), Division I, 18-8-62.

Oldest player: 46 years—248 days, S. Matthews, v. Arsenal (A), Division I, 7-10-61.

Stanley Matthews: At Fulham, on February 25, 1961, Matthews became the second oldest player to take part in a First Division match. Blackpool's inside-left, that day, was R. Parry. When Parry was with Bolton, he became the youngest footballer ever to play in the First Division.

Matthews broke W. Meredith's record—for length of time as a player in League football—when he played v. Chelsea (H) on September 30, 1961: 29 years—6 months after his League début. Meredith and Matthews both played at outside-right.

Longest time on Blackpool's Books: 20 years—5 months, H. Johnston, who registered as an amateur on May 29, 1935, and left the club on November 9, 1955.

Longest span in League team: 17 years—5 months, H. Johnston, who made his début v. Preston (A) on November 20, 1937, and played in his last match on April 25, 1955, v. Newcastle (A).

Longest captaincy: 10 years—4 months, J. Armfield, from December 17, 1960 to May 1, 1971 (inclusive).

Most seasons in League Football: 17, J. Armfield: 1954–55 to 1970–71 (inclusive).

FOOTBALL LEAGUE CUP
14 List of Matches

Season	Round	Opponents (And their Football League Division at the time the match was played)	Venue	Score (Blackpool's is always given first. A.E.T. = After extra-time)
1960–61	2	Leeds (2)	A	0-0
	Replay		H	1-3 A.E.T.
1961–62	1	Port Vale (3)	H	2-1
	2	Leyton Orient (2)	A	1-1
	Replay		H	5-1
	3	Workington (4)	A	1-0
	Quarter-final	Sheffield United (1)	H	0-0
	Replay		A	2-0
	Semi-final	Norwich (2)	A	1-4
	2nd leg		H	2-0[1]
1962–63	2	Manchester City (1)	A	0-0
	Replay		H	3-3 A.E.T.
	2nd replay		A[2]	2-4

[1] Blackpool lost the round on aggregate, 3-4.
[2] Neither club wanted the second replay to be on a neutral ground, and so the venue (Bloomfield Road or Maine Road) was decided by the tossing of a coin.

Season	Round	Opponents	Venue	Score
1963–64	2	Charlton (2)	H	7-1
	3	Norwich (2)	A	0-1
1964–65	2	Newcastle (2)	H	3-0
	3	Sunderland (1)	A	1-4
1965–66	2	Gillingham (3)	H	5-2
	3	Darlington (4)	H	1-2
1966–67	2	Manchester United (1)	H	5-1
	3	Chelsea (1)	H	1-1
	Replay		A	3-1
	4	Fulham (1)	H	4-2
	Quarter-final	West Ham (1)	H	1-3
1967–68	2	Newport (4)	A	1-0
	3	Manchester City (1)	A	1-1
	Replay		H	0-2
1968-69	2	Wrexham (4)	A	1-1
	Replay		H	3-0
	3	Manchester City (1)	H	1-0
	4	Wolverhampton (1)	H	2-1
	Quarter-final	Arsenal (1)	A	1-5
1969–70	2	Gillingham (3)	H	3-1
	3	Crystal Palace (1)	A	2-2
	Replay		H	0-1
1970–71	2	Newport (4)	H	4-1
	3	Bristol City (2)	H	0-1
1971–72	2	Bournemouth (3)	A	2-0
	3	Colchester (4)	H	4-0
	4	Aston Villa (3)	H	4-1
	Quarter-final	Tottenham (1)	A	0-2

15   Match Records

Biggest win: 7-1, v. Charlton (H), 25-9-63.

Biggest defeat: 1-5, v. Arsenal (A), 29-10-68.

16   Goal-scoring

Most goals in a match: 4, R. Charnley, v. Charlton (H), 25-9-63.

Most Goals in a season: 6, R. Charnley, 1961–62 and 1966–67. In 1961–62, Charnley was the country's top goal-scorer in the Football League Cup Competition.

Most goals in a career: 19, R. Charnley, in 23 matches between September 1961 and October 1967.

17   Appearances

Most appearances in a career: 25, J. Armfield, between September 1960 and October 1970.

Most consecutive appearances: 18, R. Charnley, between February 1962 and December 1966.

18 General

Best seasons: Semi-finalists: 1961–62.
Quarter-finalists: 1966–67, 1968–69, 1971–72.
Longest round: Second round v. Manchester City, 1962–63. Blackpool lost 2-4 in the third meeting.

19 FOREIGN OPPOSITION

Date	Opponents	Venue	Win Draw Loss	Score (Blackpool's first)	Event
9-12-35	F.C. Vienna	Blackpool	W	4-3	
24-5-47	Malmö	Malmö	D	1-1	
27-5-47	Copenhagen XI	Copenhagen	L	1-3	
29-5-47	Copenhagen XI	Copenhagen	W	6-1	
31-5-47	Copenhagen XI	Copenhagen	W	5-0	
3-6-47	Odense	Odense	W	1-0	
22-5-48	Copenhagen Combination	Copenhagen	W	2-1	
25-5-48	Copenhagen Combination	Copenhagen	L	1-2	
28-5-48	A. I. K. Stockholm	Stockholm	W	4-0	
1-6-48	I. F. K. Gothenburg	Gothenburg	D	2-2	
3-6-48	Copenhagen Combination	Copenhagen	L	0-3	
12-5-51	R.S.C. Anderlecht	Blackpool	W	2-0	Festival of Britain
14-5-51	Stade Rennais	Blackpool	W	3-0	Festival of Britain
27-5-51	St Gallen	St Gallen	W	2-0	
30-5-51	Grasshoppers	Zürich	W	4-3	
3-6-51	Geneva-Zürich XI	Geneva	W	4-0	
6-6-51	Basel-Zürich XI	Basel	L	0-2	
30-4-52	Hamburg S.V.	Blackpool	L	0-2	
16-5-53	R.W. Essen	Ghent	W	2-1	
23-5-54	Alsace Pro.	Strasbourg	W	4-0	35th anniversary of Alsace F.A.
27-5-54	I. F.C. Saarbrücken	Saarbrücken	D	0-0	
30-5-54	Alsace Amateur XI	Mulhouse	D	2-2	35th anniversary of Alsace F.A.
23-3-57	R.S.C. Anderlecht	Brussels	D	2-2	
22-5-57	Barcelona	Barcelona	D	3-3	
14-8-57	R.V. Sparta	Rotterdam	W	3-2	
29-4-58	Los Angeles All-Stars	Los Angeles	W	13-2	
3-5-58	Australia	Sydney	W	5-2	Test Match
4-5-58	New South Wales	Wallsend	W	8-0	
10-5-58	Australia	Sydney	W	8-2	Test Match
11-5-58	New South Wales	Wollongong	W	7-2	
13-5-58	Queensland	Brisbane	W	9-0	
17-5-58	Australia	Brisbane	W	4-2	Test Match
24-5-58	Australia	Adelaide	W	1-0	Test Match
25-5-58	Victoria	Melbourne	W	8-0	

Date	Opponents	Venue	Win Draw Loss	Score	Event
31-5-58	Australia	Melbourne	W	7-0	Test Match
2-6-58	Western Australia	Perth	W	2-0	
4-6-58	South Australia	Adelaide	W	2-0	
8-6-58	Hong Kong XI	Hong Kong	W	3-1	
10-6-58	Combined Chinese XI	Hong Kong	W	10-1	
6-4-60	V. V. Venlo	Blackpool	W	7-1	
4-5-60	Kumasi XI	Kumasi	W	4-1	
7-5-60	Nigeria	Lagos	W	3-1	
11-5-60	N. Nigeria XI	Ibadan	W	4-2	
15-5-60	Black Star Group	Accra	L	1-5	
22-5-60	N. Rhodesia	Kitwe	W	7-1	
24-5-60	S. Rhodesia	Salisbury	W	6-1	
29-5-60	S. Rhodesia	Bulawayo	W	3-1	
31-5-60	Nyasaland	Blantyre	W	6-1	
7-6-62	F.C. Lisbon	Valencia	L	1-3	Orange Bowl Trophy
9-6-62	Valencia	Valencia	L	1-6	Orange Bowl Trophy
14-8-63	Real Madrid	Malaga	L	1-4	Costa del Sol Tournament
15-8-63	Monaco	Malaga	W	2-1	Costa del Sol Tournament (Play-off for 3rd place)
17-6-65	Hong Kong XI	Hong Kong	W	7-2	
13-6-70	Malaga F.C.	Malaga	D	1-1	
29-7-70	Cork Celtic	Cork	W	1-0	
1-8-70	Waterford	Waterford	W	7-1	
26-5-71	Hellas Verona	Blackpool	D	3-3	Anglo-Italian Inter-League Clubs Competition
29-5-71	A. S. Roma	Blackpool	L	1-3	Anglo-Italian Inter-League Clubs Competition
1-6-71	Hellas Verona	Verona	W	4-1	Anglo-Italian Inter-League Clubs Competition
4-6-71	A. S. Roma	Rome	W	2-1	Anglo-Italian Inter-League Clubs Competition
12-6-71	Bologna	Bologna	W	2-1[1]	Anglo-Italian Inter-League Clubs Competition (Final)

[1] After extra-time.

Date	Opponents	Venue	Win Draw Loss	Score	Event
1-6-72	Sampdoria	Genoa	W	4-1	Anglo-Italian Inter-League Clubs Competition
4-6-72	Lanerossi Vicenza	Vicenza	W	2-0	Anglo-Italian Inter-League Clubs Competition
7-6-72	Sampdoria	Blackpool	W	2-0	Anglo-Italian Inter-League Clubs Competition
10-6-72	Lanerossi Vicenza	Blackpool	W	10-0	Anglo-Italian Inter-League Clubs Competition
24-6-72	A.S. Roma	Rome	L	1-3	Anglo-Italian Inter-League Clubs Competition (Final)

HONOURS AND AWARDS

20   National and International

Four "Firsts": Blackpool have a unique quartet of "firsts": the first Footballer of the Year—S. Matthews, 1947–48; the first European Footballer of the Year—S. Matthews, 1956; the first professional footballer to receive an award in the New Year Honours List—S. Matthews C.B.E., 1957; the first Young Footballer of the Year—J. Armfield, 1959.

Knighthood: On January 1, 1965, S. Matthews became the first professional footballer to be knighted. Blackpool shared the honour with Stoke City, and the whole of English football. Jon of the *Daily Mail* drew a cartoon of a blushing George Brown reminding Harold Wilson: "But surely you know he's a right winger?"

Footballer of the Year: Blackpool's captain, Harry Johnston, was Footballer of the Year in 1950–51. Two former Blackpool players have gained this award: Bill Slater (Wolverhampton) in 1959–60, and Stan Matthews (Stoke) in 1962–63.

Jimmy Armfield: After the 1962 World Cup Finals, Jimmy Armfield was voted "the best right-back in the world" by the press corps of Chile, the host nation. For three consecutive years—1962 to 1964—Jimmy Armfield was voted "the best right-back in Europe".

21   Blackpool's Player of the Year

At the end of every season, members of the Blackpool Football Supporters' Club vote for the Player of the Year, who is awarded the "Wilf Wells Trophy". The late Wilf Wells was once Chairman of the Supporters' Club. The award was first made in 1965:

1965	John McPhee
1966	Jimmy Armfield
1967	Jimmy Robson
1968	John McPhee
1969	Tony Green
1970	Glyn James
1971	John Craven
1972	Alan Suddick

22 LANCASHIRE LEAGUE

Blackpool was one of the founder members of the Lancashire League, and the club had a successful record in the Competition:

Season	Position	Played	Won	Drew	Lost	Goals For	Against	Points
1889–90	5	24	10	6	8	61	45	26
1890–91	2	20	14	2	4	62	39	30
1891–92	2	22	16	3	3	74	32	35
1892–93	2	22	17	2	3	82	31	36
1893–94	1	22	15	3	4	73	32	33
1894–95	2	26	16	2	8	89	34	34
1895–96	13	30	11	6	13	65	50	28
1899–1900	3	28	16	6	6	79	36	38

REPRESENTATIVE HONOURS

23 List of Full-International Players

KEY: An asterisk, in front of a player's name, indicates that he also represented his country while with a club (or clubs) other than Blackpool. But the international appearances, listed in this table, are only those made while a player was with Blackpool.

The column of team positions gives all the positions for which a player was chosen—by his country—while he was with Blackpool. "W" indicates that the player represented his country on both wings. Thus, for example, Alan Ball ("W") played on the left and right wings for England, whereas Bill Perry ("OL") played only on the left. Similarly, "WH ' means right-half and left-half; "FB" means right-back and left-back; "IF" means inside-right and inside-left.

The "years in international football" column gives the actual *years* (nothing to do with *seasons*) of each player's first and last appearance in international football *while he was with Blackpool.*

Name	Position(s)	Country	Years in international football	Total appearances	Appearances against home countries	Appearances against foreign countries	Goals scored
			Before World War I				
F. Griffiths	G	Wales	1900	2	2	0	0

Name	Position(s)	Country	Years in international football	Total appear-ances	Appearances against home countries	Appearances against foreign countries	Goals scored

Between the Wars

Name	Position(s)	Country	Years	Total	Home	Foreign	Goals
H. Bedford	CF	England	1923–24	2	1	1	1
J. Hampson	CF	England	1930–32	3	2	1	5
*S. Jones	LH	Ireland	1933	1	1	0	1
P. Watson	CH	Scotland	1933	1	0	1	0
*P. Doherty	IF	Ireland	1935	4	4	0	0
*F. O'Donnell	CF	Scotland	1938	2	1	1	0
*A. Munro	OR	Scotland	1938	1	0	1	0
M. Butler	LB	Ireland	1939	1	1	0	0
*D. Astley	IR	Wales	1939	1	0	1	1

After World War II

Name	Position(s)	Country	Years	Total	Home	Foreign	Goals
J. Blair	IL	Scotland	1946	1	1	0	0
H. Johnston	WH & CH	England	1946–53	10	4	6	0
*S. Matthews	OR	England	1947–57	36	16	20	3
S. Mortensen	IF & CF	England	1947–53	25	10	15	23
E. Shimwell	RB	England	1949	1	0	1	0
T. Garrett	FB	England	1952–53	3	2	1	0
H. Kelly	LH	Scotland	1952	1	0	1	0
*A. Brown	IF & CF	Scotland	1952–54	11	3	8	3
G. Farm	G	Scotland	1952–59	10	6	4	0
E. Taylor	IR	England	1953	1	0	1	0
W. Perry	OL	England	1955–56	3	2	1	2
J. Mudie	IF & CF	Scotland	1956–58	17	6	11	9
J. Armfield	FB	England	1959–66	43	13	30	0
R. Charnley	CF	England	1962	1	0	1	0
A. Waiters	G	England	1964	5	1	4	0
*A. Ball	IF & W	England	1965–66	14	1	13	1
G. James	CH	Wales	1966-71	9	5	4	0
*A. Green	IF	Scotland	1971	4[1]	2	2	0

24 Internationals—General

Most goals in a match: 4, S. Mortensen (England), v. Portugal, 25-5-47. This four-goal spree is a record for a player making his England début.

3, S. Mortensen (England), v. Sweden, 19-11-47.

3, S. Mortensen (England), v. Ireland, 9-10-48.

3, J. Mudie (Scotland), v. Spain, 8-5-57.

E. Dodds (Scotland) scored 3 goals in a war-time international: v. England, 18-4-42.

W. W. Parr scored 4 goals for England in an amateur international: v. Wales, 29-1-38.

Most matches in a season: 12, J. Armfield (England), 1961–62.

Most consecutive matches: 31, J. Armfield (England), between April 9, 1960 and

[1] Two of these four appearances were as a substitute.

Y

May 8, 1963 (inclusive). This is an England record for the right-back position.

S. Mortensen (England) is a joint-holder of the England record for an inside-right. He played in 7 consecutive matches between May 1947 and May 1948.

Most positions: 4, A. Ball (England): OR, IR, IL, OL. By having played in four of the five forward positions, A. Ball is a joint-holder of the England record.

3, H. Johnston (England): RH, CH, LH.

3, S. Mortensen (England): IR, CF, IL.

3, A. Brown (Scotland): IR, CF, IL.

3, J. Mudie (Scotland): IR, CF, IL.

Oldest player: 42 years—103 days, S. Matthews (England), v. Denmark, 15-5-57. This is an England record.

Span of years as England player: 22 years—228 days, S. Matthews (England). This is an England record. During part of this period, Matthews was with Stoke City.

Captaincy: J. Armfield (England) is the only Blackpool player to captain a full-international team. He captained England on 15 occasions, between September 28, 1961 and June 26, 1966 (inclusive).

Appearance in World Cup Final: A. Ball (England), OR, v. West Germany, 30-7-66.

Appearances in Final Series of World Cup: British teams did not compete in the World Cup until 1950. In that year, and in the final series of the four subsequent Competitions, at least one Blackpool player appeared:

1950—S. Matthews (England); S. Mortensen (England).

1954—S. Matthews (England); A. Brown (Scotland).

1958—J. Mudie (Scotland).

1962—J. Armfield (England).

1966—A. Ball (England).

England record for a full-back: On May 4, 1966, J. Armfield (England) equalled R. Crompton's England record—for a full-back—of 42 appearances. In his last international, on June 26, 1966, Armfield set an England (and British) record, for a full-back, of 43 international appearances. Nine days later, R. Wilson, playing in his 44th international, broke Armfield's record.

All 11 positions for England: When A. Waiters first played in goal for England— May 24, 1964—Blackpool became the first club since the war to provide a player, at one time or another, for all eleven positions in the England team.

Former internationals: A number of players have joined Blackpool after their international career was finished. They include:

England—E. Chadwick, J. Carr, G. Harrison, T. Wilson, G. R. Eastham, R. Parry, G. Milne, F. Pickering.

Scotland—J. Donnachie, D. Blair, F. Hill, R. Thomson, W. Cook, P. Quinn, A. Blacklaw.

N. Ireland—J. McKenna.

South Africa—B. Peterson.

Five players were England Under-23 internationals before joining Blackpool: A. Kaye, R. Parry, J. Robson, A. Suddick, K. Dyson.

Most players capped in a season: 7, 1953–54. 5 Blackpool players represented England (S. Matthews, S. Mortensen, H. Johnston, E. Taylor, T. Garrett) and two represented Scotland (G. Farm, A. Brown).

Post-war honours: In every one of the 22 post-war seasons—up to and including 1967–68—at least one Blackpool player gained full-international honours.

Most internationals in a Blackpool team: During the 1953–54 season, Blackpool fielded a team that contained 9 (current or former) internationals and 1 future international. The 11th member of the team had represented the British Army. The team was: G. Farm (Scotland); E. Shimwell (England), T. Garrett (England); E. Fenton (Army), H. Johnston (England), H. Kelly (Scotland); S. Matthews (England), E. Taylor (England), S. Mortensen (England), A. Brown (Scotland), W. Perry (England, 1955–56).

Most Blackpool players in an international team: 4, v. Hungary, 25-11-53: H. Johnston (CH), S. Matthews (OR), E. Taylor (IR), S. Mortensen (CF). Blackpool equalled the record number of forwards (3) provided by one club for an England team.

25 War-time and Victory Internationals

Blackpool did not provide any players for international matches during the First World War; but, during the Second World War, 8 Blackpool players appeared in war-time and Victory internationals. None of these matches rank as full internationals.

Name	Position(s)	Country	Years in war-time international football	Total appearances	Goals scored
D. Astley	IR & CF	Wales	1939–41	4	2
R. Finan	OR	Scotland	1939	1	0
E. Dodds	CF	Scotland	1939–46	8	9
W. Buchan	IR	Scotland	1943	1	0
A. Roxburgh	G	England	1943	1	0
S. Mortensen	IL	Wales	1943	1[1]	0
	IL	England	1944–45	3	3
S. Jones	LH	Ireland	1945	1	0
J. Todd	RH	Ireland	1945–46	2	0

26 "B" Internationals

Name	Position	Country	Years in "B" international football	Total appearances	Goals scored
J. Crosland	CH	England	1950	2	0
J. Wright	LB	England	1950	1	0
H. Kelly	LH	Scotland	1952–53	2	0
W. Perry	OL	England	1955–56	2	2
R. Gratrix	CH	England	1956	1	0
E. Taylor	IR	England	1956	1	0

[1] S. Mortensen, one of the finest inside-forwards in England history, made his international début against his own country. He was England's reserve for the match against Wales, at Wembley, on September 25, 1943. He came on as substitute for Ivor Powell—who was injured during the match—because Wales didn't have a 12th-man.

27   Football League

Name	Position(s)	Years in Football League team	Total appearances	Goals scored
H. Bedford	CF	1924	1	4[1]
J. Hampson	CF	1929–31	4[2]	9
H. Johnston	CH & WH	1947–53	4	0
S. Mortensen	IR & CF	1947–50	5[3]	6
S. Matthews	OR	1947–56	5	1
T. Garrett	LB	1952–57	3	0
W. Perry	OL	1955	1	1
J. Armfield	FB	1956–63	12[4]	0
R. Gratrix	CH	1959	1	0
A. Waiters	G	1963–65	5	0
A. Ball	IF & OR	1965–66	3	2

28   Under-23

Name	Position(s)	Country	Years in Under-23 football	Total appearances	Goals scored
J. Armfield	RB	England	1956–59	9[5]	0
G. West	G	England	1961	1	0
S. Hill	OR	England	1961–62	4	1
B. Crawford	RH	England	1962	1	0
G. James	CH	Wales	1964–65	2	0
A. Ball	IF	England	1964–65	8	2
J. Johnston	IR	Ireland	1969	1	0
J. Hughes	OR & CF	Wales	1970–71	2[6]	0
T. Hutchison	OL	Scotland	1971	1	0

29   England Amateur

Name	Position(s)	Years in England amateur team	Total appearances	Goals scored
S. J. Hoad	OR	1911	2	0
W.W. Parr	OR	1936–38	8	5
W. Slater	LH & IL	1950–51	9	7
H. Sharratt	G	1953	2	0

[1] H. Bedford holds the Blackpool record for the most goals scored in a match for the Football League: 4, v. Irish League, 11-10-24.

[2] J. Hampson scored in every one of his appearances, and he twice scored 3 goals in a match: v. Scottish League, November 1930; v. Irish League, September 1931.

[3] S. Mortensen scored in four of his five appearances.

[4] J. Armfield captained the Football League in four of his twelve appearances.

[5] J. Armfield captained the England Under-23 team in four of his nine appearances.

[6] One of these two appearances was as a substitute.

30   England Youth

Name	Position(s)	Years in England youth team	Total appearances	Goals scored
G. West	G	1960	7	0
F. Willder	IL	1962	4	0
S. Wojciechowicz	RH & IL	1970	3[1]	0

31   F.A. XI, and other Honours

F.A. XI: S. Matthews and H. Johnston went on the F.A. tour of Canada in 1950. Matthews played in seven matches, and Johnston in eight. They were both awarded a cap—as were other players—even though no test matches were played.

A number of other Blackpool players have made appearances in F.A. XIs, including T. Garrett, R. Gratrix, S. Hill, G. West, J. Kelly (who toured the West Indies with the F.A. party in 1955), W. Perry (who scored 9 goals in 14 matches on the 1956 tour of South Africa), D. Durie (who scored 4 goals against the R.A.F. in October 1957), and R. Charnley (who scored 12 goals in 8 matches on the 1961 tour of New Zealand and the Far East). J. Armfield was manager and team captain of the 1969 tour of New Zealand and the Far East.

Great Britain: S. Matthews, OR, v. Rest of Europe, 13-8-55.

England XI v. Young England XI: The following Blackpool players have appeared in this end-of-season fixture:

England XI: H. Johnston, S. Matthews, S. Mortensen, T. Garrett, E. Taylor, J. Armfield.

Young England XI: J. Armfield, B. Crawford, A. Ball.

32   Representative Matches at Bloomfield Road

Full international: England v. Ireland, 17-10-32.

Inter-League: Football League v. Irish League: 23-9-31, 25-9-35, 6-10-37 18-10-50, 12-10-60. In the 1931 match, J. Hampson, on his home ground scored a hat-trick in the Football League's 4–0 victory.

Amateur internationals: England v. Ireland: 12-11-27, 15-2-36.

TRANSFERS

The next two tables give a complete list of all five-figure transfer fees involving players who have joined, or left, Blackpool.

The records, mentioned in the footnotes, are records that were set at the time of the transfer. In an era of fast-rising prices, records such as these are short-lived: they have all been superseded, except for the Tony Green transfer to Newcastle.

[1] One of these three appearances was as a substitute.

Some transfer fees are not paid in full immediately. For example, several players have been transferred to Blackpool on the basis of: £X now, and £Y when the player has made Z appearances in the first team. In these cases, the stated fee is the *total* fee paid by Blackpool.

33   Players Transferred from Blackpool

Player	Position	The club he joined	Date of transfer	Fee
Tony Green	IF/W	Newcastle	28-10-71	£150,000[1]
Alan Ball	IF/W	Everton	15-8-66	112,000[2]
Emlyn Hughes	LB/WH	Liverpool	27-2-67	65,000[3]
John Craven	WH/IF	Crystal Palace	21-9-71	37,000
Hugh Fisher	WH/IF	Southampton	2-3-67	35,000
Pat Quinn	IF	Hibernian	10-10-63	30,000[4]
Gordon West	G	Everton	2-3-62	27,500[5]
Gerry Ingram	CF	Preston	31-8-68	27,500
Leslie Lea	IF/W	Cardiff	14-12-67	20,000
Bill Cranston	LH	Preston	4-12-64	15,000
Alan Skirton	OR	Bristol City	20-11-68	15,000
Ron Suart	LB/CH	Blackburn	23-9-49	12,000
Ray Charnley	CF	Preston	7-12-67	12,000
Fred Kemp	WH/IF	Halifax	30-11-71	12,000
Frank O'Donnell	CF	Aston Villa	10-11-38	10,500
Peter Doherty	IF	Manchester City	19-2-36	10,000
Allan Brown	IL	Luton	7-2-57	10,000
Barrie Martin	LB	Oldham	28-8-64	10,000
Ian Moir	W	Chester	12-5-67	10,000
Graham Oates	IL/OL	Grimsby	10-10-68	10,000
Ronnie Brown	IF/W	Plymouth	22-2-71	10,000
Fred Pickering	CF	Blackburn	10-3-71	10,000
Neil Ramsbottom	G	Coventry	9-3-72	10,000

Note also

Joe Lane	CF	Birmingham	5-3-20	3,300[6]

34   Players Transferred to Blackpool

Player	Position	The club he left	Date of transfer	Fee
Alan Suddick	IF	Newcastle	21-12-66	£60,000
Fred Pickering	CF	Birmingham	17-6-69	45,000

[1] Highest fee paid for a Scottish player. Blackpool received £90,000 and Keith Dyson, a forward.
[2] Record transfer between two British clubs.
[3] British record fee for a full-back, and British record for a teenager.
[4] Highest fee paid by a Scottish club to an English club.
[5] British record for a goalkeeper.
[6] Record transfer between two British clubs.

Player	Position	The club he left	Date of transfer	Fee
Dave Hatton	FB/WH	Bolton	4-9-69	£40,000
Fred Kemp	WH/IF	Southampton	26-11-70	35,000
Pat Quinn	IF	Motherwell	16-11-62	34,000
Alan Skirton	OR	Arsenal	12-9-66	30,000
Gordon Milne	WH/IF	Liverpool	13-5-67	30,000
Terry Alcock	CH	Port Vale	28-7-67	30,000
Bill Bentley	LB/WH	Stoke	9-1-69	30,000
Dave Lennard	WH/IF	Halifax	7-10-71	30,000
Chris Simpkin	LH	Hull	8-10-71	30,000
Allan Brown	IL	East Fife	19-12-50	26,500[1]
Ernie Taylor	IR	Newcastle	11-10-51	25,000
Ray Parry	IF	Bolton	18-10-60	25,000
Tom White	CF	Crystal Palace	11-3-68	20,000
Neil Ramsbottom	G	Bury	4-2-71	20,000[2]
John Johnston	WH/IF	Glentoran	13-11-68	16,000[3]
Tony Green	IF	Albion Rovers	1-5-67	15,500
Jim Kelly	RH	Watford	15-10-54	15,000
Arthur Kaye	OR	Barnsley	23-5-59	15,000
Des Horne	OL	Wolverhampton	15-3-61	15,000
Ian Moir	W	Manchester United	12-2-65	15,000
Jim Robson	WH/IF	Burnley	12-3-65	15,000
Tony Coleman	OL	Sheffield Wednesday	27-7-70	12,000
Stanley Matthews	OR	Stoke	10-5-47	11,500[4]
Willie Wardle	OL	Grimsby	12-5-48	11,500
Willie Buchan	IF	Celtic	15-11-37	10,000[5]
Frank O'Donnell	CF	Preston	30-11-37	10,000[6]
E. "Jock" Dodds	CF	Sheffield United	10-3-39	10,000
John McPhee	WH/IF	Motherwell	26-7-62	10,000[7]
Tom Hutchison	OL	Alloa Athletic	13-2-68	10,000
John Murray	OR	Burnley	12-3-70	10,000
John Burridge	G	Workington	3-5-71	10,000
George Wood	G	East Stirling	20-1-72	10,000

"Best buys"

Player	Position	The club he left	Date of transfer	Fee
George Farm	G	Hibernian	8-9-48	2,700
Peter Doherty	IF	Glentoran	10-11-33	1,500
Jimmy Hampson	CF	Nelson	10-10-27	1,000
Ray Charnley	CF	Morecambe	23-5-57	1,000

[1] Highest fee paid to a Scottish club.
[2] Blackpool paid £13,000 and transferred John Murray, a forward.
[3] Highest fee paid to an Irish League club.
[4] British record for a winger.
[5] Highest fee paid to a Scottish club.
[6] Blackpool paid £8,000 and transferred two forwards, Dick Watmough and Jim McIntosh.
[7] McPhee was signed by Blackpool on the club's 75th anniversary.

WORLD WAR I

35 Season-by-season League Records

Season	Competition	Position	Played	Won	Drew	Lost	Goals For	Against	Points
1915–16	Lancashire Section Principal Competition	3	26	14	3	9	54	41	31
	Subsidiary Competition Northern Group	2	10	8	0	2	24	13	16
1916–17	Lancashire Section Principal Competition	16	30	6	7	17	44	80	19
	Lancashire Section Subsidiary Competition	11	6	2	1	3	10	12	5
1917–18	Lancashire Section Principal Competition	12	30	9	6	15	38	67	24
	Lancashire Section Subsidiary Competition	5	6	4	0	2	18	9	8
1918–19	Lancashire Section Principal Competition	11	30	10	5	15	45	61	25
	Lancashire Section "A" Subsidiary Competition	1[1]	6	3	2	1	13	7	8

36 Match Records

Biggest win: 9-0, v. Oldham (H), 17-3-17.

Biggest defeat: 1-11, v. Burslem Port Vale (A), 18-11-16.

WORLD WAR II

37 Season-by-season League Records

Season	League	Position	Played	Won	Drew	Lost	Goals For	Against	Points
1939–40	North-west	3	22	13	6	3	73	36	32
1940–41	North	6	20	13	3	4	56	34	g.a. 1.647[2]
1941–42	North	1	18	14	1	3	75	19	29
	2nd Competition: League Championship	2[3]	22	14	4	4	108	34	32[4]
1942–43	North	1	18	16	1	1	93	28	33
	North: 2nd Championship	13	19	8	7	4	49	31	23

[1] The winners of each of the four sections qualified for the Lancashire Senior Cup semi-final: v. Liverpool (H), Blackpool lost 0-1.

[2] The League table was compiled entirely on the basis of goal-average, because the competing clubs did not play the same number of matches.

[3] The Second Championships—because they included War Cup matches: from the qualifying competition and the competition proper—were less important (as League competitions) than the First Championship of each season.

[4] Blackpool gained 32 points from 22 matches, but, in the final table which was based on 23 matches, Blackpool were credited with 33.45 points.

Season	League	Position	Played	Won	Drew	Lost	Goals For	Against	Points
1943–44	North	1	18	12	4	2	56	20	28
	North: 2nd Championship	7	20	12	3	5	53	27	27
1944–45	North	20	18	9	2	7	53	38	20
	North: 2nd Championship	16	24	12	3	9	58	42	27
1945–46	North	9	42	18	9	15	94	92	45

38   List of Cup matches in the Competition Proper

Season	Competition	Round	Opponents	Venue and Score—Blackpool's score is always given first	Result—if the round was based on aggregate score
1939–40	League War Cup	1 (North "A" Division)	Southport	4-0 (H) 4-2 (A)	won 8-2
		2 (North "A" Division)	Burnley	2-1 (A) 3-1 (H)	won 5-2
		3	Barnsley	1-0 (A)	
		Quarter-final	Newcastle	0-2 (H)	
1940–41	League War Cup (Northern Group)	1	Manchester City	1-4 (H) 1-0 (A)	lost 2-4
1941–42	League War Cup	1	Manchester City	Not played—Blackpool withdrew[1]	
1942–43	League Cup—North	1	Everton	4-1 (H) 3-4 (A)	won 7-5
		2	Liverpool	1-3 (A) 5-0 (H)	won 6-3
		Quarter-final	Manchester City	3-1 (H) 1-1 (A)	won 4-2
		Semi-final	Aston Villa	3-1 (H) 1-2 (A)	won 4-3
		Final[2]	Sheffield Wednesday	2-2 (H) 2-1 (A)	won 4-3
1943-44	League Cup—North	1	Everton	7-1 (H) 3-1 (A)	won 10-2
		2	Rochdale	8-0 (H) 1-2 (A)	won 9-2
		Quarter-final	Bradford P. A.	2-2 (H) 2-1 (A)	won 4-3
		Semi-final	Manchester City	1-1 (H) 2-1 (A)	won 3-2
		Final	Aston Villa	2-1 (H) 2-4 (A)	lost 4-5
1944–45	League Cup—North	1	Wrexham	2-0 (H) 2-2 (A)	won 4-2
		2	Bolton	1-4 (H) 2-1 (A)	lost 3-5

[1] Blackpool were unable to field a team, because Service personnel were not allowed to travel during the Easter week-end.

[2] The Cup winners of North and South—Blackpool and Arsenal—met in a challenge match at Stamford Bridge. Blackpool won 4-2.

39   Match records—Goal-scoring—General

Biggest win: 15-3, v. Tranmere (H), 28-2-42.

Biggest defeat: 4-7, v. Blackburn (A), 20-1-45.

Best seasons—League: League North Champions: 1941–42, 1942–43, 1943–44.

Best seasons—Cup: League Cup North—winners: 1942–43; runners-up: 1943–44.

Most goals in a match: 8, E. Dodds, v. Stockport (H), 8-2-41, Cup—preliminary
round. And he missed a penalty!
7, E. Dodds, v. Oldham (H), 13-5-40, League—North-west.
7, E. Dodds, v. Tranmere (H), 28-2-42, Cup—qualifying competition.

Hat-trick specialist: In the 15-3 win against Tranmere, in February 1942, E.
Dodds scored a double hat-trick. The first of the two hat-tricks was completed in $2\frac{1}{2}$ minutes. On the following Saturday, he scored a hat-trick against
Burnley, and became the only Blackpool player ever to score three hat-
tricks in two consecutive games.

Most goals in a season: 66, E. Dodds, 1941–42: 48 goals in 22 League-North
matches, and 18 in 8 Cup-qualifying-competition matches. Dodds scored in
every first-team match up to (but not including) Christmas Day. He failed
to score in only 3 of his 30 first-team appearances.

INDEX

INDEX

A